SO-CFO-325

"Moore's work recalls the international 'entertainments' of Graham Greene or John le Carré, but the hard-bitten worldview and the cynical, bruised idealism of his battered hero is right out of Chandler. Intelligent and articulate, Moore offers a rich, passionate and original take on the private eye game."
—Kevin Burton Smith, *January Magazine*

"Moore is a genuine novelist who just happens to employ the conventions of the thriller genre. His real interests are believable human behavior and way cultures cross-pollinate and sometimes clash. This is real prose, not Raymond Chandler stuff, and his motives are as close to art as to entertainment. Read him."
—Douglas Fetherling, *Ottawa Citizen*

"For those who like their mysteries dark and steamy, Christopher G. Moore's Vincent Calvino suspense series is a must read."
—Shamus and Arthur Ellis Nominee Joseph Louis, author of *Madelaine and other mysteries*

"Every big city has its fictional detective; and Bangkok's is Vincent Calvino."
—*Bangkok 101*

"Relishing another Christopher Moore novel is like receiving essential nutrients for a healthier, safe life in Thailand. Insights into the human condition of expat existence, which underpin his thriller plots, can though, be painful to swallow. They reveal us to ourselves painfully clearly but as balanced as a sweet and sour Thai dish."
—Richard Ravensdale, *Pattaya People*

Novels by Christopher G. Moore

The Vincent Calvino P.I. series

Spirit House
Asia Hand
Zero Hour in Phnom Penh
Comfort Zone
The Big Weird
Cold Hit
Minor Wife
Pattaya 24/7
The Risk of Infidelity Index
Paying Back Jack
The Corruptionist

Other novels

A Killing Smile
A Bewitching Smile
A Haunting Smile
His Lordship's Arsenal
Tokyo Joe
Red Sky Falling
God of Darkness
Chairs
Waiting for the Lady
Gambling on Magic

Non-fiction

Heart Talk
The Vincent Calvino Reader's Guide

THE
CORRUPTIONIST

A VINCENT CALVINO P.I. NOVEL

CHRISTOPHER G. MOORE

Heaven Lake Press

Distributed in Thailand by:
Asia Document Bureau Ltd.
P.O. Box 1029
Nana Post Office
Bangkok 10112 Thailand
Fax: (662) 260-4578
Web site: http://www.heavenlakepress.com
email: editorial@heavenlakepress.com

Heaven Lake Press paperback edition 2011

Cover art: Chris Coles © 2009
Author's photograph: Mick Elmore © 2009
Jacket design: K. Jiamsomboon

ISBN 978-616-75030-2-8

In evil as in art there was illumination.
—Saul Bellow, *Mr. Sammler's Planet*

When a nation is filled with strife, then do patriots flourish.
—Lao-tzu

It is certainly sordid to do the wrong thing, and anyone can do the right thing when there is no danger attached; what distinguishes the good man from others is that when danger is involved he still does right.
—Plutarch

For Tito Haggardt, John Paulos, and Chris Coles

ONE

THE THAIS HAVE an old saying about the troubles caused by a drop of honey. It goes like this. *Nam phueng yod diew.* The translation is straightforward: "a drop of honey." It doesn't sound like a big deal. More like a sweet nursery rhyme. That judgment is a big mistake. A drop of honey foreshadows a tsunami of problems. The farmer on the way to market loses a drop of honey along the way. Next thing, flies swarm over the honey; then a house lizard, what the Thais call a *jingjok*, spots the flies and starts eating them; then the cat leaps in and eats the jingjok; then a dog bites the cat, the owner of the cat kicks the dog, the dog and cat owners get into a fight. Neighbors and bystanders join in, taking sides, and soon there is a full-scale riot. In English we settle for the parable of the kingdom lost for the want of a horseshoe nail. Nail or honey, the idea is pretty much the same—something small can change just about everything. What the Thais don't tell you is that every few years there is a coup and a freight train of honey gets derailed. When that happens, the predator feeding frenzy accelerates at warp speed and anyone caught in the crossfire becomes a meal. The lesson remains the same: There is a chain of predators, each one feeding off the one below, and sooner or later even those at the top of the chain start to feel insecure.

One woman, at a funeral, sitting in the back of the church, attracted carnal thoughts and like a drop of honey had started attracting flies. Tanny Craig had been in Bangkok twenty-four hours and already had caused confusion in a land that was an "us against them" kind of place. Maybe most places had a prejudice against the outsider. But Thailand had turned it into an art, even an educational mission, teaching children about the dangers of *khon nork*—the outsider. Blame the Burmese for sacking Ayuthaya not once but twice.

Tanny Craig's polished bronze fittings on her black leather picked up the early-morning sun as she sat alone in the rear of the church. Dressed in a tailored black dress with an Aztec motif stitched around the scooped neck, her long dark hair held in place with a mother-of-pearl clip, her eyes hidden by designer eyeglasses, she might have passed as a local movie star. Tanny didn't know the deceased inside the coffin at the altar or anyone else in the church, except for Vincent Calvino. Calvino said to himself that her presence was an omen. And in this part of Asia, omens came in two packages—one with a winning number inside and one with a whole lot of suffering, pain, and loss. In a place where few winners could be found, the sudden appearance of an omen, especially at a funeral, made Old George's friends hopeful that their luck had changed for the better.

Tanny waited for him like someone determined not to lose her man. She had the looks that drew men's attention. Most would have been happy to have such a woman stalking them at a funeral. Because that was what it amounted to; their arrangement had been to meet after the funeral, but she broke the agreement and showed up. Maybe she was curious, or maybe she had other reasons.

Calvino resisted looking over his shoulder.

"Goddamn it, Calvino, how can you get a woman to stalk you to my funeral?" Calvino heard Old George's voice and in his mind's eye saw Old George slowly shaking his head, jowls swaying like an aging go-go dancer's ass, sucking his teeth and issuing a fatwa-like warning.

As Calvino shifted, trying to get comfortable on the hard wooden pew while waiting for the funeral to begin, he remembered the last conversation he'd had with Old George—it was about women. One afternoon after a couple of beers, Old George had asked a question—if you can outsource the drudgery from a marriage and make your partner happy, why not outsource the pleasure and make yourself happy?

Someone who'd been in the bar remembered Old George's rhetorical question and whispered it to a friend in the pew in front of Calvino as they waited for the service to start. Calvino felt her eyes burning into the back of his neck. But it didn't much matter; he had continued to ignore Tanny, shut her out of his mind by way of pretending she wasn't there. Giving her any satisfaction of acknowledging her presence was like ticking off an item on the checklist of what a person should do with a stalker—only Tanny was no ordinary stalker, and that simple fact compounded the problem like an accelerated interest penalty on a bad loan.

Calvino concentrated on his memories of Old George, since that was the purpose of a funeral. He visualized Old George on his perch in the bar. That was the only place where the image would reside, inside his mind. It took some getting used to thinking of Old George as that deceased person in a coffin. Calvino sat in the chapel of St. Joseph's Catholic Church on Soi Ruam Rudee wondering how everything had become clear at the end for Old George, like in a good mystery. The problem, Old George said, was, "Life's not like a book. You can't go back and relive it knowing the things you can change, the things you just gotta accept because that's how things work."

The rotating blades in the overhead fans stirred the muggy air. A fat Thai woman swept dead leaves and flowers with a broom. Attendants removed wreaths from stands in front of the coffin. The back-office crew carried out the small tasks required to run a funeral. Lined up against the rear walkway, several men smoked, looking out over the jammed parking lot of the church, wondering who would show up and who would roll over and go back to sleep. A couple of Lonesome Hawk regulars who had been trying to determine who the strange, beautiful woman in the back of the church was, turned their attention to matters of faith. One whispered about whether a Jew could get a ticket into heaven by having a Catholic funeral. Another regular said Old George had hedged his bets. If you picked only one religion, that was risky; it was better to take a chance with a couple of religions. It was a stronger hand, and you could plead your case that at a minimum you were entitled to a timeshare in heaven. "And if there ain't no God, then that meant Old George won, only he'd never know that he'd won because there's no him. That's how George figured it."

"How do you know? He tell you that? Doesn't sound like George."

"He was a lawyer and a Jew. He knew all the angles. He didn't need to tell me."

Inside the church, a woman sang a hymn. A hundred or so people filed in, sliding into the pews as the priests had already taken their position at the altar. The outer doors on both sides were open, and a slight cross breeze cooled the room. For a nine o'clock funeral in Bangkok, Old George had more *farangs* inside a church than a bishop holding Christmas mass.

George had died of old age. Everything fell apart. The faint click of the wind chimes on the roof outside the window filled the silence when the organist stopped between hymns. During the readings and the eulogy, Calvino glanced out the window. Beyond the wind chimes and battered TV aerials from the Stone Age of broadcast TV, relics of tangled, twisted metal, and potted plants, dry and shriveled, three green domes of a mosque rose like jade jar lids against a gray morning sky. George, Calvino thought, smiling, the good Jew, was getting himself a Catholic funeral in the shadow of a mosque and later in the morning would be cremated at a Buddhist *wat*. The mourners ahead of him might have been onto something. Old George was like a gambler who placed his bets on three horses—Jewish, Christian, Buddhist—in a three-horse race. Calvino imagined for a moment he heard the call for prayer coming from the direction of the mosque, making it a four-horse race.

But it was only the wind and the sound of those chimes echoing through the church.

The service ended with the singer letting loose on "Amazing Grace." The crowd had slowly risen from the polished wooden pews, bones creaking like the sound of a native clearing bamboo with a machete. While it was still early morning, the heat of the day had cranked up a notch to a couple of degrees below egg-frying temperatures, and the pallbearers groaned under the weight of George's coffin. Arms shaking, knees buckling, like a line of old rumba dancers they managed to load the coffin onto a gurney, and the attendants wheeled it out the door and to a hearse parked in front of the church. The back hatch door was open, and the pallbearers struggled once more to slide the coffin inside.

After the Catholic funeral, the cremation service was scheduled at a wat on Phetchaburi Road. The crematorium was nestled in a compound of buildings with orange gabled roofs. The wat overlooked an expressway ramp, cars lined up to pay the toll, drivers looking out their windows getting an image of the last tollgate they would one day enter. Calvino left the church and stood with other friends as George's widow stood beside the hearse, clutching a framed photograph of her husband. The widow, the photo of George in one hand, gently dabbed a tissue to her eyes. Tanny sat in the last pew away from the door, where she watched Calvino. He had seen her but hadn't acknowledged her presence. He looked away as Tanny glanced at her watch, then glanced up to see Calvino embrace an elderly man in a safari suit and with tears in his red-rimmed eyes. They patted each other on the shoulder the way men do, and then the man in the safari suit stepped forward and comforted Old George's widow.

Some of the bar regulars were dry-mouthed before ten in the morning, itchy for the taste of the first beer of the day, scratching at their collars, underarms sweat-stained from the exertion of carrying the coffin. They broke into groups, figuring out who had transportation to the wat and who had decided to cut out and find something to drink.

McPhail came to old George's funeral dressed in a necktie and a brown shirt. He looked tense, beaten down, working the kinks out of his knuckles. The knot in his tie, crooked and creased in the wrong place, along with his haggard expression would have let him pass as the foreman of a hung jury deadlocked after forty-eight hours of deliberation.

McPhail crossed over and hugged Calvino, whispering in his ear, "Don't look. But inside the door there's a *ying* who's been clocking you."

Calvino patted him on the back. "Tanny Craig."

"Second to last pew, she's seated about noon. You have to move to your left a foot or so," McPhail went on until Calvino's words sank in. "You know her?"

Calvino nodded and, to prove his point, walked to the entrance of the church and looked inside. Tanny, in her perfect black dress, sat, legs crossed, half turned, a black briefcase on the pew beside her. She lowered her sunglasses and stared at him. Calvino frowned, letting her know he wasn't happy that she'd bird-dogged him to the church. They had an appointment, but it'd been agreed that that was after the funeral. But she couldn't wait; she had to follow him, to be certain he would make the appointment. He ignored her and turned his attention to McPhail. Calvino had nothing he wanted to say to Tanny that couldn't wait until the funeral had finished and they were back at the office. And looking at McPhail, he realized that he had nothing more to say to McPhail. So he said nothing.

Had this been her idea of putting Calvino through some kind of test? The appointment was to attend a meeting with Brandon Sawyer, who was Calvino's client. She had managed to get the information about the funeral from Ratana. Calvino turned around, facing the altar, arms folded across his chest.

"Foxy," said McPhail.

"She's from New York. Strictly business." His voice was flat and dull.

McPhail's eyebrows rose. "You're joking."

Calvino said, "She's not the kind of woman you joke about."

"She's got something about her. Class."

Any Thai ying who wasn't a hooker and carried a briefcase had class in McPhail's book. Calvino saw no good reason to disclose that Tanny Craig was a private investigator in Bangkok on assignment from New York. Calvino wanted to forget that she was at the church. The prime directive was to concentrate on sending Old George off to the next life before attending to unfinished business in this one.

The service was over, and the pair of priests stood outside the church near the widow. They looked smaller, more human than when they drank from the chalice on the altar. When they'd offered Communion, it was just the wafer that was given. The chalice wasn't extended. One of the mourners had gone back to the altar and discovered that there was only olive oil in the chalice. He had badly wanted a drink. He spit out the olive oil, crossed himself, and went back outside to join the others.

A procession of cars drove to Phetchaburi Road, where a couple of the motorcycle-taxi boys in their orange vests stood in the road directing traffic, letting the procession turn into the driveway of the wat. Calvino got into his car, and then McPhail and two others from the service climbed in, slamming the doors and demanding the air conditioner be turned on full blast. "Aren't you gonna offer her a ride?" asked McPhail.

Calvino watched Tanny walk toward his car. McPhail smiled as she approached.

"I should leave her to find her own way."

"This explains why you're single," said McPhail. "You gotta sweet-talk a woman a little, Vinny. Abandoning her at George's funeral isn't gonna get you laid."

Somehow Calvino felt that George would forgive him.

She rapped her knuckles on the window. Calvino rolled it down.

"Can I have a ride?"

McPhail opened the door, climbed out, holding the door for Tanny.

"Get in," Calvino said. As he watched Tanny and McPhail change places, he was thinking that's how it always began, the "get in" part, and down the line it usually crashed into a call to "get out." As McPhail groaned getting in, Calvino avoided looking at Tanny. He was already regretting the invitation, but telling her to get out would set a record even for Calvino in terms of time together. He gave it a pass.

It was strange, looking back, how two simple, small English words—"get in" or "get out"—could become the source of so much regret. They'd deserted Calvino at the speed of buckshot, abandoning him to the pretty woman who'd mooched a ride from Old George's funeral. Inside the van McPhail and the others congratulated themselves for being heroes, giving Calvino the chance to close the deal with the hot ying. They figured that Calvino owed them a round of drinks. McPhail said, "Make that a couple of rounds. He can afford it." Calvino had a different take—the men had felt some primal instinct that told them to flee while they could. He had felt the same urge. That was the problem with driving. He was stuck behind the wheel with a woman in the passenger seat who had every intention of spoiling a perfectly good funeral.

TWO

"BRANDON DIDN'T HAVE anything to do with Kowit's murder. Achara's not a murderer." Brandon was Calvino's client; Achara came into the picture as Brandon's Thai business partner. Kowit's murder had briefly turned a spotlight on Achara, but in Thai style it was less a spotlight than one of those prison-wall searchlights scanning the swamps just outside the grounds for someone lurking in the shadows. It soon moved on to others.

She had flown into Thailand on Saturday, arriving on a late-night flight. He'd met her at the hotel for a drink. She'd worn one of those professional suits with tailored woolen trousers that a New York senator might wear.

Tanny had spent Sunday going over a number of documents at Calvino's office. It wasn't an unreasonable request given the circumstances—a desk, a chair, and a computer had been installed in anticipation of her arrival. She was moving in for a temporary period to work out the details of a business deal between Brandon and his brother Marshall. The office accommodation had been part of the deal. Brandon, who never let the money train pass without pulling off a bag or two, got his brother to fund the office-equipment expenditure, rent, telephone, and transportation. Marshall didn't blink; he wired the money to Calvino's account and e-mailed him that when Tanny left, he could keep the extra computer or give it away.

Brandon said not to consider the offer one of generosity. "Marshall's fucking with you. That's his way of doing it," he had said.

Tanny's human resources—meaning Calvino's services—had been part of the package.

Tanny Craig was the only ethnic Thai he'd ever met who didn't flash the automatic smile. That default grin had been refined over centuries to oil the hard gears of daily life, which feudalism had the tendency to gum up. Thailand had cultivated the idea of itself as the "Land of Smiles," used it to sell the place to tourists who'd do more tricks than a circus dog for one of those smiles. The smile was among those human expressions, like sex, that had been successfully repressed in the West. At least the one that had no real justification for itself; in the West, a person who smiled for no apparent reason was the village idiot. Not in Thailand, where the smiles were abundant and largely for no reason. The smile was unearned, because you never truly knew where you stood. Most everyone got a smile for nothing. But no one cared; earned or not, the smiles lit up the place, and all that grinning often kept people from one another's throats.

By the time they shook hands at the end of the evening on Saturday, Calvino had decided that Tanny Craig wore her professionalism on her sleeve, like some people wore their heart. And for the same reason: They couldn't help it. On that first Saturday, she had let him do most of the talking. The next morning, Sunday morning, and early morning, too, it was more of the same. He talked, she listened. It was a good interrogation technique. People didn't understand that in investigation the best weapon to put into the field was a patient listener. People wanted to tell their story, talk and talk, until the sunset, through nightfall, until dawn if you let them.

Brandon said Marshall had picked Craig because she would "fit in." Fitting in was something that Marshall valued as a business asset. In Tanny's case fitting in meant she not only looked Thai but also *was* Thai. She'd been born in Thailand. Her biological parents were Thai. But other than the genes, below the surface, where identity is made, Tanny Craig was 100 percent American, a wonk whose professional life consisted of taking notes and memorizing figures, forecasts, and termination provisions of contracts. Watching *American Idol,* eating McDonald's, going to Disney World with her kid. She'd bought the American package. Or another way of looking at Tanny was that she *was* the American package, right down to the bows and ribbons.

Brandon had insisted on keeping Calvino on the case. Like a punch-drunk boxer, he was in no condition to change managers halfway through a losing fight. Marshall worked behind the scenes from his New York office trying to control the financing of his brother's Thai joint-venture project. Marshall had insisted on bringing in someone from a large professional investigative firm. "An American firm," he said. And he'd kept repeating that phrase like it was a chant in some two-bit cult. Once she arrived in Bangkok, it hadn't taken Tanny long before she understood that she was stuck with Calvino unless she could figure out a way to cut him out of the deal. It would be her case; Marshall would control the ring. That was the theory. She pored over the details, searching for any scrap of fact to show over billing, corruption, conflict of interest, or a connection to the contract-killing of the journalist who'd stuck his nose into the joint venture—all possibilities that had run through her checklist. Any one of them would be a knockout blow. That's what she wanted. A one-round fight. Get the work done, get on a plane, and go home.

That was what Tanny Craig thought about on the way from the wat and the last belch of gray smoke, as Calvino drove to Brandon Sawyer's house. Tanny sat in the passenger seat staring straight ahead.

"You don't talk much," Calvino said.

"My client would be happy to pay you a severance fee," she said.

"Yeah?" He glanced at her. "He wants to buy me off?"

"Think of it as streamlining the case."

"Meaning he wants me out of the stream and for you to paddle the boat alone."

She didn't say anything, turning her head slightly and gazing out the window.

Calvino pulled over to the side of the road and set the handbrake. Cars and trucks raced past like high-speed trains that had jumped the rails. A cloud of thick dust kicked from the shoulder of the road and slowly settled over the car. There was nothing opposite the shoulder other than rows of parked pickups, motorcycles, *tuk-tuks,* and a few vendor shacks selling mangoes and oranges.

"This is Sawyer's house?" She looked confused.

"It's a wet market. I'll be back in five." He left the car engine running. Calvino had parked Thai style, with the rear half of his Honda City blocking the lane, causing cars approaching from behind to swing out into the oncoming lane without so much as a sideways glance, passing as a matter of right. As she sat in the car, one or two drivers shot her an angry, menacing look. No one honked, no one shouted. The Thais had a huge capacity to store rage until it overflowed into pure white-heat violence. Tanny puffed up her cheeks, sighed, and shook her head as if she had an audience. She glanced at her watch and then out the window. Fifteen minutes later there was no sign of Calvino, just street vendors, shoppers, throngs of students eating ice cream and smiling. As the moments passed, her sense of frustration increased until she pulled out her cell phone, and called him.

He picked up on the first ring. "I'll be right there." He hung up before she could explain how upset she was becoming. She was never late for a meeting. It wasn't professional. Men like Marshall expected punctuality. But Calvino was something else. This man had blocked the road, abandoned her in his car, and if she tried to get out on the passenger side, she'd be run over. She convinced herself that Calvino had done it on purpose, one of those macho power plays.

She waited and waited, stewing in the air-conditioned car, remembering newspaper stories from somewhere like Arizona or New Mexico that appeared now and again, about how someone had left a baby, an old person, or a dog unattended in a closed-up car in desert-heat conditions. She turned up the air conditioner. It was newsworthy if the person or dog died from heat exhaustion. He'd pulled this stunt to play with her mind, throw her off balance, and make her lose her self-control. But she wasn't going to allow that to happen. The fact was, it was Calvino who was in the stifling heat, shopping in an open wet market, gutters running with animal blood, guts, and feathers. When Calvino returned carrying plastic bags, he knocked on the glass and waved. She rolled down the window. "Flowers?" She half turned, reaching out to the orchids.

"Beautiful, aren't they?" He closed his door, smiling. "I should've told you that it was gonna be a Thai five minutes. But I keep thinking that you *are* Thai and know how things work. Like 'driver flees the scene' is a phrase of high modern art."

She didn't return his smile, turning back around and facing the windshield. He noticed that she wore her seat belt, sitting knees together, hands folded on her lap. What a careful Girl Scout this one was, he thought. "You're upset with me."

"I am not upset." She said it in a tone indicating that the "not" didn't belong in the sentence.

Calvino glanced at her, putting the car into gear. He's thinking that she's more than upset. She's on fire with rage, and nothing I say is going to do anything but stoke the flames. It was time to see how far she'd burn down. "Did your mother teach you to sit like that?" asked Calvino as he turned back into the stream of traffic.

"We should be there already," she said, glancing at her watch.

"Sawyer should fire me, right?"

She refused to acknowledge his smile, arms folded tightly under her breast and staring straight ahead. "Have you met his brother, Marshall Sawyer?"

"Brandon and his brother have—"

"Issues," she said.

He nodded, passing a truck overloaded with pool tables, stacked one on top of the other and tied with rope to the rear fender. "Am I wrong in thinking that Marshall wants me off the investigation?"

"You've finished your job. So yes, he thinks you're hanging on when you should let go."

Calvino gave her a crooked smile. She thought of him as a used-up boxer, and she'd come to tell him it was time to throw in the towel.

"That's up to Brandon." He glanced at her, the smile evaporated. "He tells me to stop, I stop. You tell me to stop, no disrespect, but that don't mean anything."

This was turning out to be more difficult than it should be, Tanny thought. "Why don't you tell me what work you did for Brandon? And what work is left for you specifically. In your opinion, of course. It can be off the record."

It was like being interviewed by a journalist. "I don't talk off the record. So why don't I be upfront with you? A moment ago you wanted to bribe me to throw Brandon under the bus. Now we're working together? And you want me to tell you all the inside information about Brandon. You're remarkable. And you want all of this to happen in a New York minute. But you're forgetting an important piece of information. This is Bangkok, where a minute is known to stretch a time zone with little effort." He could tell from Tanny's accent that she wasn't a native New Yorker. He guessed that she was from somewhere in the Midwest, one of those flyover places with accents as flat as the land outside the plane window.

"I'm learning." She was still annoyed over the amount of time he'd left her in the car. Calvino read it as one of those throwaway jabs she lobbed out of desperation when she couldn't get in close enough to deliver a couple of decisive body blows.

"I'll make it up to you," Calvino said. When a man was winning, it was no sweat to ease off. "You know about Brandon Sawyer's Frankenstein rice- and turbo-wind-driven power-generating windmills."

"That's what you call the joint venture."

"It's a nickname for it. Don't get touchy."

But she was the touchy type, and he was trying to get used to her style. She sulked, looking straight ahead at the road.

Calvino continued, "You knew before he came to Thailand that he worked a year or two as a comedian in New York?"

He watched for her reaction; she clearly hadn't known that Brandon Sawyer was a onetime funnyman before going into two businesses that comics made a good living telling jokes about. Brandon was finding that a sense of humor and business didn't mix. Losses and risks were never funny unless they happened to someone else. Tanny was in town to make certain that that someone else wasn't Marshall.

"He's unstable," said Tanny.

"The political situation is unstable."

"That's another reason Marshall's unhappy. This place seems to be coming apart."

Thousands of demonstrators swarmed through the streets of Bangkok, holding the government hostage, chanting, marching, and demanding a new political order. That wasn't exactly the kind of talk businessmen liked to hear. They liked the old order; they disliked *dis*order—it made them edgy. No one knew who had authority to set the rules. Brandon was holed up in a world of people hanging on with both hands, pretending that they might be knocked off the ride and into the gutter. Calvino understood why Marshall had sent Tanny to investigate a way to shut down the amusement park. Only thing was, Brandon was having a great time in never never land, and no one was going to push him off the roller coaster just because it was a little dangerous and badly maintained.

THREE

BRANDON SAWYER USED his right hand to rake his blond hair, moving it to the side, away from his face. A bulge of flesh hung over his trousers, ballooning out his shirt; when viewed from the side, it appeared he wore a concealed all-purpose money pouch. But the bulge was Sawyer's bloated stomach. His matted hair formed a tangle on his forehead, in the style of an old-fashioned crooner. The "look" had been part of his act.

It was the waiting to go on that was hell. Pacing backstage while the previous act worked the audience. Only he wasn't backstage; Brandon was at home. And his audience would consist of Vincent Calvino and a private investigator named Tanny Craig. He tried to occupy himself with other things. Except it didn't work. Waiting made him sweat, and his skin had that cold, clammy post-collision daze.

Calvino had never seen Brandon wear anything other than a tailored silk shirt with three buttons undone, showing a pelt of blond hair on his chest, along with dark trousers, barefoot on the marble floors. Pressing his lips firmly together, Brandon watched while his gnarly toenails the color of amber flew across the room as they were clipped by one of four yings who lounged around his mansion. Brandon sat on an overstuffed chair, holding a glass, sipping his gin and tonic, careful not to dislodge a sliver of lime snugly wedged over the rim. He had laid out all the papers Calvino had asked to examine, gotten one of the yings to spread them out on a table. Most were reports about the recently closed investigation into his partner, a thirty-seven-year-old businessman, a Thai-Chinese named Achara, who'd known the murdered journalist.

Brandon scanned the papers and felt happy. It wasn't an ideal place to work, but it was his home, not an office. He wanted this Craig woman to see him in his home and report back to his brother how Brandon's yings fussed over him. Brandon had done his stand-up work on the small-club circuit in the Village. It was something he had to get out of his system. Calvino, who'd been back to New York, remembered seeing his act. They had talked. Who would have guessed that one-day the comic would be living in Bangkok and hiring Calvino to make subtle inquiries about Achara and his family? What struck Calvino was that the gap between Sawyer's stage persona and his day-to-day personality was as tiny as the space between the bricks used to build the pyramids. You couldn't have slipped a knife blade between the two.

Calvino's uncle had owned one of the clubs where Sawyer had performed. That had been in the early nineties, when a lot of people in New York thought they were funny. Humor was changing, but Sawyer's act didn't. It was dated when he started; it had grown ancient by the time he called it quits. Why had Sawyer gone through the humiliation? Comedy was an act of rebellion against his family and his brother Marshall, who'd been their mother's favorite. Sawyer's show-business career had lasted about two long, frustrating years. And when he returned, hat in hand, humbled, to the family business, no one even seemed to notice that he'd tried his luck at comedy, stumbled, fallen flat on his face, and crawled home. Marshall grinned with satisfaction. The sound out of the back of his throat was as close to a laugh as Brandon ever got from his brother.

Brandon smacked his lips, rattled the ice cubes against the inside of his cut-crystal glass as if throwing the bones for a reading of his future. He'd been expecting the woman his brother had sent with Vincent Calvino, and they were running a half an hour late. Like most lonely men, Sawyer drank in large swallows, draining the glass. Then he lifted the empty glass and nodded. A ying massaged his ankles while a maid took the glass and walked across the room to the wet bar. The other two yings played cards at a table in the corner. The yings had the large-screen TV tuned to the cartoon station. The remote control lay on the table. One of them had pushed it into the pot of twenty- and one-hundred-baht notes and called the others. She grinned, convinced she had the winning hand. Sawyer felt agitated, as if he were about to walk onstage, going through his act in his head.

He rehearsed, mumbling to himself, the speech he'd planned to deliver to Marshall's private investigator. The plan was to start with something along the lines that the world had changed but Marshall never changed. Marshall never accepted Brandon's judgment, his recommendations, or his version of events. The same was true for his friends, his ideas, or his lifestyle. It had been that way since they'd been children. Marshall did everything in his power to retain control of every situation. If Brandon hired an expert, Marshall found something to discredit the person. He'd been trying to do the same thing with Vincent Calvino. Marshall had sent his own hired gun to find a way to kick Calvino off the case. That would leave Brandon alone, isolated, and Marshall would again win the toss. But Brandon hadn't given up; Calvino was still on his side. He had a fighting chance.

Brandon fidgeted, brushing his hair, wringing his hands; a nervous, unsettled stomach revolted against the gin and tonic. He counted the toenail fragments flying across the room, yelling, "Incoming!" He belched and took the refilled glass from the maid, moving across to stand in front of air circulating from the blades of a couple of floor fans. "Other leg," he said to the ying in white shorts and blue tank top, braless, a gold chain swinging as she massaged his leg. She shifted to his other leg, diving in with hands shaped like claws. "Softer," he protested. "That's my leg, not a hunk of Kobe beef."

The ying, who was twenty-one, had no idea what Kobe beef was, but understood he wanted a gentler touch. She smiled, blew him a kiss. That was the kind of audience Brandon loved best—adoring, responsive, tireless, and at his feet. All morning a crew of electricians had been fixing the air-conditioning, and several fans circulated the hot air without doing anything to reduce the temperature. The yings and the other staff couldn't have been happier; they hated air-conditioning, saying it gave them headaches, colds, bladder problems, skin eruptions, that it attracted rats and ghosts. Sawyer just stared at them when they carried on conversations that defied cause and effect. How such irrational beings had occupied every room in his life sometimes troubled him. It was the trade off for nonstop massage and refilled glasses, he told himself. Living in Thailand, he had grown to accept many peculiar aspects of living.

Where the fuck is Calvino? he wondered. His man was running late. He remembered something about a funeral. People died every day. Running late because of death was hardly an excuse. If anything, it was a good reason to speed up, he thought. Maybe something had gone wrong. He started to worry about the things that might have happened— that Marshall had gotten to Calvino. Sawyer's mind, heat-addled and gin-plied, had begun to play tricks, throwing out images of Calvino sitting in his office, unknotting his black funeral tie, having tossed the case file into the wastebasket.

Brandon's brother could have paid him off. The implication had been that Calvino was a local hire and wouldn't be up to the job required. Would Vinny have taken his brother's money and not have told Brandon? Calvino was a lot of things, but money-driven wasn't one of them. Yet Marshall said every man has his price, and every woman sooner or later morphed into Lady Macbeth. With their mother, Brandon never questioned the last part of Marshall's equation.

Most people in Sawyer's family suffered various degrees of paranoia, and if scientists ever figured out the gene sequence, he was certain they'd find that it came from his mother's side of the family. That's where the money had come from, and if he gave up always looking over his shoulder, assuming that someone was trying to get him, eventually someone just might get lucky. Paranoia was a major corporate asset; it never deflated, and retained its value, especially in hard times. Sawyer had never liked his brother's attitude. Marshall was always causing trouble, and looking for some angle to trip Brandon up, make him fall flat on his face. As far as Brandon was concerned, this imported investigator from New York was part of a conspiracy intended to get his money, kill a profitable deal, and drive him out of Thailand. "I've got a cramp in my right foot," he said, making a face.

The ying sat back on her haunches and called over to one of the other yings at the card table. Another ying sighed, put her cards down, and, like a good relief pitcher, left for her tour of duty. "Right foot, darling," he said. "This foot. The one you're holding is the left. This one is … guess which one it might be."

She picked up his right foot, wrinkling her nose.

"Let me introduce you to Mr. Right." He wiggled his toes. "Hello, glad to meet you. I am Mr. Right. Who are you?"

"*Baa*," she said, which roughly translated to "crazy."

"Totally," he said.

As the massage continued, Brandon thought that maybe Marshall wasn't trying to kill the joint venture—it was too good a deal—but what he wanted was control over it. That meant pushing his younger brother into what the Thais called an inactive position, like inspector-general of sewers, a position at the bottom of a slope, where it was hard to support a certain way of life. There will always be enough money for gin and tonics. But a mansion and servants? He felt sweat forming on his forehead. No more unlimited supply of toy girls to clip his toenails and massage his tired dogs. A line of sweat dripped down, rolling off the tip of his nose. No more expense accounts to entertain as he pleased. Brandon sighed and wiped his face with a tissue. He balled up the tissue and threw it on the floor. He'd have to pick up for himself if that happened. The worst of it was, he was too old to tell jokes in front of a roomful of strangers. The meeting with Calvino and the investigator from New York was part of Marshall's power squeeze, and that was why Brandon needed Calvino. Damn, where the fuck is he? Maybe Brandon had played it too cool with Calvino, not letting on how miserable and upset he was over the due diligence his brother had ordered.

Marshall had said on the phone that sending an investigator hadn't been his idea; it had been the board that had insisted. An outside director of the company, the prick, had recommended hiring a specialist to check out the books and operations. Kowit's murder had given Marshall a justification for his move. The air needed to be cleared, as there'd been a suggestion that Achara had been on the possible suspect list. That was a half lie. The suspect list was the size of the Manhattan telephone directory. It gave Brandon digestive problems to think about the idea that Achara's name had been included. He tossed back his tumbler filled with gin and a splash of tonic.

The cramp had moved up his right foot to his leg. Brandon wondered if he might be suffering from a heart attack. He sat forward with the empty glass. The maid's face went on alert, like a retriever who had seen his master throwing a ball. "Massage higher," he said.

The ying made a grab for Brandon's balls. "Not that high. Massage my leg." He caught her wrist and pushed her hand down to the muscles just above his knee.

He started to laugh, and that convinced him he probably wasn't having a heart attack after all. Sawyer rose, stretched, feeling much better, and walked out of the room, down the corridor, and into the expansive entrance, where he opened the door and looked down the driveway as if staring hard enough would cause Calvino to materialize.

Sawyer's shoulders slumped as he stepped back inside. He stared at his glass, thinking about the boardroom in New York, with his brother occupying the seat at the head of the chrome-and-glass table. Relatives, lawyers, accountants, big shots on both sides of the table sifted through piles of papers. The board never did anything that his brother didn't agree with. He thought of how his brother Marshall would have looked at those around the table, drilling him with his stare, holding up a newspaper clipping and saying, "This joint-venture partner, Achara. The police connect him to a murder. We can't let this pass."

There was nothing funny about Achara, the deal, or the potential profits involved, which were enormous. But someone had murdered a journalist named Kowit, who left behind a wife and a couple of kids. Widows and orphans made good copy. The story had some legs for a murder, which, like a bribed boxer, was supposed to go down and stay down after the third round. This one kept fighting. And that had been the problem, and why Brandon had brought Vincent Calvino into the matter.

Calvino's report cleared Achara. True, in the early stages of the business venture, Achara's lawyers created a shareholding structure that gave the power to Achara, and

Brandon had gone along with the lawyer; Marshall had been told that they'd been forced to work within a set of informal conventions, structuring deals that looked like one thing but were actually something else. Marshall thought Brandon had been sucker punched. Calvino found nothing to link Achara with the murder; Achara, if anything, was an ascetic type, even eccentric, raising lions on his grounds. More than that, Achara had a record of good deeds. Thais would have said he had a "good heart." In other words, Achara was a fair, honest man, a man of his word who'd locked himself inside a world of ancient Chinese beliefs and rituals. Such a man didn't go around killing people or ordering someone else to do so.

After reading Calvino's report, Marshall had phoned Brandon. Marshall cleared his throat on the other end of the line—it was one of those habits that made one brother want to strangle the other—then explained that no matter what Calvino had found, the fact remained that the journalist had been murdered upcountry, five kilometers from the land with cultivated, genetically modified rice and a wind farm. Kowit's articles suggested that kickbacks and cronyism were involved in both projects. Each had received government backing, tax write-offs, import-duty concessions, making them sweet but at the same time generating controversy.

"No one gets something for nothing in Thailand," said Marshall.

FOUR

CALVINO GRIPPED THE steering wheel and made a left turn, but in his mind he was inside Brandon's enormous lounge, explaining, "Achara's name had been on a long list of people with a motive to kill the reporter. But that didn't mean he had anything to do with it."

"Of course, not," Brandon would reply. "Why would he do something so stupid? Achara graduated from Stanford University. Duh. He's like you or me. Maybe smarter than you. Certainly smarter than me. Smart people don't shoot reporters in the head. It's bad for business." It was the kind of logic followed by a conclusion that a bargirl might make, thought Calvino. Rich, Ivy League–educated people killed but brought more cunning and resources to the job. Since they mostly ran the government, it was usually called an execution rather than a murder. An argument along those lines was pointless with someone like Brandon. Calvino would ignore him and ask for a drink. Without alcohol, a world of Brandons was difficult to bear.

He wondered what kind of shape Brandon would be in for the meeting, as he tried to get a better reading on Tanny's intentions. Brandon's drinking would be something she'd pick up on immediately. Not that Marshall was unaware of his brother's drinking problem, but having it confirmed in writing wouldn't be exactly advancing Brandon's position when it came to retaining power in the joint venture.

"Running probability analysis, what are the chances Achara was behind the murder?" asked Tanny.

She was one of those women who had a knack for reading a man's mind. And after two meetings, he'd concluded that she was likely the kind of woman who didn't take much flak from anyone and who fought like a rattlesnake when faced with resistance to what she wanted.

"I said the chances of his being involved were less than twenty percent."

"Brandon told Marshall that you said Achara was clean."

Calvino wondered if Brandon had said that; "clean" wasn't a word he ever heard Brandon use. "Eighty percent is as clean as you can get a body in these parts."

"The problem is, Marshall saw 'less than twenty percent' in your report and knew that Brandon had lied. He'd already factored in a thirty-percent risk for doing business in a country known for political instability, street demonstrations, and—to use Marshall's words—with a reputation for fucking foreigners around, so he recalculated the overall risk, marking it up to fifty percent."

"Meaning it's fifty-fifty the joint venture could float down the river belly-up," said Calvino, having some respect for the brother.

"Doing a deal in Thailand is like buying subprime mortgages. I've been sent to see if the joint venture is toxic. Have a look at that twenty percent of baggage. See if we might find a solution."

"You came to double-check my work."

"That's one way of looking at it." Letting the arrow hit flesh and bone.

"Can you think of another way of looking at it?"

Tanny thought about other options in silence. There wasn't any other way of looking at it. They both knew it.

Brandon Sawyer liked that, in the distant past, before Calvino became a nobody sneaking around taking pictures of farangs' cheating bar ying girlfriends in Bangkok, they'd palled around New York together. They had a history. In Brandon's way of thinking, Calvino understood the cultural bullshit of doing things in Thailand and the rules of the street in New York. That made Calvino, in Brandon's view, qualified to look into matters that Brandon labeled as of vital interest, and to report back what he found with authority and credibility. "You could've saved yourself a lot of trouble if you'd read my report," said Calvino.

"Thirty million dollars is a major investment. One report isn't enough comfort." She offered a thin smile.

"If Marshall wants comfort, tell him to put the money in a savings account. Assuming there's a New York bank left standing," said Calvino.

Tanny had read through Calvino's reports: Who, what, where, and how kind of reports. "Risk, Mr. Calvino. It's all about risk. And credit. The appetite for risk has vanished along with the credit needed to finance it. Marshall has money at risk in Thailand, and he wants to find a way to eliminate the risk."

A number of foreigners Calvino worked for didn't like making decisions about risk, and hired him to tell them what to do. He included Brandon in that category. It hadn't taken Brandon long to expand Calvino's brief, asking him to make recommendations or come up with solutions, shouldering the responsibility for the outcome. Brandon wanted Calvino to predict the future and make the right decision for him. That was dangerous territory; it involved judgment, cash, opportunity, and random bad luck.

Calvino told Brandon before Tanny turned up that sometimes there was no clear reason to choose one option over another. And that he was a private investigator, and if Brandon wanted predictions about the future, then book an appointment to see a fortune-teller.

"You want me to throw a dart? Flip a coin? Is that what you're telling me are my options?" Brandon had asked as he'd sat in Calvino's office. It had to be something deep inside his upbringing, decided Calvino.

"You ever meet Brandon's mother? I have," he said, answering his own question. Then he told her the story about meeting Sawyer's mother in the old days in New York. She wore a white hat, an expensive knee-length leather jacket, and high black lace-up boots. Up close it looked as if a younger woman's face had been sewed onto her own, leaving her sagging neck as the material evidence of plastic surgery. It had been late October, and she was carrying a Saks Fifth Avenue shopping bag. Brandon walked next to his mother. They stopped briefly on the street for an introduction. She gave Brandon the bag to hold and, flashing her emerald green eyes, she said that she liked Italians... "You meet her or not?" he repeated to Tanny now.

Tanny's tongue darted over her lips—moist, large lips, Calvino had noticed. She also had the habit of pushing her tongue against the inside of her cheek. "Yes."

Her resolute firmness, her devious, nasty, ankle-biting nature had been passed on to Marshall. But Brandon must've had a letter or two in his genetic code scrambled. Brandon got a double shot of the single-malt-whiskey DNA sequence instead. Sawyer's mother surrounded herself, like a Chinese empress, with a court of professionals, courtiers who gave advice garnished with colorful flow charts. Brandon Sawyer had a court, but they were yings who spoke twenty words of English, sufficient for him to order them around; for business he had come to rely on Calvino's advice. There'd been something in Calvino's style and attitude that Brandon liked.

Brandon leaned back like a good audience of one, holding a single-malt whiskey, and watched Calvino perform; he usually found that it was good entertainment. Wasn't this act a variation of what his mother had done throughout his childhood? At some point Calvino had rolled over his investigation work into a more general consultancy to the joint venture. Though the revised arrangement had cost more money, that didn't matter to Brandon, because Calvino had a knack, like some men at poker, and in the end what Calvino saved the joint venture came to vastly more than his fees. It was the way some people got very rich and others, who relied simply on their own talents and brains, just got along the best they could.

"I wrote two reports for Brandon," said Calvino.

Tanny raised an eyebrow, her tongue dancing against the inside of her cheek. She'd seen only one. "I saw one of them. It was dated the seventeenth of August."

"What about August ninth?" He thought she'd be a terrible poker player. Her tics would have done all but show her hand.

She mouthed, "No. Didn't see that one." Tanny shifted in her seat, sighing. "This isn't good. How can we move ahead if people here aren't going to be straightforward?"

Tanny's net of "people here" was wide enough to cover Calvino and anyone else within drinking range of Brandon. Had she gone out of her way to insult him when he'd been upfront and when he could have had her running around in circles chasing her own tail?

"Isn't that why Marshall sent you?" The anger stirred just below the surface of his voice. "Aren't you supposed to be doing *your own* due diligence? That way you can decide if I'm making stuff up. I can understand Marshall's concern. The Sawyer family doesn't know me. Brandon hired me. The family knows Brandon and thought with all that money riding in this business, they'd better get a second opinion," he said, stopping at a traffic light. Motorcycles filled up the gaps on both side of the car, the riders looking in at Tanny the way lions look at a lamb. The light changed, and the motorcycles shot off.

She turned and watched him gliding in and out of the traffic.

"What's your end of the deal?"

Calvino shook his head. "I've got no end."

She shot him a look as if a *katoey* had stuck her hand into her handbag.

"You're doing this just for a fee of a couple grand?"

By New York standards, he was working for free. "You're saying I'm a cheap date? That's okay, too. Why don't you ask Brandon to throw in another grand a month?" he said, winking at her.

"Why would I do that?"

"No reason," he said. *Combat pay* was on his lips. Call it the Tanny Craig factor, chauffeuring a woman whose brief was to bust his balls.

It hadn't helped that Brandon had considered passing along his reports. Calvino understood why Brandon hadn't sent Marshall the August report. Calvino found out that Kowit, the dead reporter, had interviewed Achara in January. The police investigation had placed them at a restaurant with tables outside overlooking the street. Kowit and Achara had exchanged *wais*. Performed the little polite Thai social dance.

Not once but twice, Brandon, under pressure from New York, had asked Calvino to check out every aspect of Achara's business, his associates and his family. They were clean; nothing much connected them to the murder. The interview was conducted six months before the murder. One interview was a slender reed to support a murder charge. Kowit had interviewed dozens and dozens of people during the same period. That's what journalists did; that's what investigators did as well.

"The reporter had interviewed Achara half a year earlier," said Calvino.

"I feel Brandon should have revealed that. Don't you?"

"It was a background story on real-estate speculation. Three other people were interviewed for the same story. I checked Kowit's report. He interviewed sixty-three people before he was shot. So if being interviewed makes Achara a suspect, he needs to take a number and wait, because there's a monster lineup of suspects."

"Do you have copies of Kowit's newspaper articles?"

He nodded, a smile spreading across his face. "The clippings are in my office."

It had taken Calvino a couple of weeks to assemble a file cabinet of background material.

"Of course you read Thai," he said in a flat, matter-of-fact voice.

Tanny didn't read or speak a word of Thai. Calvino decided this was a good time to get that limitation out of way. She'd been sent to investigate a deal in a language she couldn't read or understand. Only someone from New York would have shrugged that obstacle off as insignificant. Calvino always found it comforting to work with people who underestimated the importance of being culturally fluent. They inevitably fell down an open sewer marked by a sign in Thai.

She cleared her throat. "How quickly can you have them translated?"

"Three, four months." He smiled, waiting for a reaction.

She ignored his time estimate, meaning that was a problem. "Three or four days," she countered.

Calvino replied with a broad grin. "It's not just money. Only a handful of people can do a good translation. And the ones who can aren't available. They're working at embassies, the UN, the multinationals. You ever see that Johnny Cash biopic? I remember the English subtitles. Johnny Cash in the early days is a door-to-door salesman. He introduces himself to the woman who opens the door. 'Hi, I'm Johnny Cash.' The subtitle underneath translated it as, 'Hi, they call me Johnny Fresh Money.' "

Tanny neither laughed nor smiled.

"When you see a movie, you can figure out what's happening. But when you read a paper translation, all you're left with is trying to figure out why anyone would be called 'Fresh Money,' " he said.

"I'm certain that you can figure out something," she said. "Put someone on the job." Tanny understood Marshall well enough to think that if Achara had investigated the background of Sawyer's family, he would have required a roomful of file cabinets for the divorces, committal orders, arraignments, depositions, suspension-of-shares reports, class actions, security-commission hearings, shareholder lawsuits. None of the allegations involved common crimes; nothing stuck, but a lot of mud had been thrown against a lot of people. The most secretive decisions and discussions were done behind a secure boardroom door, in hotel suites, on yachts, at first-class airport lounges. Nothing any investigator could find, no matter how hard he looked.

Calvino pulled to a halt in front of a gate and guardhouse. Uniformed guards asked for his identification. "You need to show some ID." Calvino handed the guard his Thai driver's license.

Tanny dug out her American passport, the wings of the golden eagle catching the sun.

"I wouldn't give them that," he said, noticing her birthday and place of birth. She was thirty-two years old and had been born in Ayuthaya. Her name appeared as Tanny

Craig. He pointed at the New York driver's license in her wallet. "That will do it."

The guard returned the documents and Calvino drove gently over the speed bump into the gated community. Next to him, riding shotgun, was a Thai who neither spoke nor wrote Thai. She didn't wai, or, even worse, she hadn't developed the habit of returning a wai she'd received; she didn't smile, and she held herself with the tense posture of a combat infantry solider waiting for the order to advance. That was a first, he thought. He filed the information away; sooner or later he'd find out how that had happened. The Land of Smiles was good at producing laughter, sunshine, and mystery. She'd managed to filter out any personal feelings. Whoever she was, her life in New York, what made her laugh or cry, had been buried under the professional mask. Calvino found himself wondering, if he chipped away at the façade, what he'd find underneath. With his stockbroker and neighbor, Siriporn, he'd been on the other end of the chipping away. She had been looking to get inside him, and he'd been backpedaling. Considering Tanny's personal coolness while working on a case, he thought he was looking at someone very much like himself.

FIVE

BRANDON SAWYER'S HOUSE was inside a *moo ban*, a private gated village, with uniformed security working control gates in and out of the complex of houses. Thailand existed outside the gates. It was no different from similar enclaves of seriously wealthy people in California, Arizona, or Florida. Places with good weather and cheap, illegal alien labor. The moo ban had a network of wide avenues with mansions hidden behind high fences and bamboo, speed bumps twenty meters apart. The Thai ground crews worked under the hot sun setting up sprinklers, cutting the grass, and trimming trees. They could have passed for Mexican laborers in their oversize hats and baggy clothes. The houses had been built on an epic scale, with enough stone, brick, and concrete to erect an upcountry village. The main difference was that this village was the end of the rainbow. Most of the owners stayed locked inside their castles, terrified that upcountry people were under the spell of French revolutionary ideas and one day might invade, break open the gates, knock down the walls, and walk away with everything inside. Sawyer accepted the communal paranoia of the rich as normal; he'd grown up with it. The fear of having one's rich throat slit in the middle of the night cut across race, culture, ethnic divides. Those at the receiving end of the pipeline dumping mountains of money created their own villages to house victors and to keep out the losers who could turn vengeful at any moment.

"Here's where they'll build the farang guillotine," Calvino said as the east wall of Sawyer's estate came into view.

"I don't understand," she said.

"You're not following the politics? Doesn't matter. Most people don't. After the revolution it's too late."

"The guillotine is French. Not Thai."

"Crushing by elephants is an old-time favorite Thai method of execution," said Calvino. "The guillotine is more humane, don't you think?"

She shivered at the thought, let out a small sigh before she shrugged off Calvino with a disapproving look. Then he pulled into Sawyer's driveway, and a gradual change, subtle at first, overtook her. Money did that to people. Parked in the driveway were Brandon's silver BMW, an eight-seat van, a black SUV, and several motorcycles, including two Harleys, the chrome polished like mirrors, catching the sun. Two women were wiping down the BMW as Calvino shut off the engine of his Honda.

"He lives here?" Her mouth dropped.

"Brandon calls it Castle Sawyer."

Brandon Sawyer's house was a mansion that a nouveau riche Chinese merchant built in homage to Tara, the southern plantation house from the movie *Gone With The Wind*. Regal and elegant, it was ringed by a circular driveway, and inside the house a circular staircase spiraled to the upper floor. There were African black marble floors and Burmese teak tables and chairs, two *salas,* and a pond with carp and goldfish swimming in it, nestled in the garden behind the main house. They stopped in the redbrick drive sheltered from the private street by banana and mango trees. Barefoot servants ran up to the car to open Calvino's door. They remembered him from his last trip, when Calvino had brought them a basketful of durian.

The car door swung open, and Calvino stretched out his right leg. Two maids and gardener waied him, pulling at his arm and shoulder, staring at Tanny in the passenger seat. She sat quietly, gazing straight ahead. One of the maids waied and spoke Thai to Tanny, who looked blank and ignored her. The maid, confused and hurt, had been deflated.

"She doesn't speak Thai," Calvino said in Thai. "Don't take it personally. She speaks only English."

The maids smiled, thinking Calvino was telling them some kind of farang joke. Anyone who looked like Tanny was expected to speak perfect Thai. That was a given.

He looked up at the house. Sawyer's large bulk stood framed in the open door.

"I hope to hell you didn't bring durian again," Brandon called out.

Calvino walked around to the rear of the car and opened the trunk. He pulled out a basket and handed it to one of the maids. She removed the top, smiled, and the others looked inside. "Sticky rice and fresh mangoes," said Calvino.

"I've got mangoes coming out of—" Sawyer stopped as he watched Tanny get out of Calvino's car and walk toward the house.

She held out her hand. "I'm Tanny Craig."

"I can see why my brother hired you. You're beautiful."

She didn't return the smile. "Actually, I work for Sawyer Corporation."

"Okay, his corporation hired you, if that's how you want to play it. But you're still a dish. And I approve of Marshall's taste. He pumped her hand in the kind of shaking exercise that gives the appearance of no probable ending point. Brandon smacked his lips and rolled his eyes. "I'd like a taste of that dish."

"Does that mean you won't need Mr. Calvino's services?" she asked as Calvino walked up, surrounded by Sawyer's servants. His vulgarity hadn't fazed her in the least.

Calvino grinned. This woman, despite her accent, had to be from New York, he thought. She had balls.

Sawyer's smile vanished. "Hey, you're kinda pushy, aren't you?" That was his first shot, fired wildly and, more important, missing the mark. It was an example of a Sawyer statement that began as a declaration and ended as a question mark. Calvino was accustomed to Brandon and tried to think what someone who didn't really know him would be thinking at that moment.

She let go of his hand.

"I like to get to the point," said Tanny. "I find it's easier."

"She's a professional, Brandon," said Calvino. "That's what she told me."

Sawyer grinned. "Sweetheart, you never want to call yourself a professional in this town. It has an entirely different meaning. You could give a man the wrong idea."

She had expected to be baited. He waited a beat, thinking she would slap him.

Instead, Tanny checked the time, then the door. She half turned, her eyes on the move as she swept the grounds. "Perhaps we can we start to work?" One of Brandon's small yappy dogs with rat-size teeth yammered at her ankles until a maid called him: "Benjamin, Benjamin, *pai loey*." Enough already. Off.

"I have another one just like him. His name is Marshall," said Brandon. "That one over there is Vincent. If I get a fourth, I'll call him Tanny. Good name for a bitch."

Three Chihuahuas, white with brown markings on the face and body, ran around yapping and jumping, baring their teeth, the maids in hot pursuit; they had all been from the same litter. The yings were forever feeding them cookies, raising their blood-sugar levels, causing them to go into hyperactive cartoon mode. The one that answered to Vincent spun like a top as a servant brushed him away.

At the entrance to the house, Calvino stopped, braced himself against the doorjamb, and removed one shoe, then the other, and lined them up behind some of Sawyer's shoes near the wall. Tanny had gone halfway inside with her shoes still on.

"You mind removing your shoes?" asked Brandon, making his question sound more like a declaration.

Calvino had to give it to her. She was a quick study. She glanced around at the others; none of them wore shoes. "I keep forgetting," she said.

"Is that right? You forgot?" asked Sawyer, his tone in the Sawyer-like way of not asking.

After she removed her shoes, Brandon, walking barefoot, led them upstairs to the main sitting room. The windows overlooked the large salas, a swimming pool, and the Chinese carp pond in the garden. Calvino stood and looked out at the garden. He liked the view—water, flowers, and coconut trees. Birds singing. One of the maids was playing with the dogs.

Brandon started the meeting while Calvino continued to take in the expanse of green below. "I don't really know why Marshall had to send you business class from New York to look over Calvino's work. Does Marshall think Calvino's stupid and you're Einstein?"

Tanny raised a finger to her lips to signal silence. Brandon replied with an arched eyebrow and a shallow sigh. She nodded at the three yings in short shorts and halter-tops sitting around the table, eating strawberries and whipped cream, dangling bare feet not quite touching the floor. They moved like a troupe of mimes who'd been hit thigh high with a tranquilizer gun. "Who are these children?"

"There're not children. They're support staff," said Brandon. He had intended it as a joke.

"I'd asked for the meeting to be private. That means no one else."

"*I* understand what it means. But *they* don't understand a word of English," said Brandon.

One of the bored yings shuffled a deck of cards.

"They might have picked up more English than you think," she said. "Security is essential. Marshall told me he briefed you on that."

"Marshall's been briefing me on shit my whole life. I am twelve thousand miles away, so I don't have to listen to his briefings." He walked over to the yings and asked them to go outside for a swim. "It will be fun." The invitation had been issued with the magic word, and they were out of the room in under a minute.

"Thank you," Tanny said in a half whisper, as if she were in a library.

"Why do I have to be silent? Can you explain that to me?" asked Brandon.

"Routine precaution," she said. Tanny laid her briefcase on his desk, snapped open the latches, removed an antenna from the inside until it stretched two feet in height, and then pushed several toggle switches before securing a pair of earphones over her ears. Calvino glanced back from the window and smiled at Sawyer, who shrugged, rolling his eyes. "You'll let me know when I can talk, won't you?" he asked her.

Calvino sat in a chair next to Tanny. "She thinks someone might be listening to us." He whispered, smiling as he caught Brandon's eye.

"No one listens to me. Not the staff, the women, my brother—why would a stranger want to listen to what I've got to say?" Inside Brandon's world of maids, drivers, handymen, gardeners, security guards, the help acted like a fifth column; they worked on the inside for those with money, sometimes acting as nominee shareholders, signing documents they didn't read. They had all kinds of sensitive information that could be easily converted into fast cash. This was a downside to living in the moo ban. The staff had a community of eyes and ears watching and listening.

"Now we can start," she said.

Playing meeting leader seemed to come naturally to her. Brandon grinned and winked at Calvino. "Don't you wanna eat something first?"

Calvino had a history of clients who'd been in Thailand a long time. One of the things that rubbed off was the Thai preoccupation with food.

Before Tanny could say anything, two servants appeared from the kitchen, in that submissive half crouch, one with a vase containing freshly cut orchids and the other with a silver tray bearing a bowl of coconut milk, a bowl of sticky rice, and a plate of fresh-cut mangoes laid out like tiny bars of gold. The servant set the tray on a coffee table. She resumed her bent-over position and backed away. The older maid sucked her teeth as she cleaned up the mess of splattered strawberries and whipped cream left behind by the yings. The attitude of the maids made it clear that Brandon's latest collections of yings not only didn't bother to be neat, they used the house servants to do their laundry. It was the domestic struggle between bar yings and house servants—same class, same background, but they'd been assigned a different set of duties. The younger maid finished arranging the flowers and the food, and then both women beamed as they stood back from their offering.

"Ms. Craig, enjoy the mangoes," said Brandon.

"Why don't we go through some talking points first?"

She was negotiating already.

"Vinny, what about you?" Brandon asked, ignoring her. "I thought only politicians had talking points."

Calvino held up two fingers. Brandon beamed. "Bring Khun Vinny some of that single-malt whiskey and mangoes. Do you want a drink?"

They sat at the table while Tanny, controlling her anger, waiting near the door, managed to shake her head and retain some sense of dignity.

"Feel free to sweep the room again," said Brandon. "You never know if the tray is bugged. The maid who sliced the mangoes used to work for the CIA bureau chief."

"I'm not certain if you realize how serious this is, Mr. Sawyer."

"In the land of fun, being serious is fucking bad manners, Ms. Craig. It's also said to cause headaches, make people depressed. As a Thai you should know that seriousness only has downsides. No one would be in the streets protesting if the government could offer them some fun things to do."

Brandon finished his sticky rice and mango in several greedy swipes, like a bear devouring a couple of baby salmons. He held the plate out for a servant to collect. He didn't even have to put the plate down. "I want to say something. The joint venture with Achara is one of the best deals Sawyer Corporation has ever made. Financial meltdown or street demonstrations, none of it matters to our business. It will remain highly profitable. We've checked him out. Meaning, of course, Vinny and me asked the right questions of the right people. And Achara's as straight as a line of Colombian coke." Brandon tapped a finger on Tanny's electronic device.

"Tell me why the police investigated Achara in the murder of the journalist," she asked.

"Because that's what they get paid to do. The more people they interview, the more chances they have to shake down the nervous types. Everyone has something to hide. They slip the cops a white envelope and get their name checked off the list."

"You're saying Achara bribed the police?"

"Never, my dear Ms. Craig. Achara's a good man. He doesn't need to bribe anybody."

"That's only your conclusion. 'A good man' and that's it? The board wants slightly more than your opinion about his goodness."

"My brother said he was sending a Thai investigator. You don't seem very Thai," said Brandon. He winked at Calvino. "You look the part. That's why you were cast. But you're not really Thai. I'd say it's my brother who's dealing in some misleading generalizations."

"We can't progress if you keep changing the subject," she said.

"We keep our shares. Achara stays in the picture. That's the way it is," said Brandon. "Work with Vinny, and after you're finished next week, go back to New York and tell my brother to fuck himself."

"Why didn't you tell Marshall about Mr. Calvino's August report?"

Brandon's eyes widened, the crow's feet spreading outward. Calvino looked away from the window, where he'd been watching the three yings playing like dolphins in the swimming pool. "Pool decorations" was how Brandon had once described the young women who came to visit and stayed on, from a couple of days to six months, before new ornaments appeared to replace the old ones. "Who told you about that?"

"I told her," said Calvino.

Brandon's jaw dropped. It wasn't his best look. "Goddamn, Vinny. You're supposed to be on my side. That report was confidential." His fist clenched around his glass, and for a moment it looked like he might throw it against the wall. But there was no clear space between the art and windows. He set the glass down. Tanny cracked a smile for the first time. She had gotten to him, and she knew it. It was more of a smirk that comes with having scored a small victory. Brandon exhaled loudly, rolled his head like a swimmer coming up from the bottom of the pool for air. She'd won a toehold on the beach, and she gave every indication of intending, like a good Marine, to fight until she captured the position she'd been sent to secure. "You led Marshall to believe there was just the one report. I don't think he'd like that. Do you?"

"Judas," whispered Brandon, baring his teeth at Calvino.

"I didn't mislead anyone," said Calvino. "It's no secret that Kowit interviewed Achara last January. That's on public record. You asked me to cooperate with Marshall's investigator. You said give her a desk, a phone, a computer. It's a due-diligence exercise. 'We've got nothing to hide. Give her whatever she asks for.' Do you recall having that conversation?"

"Well, give me a dead fish to eat. It's obviously all my fault."

"Anytime you want me off the case, let me know," said Calvino. It took half a minute before Brandon broke eye contact.

Lost in thought, Brandon swirled his drink around the inside of the glass like a chemistry student conducting an experiment in a beaker. He looked up, shook his head. "That's what Marshall wants. Work together. I've got it. Like you said, there's nothing to hide. We've got some important contracts to sign next."

"Correct. There are some important contracts to sign," said Tanny.

Brandon rubbed his fingers together. "Money. That's all Marshall thinks about, cares about. I've got a relationship with Achara. It might mean nothing to Marshall, but it means something to me."

"I'll leave you a set of documents. Please sign them. There's a signing tab so you'll know where to. Let me know when you finish, and I'll arrange to have them picked up," she said, pulling out a sealed envelope and sliding it across the table.

Calvino waited for Brandon to pass it to him with the instruction, *Have a look at these and let me know what you want me to do.*

Only Brandon didn't say that. "You can work out of Calvino's office until then," he said. His hands folded over the envelope.

"I'll let you know what I find," said Tanny, and then she rose from the table.

That's the way Brandon wants to play it, thought Calvino. Cards so close to his chest that you'd need a scalpel to peel them off. As the meeting ended, Brandon walked over to the windows and rattled off a set of specific instructions to Tanny: Use Calvino and his office so she could go through the information, study the evidence, evaluate the risk, and interview Achara. Then submit her final report to Marshall.

"It's up to Marshall whether you see my report," said Tanny. "Don't take too long in signing the documents."

Brandon's slightly deflated grin faded. Calvino waited for showman's comeback, but Brandon fell into silence, leaving Calvino and Tanny to discuss the details of their working arrangements over the next few days. A couple of times Calvino glanced at Brandon, who was half listening, but his mind was somewhere else—maybe outside in the pool splashing around with the yings. But there was a hint of seriousness in the silence, and as Brandon had explained, that was something you weren't supposed to be in Thailand, unless, of course, there was some major problem.

Brandon's stare fixed on a distant point, a space beyond the swimming pool, the yings running around the pool edge in their tiny bikinis. It was as if he had seen an invisible force approaching, one that couldn't be easily stopped, a strong, determined, and unyielding wall of trouble. "That's it. Why don't you work out what you need to do at Calvino's office?" said Brandon. "You don't need me."

45

"You've got things to do," said Calvino, looking at the envelope on the table. Brandon shrugged and waited for a servant to pour him another drink. Once he'd sipped the fresh drink, he went to the door and shouted for the yings to return to the nest. It wasn't so much that Brandon was interested in talking to them as that the yings shielded him against the isolation and the waiting for the wall that was closing in and about to entomb him. Marshall had used the financial crisis and political unrest in Bangkok to set in motion forces that couldn't be pulled back. Only Brandon didn't fully believe that; he had a plan to stop Marshall. And sooner or later he'd have no choice but to let Calvino in on the plan. But not on this day, or inside his house in the presence of Tanny Craig, a dark angel dispatched from New York with an envelope delivered in front of a witness.

She'd handled Brandon like a veteran bullfighter, showing the cape, letting him charge, stumble past, a look of dumb surprise on his face as he missed and circled for another run, then missed again and again, until he got tired and told them to leave. Calvino found himself attracted to this messenger. She had class. And she excelled at something Calvino liked—letting a bull run himself around in circles until he collapsed. He had an idea she would be waving her cape at him next, and that made him smile. It'd been a long time since Calvino had come across a worthy adversary whose first instinct was to unholster her sexuality and use it as a weapon to get what she wanted. Tanny had revealed at the funeral, and now at Brandon's, that she had other, more powerful weapons. Her instincts made her effective in the field and more than a little dangerous inside a room. She worked like a long-distance runner, who, unlike Brandon, never broke a sweat.

SIX

CALVINO, HIS NECKTIE unknotted, jacket slung over his shoulder, strolled into the Lonesome Hawk. World-weary, absorbed in private thought, he walked past the bar without acknowledging any of the regulars. But it didn't much matter; most sat on their barstools, heads down, concentrating on their food, their women, their troubles. Old George's death acted like a hydraulic pump, filling the bar with a deep sense of gloom. Outside, a jackhammer vibrated. Men slowly drank their Singhas from the bottle, peeling the labels off with a thumbnail. A thick fog of cigarette smoke hung over the bar counter. A law had been passed making smoking inside restaurants and bars illegal. No one cared. George's death had dragged everyone down a couple of notches, looping their thoughts to the future, when it would be their turn to be transformed into a thick rope of gray smoke coiling against the Bangkok sky.

McPhail climbed off his barstool, picked up his cigarettes and drink, walked over to Calvino's booth, and slipped inside, grinning. Given that George had been cremated and everyone was drunk or nearly drunk in grief over the old man's death, Calvino tried to read some meaning into McPhail's larger-than-life smile.

"The woman picked you up at a funeral. George would have been looking down applauding. Everyone's been talking about how you scored. Calvino had a ying crawling into his car at George's funeral." He winked at Calvino, leaned over and shook his wrist. "You're the man."

Calvino stared at him. This was how false legends were launched.

"You think that you did the right thing?" asked McPhail. The ethics of picking up yings at the funeral of a fallen comrade had obviously been a topic of discussion at the bar. The speed at which McPhail had joined Calvino indicated that he'd been anointed with the task of finding out the details.

"It wasn't a score. It was work, McPhail."

"Sure. You don't want to talk about it. Spoil her reputation. That's noble."

"She's an investigator from New York."

McPhail frowned. "Everyone said she was Thai. New York? Vinny, cut the bullshit. Who was she, and does she have a sister?"

"Tanny Craig. And she's as American as you. I take that back. She's more American than anyone in this bar."

It wasn't an explanation that McPhail had expected. The rumors had already had the ying working in one of the "dead artist" bars on Soi 33. A couple of the regulars swore they recognized her. One claimed to have bar-fined her five weeks ago. McPhail had the unpleasant duty of passing this along to the others waiting at the bar.

"Believe what you want. She only looks Thai."

"An American?" McPhail rubbed his jaw.

"I saw her passport. She's an American."

McPhail lit a cigarette and blew smoke to the side. "George's ashes would roll over in a little wave inside the urn." He shouted at a passing waitress who was already a grandmother. Her eyes were red from crying. She sniffled as she took Calvino's order for a double Mekong and Coke. "She was one classy-looking broad. Everyone else who was at the funeral was talking about her. When are you seeing her again?"

Calvino figured that "everyone" covered McPhail and maybe Arnold.

"In half an hour," said Calvino.

"You animal. Your place or hers?"

"In my office."

"Kinky."

"She has a desk and computer at the office."

"She's working for you?"

"The other way round," said Calvino.

"You're doing her. I can tell."

"Don't quit your day job. You're no mind reader."

"I don't have a day job."

"That's your problem."

"She's *your* problem. You picked her up at Old George's funeral, and now she's moved into your office. You're like some guy fresh off the boat."

"Did it look like I picked her up?"

"Was she or wasn't she at a fucking funeral?" He studied Calvino's reaction. "Gotcha."

"I told you she's not really Thai."

The regulars were going to be disappointed that Vincent Calvino had walked out of Old George's funeral with an American who only looked Thai. "Did she know George?"

Calvino shook his head and drank a long pull from the Mekong and Coke. "Never heard of him."

"She crashed George's funeral? How sick is that?"

"Trailing me," he said.

McPhail smiled again. "What did you do to her?"

A couple of the regulars turned from the bar, and their attention focused on Calvino. They wanted to hear his answer to that question. "It's not personal. She's in Thailand investigating a murder."

That was the kind of answer McPhail and the regulars liked. "She's tough, then?"

"She's like someone with a new hammer. She sees the world full of nails that need a good hammering down."

McPhail's eyes widened as he looked back at the kitchen. The cook walked out fanning herself, her blouse tied to expose a large, flabby stomach. "I'd like to have nailed her. So would have everyone at the funeral. But she went with you." Metaphors never worked all that well on the Lonesome Hawk crowd; they stuck with beer and literal explanations.

"She thinks I can help her."

"Can you?"

"I've done about all I can."

"But she wants more! Like all women!" shouted one of the men from the bar.

It was easier to cure a man of his addiction to drugs and alcohol than to wean him off his stereotypes, thought Calvino. Tanny didn't fit their mode, and that made some people in the bar confused and angry, the signs of cold-turkey sweats.

Old George's booth remained empty, the water buffalo head on the eternal wait for its master's return. Men with bloodshot eyes lifted their bottles of beer more slowly than usual, slightly drunk, more than a little anxious about what came next. Like most foreigners in Thailand, they were either too afraid or not afraid enough. It was the rare man who got the balance between paranoia and complacency pegged without some delusion intervening to throw him off course. By leaving George's funeral with the beautiful stranger ying, Calvino had given them something to cling onto. He tried for a moment to see Tanny Craig through McPhail's eyes, the eyes of the other men around the bar. But what he saw was an all-business professional sweeping

Brandon Sawyer's room for bugs while three stunning yings splashed outside in a swimming pool.

"Hey, Vinny, who's the new girlfriend?" Convict Carl shouted across the bar.

The bar chatter subsided as all eyes were on Calvino. The demons of prison life still haunted Carl, gave him an edgy tic in his right eye. McPhail lit a cigarette, allowing the smoke to curl out of his nostrils.

"Carl, when I find a new cellmate, you'll be the first to know."

Calvino paid for his drink and slid out of the booth.

The guy next to Carl nudged him in the ribs and laughed. "You know about cellmates," he said.

"But you just got here," said McPhail.

"I need to get some air. And I've got work to do." He looked around at the men. He knew the faces. What he didn't know was what was behind most of those faces. Except today their masks had come off; grief was the great paint stripper, taking off layers of pretense, petty emotions, and secret grievances, exposing the bare cement walls of life and death underneath.

"The American government has a plan to put microchips in everyone," said Norris, his hairy arms and chest exposed in the one-size-too-small T-shirt with the word "Bangkok" and a stylized garuda on the front. "FEMA has built hundreds of prisons in California and on the East Coast. Some of them can hold fifty thousand prisoners. These prisons have the razor wire strung along the fence facing inside. And another roll of the razor wire is laid down but not facing the inside. You hear what I'm saying? That razor wire is for the outside world. You tell me, has there ever been a prison built with the barbed wire strung to keep people out? They don't want anyone looking inside, snooping around, and putting shit on the Internet. George saw what was happening. Everyone sees it. They plan to use chip implants to download credits for work done. That's a fact. You're told to spend what's on that chip each month or lose it. No carry forward is allowed. They don't want anyone saving up to buy their freedom. The government will be able to track you wherever you go. They'll know what you spend and what you buy. They'll sell that information. It's a circle, Vinny. And if you try to break free, then you'll find yourself in one of those prisons. No more rights to challenge the police. They can hold you for as long as they want, and there's nothing you can do about it."

Norris had spent hours trading conspiracy theories with Old George. George's death would be hard for Norris, who had lost his best audience. Norris took a long pull from his beer. Some men needed a good excuse not to return home. Norris had found his.

"I didn't see you at the funeral," said Calvino.

Norris shook his head, sighed. "They would be taking pictures of everyone who went. You can be certain they got your picture. It goes into a file."

"For the chip implant," said Calvino.

Norris nodded, smiled. "They didn't get my picture."

"But they will, sooner or later," said Calvino.

The muscles in Norris's neck tensed. His lips folded around the bottle as he tilted his head back, eyes nearly closed. He looked up and sighed. "I hope that day never comes."

"Norris, I wanna see a picture of one of those secret prisons," said McPhail.

"You don't believe me?"

"I want to see the razor wire. With hundreds of prisons, someone somewhere must have taken a picture with their cell phone," said McPhail.

"Close the goddamn door!" shouted one of the men three stools down the bar.

The noise of the jackhammer roared through the bar as Calvino stood holding the door open, letting a blast of hot, polluted air roll in. Getting away from Norris was as challenging as finding evidence to support his various conspiracies. Once Big Henry started bellowing about the noise from the jackhammer, Calvino found the opening he needed, and he slipped out of the bar, leaving McPhail and Norris to argue over the existence of America's secret detention centers.

SEVEN

OUTSIDE, IN THE heat, Calvino turned right and walked toward the Irish pub, stopping outside the muay Thai joint on the corner. Two farangs wearing trunks and gloves, their feet wrapped, danced around the ring, and a Thai trainer, a head shorter and darker, shadowed them. No one had ever seen a Thai kickboxer in the Lonesome Hawk; they were young, hard, lean men, two generations younger than the bar regulars. Calvino watched the two young men with cropped hair, square jaws, six-pack abs, and bulging shoulders and arms. They had the physical capacity to inflict a lot of damage using only their hands and feet. Both men wore headguards and plastic mouthpieces, making them look like advanced alien invaders in baggy silk shorts. McPhail came up alongside and stopped beside Calvino.

"To listen to Norris, you'd think a conspiracy got George," said McPhail.

Calvino nodded, watching through the window. "There was no conspiracy. Only old age—that's not a conspiracy. That's called a good enough reason to die."

The glass doors of the muay Thai joint stood wide open. The jackhammer noise made no difference to the boxers or the trainers. The entryway to the gym was littered with cheap plastic sandals and chewed-up tennis shoes. The large tennis shoes belonged to the young farang boxers. Beyond the door, in the ring, the boxers circled, threw a tentative punch, arched a foot into the strike position, all concentration and focus as they moved around the ring, looking for any edge, any opportunity to connect with a takedown blow. In the corner a middle-aged Thai sat with his legs crossed, eyes closed like a monk in deep meditation, a thick layer of calluses on bare feet that rested on a desk, tattooed arms stretched behind his head. The boxers didn't seem to mind. They sparred, lost inside the moment, unaware of Calvino and McPhail watching them. One boxer twisted to the side, landed a punch; the other reeled against the ropes, and then backpedaled before responding with a flurry of punches.

"You know the secret of muay Thai?" Calvino asked.

"A good kick in the nuts," said McPhail.

Calvino didn't respond as he watched another series of punches knock the fighter in the blue trunks onto his ass. The boxer sat with his knees raised on the mat, looking dejected or shaken or both. Catching his breath, he counted to eight before rising to his feet, touched gloves with his sparring partner in the red trunks. There was a brute elegance in the way they moved around the ring, mindful, focused, in perfect harmony. A flurry of punches was followed by kicks. An explosion of hands and feet, a blur of motion, and then the boxers fell into their dance, reconnecting to a zone where everything is in balance, if only for an instant.

"The secret is waiting until the other guy makes a mistake. Then a good kick, a fair one, not one in the nuts, lands where it should and hits home." He pushed his fist against McPhail's chest. "Then his wind is knocked out. And he goes down."

McPhail shrugged and lit a cigarette. "Speed's more important. If you're fast enough, you don't need to wait for the other guy to screw up."

"One or two such boxers who come around once every generation are that fast. But most men, they look for the weakness, the lack of concentration, and some hint that the opponent is distracted, and then they act, fast and with all the weight they can put behind their punch. That's how a man wins at boxing. It's how a man wins at most things."

Muay Thai was the national sport. It was the negative image of their worst fear: Making a mistake. Even the *thought* of making a mistake paralyzed most Thais. Better not to act than to get something wrong. But muay Thai let them witness firsthand what happens when a mistake is made. Blam. The heel of someone's foot strikes under your jaw, lifting you off the ground. To make a mistake in ordinary life risked the loss of face; to make a mistake in muay Thai was a surefire way to have your face smashed in.

The boxer in the blue trunks hit the mat a second time. He leaned forward from the waist, his face almost touching his outstretched legs. A sense of loss, a struggle ended, crossed his face. The boxer in the red trunks knelt beside him, touched his glove to the man's cheek, and started to remove his gloves. The fight was over. One man had won, the other sat in defeat.

As they walked on, McPhail had his hands stuffed in his pockets. "I used to box. I could take a punch. I was one tough bastard," he said. "But that was a long time ago."

" 'I coulda been a contender,' " said Calvino. Sometimes an old movie line summed up a public library's worth of weariness and regret.

McPhail nodded. He shot Calvino a sober, grim, distant look, as if he were somewhere else. "I really was. No bullshit."

Calvino nodded in agreement as McPhail scored a direct hit on one of Calvino's law: Everyone can throw a punch, but only a few can take one.

They walked a while until Calvino stopped under the marquee of the old cinema house opposite the entrance to the square. McPhail said, "See you around." He looked like he wanted to say something else but couldn't find the words, so he said nothing and kept walking—hands in his pockets, shoulders slumped, head down, feeling his age in the heat of the day. It wasn't like McPhail. But the world was changing all around him. He was looking to find his place, like everyone else. The young reminded a man that his place was a temporary accident. McPhail headed in the direction of the bars on the other side of the square, a place with enough old rednecks to make him feel young. At a certain age, it took a fair amount of alcohol to ride the illusion train of youth when just about everyone knew that that train had left the station ages ago. It was the kind of illusion that rolled through a man, putting him in the right frame of mind to do a lot of serious drinking.

Calvino left Washington Square, stopping on Sukhumvit Road and waiting to cross over to the Soi 31 side. He waited not for the cars to stop at the marked crosswalk—that would rarely happen—but for the first person to edge into the road, making himself a human shield, and then gradually for one car to stop, followed by another, until the traffic briefly halted. As he waited, Calvino thought about Marshall Sawyer, wondering if he really thought he'd made a mistake in the risk assessment of the local Thai partner, or if that was a smoke screen for what was inside the envelope Tanny had handed to Brandon.

Men like Achara didn't get arrested or go to prison. Calvino regretted that he'd not written that in the report instead. These were careful men who avoided silly mistakes, because only a boneheaded mistake would land them in trouble. He should have written that as well. All the things he wished he'd written and had never thought of at the time would have made a reasonable library. An office worker with a thin mustache, a white shirt, and dark trousers stepped into the road. Calvino followed the volunteer, half a step behind. Locals made much better human shields for crossing

Sukhumvit than did tourists, who tended either to freeze in the middle of the road or start screaming and shouting, shaking their fists, making angry faces. That kind of farang behavior amused Thai drivers to no end, and they took it as an invitation to jam down on the gas pedal. Local drivers thought of it as target practice.

Inside Calvino's office, two Thai women talked with an intimacy that suggested they'd known each other for years. Tanny sat in a chair facing Ratana, who positioned herself on Calvino's desk. It was the first time he'd ever seen her sitting on his desk, ankles hooked like a schoolgirl, acknowledging him with a sideways glance without a break in the conversation. Tanny told her about Brandon Sawyer's wrinkled brow as he'd watched her walk into his house with her shoes on. Ratana had seen Brandon in operation, and he never struck her as being a defender of Thai ways. Ratana saw Vincent standing in the doorway listening to them.

"Tanny told me the story about Brandon and her shoes," Ratana said.

"You had to be there," said Calvino, nodding at Tanny, who had turned around in her chair, facing him. "There's something not quite right about a farang enforcing the shoes-off rule against a Thai who isn't Thai."

Ratana laughed, and that eased the atmosphere back to the fun zone. He'd interrupted one of those "Isn't the world of farangs a strange one?" conversations Thais have among themselves. Calvino circled behind his desk, removed his jacket, and sat down in his chair.

"Nice building you've got here," said Tanny. "Your wreck of a car is a good cover for the poor-farang act."

It didn't take much of a leap for Calvino to fill in the blanks about what Tanny had been digging around for. Looking for dirt that was as good as gold. The two of them had been bonding while he'd been at the Lonesome Hawk.

Ratana looked annoyed. Why shouldn't she look upset? Calvino thought. She had just been double-crossed. Given out confidential information to someone who seemed a little too pleased at her luck. Ratana had told Tanny about his financial windfall. How he came into a great deal of money, which had, among other things, allowed him to buy the building that had for years housed his office. If Tanny checked it out, she'd find that it was legitimate money—or at least clean enough under prevailing local standards.

Ratana moved to the door, halfway between Calvino and Tanny. She stretched forward and handed Tanny a photograph of a child. "Your boy is lovely," said Ratana.

One of the things Calvino liked about his secretary was that her emotional recovery time was a couple of minutes. Whatever annoyance she felt toward Tanny for encouraging her to discuss Calvino's increase in wealth had receded, vanished.

"Jeffrey. That's my son's name," said Tanny, taking back the photograph. Calvino glanced at the boy's photo as Ratana handed it back. But the passing of the photo happened too fast; the boy was a blur.

Marshall Sawyer sent the mother of a youngster to walk the front lines in Bangkok, thought Calvino. That was how capitalism worked. You deployed any asset that gave you an edge. Business always came first.

"Let me have a look," said Calvino. "Seven years old?"

"Six," said Tanny.

Calvino couldn't help but wonder about the boy's father. What kind of American would Tanny Craig have married? Was Craig his family name that she'd used on her passport? The kid looked *luk-krueng,* with the straight nose, brown eyes, and light-colored hair. He wore a New York Mets T-shirt and posed with a baseball glove on his left hand and a baseball held in his right. He had that Little League ready-to-play intensity. "Looks like a future Mets shortstop. Your husband's influence."

"We're divorced. He has no influence."

"None?" asked Calvino, raising an eyebrow.

"He's in federal prison. Five years for insider trading. But you don't want to hear about my little dramas. The point is—" She paused as the phone rang on the other side, and Ratana walked to her office and answered it.

"The point is?" asked Calvino.

"I get what I need. I'm on a plane and back with my son. That's the point," she said.

Ratana, standing in the door, nodded, her smile confirming the meager influence of men in the child-rearing game. The father of Ratana's son had the best excuse. He'd been murdered in Bangkok. Tanny's husband, from the way she'd described his role in the boy's life, was as good as dead.

"Anything you need to get you on that flight, you let me know."

"I will," she said.

Calvino was starting to get an idea what Tanny was capable of doing to get what she wanted. Making Ratana her ally was another step along that path. He should have seen it coming, but Brandon Sawyer had authorized payment for the additional office equipment to be bought and delivered to Calvino's office. He had insisted, and Calvino, not thinking it through, had given in. He'd never shared his personal space. Suddenly Tanny was in that space, in his face, budding up to Ratana, gathering information.

"That was your Mr. Sawyer on the phone," said Ratana.

Calvino looked up from his computer screen. "What did he want?"

"He said to tell you that Khun Achara will meet Khun Tanny on Wednesday afternoon at his office. He said you should go along. I asked if he wanted to talk to you directly. He said that he didn't. I could hear splashing of water."

Tanny shook her head, her lower lip in a pout. "Brandon would never get away with such behavior with young girls in America. He'd be thrown in prison as a sex offender."

"He's not living in America," said Calvino. "For the record, the women at his house are not underage."

"And next you'll tell me he hired you to verify their age."

In fact Brandon had. "It's what I do," said Calvino. "Verify facts."

She'd had some hard knocks, and, like a lot of people who had suffered from disappointment and anguish, Tanny Craig had a sala's worth of teakwood on her shoulder.

Ratana saw no point in getting into the middle of something that had the smell of conflict, and returned to her desk.

Tanny sat in her chair, her back to Calvino, and flipped through papers inside a file. She slammed the file on the desk, reached into her handbag and pulled out a pack of cigarettes. She shook one lose, lit it, tilting back. "I tried to get you kicked off the case," she said, exhaling smoke, slowly turning her chair around in time to watch his reaction.

"The thought passed my mind that you'd try," he said. "Nothing personal."

She nodded. "Not personal at all."

"It was ... professional," he said, smiling.

Tanny blushed, took a long drag on her cigarette, tapped the ash into a black oval ashtray with an advertisement for Singha beer. "I had no idea it meant that."

"Life is a string of saying one thing but finding out it means something different in another country."

"And you've got Thailand all figured out? Like what everything means?"

"Can we start over?"

Before she could answer his question, Calvino extended his hand. "Hi, my name's Vincent. I'm from New York. I work as a private investigator in Bangkok. What kind of professional are you?" asked Calvino.

A long moment of silence fell between them.

"Aren't you going to shake my hand?"

"Don't be ridiculous," she said.

He was going to ask her how a professional investigator married someone who ended up committing insider trading, got himself convicted and sentenced. It said something about her judgment. The same judgment she brought to work, inside his Bangkok office on a corporate due-diligence case. For the moment, he decided to let it ride.

"Corporate investigations," Tanny said. "And you, what does Vincent Calvino specialize in?" She shook his hand.

"Whatever walks through the door," he said. "That's my specialty."

"But you graduated to become a senior consultant to Mr. Sawyer."

"In life the unexpected happens. One minute you're married and living the good life, the next your ex-husband is in jail and you're a single mother. You didn't graduate into that life. That life wormed its way into what you do and who you are."

He had made it personal once he decided she was spinning him. Before she'd even left New York, she would have run his name through a criminal search website and found his old problem with the law in New York and his removal from the list of lawyers licensed by the New York bar association. On her computer screen was the result of her latest Google search. She made no attempt to block his view of the screen. In fact, she seemed to invite his attention to the fact that no matter how private his life seemed, she found ways to explore inside; no locked rooms remained. She carried a thumb drive that had fifty pages of documents from searches on Calvino and thousands of pages on the background of the joint-venture deal. His part of the overall position in the deal universe was a moon around a distant planet, circling an obscure star.

"You sound like an existentialist," she said. " 'The unexpected happens' is something my ex-husband used to say."

Calvino smiled as if he'd ducked a bullet. "I don't believe that most people have many good choices, if that's what you mean. Mostly they're left with the least-bad choice. I'm not so much existential as realistic. My opinion I draw from working the street, investigating people's lives, seeing what has gone wrong and what they can do about it. In most cases they get around to doing something about their life, but it's too little, too late; life has closed in, grabbed their collar, pushed them against a wall like a seven-foot mugger with a knife pressed against the throat. And they come through my door to ask me to help them."

Tanny finished her cigarette and ground the butt in the ashtray. "Then why does Brandon Sawyer still have a knife against his throat?"

Calvino shrugged. "Some clients love the proximity of the blade."

"You're talking about Brandon," she said.

He waited a couple of seconds, letting her wonder what was going on inside his head. "What was in the envelope you gave him?"

"That's between Marshall and his brother."

Small talk ultimately was a dance around the trajectory of the blade. The dance had started, and there was still a big question about who was leading and who was following. Tanny had gone secretive about some documents. Brandon wasn't talking. It was just a matter of time before who was in control on the dance floor would become clear.

EIGHT

INSIDE MONTRI'S MANSION was a gallery, the size of an airport hangar, had a cathedral-like ceiling, walls slanting upward to a bank of glass skylights. On each wall was a framed Chini painting, perfectly lit, guarded by a small red velvet rope suspended between two brass stands. Beneath each painting was an elegantly handwritten description of the painting. The twenty-seven men in black ties and dinner jackets gathered in secret, showing no guilt or remorse about their wealth. One man was dressed in white, his neck heavy with amulets—that was Ajarn Veera, a professional medium (meaning that was how he made his fortune-telling livelihood, and not that he had any real science behind his predictions) picked by Montri to choose the auspicious time for the opening. Owning most of the commercial enterprises in country was their day job. They were public figures, but not the kind who had their faces plastered on highway billboards, one of those smiling faces on the way to the airport, inviting a driver to buy a washing machine, a premium whiskey, or a condominium. These men were the ones who got the lion's share of the money from such white, gray, and black commerce—it was hard to know when one color bled into the next.

They had come to see a private showing of paintings. Moguls, generals, a couple of cabinet ministers, a sea of big smiles, men who waied each other, cradling champagne glasses between their money-counting fingers. Men with real money never bothered to count it; the counters were in the wannabe category. But in Montri's gallery the wannabes circulated with the real power brokers.

Twenty-seven distinguished men who'd come to see a private exhibition of twenty-seven paintings. Not just any art, but a private collection that had been in Siam for nearly one hundred years.

Calvino had never seen Colonel Pratt in black tie and dinner jacket. He looked like a different person, blending in like a penguin into an ice-shelf colony. What was on the surface and what was buried beneath the ice were two different things. In this colony, relationships followed clan lines, detoured through intermarriage, bonded at elite schools, and exchanged benefits and favors through overlapping business empires. It was like being in a room where everyone shared the same birthday. Colonel Pratt had been invited only after Calvino refused to attend without his presence. Finally Montri thought it was a good idea to let each person invite a close friend; it was a brilliant way for the guest to get an extra dose of face.

A couple of months before the economic collapse, Calvino had sold twenty-seven oil paintings by the Italian artist Galileo Chini to Montri, a billionaire real-estate investor. It had been love at first sight—Montri and the Chini nudes. And Montri was a man who easily fell in love and just as easily fell out of love—a cycle that sometimes completed itself in the space of the same evening. With the Chini paintings, Montri couldn't help himself from falling madly in love twenty-seven times over. It was as if the nudes had been painted according to his personal instructions and sexual tastes. As Montri gave an explanation of each painting, his guests stared at the nubile bodies of Siamese dancers, peasants, workers, and prostitutes, a few giggles and sighs rising whenever Montri paused.

The artist had completed the paintings during a Vincent Van Gogh—like feverish period of near madness between 1911 and 1912, and he employed the same wild splashes of movement, color, and texture. Chini left viewers of his paintings a choice: Images of prostitutes weary or dreamy, sad or contemplative, drifting out of time or thinking about their next meals—which side one came down on matched one's experience of the world. The women with big eyes, painted mouths, awkwardly standing or sitting, seemed to have sprung from an agitated mind infected by a torrent of feelings—attraction and repulsion, want and desire, hope and despair.

Chini painted canvases populated by prostitutes because he had needed the money. Calvino understood the impulse; he, too, needed the money. Were the paintings pornography or works of art? The buzz saw of doubt never made a clean, final-cut answer and never would. For Montri—and he was the one who had paid for them in cash—the Chini nudes were an expression of high art.

"Which is your favorite?" asked a guest.

That was expected.

"I love them all," he said as the guests shook with laughter, refilling their champagne glasses.

Montri had cultivated a reputation for collecting women for a season, cutting them loose, taking on replacements with the dedication of a World War I Allied general. What Montri neglected to mention was that the one he coveted the most was a painting that Calvino had refused to include in the sale.

Montri was the perfect owner. The sale to him had been Pratt's idea. Montri was rich. The paintings would stay in Thailand. That had sealed the deal. Chini's paintings would be in the possession of a collector who valued them and had no incentive to sell them off. Montri hinted, in a subtle, indirect way, that the Chini paintings might be haunted by a family curse. He had consulted his spiritual adviser, Ajarn Veera, who had raised the possibility. The last owner had died a violent death. The artist might have been an opium addict. The bad karma had built up over nearly a century and needed cleansing. The black-magic ritual had been held two days before the exhibition opened. The *sadoh kroh* ceremony was performed to appease the ghosts of the dead artist, his opium-laced friends, and all the accumulated bad karma that had included the death of the previous owner. The past lives had to be taken into account.

The dead had their influence and their role to play. To ignore them was something Montri would never have considered.

The auspicious time and day had been selected by Ajarn Veera. Montri waited until precisely 9:19 P.M. before he announced that the exhibition was open. Calvino had met Ajarn Veera, the medium or *maw doo* as they were called in Thai, a birdlike man with a shaved head and bushy eyebrows, a long thin face, and full lips. It hadn't been easy to book Ajarn Veera, since he was in great demand as the voodoo wars had escalated between the political factions, each side using black magic to cast a spell of bad luck on its enemy. Curses loomed in the thick, rain-filled air. Each side had rolled out their favorite maw doo, instructing him on the next cosmic counterpunch—kickboxing at clouds, some said, but that insult never stopped any of them from dismissing the power of the maw doo.

"You could always sell them to a museum in Italy," said one of the guests, who had been a minister in a previous government.

"Never," said Montri, finding Calvino in the second row.

"If we lose our heritage, we lose everything," said another guest, nodding over to the group huddled around a Chinese man. "That's why we need great patriots like General Suchart. And Khun Wei is the general's man."

The mention of the general's name caused Pratt to stop his conversation and look over his shoulder at Zhang, who was standing a few meters away. He had attracted a small, appreciative audience.

"That's Wei Zhang," whispered Colonel Pratt.

In a sea of black ties, he stood out. People noticed him, were drawing into a semicircle around where he stood. People were drawn to Wei Zhang. Several features marked him: Zhang was uncommonly tall for a Chinese. Calvino made him for six-three. The other thing was his attitude, which projected calm, supreme confidence—in himself, his abilities, and his vision of the future. To look at him was to see a man who believed in himself—his diamond-crusted Rolex, designer gold-framed glasses, manicured nails, groomed eyebrows, narrow eyes that gave away nothing. Calvino guessed that Zhang was mid-forties; his waist was no longer small, a hint of flesh gathering around the belt-line. It was his height and attitude that cloaked Zhang with a mandarin-like detachment.

Colonel Pratt leaned over to Calvino and said, "Chinese. Wealthy. Connected." He had one of Wei Zhang's business cards. Expensive paper and gold lettering that said he was "Special Adviser to General Suchart, the founder of the True Sons of The Soil Party."

Colonel Pratt had already nailed these essential qualities about the Chinese businessman.

"Art and the sacred go together," said Montri with a grin. "Like a woman and a bed." He drew more laughter from the assembled guests. He gestured toward Ajarn Veera, who was deep in conversation with Wei Zhang. "That is Ajarn Veera, and he is the best maw doo in Asia. To have him here tonight wasn't easy. He's very busy." Ajarn Veera glanced over, and Montri gave him a deep wai.

Pratt had been right about Montri—once he'd seen the collection, he had to possess the paintings. It was only a matter of price. It seemed natural, so Pratt had told Calvino that on the evening of the special exhibition, Montri would want Calvino, given his family connection to the artist, to attend the private party. Calvino understood that it was a face thing. Montri wanted to parade before his guests the farang whose lineage provided a direct connection to the dead farang artist. The man who'd sold his heritage.

Close to Zhang, Brandon's business partner, Achara, was looking at one of the paintings, captioned "Siamese Dancer."

Calvino looked up in time to catch Achara's eye. "Hey, Khun Achara, you like the dancer?" asked Calvino. His face, thought Calvino, looked as if the bandages had just been removed and the healing process had some time to go before it was complete. A small scar here and there, a red ridge along the cheek, and a smile that exposed both lower and upper gums.

"She's very beautiful," said Achara. He turned to Wei Zhang. "Wei, Vincent Calvino. He's an American friend of Brandon's."

Calvino found that to be an interesting characterization of his relationship with Brandon Sawyer. Wei offered his hand, and Calvino shook. Before they could talk, Montri called for everyone's attention.

Montri pinged the rim of his champagne glass with his overlong pinkie nail—the sound echoed off the vast walls and ceiling, and the conversation came to a halt. "Gentlemen, welcome to the exhibition of Galileo Chini's collection of exotic Siam."

He paused until the last scattering of applause faded. It was 9:19 P.M., precisely. Montri smiled and continued, "And as I told each of you, I have a special surprise this evening. Tonight I'd like to introduce the grandson of Galileo Chini.

Khun Vincent will tell us about his famous grandfather. I have promised Khun Vincent that he can come out and visit this gallery and the Chini paintings every three months. It can be his visa run. I will even stamp his passport. Or get Khun Prinya to do it."

Prinya was a cabinet minister in the current government, and he laughed along with the others.

As the laughter died away, Montri said, "Khun Vincent, everyone wants to know the story about these works of art. Later I'll tell the story of how Vincent installed the security system."

Pratt and Calvino exchanged a look. They knew the story of how Calvino came to possess the paintings—he'd killed the man who'd owned them, because the man had tried to shoot him first on the eve of the coup in 2006. Even in Thailand there were large parts of a story that no one told, but that hardly mattered, because no one had the slightest hesitation to fill in the gaping holes with self-aggrandizing stories.

A roomful of penguin impersonators turned their attention to Calvino. He hadn't expected to speak; Montri hadn't warned him to prepare a speech. A bead of sweat formed on Calvino's forehead and slid down his nose, splashing on the floor. Montri, to be fair, hadn't expected that Calvino would speak either. The invitation had been one of those spontaneous acts, and once Montri had made the announcement, it seemed perfect and natural that Calvino, as the only farang in the room, should be called upon to explain what he was doing at the party. Montri got their attention by drawing on the family connection between the artist and Calvino. Family, connection, and influence were like an abacus in Thailand, and in their minds the guests waited to hear how this farang could weave his tale of privilege, power, fame, and wealth. That was the only kind of family that mattered.

Calvino cleared his throat, deciding whether to speak in Thai or English. Calvino's law: In case of doubt, when called upon to speak in public, always choose English. Once in a while, slip into Thai; that makes them grateful forever. "One small correction: Galileo Chini was my *great*-grandfather. He died before I was born. What I know comes from my grandfather, who was Galileo's son. What my grandfather taught was the importance of family to Galileo. Without our sense of our ancestors, we would be lost. As this gentlemen said, it's about heritage. I'll share a secret with you."

They nodded their heads, just like penguins. Secrets always caught their attention, and they waited as Calvino drew in a long breath.

"My grandfather taught me when I saw Chini's paintings to remember he wasn't asking anyone to look at him. Galileo was an ordinary-looking guy. My grandfather said, 'You look at the paintings and you see Siam through his eyes.' A great artist reveals a sensibility that is timeless. He asks the audience to experience his subject as if each viewer were the artist. Audiences come and go over time, as do the owners, but my great-grandfather's sensibility is alive in this room tonight and will stay alive so long as there are rooms for paintings to hang in. Galileo also loved Siam. These paintings are what he left behind, along with that affection for its people. His art opens a window into what Siam looked like almost a hundred years ago. He painted much more than nude women. But a collector like Khun Montri favors these paintings. They touch the inner old Siam in his heart."

Laughter and applause interrupted Calvino. Looking around the room, no one would ever guess from the attitude of the guests that revolution was gathering outside in the street.

"Khun Montri fell in love with them. If you know what I mean."

"They know exactly what you mean," said Montri, smiling, a proud, preening smile that spoke of being in total possession of a larger-than-life identity.

"But the feeling of family isn't just about a bloodline. Colonel Prachai is as close as any brother could ever be. He brought me into his family and made me feel that I belong. Without Colonel Prachai—I call him Colonel Pratt—these paintings wouldn't be hanging in this gallery. I wouldn't be standing here talking about my great-grandfather. Khun Montri is the custodian of Galileo's vision of old Siam. Wherever he is, Galileo is smiling down on all of you tonight and is grateful to Khun Montri for seeing to it that his dream of Siam can never be extinguished so long as his paintings continue to hang in this room."

Calvino raised his glass. "To Khun Montri, Colonel Prachai, and distinguished guests, on behalf of my great-grandfather—thank you."

Applause rose like heavy thunder from the penguins in the gallery. Champagne flowed. Montri slapped Calvino on the back. "Good speech." At Montri's elbow was Achara, who pushed his way into the circle around Calvino and Pratt. "You know my good friend Khun Achara?" asked Montri.

Calvino nodded. "Good to see you again, Khun Achara." Brandon's Thai partner seemed more subdued than last time they'd met, as if he were preoccupied, lost in his thoughts.

"And this is Wei Zhang. He's my very good friend from China. He's a special adviser to General Suchart."

"I liked your speech, Mr. Calvino," Zhang said in excellent English.

Montri raised his glass. "I forgot that you and Khun Achara already know each other. Khun Vincent seems to know everyone."

"Tomorrow we meet at my house," Achara said to Calvino. He was about to say something else before he was distracted by a look from Zhang and immediately changed the subject.

Up close, Achara's face showed signs of being banged up, as if he'd been in an accident. Achara saw Calvino staring. "I had a bad spill skiing at Whistler," he said, assuming that anyone at such a gathering would automatically be able to place Whistler, two hours north of Vancouver.

"I witnessed his fall. It was a nasty one," said Zhang.

"I was his guest at Whistler," said Achara.

"I didn't know you skied." Montri arched his right eyebrow into a question mark.

"There *are* things you don't know, Khun Montri." Achara turned to Calvino. "Do you ski?"

Calvino shook his head, trying to figure out what kind of business Zhang had with Achara. "I'm from New York. Skiing wasn't gonna help anyone with anything. I was taught to run in a zigzag pattern. Between school and home, so I wouldn't get mugged."

"It's different now. New York is safe," said Wei Zhang. "I was there last month. Skated in Rockefeller Center."

"Thinking of buying Rockefeller Center?" asked Calvino.

"Didn't know it was for sale. I thought the Japanese already owned it. Besides, the Flatiron Building is more interesting."

"That's kind of a big place for a Chinese takeout," said Calvino.

"But just the right size for a Chinese take-in," said Zhang. He flashed an insincere smile. The kind you see on insurance salesmen when they finally get that you don't want to buy the policy and nothing's going to change your mind. That kind of fixed, default grin that masked whatever true reaction lay beneath. He was a man who patiently waited for the right moment before he made his next move.

"You two sound like a couple of New Yorkers. Vincent, did your great-grandfather have this humor?" asked Montri. He squeezed Calvino's shoulder, lips pursed. "You're my family, too. If you ever need anything, you let me know." He removed his hand from Calvino's shoulder as a waiter brought another round of champagne. Zhang helped himself to a chilled glass.

"Come, I want to show you something," said Montri, who led them like penguins over an ice bridge to where a large, ornate grandfather clock stood, gold and silver inlaid in teakwood. The clock face had an animal representing each of the Chinese zodiac signs, and each of the twelve had a single diamond fitted into its eye. Dog, pig, dragon, chicken, and monkey along with the rest of the animals—all shared the same diamond eye.

"This is a gift from Wei Zhang. It is an object worthy of a gallery of Chini's masterpieces. Every hour, it strikes a tone from another world."

The clock was beyond any reasonable definition of friendship, and that gave Montri all the more face in the crowd. He might have paid hard cash for the Chini artwork, but the magnificent clock had been a gift. Not free, but a gift nonetheless. The other penguins nodded in awe and wonder at the dazzling timepiece. The financial system had melted fast, like the spring thaw revealing an outcrop of rugged edges where survivors clung, and the strongest of them raised a fist. The gallery featured the clock, a double helix sculpture constructed of chrome, mirrors, and glass, and the Chini paintings, and those gathered in the gallery were outside of time, in a space waiting for Zhang's clock to sound the hour.

"You have someone who designed security for the room?" asked Colonel Pratt.

"Colonel, I have installed state-of-the-art electronic surveillance, bugging equipment," said Montri. "The art is safe. And so is the clock."

It was a smug reply delivered in a joking way.

"Relatively safe," said Calvino.

Montri raised an eyebrow.

"You wouldn't want to challenge a professional thief," said Calvino. "Or a worked-up mob who've decided to turn on the rich."

"That's why Khun Vincent works for my partner, Brandon Sawyer," said Achara. "He has an ability to slip inside the black house and read the minds of professional criminals. To know what they are planning, how they will do the job, and how to stop them before they get the chance."

Zhang smiled, looking at the clock, until a new group formed around him and his time masterpiece. But Montri, who looked slightly disappointed, then slipped away to another small group. This left Calvino and Pratt shifting their feet in silence as Achara made polite conversation about the stock market, skiing on fresh powder, and the virtues of shark-fin soup.

"I will see you tomorrow, Khun Vincent," said Achara.

He locked eyes with Calvino as if he wanted to say something more but thought it better to remain brief.

Achara didn't fit the profile of a murderer. But Calvino had been an investigator long enough to know that a killer had no special look. They came in a variety of ages, shapes, backgrounds; men and women and, like everyone else, they bought and sold shares, skied, ate soup—even shark-fin soup. It was a lost cause trying to read anything in Achara's battered face. Calvino had found it of interest that Achara and Zhang had been skiing together in Canada. Also, Achara had managed an invitation to the opening. Calvino hadn't thought of Achara running on the inner ring of the track at the highest elevations of Thai society. Pratt glanced at his watch.

"Tomorrow," said Calvino, raising his glass. Achara touched the rim of his glass to Calvino's. The gong on the clock sounded, like the roll of thunder heralding a distant storm rolling in.

Calvino and Pratt waited outside Montri's mansion for a valet to bring Calvino's car. Inside the mansion the Thais mingled, told stories, exchanged gossip, and bragged about their business deals and political connections. It had been time to leave. Chini's artwork was on the wall, the ceremonial part of the evening had ended, and they could get down to business.

" 'Men's evil manners live in brass; their virtues we write in water,' " Pratt said, quoting Act 4, *Henry V*, as he got into the car.

Calvino smiled, starting the engine. "Only it's the other way around. Men's evil is written in water and the amount of wealth in brass."

"Does that mean you regret selling the paintings?" asked Pratt.

Calvino shook his head, checking his rearview mirror. "For the money Montri paid, I don't care what he writes in brass or water. Besides, remember, I've got visitation rights."

"Do you know who Zhang is?" asked Colonel Pratt.

Calvino shrugged as he drove away. "Wealthy Chinese."

"One of the *most* wealthy."

"He made the point that wealth and taste don't necessarily go together with the tacky clock," said Calvino. "It was a perfectly-timed gift. Listening to the tick-tock reminds them that their time is running down."

"Most people were impressed. They don't think their time will ever end."

Calvino glanced over as he entered the highway. The car backfired, belching a cloud of black smoke. "Wasn't that the whole idea? To gain face with Montri's crowd, who

76

are feeling a little nervous about what's happening on the street."

"Is your car going to get us back to Bangkok?"

"Old George's car is for sale. The widow wants fifty thousand baht."

Pratt looked straight ahead, nodding as if he were thinking about the possibility of Calvino's driving an even bigger wreck on wheels. "You're thinking of buying it?"

"It's twenty-five years old. But it doesn't have a lot of miles on it." He glanced over at Pratt, whose face revealed nothing.

Calvino's description sounded a lot like Montri talking about one of his women.

"You should keep this car," said Pratt.

"Thanks, Pratt." They both knew the gratitude had nothing to do with cars. It had everything to do with the art collection. The evening had been the end of a story that had started a couple of years earlier, on the evening of the coup. Pratt had removed all the paintings from Weerawat's house—the deceased owner of the Chini collection—near the Chao Phraya River. The colonel and his men could have kept them, sold them off. But Pratt never had any doubt as to what he should do: Deliver the paintings to Calvino. Plundered art should be restored to the rightful owner or his next of kin. Calvino was Chini's next of kin. In the colonel's mind, it was a straightforward and appropriate restoration. After the sale of the paintings to Montri, Colonel Pratt had refused to accept any compensation.

Calvino used part of the money to buy his old office building—and registered it in Pratt's and Ratana's names—and then he moved into a large condo overlooking the lake near the Queen Sirikit Center. Gradually he wore better clothes, shoes—everything had been upgraded over the one-year period except his car. It had been a long haul, Ratana guiding him through the process one pair of shoes at a time.

NINE

CALVINO AWOKE THINKING a five-hundred-pound bomb had exploded outside the building. He shook off sleep and listened for another explosion. Weeks before, a bomb had been thrown from an overpass onto a group of Klong Toey protesters. One man had been killed.

Calvino sat up in bed, peeked through the blinds, wondering if the bombers had returned. But it wasn't a bomb—the explosion came from the direction of a tangle of overhead electrical wires hooked in a crazy-quilt patchwork to a vertical wall of transformers. The coils were tied to metal crossbeams bolted to forty-foot-high concrete pillars, along with switches and fuses, insulation peeling off, flapping in the wind. Like an old star, the magnetic core became unstable and the transformer exploded in a shower of fireworks. No black hole. Just a smoldering meltdown of wires and insulation, sending a pungent column of smoke over the shophouses, as the owners waited for a repair crew to restore electricity to the neighborhood.

He lay back in bed, careful not to disturb Siriporn, who had slept through the blast. Partitioned off from the rest of the world by her wall of dreams, she hadn't moved. For all he knew, exploding transformers may have been a traditional part of her upbringing, and she no longer took notice when one blew up. Calvino liked that about Siriporn, who slept in the nude, her long, thin legs sticking out from the rumpled sheets as she lay on her stomach, her hair splayed out like a fan over her back. Looking at her in bed, Calvino had to remind himself that she was his stockbroker and financial adviser.

Siriporn lived in a unit on the ninth floor of his building. The night before, she had stopped by his condo to discuss his portfolio of shares. Halfway through the briefing, she smiled in a way that made him forget profit-and-loss and balance sheets, and once she let her hair down, he no longer cared about the market crash. Naturally enough, or so it seemed at the time, Siriporn spent the night. It was one of those small changes that friends like McPhail had pointed out to prove that money changed the kind of yings a man attracted. Especially the pool of yings willing to take off their clothes and slip into bed, talking about commodity prices, Eastern European foreign policy, or the science of the mind. The shift away from the ranks of cartoon-watchers, comic-book-readers, and ghost-fearers had come gradually.

Calvino was amazed at how his stockbroker had slept through the explosion. Losing other people's money didn't seem to trouble her. He worried about his investments. The stock market had exploded, too, and she hadn't heard that one either. Another look at those long, tapered, sensual legs, thin arms like a catwalk model's, and he quietly rolled out of bed, slid back the wooden door, and walked into the living room to open the blinds and look down at the street. He stared at the wall of ruined transformers, which continued to spit sparks and flames. The fire brigade came to watch the flames and thick smoke. He looked back at Siriporn still sleeping, unmoved and silent.

Calvino sat, hands folded, on the balcony of his condo overlooking the skyline, meditating. He tried to watch his breath entering and leaving his body. But he kept thinking about the party the previous night. The heinous clock,

79

Achara's bruised face, Colonel Pratt's questions about the security—all of it spun around inside his head.

No one inquired how Calvino became rich overnight. A collective shroud of silence cloaked such matters in Thailand. There were certain questions people didn't ask— where you made your money, where you met your wife, what were you running away from. It was better not to ask. But it didn't stop people from thinking that wealth came from avenues that were fed by underground streams. No one ever thought it was the result of a miracle or of good work. A deeper, more fundamental connection with karma kicked in, justifying the newfound wealth. Calvino's turn of fortune for the better had raised no eyebrows, launched no investigations. With the receipt of Montri's money came a new freedom for Calvino to turn down cases. He could take a case to help someone who needed assistance but didn't have money. At least that was the theory of how he'd take on new clients. Instead he found himself working for a rich deadbeat with a drinking problem and a dysfunctional family. Brandon Sawyer hadn't fit the bill as the prototype of Calvino's new client. Tanny Craig represented the blowback from taking on Brandon's work. Someone had been sent to check on the quality of his investigation and to bring pressure on Brandon. Poor people were just grateful for whatever help he could muster. Men like Brandon attracted nothing but problems, and their cases had little to do with securing justice but amassing and maintaining power.

Calvino went back inside. He walked into the kitchen, opened the fridge door, and filled a glass with orange juice. He picked up his cell phone and checked the new messages. He drank his juice as he scrolled through them. Two were from Brandon Sawyer: TURN ON RADIO THAILAND NEWS. NICE SURPRISE. He ended the message like a bar ying, with a happy-face icon. Calvino put the orange-juice carton back in the fridge, carried his glass and cell phone into the large sitting area. He settled in, finding the remote-control device, aiming it at the radio, and flicking through the channels until he reached Radio Thailand. An English-accented newscaster read the news. The police had arrested a twenty-three-year-old man who confessed that he killed Kowit, the reporter for the *Daily Asia Times* Thai-language newspaper. The man was identified as Tongchai Silavipah, an ex–police officer. Tongchai said that he shot Kowit because a piece on police corruption written by Kowit caused him to lose his job. He told police that he acted alone.

Calvino switched off the radio. He walked back to the sliding glass door and walked out onto the walled balcony overlooking the lake and the city. A few minutes later, Siriporn joined him. She leaned against him, hugging him. "I was surprised. I woke up. And you were gone."

Calvino nodded. "You slept through an explosion."

"Another bomb?"

He smiled. "A transformer blew up." The explanation seemed to reassure her. He pointed to the power lines below, where the transformer still smoldered and kicked out sparks that would have impressed the guests at a Chinese wedding celebration. But there was no wedding, no guests. There was a small crowd of people from the shophouses on the *soi* gathered below the transformer. Explosions attracted an audience. But there was no encore, and soon people moved on. Except for Siriporn, who had wrapped an arm around Calvino's waist, signaling that she had other ideas. She wore his favorite Hawaiian shirt, the one with bottlenose dolphins, taken from his closet. Slipping it on, fastening a couple of the bottom buttons, and wearing no bra or panties, Siriporn no longer remotely looked like a stockbroker.

Calvino's problem was how to get her out the door without her taking offense, selling his well-diversified holdings, and investing in Russian junk bonds. It was all about money—the only difference was the nature and scale of involvement. Dressed in a Hawaiian shirt and nothing else, it was difficult to distinguish a working ying broker from one who carried out the brokerage business at night.

"My mother said I could sleep through World War Three and not hear a thing."

He glanced at his watch, his eyes narrowing. "Time to go to work."

She squeezed his waist. "Why would you need to do that?"

She has strength in her fingers, he thought. And she was letting them do her talking.

He watched the traffic moving below.

"I want the information on Achara's listed companies. We discussed it last night. I'd like it in two hours."

She removed her arm from around his waist, taking a deep breath. She had remembered *that* discussion and hoped that it was an icebreaker to another level. If it had broken any ice, the sea had frozen up again, the illusion of a Northwest Passage into Calvino's life vanished against a dreamy blue horizon. "I'll e-mail it to you in the next hour."

He had led her to think that his interest in her was strictly on the investment side. But keeping her in that compartment was doomed once he got a good look at her legs. Mission creep had come to dominate his life. He slept with his broker. His only client had roped him into advising on business deals. Next he would be writing letters to the editor of the *Bangkok Post* to start a campaign to inspect transformers before they exploded, disturbing the sleep of good people. All he could salvage was that Siriporn hadn't asked him why he wanted the information on Achara's companies. He could love a woman like that. She lingered as if waiting for him to say something else. When he didn't, she turned and slipped back through the sliding door.

She told herself that Calvino had a lot on his mind. In the doorway she looked back and caught him grinning at her. "Thanks."

The warm smile said it was all he needed from her.

"Sorry, I'm a little distracted."

"It's no problem. If I can do anything else, phone me."

He caught himself before inviting her to stay. "Yeah, see you later," he said.

What was reeling through his head wasn't about her. Her sister, nicknamed Film, had once told her, "A man with too much money can have any woman. No good for the woman. They are different from other men." Film hadn't meant it in a good way, and when Siriporn had asked her how they were different, Film had said, "Rich men are indifferent to the needs of women. That's what all that money buys them—the freedom to ignore what you want. They don't need to care about you."

Film pretended to be an expert on men, but as far as Siriporn could tell, the expertise hadn't brought her the right man or any amount of happiness living on her own.

After Siriporn left, he thought she was exactly the kind of woman he'd been looking for and wondered why he'd pushed her away. Tanny had lingered inside his mind, the kind of woman he should push away but who was now sitting in his office. He walked along the balcony, hands on the rails, following a spidery network of narrow sois—a scribble of micro roads that, from a distance, might have been designed by a drunk. Craig—what was she really doing in Bangkok? And was there some way he could get her out of his office? He didn't have the answers.

He watched the cars below his building navigate the looping, winding, spidery network of roads that brushed against the edge of shophouses, condominiums, a couple of small factories, straightening out past the bottled-water storage facility, the auto-body repair shop, and the YMCA. Trucks, vans, cars, bicycles, motorcycles, vendors pushing metal food carts, and pedestrians shared the narrow sliver of dull concrete. Understanding people came from watching how they used their common space.

In Thailand that space was used according to the Zen of Thai Traffic, which meant there was a consensus on applying the non-rules of the road. Watching the traffic bump and grind to a stop, then barrel ahead, cars overtaking on blind corners, Calvino was certain that Tanny Craig had no idea how the Thai rules of the road and the rules of business came out of the same playbook. He was proud of himself, thinking this might be a way of reaching out to her. A few lessons in the Zen of Thai Traffic might help give her insight into the movement, gesture, and body language— the ballet that Thais performed daily, both on the road and in the boardroom.

Thai drivers were part ballerina, part bullfighter, and part hockey-night thug, hidden from view by iron, steel, leather, and tinted windows, in love with acceleration, alienated from the idea of braking, crazy about flashing their running lights and smoking rubber on titanium wheels. On the soi below, an Audi performed a perfectly executed arabesque around a hairpin turn, avoiding a head-on collision with a BMW coming from the opposite direction. It wasn't long before new players entered the hairpin. Near misses, one after another. None of the drivers kept their cars within the yellow line. Each assumed that the road belonged exclusively to him. In a way, the yellow road-dividing line didn't matter. Everyone claimed both sides of the road when it suited him. Nothing in any driver's behavior suggested that crossing the line had any meaningful consequence. After all, it was only a hairpin turn—why shouldn't the entire road be available for each one alone?

Am I any different? Calvino asked himself. He'd started the evening painting a yellow line down the road in his relationship with Siriporn. At the first chance, what had he done? Crossed the line. Not just crossed but erased it, only to find her standing there in his Hawaiian shirt looking like a girlfriend, and his immediate instinct was to pick up a paintbrush and redraw the yellow line. Any other woman would have been enraged. Not Siriporn, who responded with a smile and a hug. She possessed one of those line-erasing smiles that made a man think there might not be enough yellow paint in the world to keep that road divided.

TEN

CALVINO WALKED ALONG the street. Under a gray bank of clouds, the motorcycle boys looked up as a clap of thunder tore a jagged white streak against the far horizon. A couple of minutes later, the rain fell, a heavy curtain, splashing off the gutters, scattering the motorcycles to shelter under bypasses and trees. The rain killed the motorcycle-taxi business stone dead. A brave passenger fighting with an umbrella as the taxi sped down wet streets was closer to Russian roulette than to public transportation. The world had already seen enough of the mayhem of risk-taking fools—that was for sure. But the rain and accidents, in Bangkok, had a natural way of whittling down their numbers.

Ever since Calvino came into his windfall, Colonel Pratt no longer felt restrained from suggesting an upscale meeting place. There were a number of them around the corner from Pratt's office at police headquarters. A farang showing up on a regular basis at his office set tongues wagging. Two doors down from Pratt was a senior officer whose ultra-nationalistic views had come into fashion, and he was said to have powerful allies. This was General Suchart—whose political aspirations were well known. Suchart looked with disfavor on the colonel's friendship with Calvino.

Some said that Suchart was an ultra-nationalist; others said the general was merely another example of a successful product whose mind had been molded by childhood textbooks. The prevailing sentiment about foreigners shifted along with the heavy weather of politics in the streets. Mobs had taken to the streets in Bangkok, and followed self-appointed leaders to occupy Government House. The mob were promised an escape to a glorious past, a distant point in time when foreigners were few, and those on the ground were remote and mostly hidden and kept their opinions to themselves. Suchart had appeared at some of the rallies, his supercharged speeches bringing the audience to their feet, and their clapping hands beating in unison.

Calvino had told Pratt that the Chinese process of selecting the Panchen Lama had as much to do with spirituality as General Suchart's proposal to select a new government had to do with democracy. Deception and manipulation in the name of some larger purpose was Suchart's game, and he had made it clear that there was only one true vision of Thai goodness.

This wasn't a suitable time for a Thai police colonel to explain his motives for helping a foreign private eye to sift through the details of the investigation surrounding a murdered Thai reporter. The mood created the risk of someone starting a rumor that Colonel Pratt was disloyal, or worse. While the Thais might ignore the rules of the road, there was a yellow line that foreigners were forbidden to cross. Investigating a murder case was one such line.

Inside the entrance to the restaurant, Calvino handed his dripping umbrella to the waitress, who acknowledged him with a smile. She pointed at the back of the room. Colonel Pratt sat alone at their usual table. He looked up, saw Calvino, and nodded. The waitress smiled again. "Mr. Calvino, your friend is waiting for you."

Colonel Pratt's hands were clasped around a cup of tea. He looked tired as he watched Calvino cross the length of the restaurant. As Pratt slipped his glasses back on, Calvino had slipped into a chair. Fatigue etched lines around Pratt's eyes. He muffled a yawn.

"You look terrible," said Calvino.

"Thanks," said Colonel Pratt. "I'm working to improve my image."

"Forget about it. So what's the latest at Government House?"

Pratt wrinkled his nose in disgust. "The stench is too much." The stink of unwashed bodies, garbage, and human waste clung in his nose.

"Perfume and revolution. They don't really belong together," said Calvino.

The official name of the occupied building was Thai Khu Fah, and thousands of protesters had taken over and settled into the premises, planting rice and vegetables as if they had some long-term plan to stick around to harvest the crop.

"The protesters are demanding the city supply them with toilets and food," said Colonel Pratt.

Calvino smiled. Only in Thailand does the mob expect to be supplied with rice by the government it sought to overthrow. "And your buddy General Suchart is trucking in the portable toilets and pillows. What next? Someone's going to establish a mob catering policy?"

That brought a smile from Colonel Pratt. "Something's cooking, but I can't tell you exactly what's on the menu. Not yet."

Calvino understood that there were limits as to what the colonel could disclose; he lived inside a network of loyalties, and nothing could tempt him to cross the border that separated where foreigners and outsiders dwelled. The harsh smell of betrayal rose hot and dense in the air above Bangkok. No one trusted anyone; no one felt safe or secure. Old alliances were being redrawn, as if crooked politicians were redrawing election districts. Children were weeping in the heat against their mothers' breasts. No one was making the first move.

Colonel Pratt explained how the grounds of Government House had been turned into mud and garbage, bras hanging out to dry on bushes, how children were running around the mountains of empty plastic water bottles, discarded newspapers, and discarded food that had been colonized by insects and rodents the size of small cats. People as far as the eye could see were camping out on rattan mats, squatting on cushions, sitting on chairs; others hunkered down in makeshift shelters made from plastic sheets and hung from poles sunk into the dirt. It might have passed for a medieval village, except that it was buried under a mountain of Styrofoam. Or a modern relief camp, squalid and hopeless, crammed with refugees escaping massacre by invading forces. The Venetian Gothic structure of Government House—Khu Fah, translated as "Partner of the Sky"—had been designed by Italians in 1908 as a symbol of power, and the demonstrators who occupied it announced that the partnership with the sky was at an end.

Calvino and Pratt sat in a restaurant inside an upscale shopping complex and frequented by Chinese-Thai businessmen, rich housewives, high-level government officials, and playboys with their latest trophy ying to impress their friends. The restaurant was the kind of meeting place that Calvino could now afford. If the colonel were spotted in the presence of a farang, then the main room laundered the meeting as something social, and no one at the surrounding tables, even if they recognized the colonel, would think much about it. In other words, the place was another universe away from Government House and the cramped and hungry mob. It was business and social. Politics was only whispered between courses.

"Nothing has gone right since the coup," said Calvino.

"I recall that you came out all right," said Colonel Pratt.

Calvino had to give it to him. "Don't confuse causation with correlation," said Calvino.

"The point is, you went from a slum to a penthouse. That's a bigger jump than most of the coup-makers got." The colonel drank his tea and sighed.

"It seemed like a good thing at the time."

"That's the definition of a coup."

The chaos on the night of the coup had provided cover for Colonel Pratt; he used it as an opportunity to remove the Chini paintings from an old row house near the Chao Phraya River and take them to a secure location. In normal times the fact that there had been bodies riddled with bullet holes inside the house would have been a problem. During the chaos of a coup, normal policing wasn't possible. But even in abnormal times, the violent death of an influential person couldn't be ignored. It was complicated getting the bullets from the bodies to disappear after the autopsy had taken some effort to organize. That was just as well, since the slugs would have matched Calvino's handgun.

"We're at that same point again," said Calvino. "When things go sideways, strange things happen and are accepted. It looks like a cutoff killing. Maybe the triggerman took a contract. But is he going to drop the dime on the mastermind?" Calvino shrugged his shoulders, looking straight at the colonel. It was the same reasoning that the police had often used. There was hardly a distinction between a cover-up and a real investigation; both followed the same internal logic.

Colonel Pratt motioned to the waitress. He ordered sticky rice and mangoes, thinking it might help kill the smell of decay that refused to dislodge from his nose. After the waitress left, Calvino watched a table at the other end of the room erupt in laughter.

"We got the right man," said Colonel Pratt.

The sticky rice and mangoes arrived on a large blue and white China plate.

"No one hired him for the job?"

Colonel Pratt shook his head, his spoon and fork working on the fruit.

"He had personal reasons to kill Kowit."

"An old-fashioned crime of passion," said Calvino, sipping coffee.

"That explains most crime," said Colonel Pratt. "Passion pressed too far." His attention drifted, eyes wandering to those at tables in the front.

Calvino felt a surge of guilt. He'd asked for help. But it had been the wrong time to ask for such help, and a worse time to follow up on what Pratt had found out about the murder investigation. "Have I told you that Brandon Sawyer is under a lot of family pressure?" He regretted saying this almost immediately. The duress Sawyer suffered at the hands of his family wouldn't have shown up on Colonel Pratt's radar screen, except for Calvino's pressing him.

"Get a different client," said Colonel Pratt.

Pratt had met Brandon; he hadn't liked him. And the colonel didn't have an especially high regard for Achara either. Pratt remembered him as an officious, pompous, and proud man. Someone who spoke Thai with a Chinese accent— an affectation, as Achara had been born in Thailand. Pratt saw Achara as part of a rich, closed Thai-Chinese circle that excluded Thais like him. As much as Colonel Pratt would have liked that the evidence of the murder had pointed to Achara, the fact was, it didn't. Achara was the species of Thai businessman whose empire had grown exponentially as a result of his high-octane political connections. Achara was the sort of man who could have the colonel transferred to a Burmese border posting. The sort of man who skied Whistler in Canada and received invitations to Montri's mansion.

"Vincent, you can let Brandon know that his partner didn't murder the reporter."

The colonel had read the confession, he'd talked with the officer who'd been present at the interrogation, he had reviewed the evidence—nothing had tied Achara to the Kowit murder case.

"Thanks, Pratt." Calvino pulled out a roll of notes and signaled the waitress for the bill.

Pratt remained silent as the waitress came and collected the money.

"They've made a big investment. Not a lot of people are lining up to invest in Thailand," said Calvino. "It means jobs."

Colonel Pratt rolled his eyes. "I don't know what it means. And neither do you."

Achara and Brandon's company controlled over two thousand acres upcountry. Half had been planted with seeds from a modified rice stock. If the projected yields came about, their consultants told them, they could duplicate the project hundreds of times over, feeding billions with a steady supply of rice that would not rot—firm, strong, engineered rice. No mathematical genius was required to see the potential upside for a business that got it right. The other half of the land had been earmarked for wind turbines. Kowit had been investigating the story about this genetically modified rice at the time that someone slipped into his house and pumped several rounds into his head as he stirred a pot of soup over the kitchen stove. His wife was on the way home from school with their three children.

"Kowit's investigations caused Achara and Sawyer a problem," said Calvino.

"I am more concerned whether we are going to have a country to live in. Foreigner investors worrying about if their money is safe ... well, it isn't a priority." Colonel Pratt sipped his tea. Like everyone else in Thailand, Pratt had read the local newspapers, which had circulated rumors about those who had a motive for killing the reporter. Certain newspapers shilled for powerful families who would have been happy to take Achara down a couple of notches. By the third day of reporting, Achara had dropped to the number-four spot on the list of suspects.

"Achara's not in the medals!" Brandon would later scream at his brother over the phone. But business in Thailand didn't play by the Olympic rules. The other suspects with a motive included a government official, a high-ranking cop, and a firm with a contract to lay a pipeline. All this speculation only led to the huge disappointment that it was none of the above. It had been a petty domestic murder, nothing political. His murder hadn't come from the usual combination of stupidity and greed but had been done by someone outside the money loop. The killer had the best wishes of many people who'd been grateful for his intervention. Looking at the history of Kowit's investigative reporting, it had been a minor miracle that he'd lived as long as he had. Thirty-seven years.

"I'm up to my eyeballs in scorpions with the investigator Brandon's brother sent. They're checking out whether there's been a cover-up."

"She's wrong," said Colonel Pratt.

"That's what I said." He shrugged his shoulders and sighed. "Some people don't listen, except to take in what they want to hear. Craig's one of them."

Pratt nodded as if he understood. Some people plainly had been overwired for talking, and the wires for listening had never been connected. "Then you've done all you can. It's her problem. Brandon's problem. I don't honestly see why you're making it your problem. You have enough money. Why put yourself through the agony?"

"Mission creep." Calvino considered for a second telling the colonel about Siriporn. Parts of his life were better left out of sight, he decided.

"Brandon is a creep. You shouldn't have let him define the mission."

"Saints and Nobel Prize winners don't coming knocking on the door of a private investigator in Bangkok. It's usually a farang with a suitcase full of great expectations, as if he's a character from Charles Dickens but all he got from Dickens is a miserable, fucked-up family life and a football-stadium-sized delusion about starting over in Thailand. And what inspires most of my clients? He's in love with a bar ying but has some doubts whether she truly loves him. So he hires me to confirm his brilliance in character analysis about his loved one. And pays me before I lay out the photos that expose his stupidity. Is that what you're trying to say?"

"Get a hobby."

"Brandon's case gives me a reason to get up in the morning. Don't tell me you don't need the same thing. When I tried to give you a bunch of money so you wouldn't have to work as a cop, what do you do? Something that should get you kicked off the force if your colleagues knew. You wouldn't take the money from the farang. How crazy is that? I asked you, and you said, 'It's the only life I know. It's the only life I wanna know,' " said Calvino, gesturing with both hands. He observed his hands in midair, and suddenly they seemed to belong to someone else. He thought how his father used to do the same thing and how it had disturbed him. Now he was sitting across the table from Pratt, doing his father's gesture. "I need a reason not to hang out in a Washington Square bar in the afternoon and drink."

"Your father used to gesture like that with his hands," said the colonel, smiling.

"I was thinking the same thing. We repeat this stuff and don't even know we're doing it. Like the way you're smiling, tilting your head. Just like *your* father."

Colonel Pratt sighed and nodded.

Calvino dropped his arms, resting his palms flat on the table. "Brandon's okay. Strange but harmless, and living like a raja."

"We know what happened to the Raj," said Colonel Pratt, who not only knew Shakespeare but also had studied Chinese and Indian history.

There was no denying that the colonel had grasped the essential nature of Brandon's problem. Calvino admitted that he'd gotten sucked into an ego ride, letting Brandon Sawyer gradually expand his brief from investigator to adviser. As an investigator, Calvino could find people who didn't want to be found, or information hidden in layers of passwords, or objects disguised as other things—he had a knack for tracing the lost into the most unlikely hiding places—which resulted in his clients' assuming that those skills qualified him to advise on their business and their life. Bangkok was lousy with schmucks selling advice. He avoided these farangs in their dress shirts with French cuffs, expensive neckties, and gold-embossed business cards. Opinions were as cheap as life in Asia. Voicing the wrong opinions made life even cheaper. Pratt warned him that Brandon Sawyer was asking Calvino to take on way too much responsibility; and Calvino wasn't paying close enough attention to see where it was leading. Pratt had warned Calvino to stay away from giving an opinion on whether the Thai partner was involved in the murder and to keep out of the business.

"Tell Brandon the police have caught Kowit's killer. And it wasn't Achara. Then tell him that you are moving on."

"There's something else going on, Pratt."

"That's the definition of life. There will always be something else going on."

"If Brandon's brother backs off. Then, yeah, I'm outta the case."

"This investigator his brother sent from New York. Ratana says she's Thai. Attractive. Single. She says you look interested."

The colonel had been talking to Calvino's secretary. If there'd been a two-person committee appointed to run his life, they were the two permanent charter members.

"Craig, Thai? If you put her behind a screen and told her to talk and then she walked out, you'd fall over. She got adopted from some orphanage when she was a baby. She never knew her Thai parents. Interested? I can't believe Ratana said that. She knows that woman's occupying my office. How can I help but look at her? She's sitting in my line of vision."

Colonel Pratt's smile softened his face. Family talk was something he liked. "Ratana told me you were spending more time in the office."

"Am I in my office?"

"You protest too much."

"You should be telling that to the people at Government House."

The colonel smiled, again that half-bemused, knowing smile of his father. Calvino shuddered to think what kind of crazy idea his sleep-deprived friend was about to offer.

The waitress who had already cleared the bill returned and asked if Calvino might want another cup of coffee. He nodded. "Make it a Spanish coffee."

"Tanny brought along her Thai birth certificate," said Colonel Pratt. "That might mean something. Show her your stuff. Find her Thai parents. How can a Thai woman be whole without knowing her mother and father? It will get you out of the office."

It was, in other words, incomprehensible to Pratt and Ratana to conclude that this hadn't been Craig's real mission. In their collective view, Tanny Craig had obviously come to Thailand on Marshall Sawyer's dime with the intention of finding her true identity. Brilliant. It made her straight-from-the-mint Thai. For Colonel Pratt and Ratana, her presence in Bangkok made perfect sense.

"Track down Tanny's mother?" asked Calvino, warming to the idea.

"And wash your hands of Brandon Sawyer. It's a reason to get out of bed."

"Get out of bed for Tanny? Is that what you're saying?"

Colonel Pratt nodded. "Or is there someone else you're not telling me about?"

As the Spanish coffee arrived, Calvino held the large mug to his nose and inhaled deeply. After a long drink, he sighed, wiped his mouth with the back of his hand, and said, "I'll think about it."

At least Siriporn lacked Tanny's identity problem, Calvino thought. But it was far more complicated than that. Two women had tumbled into his life: Tanny, who didn't know who her birth parents were, and Siriporn, who didn't know that her wearing his Hawaiian shirt and sleeping through an early-morning explosion had him fearful about what lay waiting around the hairpin curve. He thought about both of them on the way back to his office.

"Get in," he'd said to Tanny Craig, who hovered at the door of his car, as he was about to leave Old George's funeral. Calvino tilted his chin down, looking at the floor and wondering what he'd done. He had grabbed Siriporn's hand, given it a squeeze, and walked her into his bedroom.

There were a couple of things wrong with the picture inside Calvino's head. First, investors didn't hold hands with their broker and take them into the bedroom. And second, brokers only metaphorically fucked their clients who paid them fees for the privilege. But once Calvino had done the hand-grab-and-squeeze operation, it sent a powerful message—by crossing the line from the sitting room to the bedroom, Siriporn had stopped being just his broker. She

97

had the potential to be something else, and what that else might be was left unsaid. Calvino's actions had spoken the magic words: Here's your invitation. Get into my life.

One way of looking at it, thought Calvino, was to visualize that he was occupying the space between two drops of honey. How long before the flies, house lizards, cats, dogs, and fighting crowds gathered?

ELEVEN

CALVINO WALKED INTO the office in a good mood. Tanny watched him ease into his chair, check his e-mail, humming to himself.

"Ratana's upstairs with her son," said Tanny.

"That kid loves books about dragons," he said.

"You've got something you want to tell me? And tell me it's not about dragons?" Tanny asked. She smelled the Spanish coffee on his breath and twitched her nose in disapproval.

He looked away from his screen, pretending without much success to appear surprised. "Good news."

She wondered whether he was drunk. "Yeah? I could use some of that. Pour me a double."

"We can cancel the appointment with Achara. You can return to New York tomorrow or hang around, if you like. I was just getting used to you in the office. But it is a little crowded. You know, for two people trying to work."

Tanny raised an eyebrow. He was only a few feet away, but his attitude was in another universe. "Why would we cancel the appointment?"

"The police caught the guy who popped your reporter. I just got back from a meeting with Colonel Pratt. The guy the police arrested *is* the killer. They've got the gun.

99

He acted alone. They've got his confession, and they've got a motive. They didn't beat him up or anything. Guess he had a guilty conscience. You don't find many of those around. The main thing is, the murder had nothing to do with Brandon and Achara's joint venture. There. Aren't you happy? I'm happy."

"I can see that," she said. It suddenly became evident why Calvino had danced into the office like someone who'd just won the lottery.

Only, when he studied her face, he had the sinking feeling maybe he'd misread the number on the ticket.

She paused, broke eye contact, glanced at her watch.

"Something on your mind?" he asked.

"There are some other issues," she said.

Calvino inhaled deeply, held in the breath, trying to calm the voices screaming random directions inside his brain. The unthinkable unfolded—the specter of a hard, pointed blade finally pulled from the sheath. "Like the issues in that envelope you handed Brandon?"

She studied his eyes, confused, angry. It's turning into a situation, she thought. "Marshall Sawyer has information that Achara took commissions from a couple of local suppliers. The kickbacks went straight into his pocket. I call that activity raising issues of corruption."

He heard for the first time the real reason the Sawyer family had sent her to Thailand. She had said her specialty was corporate investigations.

"Marshall could live with Achara's being a killer but not a thief, is that the executive summary?" asked Calvino. "The murder case was just a phony cover."

"Of course Marshall wanted the murder case cleared. But it doesn't mean that was the only concern he'd put on the table."

It was as if someone had fired a flare gun and illuminated the landscape so that Calvino could see the real advance of troops on the unguarded flank. "Brandon isn't expecting this."

"That was the intention."

"You didn't trust Brandon to follow up about the commissions?"

He unbuttoned his jacket and leaned back in his chair. This woman doesn't trust anyone, he thought. Her mother had put her up for adoption. How could she trust another human being with that kind of history?

"It wasn't my call. Marshall doesn't trust him."

"Or me," said Calvino.

She didn't say anything; there was no need to.

Calvino nodded, got up from his chair, put on his jacket. "Let's get out of here."

"Ratana said it was a thirty-minute drive to Achara's office."

She'd been pumping his secretary for information. Had Tanny also asked Ratana for the password to access his computer files? He had a bad feeling that came from a sudden punch thrown hard and in close quarters. It was an hour before the appointment. "I want to show you something," he said. "Don't worry. It's on the way, and it won't take long."

"Unless it's directly connected with the investigation, I'd rather take the extra time to go through some documents," she said, holding up a thick folder.

"It's connected. Trust me."

She drummed her fingers on the folder, never once breaking eye contact, never once smiling, as if she were staring through him. In an ideal world, no one laid snares to trap the unsuspecting. In the real world, traps were the rule. Avoiding them an obsession. Calvino felt he'd been caught in an unnecessary trap set by Tanny. He didn't like it. He'd assumed that she had come to Thailand to investigate Achara's possible involvement in the murder

101

of a reporter. That, as it turned out, had only been the bait. Like any animal caught in a trap, he at first struggled, and gradually resolved to find another way to reverse his misfortune.

Calvino wheeled his Honda to a stop, kicking up dirt on the shoulder of the road. His eyes narrowed as he looked up ahead about twenty meters, to where the road fell away as it disappeared into a blind curve. He waited until Tanny looked at him, then smiled. He switched on the car radio.

"There's a good reason you pulled over?"

"Do you like Grover Washington Junior?"

Her sigh sounded as if the rubber rings on a valve had collapsed, allowing a bolt of steam to escape full throttle. "Please, Mr. Calvino."

"Thank you, Ms. Craig. Now that we've got our pleases and thank-yous out of the way, we can settle down to serious business."

"I would like nothing more. But I don't see the point of why you parked here."

"I've been thinking that you've got some gaps in your Thai education. And that's holding you back in your job."

She raised an eyebrow. "And you've decided to fill them in? No thanks."

"That's the wrong attitude. If you don't learn, you don't grow. If you don't grow, you get washed away." He paused, glanced over, finding her face stern, unyielding. "You'll really thank me."

"I seriously doubt that."

He ignored her doubt and focused on the blind curve. From his condo balcony, Calvino had studied the activity around that spot, though distracted by Siriporn, who was wrapped inside his favorite Hawaiian shirt. She had slipped her arm around his waist, lifting herself up on her painted toenails, and sniffed his neck. Sniffing necks and cheeks was an old custom. Smells mattered. Smells mattered more than, say, keeping within the lines. Or watching drivers stay within the lines. He'd looked away from the road. Calvino had started to believe that was the story of his life. With Tanny he didn't need to worry about taking his eye off the ball. It gave him the opportunity to explain how blind curves had no smell, touch, or feel but, just like a woman, could be deadly if ignored. He opened a brown bag, exposing the neck of a bottle, screwed off the cap, and took a long pull, then held out the bag for Tanny.

She waved it away. "You shouldn't drink and drive," she said.

"I'm parked. I'm not driving. It's Gatorade." He held it out again. "Want some?"

She shook her head. His smile faded. She was not only tough; she was unyielding, demanding, and bullheaded. Was she willing to learn? The last question was the essential open-ended one. If her mind were open just a fraction, then what she was about to witness could help her understand some of the basic wiring of people in Thailand. He wasn't encouraged by her reaction. So far, her mind was as open as a fundamentalist preacher's listening to a bearded college professor explain the theory of evolution.

Her eye roll told Calvino that he had an uphill battle on his hands. Being in a good mood made it easier to shrug off her stubbornness. He listened to the music, moving his head to the beat of Grover's saxophone, as the memory of a naked Siriporn suddenly reappeared in his mind.

"The meeting with Mr. Achara is important. Shouldn't we go?"

"We've got time. I'm asking you to do something for me. I want you to keep an eye on the yellow line. I'll give you a hundred baht for every driver who turns in to the corner and stays within the yellow line, and you give me five baht for everyone who doesn't."

She thought about this, looking at the line, watching the first couple of cars wheel into the oncoming lane as if the yellow dividing line didn't exist. "What's the point of this game?" she said.

"It's to teach you traffic lesson number one," said Calvino. "It's a Zen thing. You know about Zen, right?"

She folded her arms like a teacher whose head was about to explode. "It's the name of a department store."

Nice answer, Calvino thought. Brandon Sawyer wasn't the only stand-up genius working the audience in this case. He had some competition imported from New York. There was an outside possibility that this was really the only Zen that had entered her private universe.

"Zen's a philosophy. It's a way of looking at things. Understanding their true nature. It works on people, too. So you want to understand Achara? Zen is a good place to shop for insight," he said.

"That's why I'm meeting him." She paused before whispering to herself, "Duh."

Like an American passport, the origin of her response was unmistakable.

"Traffic lesson number one is your homework for the meeting. It will help you understand how someone like Achara thinks. It only takes a few minutes. Trust me."

She stared ahead as if trust weren't anything that came naturally to her.

The curve coiled like a narrow belt around the waist of a condominium. A sharp corner of the building had been built close to the inside of the curve, obscuring vision from both directions. The six-story redbrick building looked like a fort jogging out into the bend of a river. The structure would have slowed down a boat, but it did nothing to slow down cars, trucks, and motorcycles on the soi. Once in a blue moon, a taxi, driven by someone in the know, hugged the corner tight in order to avoid the oncoming traffic, which ignored the yellow line, turning into the oncoming lane.

"Ratana said the corner had bad feng shui," said Calvino. "When the gods of feng shui were angry, then what? Tear down the condo? Forget about it. The gods never got that angry. Instead someone sends out a crew to paint a yellow line down the center of the road. The yellow-line rule goes something like this: Stay on your side and I'll stay on my side. But no one ever drives inside the line dividing the road. Their side is both sides. That's the Zen lesson. The yellow line's decorative; it's a suggestion, take it or leave it, a way of seeing the curve in the road. It's roughly the same Zen principle that applies to business in Thailand—the local partner knows where the line is but never bothers to stay inside it. Not so much because he's cunning; it's mostly inattention and the convenience of the moment. It's easier to cut across the line than to stay within it. It's more like a natural right. To ignore the yellow line is to be free."

Tanny screwed up her face. "Free of what? That makes no sense."

"In the land of the free, sometimes things don't make much sense. But it doesn't mean they're not real and you don't have to deal with them."

Ignoring lines painted on the road might have had some larger cosmic meaning, but for purposes of day-to-day driving, the yellow paint might have been just one more feature of the scenery, like trees, security guards, and garbage cans—a stream of people and things that didn't register as having much significance or purpose.

Calvino answered his cell phone, keeping his eyes on the traffic ahead.

"The prime minister has declared a state of emergency," said Ratana. "It was just on the news. And Achara phoned in with the news. He wanted to cancel the meeting."

Calvino relayed the government order to Tanny.

"He doesn't want to cooperate," she said, arms folded on her lap, looking straight ahead as if it had all become perfectly obvious that Achara was avoiding her. "That's not acceptable."

"I said he wanted to cancel because of the state of emergency. Ratana already told him we'd left. We were on our way. And he said never mind, he'd meet us." Calvino still had Ratana on the line as he spoke, letting her listen in. He expected Tanny to ask what a state of emergency meant, whether it meant danger, tanks, soldiers patrolling the streets, the possibility of gunfire. She was strangely incurious. Her lack of interest in anything other than the case had started to bother him. It was also a challenge, making him wonder how he might bore through her shell.

Colonel Pratt had warned him, "Get rid of the Brandon file. Bury the case in your filing cabinet and get a new case. You don't need the money. You don't need the grief. And you don't need to get in the middle of a conflict that isn't yours to resolve."

"Why don't you talk to Ratana?" he asked Tanny now.

She shook her head. Her frustration, like a bad earache, drained her energy, her strength, and made her tense, cranky, and miserable. So much for the depth of Tanny's new girlfriend-to-girlfriend relationship with his secretary.

He ended the call and slipped the cell phone into his jacket pocket. Another BMW swung into the wrong lane as it headed around the blind curve. He took another swig of Gatorade, removing the bottle from the bag. Tanny noticed, but the show did nothing to lower her contempt level—she had a full tank. They waited in vain for the sound of metal and glass crunching. Calvino sat with both hands on the steering wheel, keeping the beat as if to a tune inside his head.

"Does the state of emergency restrict our travel?" she asked.

"It suspends the rules of the road."

"Are you ever serious?"

Calvino shrugged. "When desperation intervenes. I'll let you know when I hit that point."

He leaned forward, changed the radio channel to the news, and turned up the volume. Grover Washington Jr. gave way to an announcer who read from a script about how the army had agreed to remain neutral. The demonstrators at Government House would be allowed to continue their Woodstock-like festival. For the moment no cracking of heads or ribs, no breaking of arms and legs.

"I understand the message, Mr. Calvino. Perhaps we can go to the meeting. Let's find out how Mr. Achara manages to drive over the yellow line and not crash into cars coming at him. That's a discussion I wish to have."

As Calvino pulled back onto the soi, an SUV almost slammed into a Toyota at the blind curve. As the SUV came closer, Calvino expected to see a face twisted by terror and anger, but instead the SUV driver smiled, eyes dreamy and distant, a face unchanged by the possibility of a head-on smash-up that hadn't happened. As the government prepared to crack down, all near-death experiences became more tangible, urgent, and immediate. The two drivers had been dancing a ballet, and they'd been taught from birth that all Thais were members of the same extended family. And no one died so long as they followed the same steps in the ballet. People in the same family automatically forgave each other. Brothers and sisters all glued together with their *samakki*. Until the moment when the glue cracks and breaks and everything it's held together flies apart.

TWELVE

THE HIGHWAY RAN south of Bangkok toward Malaysia. Calvino ran his hand through his hair as he drove in silence. Sometimes, out of nowhere, that ancient feeling of wanting a cigarette hit with the surprise force of a mugger's knife. The presence of Tanny Craig had set off a need for nicotine. Women who triggered a former addiction usually spelled trouble.

As they passed signs for Hua Hin, he thought about Colonel Pratt's idea of finding Tanny's birth mother. And her father. But from the Thai point of view, everything depended on finding the mother. Fathers were optional in constructing and operating the family vehicle. Another Hua Hin sign flew past. He glanced at Tanny. Did he really want to find this woman's mother?

"Do you ever think about what happened to your Thai mother?"

She cleared her throat. "Are we close to Achara's office?"

That was the answer he got, another question that had nothing to do with her biological mother. At least he could tell Colonel Pratt he'd tried.

"Not long," he said. "When are you going to tell me what was in the envelope you gave to Brandon?"

"It's confidential."

"Give me a hint."

"Give me a break."

Calvino slammed on the brakes and pulled off the road. "There's your brake. Where's my hint?"

"It's a way to end the problem between Marshall and his brother."

That was about as much as he would get out of her. He put the car into gear again and pulled back onto the road. Achara's office was situated in a compound near Samut Sakhon, a small hamlet on the outskirts of Bangkok. They passed a scattering of skinny dogs with blotchy, infected skin lying by the road, thin bags of bones with ribs showing. Along the road ran canals, the water brackish, still, as if a shaky hand had cut the earth with a dull tool. In the distance, pools of water formed as smooth as glass—malaria factories, with fast-moving overhead clouds reflecting the sun off their surfaces.

As they came to the outskirts of Samut Sakhon, the land flattened as if it had been hammered until every dent, wrinkle, or gully had been smoothed into one continuous sheet of earth. Vendors sat on chairs under umbrellas at their roadside stands. Behind them were bags of salt stacked into high pyramids. There were no customers. Given that the state of emergency had just been declared, there hadn't been time for panic buyers to converge on the stockpiled salt. Behind the vendor stands, salt flats stretched to the horizon; leathery men and women in rattan hats bent from the waist, working the fields. A couple of children shuffled, rakes in hand, against the horizon, clawing the salt from the cracked ground, dragging it into piles as if it were sand and they were at the seaside. As the car passed the latest stretch of billboards screaming in flashy smiles, heads the size of cars staring out, hawking insurance, soap, mouthwash, and condominium developments, Calvino wondered if Tanny had a reference point for what she saw.

"That's a spirit house," he said. The modest spirit house, which looked like a wedding cake from a dangerous cult, abandoned on a concrete platform, passed in a blur.

"That's a car dealership," Tanny said a moment later, mocking him.

Calvino absorbed her verbal right hook. He knew how to take a direct punch to the ego from a woman.

"Another spirit house," he said.

"You don't ever give up, do you?"

They drove past rows of shophouses, the concrete painted like Wedgwood china plates, identical balconies suitable for potted tropical plants and a birdcage. Large factory complexes, all gray cement and blue-tiled roofs, smokestacks looming in the distance. Now and again, with the regularity of a McDonald's franchise, a complex with a wat and salas, each wat identical to the last, bearing the same traditional Thai gabled roof with the buffed gold and red trimming like a fairy-tale castle. The chimney sticking upward was as black as an eighteen-wheeler's exhaust pipe. Each time the dead were burned, another thin layer of smudge was added. He thought of Old George as they passed lumberyards and a police station. Dust flew up as he pulled off the highway and into a narrow side road that was half dirt. "Almost there," he said. She fidgeted in her seat, never taking her eyes off the scenery passing in a dusty blur on her side of the car. After a kilometer on the country roads, Calvino stopped the car at a security gate. The guard looked inside, took Calvino's driver's license, then stood back from the car and waved them inside the compound. Calvino cut the engine and got out of the car and had walked to the other side as she emerged. "See the canal?"

She saw the light glitter off the water's surface. "Achara has a private boat. He claims he can follow the canals all the way into the city."

"He's a man who makes lots of claims," she said, unimpressed.

A servant showed them into a large combination banquet hall and meeting room used to greet VIPs. In the center was a long table lined with high-backed chairs. She disappeared and returned with glasses of water. But she avoided answering Calvino when he asked her if Achara was on his way.

"What did you ask her?" Tanny wanted to know.

Calvino drank from the glass of water, looking at a huge carving of a winged red-breasted garuda—fierce eyes and mouth, snapping-turtle beak, eagle claws, the talons extended ready to seize prey. "I asked her if she had any whiskey. To bring the bottle."

That answer satisfied Tanny, and it showed with her tiny smirk, as if she'd seen the talons in the wall dig into Calvino's hide. "I'm glad she ignored you."

"I thought she was ignoring *you*."

Along one wall a dozen French doors stretched the full length of the room. All the doors opened onto a garden lavish with coconut trees, bamboo shoots, rubber and banana trees, and a row of mango trees lining the edge of the canal. A couple of the doors stood ajar. A light breeze, first ruffling the yellow bamboo, lazily blew through the openings in the doors, buffeting candle flames with the calm, firm hand of a mother rocking a cradle. The candles were lit even though it was afternoon, and the fleshy white petals of lotus flowers puckered tight like innocent lips in the midst of a first kiss, lending the flowers a rich, sensual look. The smell of the canal and bamboo and lotus lingered like the perfume of a familiar lover.

Tanny sat underneath the high-vaulted ceiling that sloped as if into an ancient cathedral. Calvino looked down the table, past the candles and flower arrangements—three

111

separate arrangements, dwarfed by the length of the table, like lights on a taxiway.

"The position of the flowers and candles follows feng shui. That stuff about the yin and yang, water, earth, fire, wood, and pizza," said Calvino to see if she was actually reading the papers in her folder or just pretending.

"Feng shui is Chinese," said Achara.

He had slipped in through a side door at the back, drying his hands on a towel. Observing Tanny and Calvino, he stood beside a lacquered Chinese cabinet, black ebony, inlaid gold outlining a fairy-tale kingdom populated with angel-like figures in flowing robes, men in boxy hats, while the women, thin-necked with heart-shaped faces, flew above a forest and villages. He finished drying his hands and held out the towel for a servant to take away.

Achara wore a tan safari suit, the top button undone, with his skinny arms sticking out of the short sleeves. His hair, combed to one side like a schoolboy's, was pure white. He looked smaller than the other night when he had suited up in a dinner jacket to attend the Chini exhibition. The black jacket and tie had inflated him into a larger man. Achara's face, kind and open, had a hint of worry, but his large brown eyes, clear and shiny, unencumbered by uncertainty or anger, focused on Tanny Craig. Then he looked away as he walked past the twin larger-than-life bronze busts of an elderly man and woman. Achara brushed his fingers against the spray of orchids placed as an offering at the base of these busts of his father and mother, their hollow, lifeless eyes in a perpetual gaze at the throne.

"Vincent, it is good to see you again. The Chini paintings are remarkable. You are blessed to have such a famous ancestor. It explains how your karma brought you to live in Thailand. And, Ms. Craig, I'm so sorry there was a misunderstanding about our appointment. Last night I had a medical emergency. Not me personally, but two of my animals, and I needed to call in the vet. You've no doubt heard the news about a state of emergency." He sighed, studying his two guests as he broke into a smile. "Our lives are, for the moment, one emergency after another."

If he were lying, Calvino gave him full marks for creativity—he'd substituted the word "animals" for the normal usage in those circumstances: Water buffalo. He might have done better just sticking to the government's declaring a state of emergency. Tanny gave no indication that his explanation made the slightest difference.

"We heard," said Calvino.

Achara sighed, shaking his head. "Why don't I tell you something about this room?" Achara walked to one end and stopped in front of an elaborately carved throne. The back and arms of the throne were embedded with hundreds of semiprecious stones and sported gold filigree and spires rising like flames from a skyline at dusk. A thin red cushion covered the seat.

"I bought this chair in Chiang Mai. The previous owner was a wealthy Chinese merchant. The merchant had bought it many years ago during his travels inside the Shan State. But he'd fallen on hard times and was forced to sell it. The dealer said it was one of the last of his possessions the merchant had sold. After the rest of his fortune had been exhausted, he sat in the chair and pondered his adversity. Six months later the owner shot himself in the head. The antiques dealer hoped that the new owner would have a better karma, one that would entitle him to sit in harmony on such a chair for a lifetime, an old Chinese blessing."

"Blessings can be hit and miss," said Calvino.

"So true, Mr. Calvino. It all depends on your karma." It was the second time Achara had referred to karma in speaking to him.

Tanny stared at the throne, tapping the end of her pen against the file folder on the table. She figured that the chair was worth a small fortune. In a smaller room, it would have looked pretentious, but in the vastness of the banquet hall the dignity of its lineage had found a home.

"You mean luck," said Tanny. Having let the first reference pass without comment, she found herself drawn out.

Achara smiled again, nodding toward her, leaning over the table. "And your luck depends on how well you lived your last life. That is what Thais believe."

He gestured at the wall. Two fire-breathing, gold-lacquered dragons hung there, two beasts each forever struggling to slay the other and eternally frozen in deadly strike position, never able to pull back or deliver the blow. Colonel Pratt was in the habit of quoting Shakespeare. Calvino remembered a line from *Othello*: "I am one, sir, that comes to tell you, your daughter and the Moor are now making the beast with two backs." It came to his mind as he gazed at the dragons and at Craig.

Achara's talk of karma, of luck, of the throne chair and dragons and garudas had begun to seem more like a stalling tactic than a speech by a proud householder on the meaning of his possessions.

Achara had pulled back his chair when a Thai man came in through one of the French doors and, barefoot, crossed over and whispered into Achara's ear. He nodded, and the man, like a ghost, left by the same door through which he had entered. "If you will excuse me. My vet wants me to come and look at my lions."

Calvino's crooked smile caught Tanny like a sock puppet thrown by a child.

"*Singtoh mai sabai*," said Calvino in a matter-of-fact tone, using the Thai expression for the condition of the lions.

Achara nodded in confirmation. There was no misunderstanding.

"Ms. Craig, Khun Achara has a sick lion," said Calvino.

Achara corrected the math. "I have two sick lions."

It seemed she had little choice. She could either join them outside or stay seated at the long table and watch the candles flicker and wait until they returned. She closed her file folder and pushed back her chair. It would be something to put in her report to Marshall Sawyer. Business partner keeps lions on his property. Not that amateur zoo keeping necessarily violated any contractual provision. But it did reflect upon the habits, lifestyle, and priorities of the Thai partner.

THIRTEEN

ACHARA LED THEM to the enclosure housing his lions. Calvino and Tanny followed him along a flagstone path, weaving between the bamboo and banana trees. They watched a boat slowly gliding down the canal as they walked. After a few more steps, like a rope thick with algae, a green snake dropped from a banana tree in front of Craig. She screamed, frozen in place, her fingers splayed over her mouth as if holding back a primeval howl. Calvino leaned down and snatched up the snake, holding its head between his thumb and forefinger. He stared at its shiny, beady eyes, its forked tongue licking the air. "It's harmless," he said, putting it back on the banana tree.

Ahead of them two enormous granite lions flanked the path. Later, Achara would tell them that the features— Rastafarian-like manes, muzzles in a snarl, right leg propped on a ball, with claws extended—had been carefully modeled from Ming-dynasty lions. But the snake had had a more immediate impact. It wasn't clear that Tanny even noticed the stone monsters as she passed by them.

The snake had unnerved her, rattled loose the tight control she kept over herself. "Mr. Calvino is quite right. Snakes, lizards, and spiders are all part of a tropical garden," Achara said, smiling like a professor giving an impromptu lecture on God's little creatures. She regretted not staying in the banquet hall, but it was far too late to retrace her steps alone.

In the distance the roar of a wild animal rolled like a clap of thunder. Then another lion roared as if part of a duet. The blood had drained out of Tanny's face as she instinctively grasped her throat. Some ancient roaring-lion gene had automatically kicked in, and she suddenly felt wobbly on her feet. "Are they caged?" she asked.

Achara smiled. "Don't worry. I keep them caged this time of day. I only let them out into the compound for an hour before sunset."

She examined Calvino for some clue in his body language signaling an intention to run, laugh, or ignore the lions' roar. She found nothing. Distracted by watching the green snake slither along a large coil of banana leaf, Calvino seemed to take the roar in stride, as if he were sitting behind the wheel of his car, watching vans and cars cross the yellow line as they turned sharp curves. Achara walked ahead. "Yes, they are in their cages this time of day. Come, let me show you."

Calvino carried on a few steps before stopping again, waiting for Tanny, who stood stock-still on the path. "You want to go back to the house?"

"Thanks for being supportive," she said.

In a voice thick with irony, Calvino took her hand and said, "You worry too much."

"Did you ever think that you might not worry enough?" The answer, wrapped in fear, rolled across the garden.

"It's safe. I promise," said Achara, waving at her.

They came to a small grassy clearing. The assistant who'd earlier come into the banquet room worked next to the vet near a large structure, a concrete pad that measured ten meters by five meters and was enclosed with heavy bars, at one end a metal gate with a brass padlock. The assistant, a young man, was alert, his excitable eyes scanning the lions inside the enclosure like a bank robber glancing at the

117

CCTV camera, figuring that his time was running out along with his luck.

Inside, two sleep-groggy lions lay in the shade, their rib cages slowly rising and falling.

"They've been sedated," said Achara. "I've never had a break-in. Living on the canal, you sometimes worry about someone coming in a boat and stealing your silver. The one on the right is Fu. She's one hundred sixty kilos. Fu means "happiness" in Chinese. I don't worry so much about her. She is recovering well. But Shi's a male, and he's not responding so well to the medication. In Chinese tradition lions are the protectors, the gatekeepers. Perhaps you've seen the stone lions at Chinese temples?"

"I had a client who lived in a mansion outside of Pattaya. He raised goats. Someone murdered his gardener. But this is my first case involving a client who raises lions." Calvino paused, scratching the back of his head. He wished he had a drink. His mouth felt dry. If Achara, with his low-key excuse of a medical emergency for his animals, had intended to play it cool, then he had succeeded. Calvino had thought Achara had been talking about his dogs.

He glanced at Tanny, who shrugged, still pale, shaky on her feet. "Is he dying?"

Achara sighed, looked longingly at Shi in the back of the enclosure. "Let's hope that's not the case. To lose a protector is an omen," he said. "You see, it impresses my friends when they come out and see Shi and Fu. It makes them feel secure."

Tanny looked as if she felt anything but safe. Achara turned away and entered into a discussion in Thai with the vet, gravely nodding as the vet spoke.

Calvino overheard the vet talking about medication, a regime of shots, and his belief that both lions would recover. There had been a legitimate reason to cancel the appointment after all. Calvino gave Achara credit for coming up with an excuse that he'd never heard before. "Are you okay?" he asked Tanny. Her eyes were wide as she watched the vet and Achara enter into the enclosure and squat down beside Fu.

"Fine. Just fine." Her teeth chattered as she spoke, gooseflesh on her bare arms.

Calvino squeezed her hand; it felt ice cold.

After Achara came out with the vet, he locked the padlock and smiled. "Aren't they beautiful animals?" He beamed like a proud parent.

"Lovely," said Tanny as if pronouncing a dirty word.

"They look powerful," said Calvino, regarding the thick necks, the strong, muscular legs and chests.

"Yes, they are also surprisingly fast for big animals. No one should ever underestimate the true nature of a big cat. They are wild deep, deep inside. The Discovery Channel always shows them at a distance. Hunting. Killing. Sleeping. Having sex. I've had Fu and Shi since they were cubs. They know me as part of the pride. I play with them. But would I turn my back on them, and pretend to run so they would chase me? That would invite trouble."

"What's wrong with them?"

"Fu killed a stray dog. Shi helped her eat it. They contracted canine distemper virus, and it made them sick. It can easily kill a lion."

"They ate a dog?" asked Tanny in horror at the image of the terrifying scene.

"That's rare," said Achara, defending his lions.

"How much do they eat?" asked Calvino, staring into the enclosure.

"Fifteen kilos of red meat. Each. They'd eat a lot more in the wild. But that's because they never know how long they might have to go between kills."

"Thirty kilos?" asked Calvino, thinking that was a fair chunk of cow to carve up and parcel out on a daily basis.

Achara nodded. "I have it delivered fresh. The blood's not yet curdled." He gestured with hands like a Muslim in prayer. "We have business to discuss. Ms. Craig has questions for me. We can go back inside if you like. Or talk in the garden. Up to you."

If you like, thought Tanny. "Like" didn't come close to describing how much she wished to return to the table inside. It no longer matter where he put her, on the blessed or the cursed side; she just wanted to be inside the confines of a room.

"The vet says they should get their appetites back in a few days." Achara shook his head as if worried about the vet's opinion.

Back inside, Tanny shivered as she sat down at the table where she'd left her files. She sipped from her glass of water, the surface making tiny wakes as her unsteady hand struggled to keep the rim to her mouth.

"I am sorry if you aren't feeling well," said Achara.

She used both hands to put the glass on the table. "I'm fine. Perhaps we might start."

Calvino watched as she tried to compose herself. A couple more inches and that snake would have landed on her head, converting her into an unwilling Medusa look-alike. The near miss had been bad enough, making her heart pound, her palms sweat, and her eyes dilate as if she'd gone into shock.

Once she cleared her throat, Tanny dug deep down to find her private investigator's voice. "I understand that the police have arrested a suspect in the murder of the journalist."

Achara nodded. "Technically he remains a suspect. He has confessed, that's the end of it."

"That's not the reason I asked for this meeting."

"Please continue," Achara said, leaning forward, hands on the table, an arm's length from the throne.

120

Calvino had been happy that he hadn't sat on the throne. All that coolness from the lion enclosure would have gone out the French doors. Achara grinned at Calvino as if the party they'd both attended had somehow made them best friends.

Tanny removed a document and passed it down the table. Achara's long fingers stretched forward, and he pulled the paper until it rested in front of him. He put on a pair of rimless, gold-framed eyeglasses, reading with the same intensity Calvino imagined he put into the weather reports at the ski resorts he booked. Calvino had no idea what was in the document. He smiled at Achara as if the weather report had promised fresh powder on the higher slopes. Achara had a face that the hint of a smile softened into a state of polite, if not tender, concern. That smile had vanished.

"Is it true?" asked Tanny.

Is what true? Calvino asked himself.

Achara removed his glasses and pushed the document to the side. "It's true."

"Everyone agrees," said Calvino. "We can move on."

"I gave him two million baht. It was my obligation. Khun Direk's father and my father were from the same village in China."

"Direk is an *active* Thai government official."

"That is true."

"And he is also the official who approved tax relief for the GM and wind-power projects. You paid him after the approval was granted. Sir, you've just admitted to an act of corruption. You've just said that you bribed a public servant. I'm sorry, but Mr. Sawyer can't do business like that. It's illegal under American law. A grand jury might find it interesting to look into the files of a CEO in New York based on what you've just told me." She started to collect her papers, taking another drink of water. "You apparently didn't mention this payment to Brandon."

The final statement stabbed Achara like a knife. He visibly flinched.

"The money wasn't a bribe," he said.

"Then what was it?"

"Are you Thai?"

"I'm American."

Calvino waited as the silence grew near the throne end of the table. The deal was starting to look very much like the sick lions.

"I don't think that you understand our customs and traditions. Khun Direk's father, like mine, came from a small village near Shanghai on the Yangtze River. They were boatmen who came to Thailand together. They left to start a new life. The two million baht was only one payment. There was an earlier one for one million baht. I am surprised you didn't find that one, too. You seem quite thorough. But unfortunately you aren't as careful in drawing your conclusions. The money was used to build a Chinese temple to our fathers and our ancestors. It is like a lodge, an ancestral meeting place. Khun Direk and I are from the same clan; we have a common ancestor. Like me, he is an eldest son of an eldest son. That means our names can be traced in the book of eldest sons uninterrupted, stretching back four thousand years. Is that against your laws in America?"

"As a matter of fact, it might be. I'm not the person to ask. You'll have to contact Mr. Sawyer's law firm in New York. It's just that no one wanted to make a mistake. You've confirmed the payment."

"Can I ask how you know I made the payment to Khun Direk?"

"I'm afraid that's confidential," she said.

Achara sat listening to this with the balance and skill of a downhill skier. At some point, over the distant roar of one of the lions, Calvino half expected him to reach across the table and throw Tanny out. She'd called him everything but an untrustworthy crook, which was fine for her. Instead Achara nodded at Calvino, smiling. "I remember Mr. Calvino's speech the other night. You spoke eloquently about family. About your great-grandfather, the famous painter, your grandfather and father. And how you had become part of your Thai friend's family. Not everyone understands how deep family runs for many people."

"Foreign custom isn't a defense to corruption in America. I really don't have anything else," she said, gathering her papers and file folders and sliding them into her briefcase.

"You can tell Marshall Sawyer that if he wants to sell me the Sawyer shares, I have no problem. An old Japanese friend will buy them. My friendship with Brandon, who came to me first, prevailed. I included Brandon out of friendship. You let me know in the next couple of days whether Mr. Sawyer wants me to make that call."

"Marshall Sawyer has another idea. He wants to buy your shares."

"That's not possible."

So that was Marshall Sawyer's play—go after the bribe angle, put the squeeze on Achara to unload his shares at a fire-sale price. It fit a pattern. Marshall Sawyer looked for an edge, starting with the murder possibility, and when that failed, without missing a beat he got Tanny to hammer Achara with allegations of a bribe. What else did Marshall have hidden up his sleeve?

Achara had a good business plan, received the necessary permits, and after the first year cash-flow projection had started to look good; the problem was, it looked *too* good for Brandon to have brought in the door. When Brandon bragged about the payment Achara had made to the government official, it had been just that—a boast, an ego-sodden howl, that said, "Look at me. See. See. I'm connected. I've brought us a moneymaking machine."

Calvino sat quietly, glancing out at the grounds, thinking he had a good idea what papers Tanny had delivered to Brandon—buyout documents for Achara's shares.

"In your country you love to talk about the rule of law," said Achara. "But in my country, Thailand, we talk about the rule of compromise. It's the same, but different. Americans don't consider a compromise that violates the law, even though the compromise results in peace and harmony between parties. For us, we would set aside the law if both sides agree to a compromise and end their conflict. That is what we are working on now in Thailand. When we have a state of emergency, that means both sides must reach a compromise. No one will get very far talking about who broke what law. The point is, how do people agree to live together? Most of the time, the law allows that. Good, apply the law. But sometimes the law is not your friend. It can get you into conflict, and once that happens, then nothing stays stable. What good is a law if it leads to people shooting each other? Compromise. That is our politics. Our way. Not democracy, not dictatorship, it is our own ideology."

"I don't think the state of emergency would stop the right investor from buying your shares. Now would be a good time to make that deal. Governments change. Permits are revoked. Plans shelved. It happens," Tanny said, snapping her briefcase shut and rising from the table.

Calvino raised a finger and brushed against the chin of a terracotta warrior; he stood at eye level with the warrior made of clay, thinking how the shape of the ears, eyebrows, mouth, and chin on one of the bronze busts and on the terracotta warrior were identical. Achara had used his father's face as the model for two powerful artifacts. Lions in the large garden, terracotta warriors standing guard at the front entrance to the house. Achara was a man who took his links to the past seriously. Replicas of what the ancients had built were everywhere. Paneling in the style of the Forbidden City. The furnishings were from the region—Ming vases, a Shan throne, a flying garuda, and golden dragons.

Achara's faith was in his lineage, and here he had found his protectors and a way to surround himself with them. Calvino had taken one more look at the bust of Achara's parents, wondering not so much how he was going to break the news to Brandon—that part would be easy—but how much fight Brandon had left in him. Whether he'd go head-to-head with brother Marshall. If Calvino were a referee filling out his scorecard, he'd have to score round one to Marshall. And Tanny.

FOURTEEN

A VIOLENT AND sudden emotional outburst hit like a monsoon storm—without warning, hard and fast. As they drove back to the city, Tanny's face clouded, her eyes filling with tears. Her first sob sounded like a hiccup. The Lonesome Hawk had full-time drinkers who'd mastered the squelched hiccup as they wiped the beer suds off their lips with the back of their hand. Calvino looked over as the rain started pelting her cheeks, a river of tears. He reached into his jacket for a handkerchief and, finding it, held it out with one hand, keeping his eyes on the road. Tanny's shoulders twitched, and she shuddered, a spasm of sorrow cocooning her as she blew her nose.

"Thank you," she whispered.

He could tell that she was embarrassed and disappointed with herself. She was tough, implacable, one of those women who looked a man in the eye and didn't look away when he lost his smile. A green snake, a couple of sick lions, and a temple project had stripped away her protective shield, exposing what lay beneath. For the first time, Calvino got a look inside.

"Is there something you want to talk about?" he asked.

She'd been holding something back ever since they got into the car.

"I've never been so scared. I felt like a fool. I must have looked like one, too," she said, fishing for Calvino's observation.

"The snake, the lions, the strange banquet room. Okay, it was a little weird."

She laughed, shaking her head.

"I make a pretty good pasta and salad. Why don't you come back to my place, we'll have dinner, relax, and I'll drive you back to your hotel. You don't look like you're in any shape to go to the office or to your hotel."

"What kind of pasta?"

Calvino grinned, glanced over, catching her eyes. "Campanelle, rotini, manicotti, penne rigate, you name it."

"Farfalle?"

"I don't do little bow ties," he said.

"Somehow I'm not surprised. But for the record, it is my favorite pasta." She'd stopped crying, but the tears had streaked her face.

Once they reached the outskirts of Bangkok, the traffic slowed to a crawl. The cage doors of every office opened at the same time, disgorging employees who, like escaped prisoners, rushed into the streets in one large tidal wave. The traffic jammed. Stopped. Calvino sat back from the steering wheel looking out at Rama IX Bridge, the superstructure an infinite span of individual filaments flaring out and creating something that reminded him of the hood of a frilled lizard who had spotted a mating opportunity. This also gorged on the flies swarming above the drop of honey.

By the time Calvino had unlocked the door to his condo unit, Tanny was complaining about being hungry. He had the feeling that despite her American upbringing, some Thai gene triggered the primal desire to eat every three hours or collapse into a coma. He turned on the lights, leaning against the door to remove his shoes.

"You do this even when they're not watching," Tanny said, taking off one shoe, then the other, and standing in the doorway with the patience of a yellow Lab.

"Funny thing about habits," he said. "I never thought about it. Yeah, it's natural. You wanna keep your shoes on, no problem."

"That's what the Thais say, too. 'No problem.' "

"You got me. Shoes off. No problem. That's about all you need to know. I don't understand why they don't give me a passport."

But she wasn't listening. She walked into the living room, to the bank of windows overlooking the Queen Sirikit Center and the lake. The blinds had been left open, giving an unobstructed view. "You do all right," she said, not bothering to look back at Calvino. "Famous ancestors, luxury lifestyle, and a way with snakes."

A light went on in the kitchen hidden behind a shoji screen. Calvino peeked around the corner. "If you're living in New York, you're not doing too bad yourself. If I were really Thai, I'd come straight out and ask how much you make," he said.

"But you're not that Thai," she said.

"So how much *do* you make?"

"That's none of your business." There was something almost playful in her voice.

"And now that we've established that neither one of us is Thai, let's get something to eat and relax."

He found the remote, pointed it across the room, and a smoky jazz saxophone opened from recessed speakers, Pratt's riff sending a mellow harmony into motion like a languid cat stretching after a long sleep, beginning to find its legs.

"That's nice. Who is it?"

"A friend named Pratt. That's Pratt playing at the Java Jazz Festival a couple of years ago. He wrote it, too." The man is a musical genius who never should have been a cop, thought Calvino. But that's how his life had turned out. "Destiny" is what Pratt called it, proving his point by quoting Portia's line from *The Merchant Of Venice*: "The lottery of my destiny bars me the right of voluntary choosing."

"Ratana tells me that Colonel Pratt's a very good man," said Tanny.

She turned away and walked a couple of steps, crossing the black marble floor illuminated by a large globe that slowly rotated, throwing flashes of red, yellow, and green as Africa, Europe, North and South America floated in a deep sea of blue. Her fingertips brushed against its surface, the sea and land in her reach. "Also, Ratana said that Brandon was your only client. If he's paying you to live like this, then Marshall should be more worried about you than about Achara."

"I inherited some money," he said. She'd been pumping Ratana for information, not necessarily knowing that what came out of that well would be just enough water to whet her thirst.

Tanny nodded, confirming that she'd heard the same story from Ratana.

Inheritance was the official version. It left out a couple of details like the shooting of a Chinese-Thai businessman, who had been the previous owner of the paintings. The idea of inheritance wasn't the full story, but it had a clean, legal ring to it.

Calvino boiled water. The lights in the hood above the gas burners shone on the built-in kitchen cupboards and counters. He glanced at the jars of pasta as Tanny hovered near the counter, watching him. He had decided on the rotini, and scooped up a handful out of a glass jar on the counter. Leaning over the counter, he opened his hand. "Rotini," he said. The pasta looked like something a chef had made by carving a fan belt of rings around a slug. Calvino turned and dropped it into the boiling water. Opening a cupboard, he pulled out a bottle of Pomerol that he'd been saving for a special occasion.

"You've got to drink wine if you wanna enjoy pasta," he said. "It's the law. No compromise when it comes to pasta and wine."

He set the bottle of Pomerol on the counter next to her. Tanny's eyes widened as she read the label on the 1983 vintage. It wasn't just any Pomerol but a Petrus, and it had the desired effect, bringing a slow, smooth smile. Not waiting for her to answer, he pulled out the corkscrew and had begun to peel back the silver paper surrounding the cork when his doorbell rang. His hand froze on the corkscrew as he tried to figure out who would be at his door this time of night.

"Aren't you going to find out who that is?"

He rubbed his hands together, turned down the heat on the pasta, and covered the pot. "I'll be right back. Don't go anywhere."

Wiping his hands on a kitchen towel, he opened the door. Siriporn stepped forward, wrapping her arms around his neck, kissing him on the mouth. It took her a couple of seconds before she realized that Calvino wasn't kissing her back. She looked down and saw Tanny's shoes, black high heels, lined up perfectly with Calvino's. Around the corner from the door, she saw the light coming from the kitchen, smelled the pasta sauce coming to a boil on the back burner. "This morning I realized I must've left an earring last night. I'm sorry if it's a bad time. It's probably in the bedroom."

Before Calvino could say, "Tomorrow would be better," Siriporn slipped through the door and into the master bedroom, switching on lights as she walked. It was uncanny how she knew the location of each switch. He'd been in the unit for six months and still hadn't memorized what switch was connected with which light. The "left earring" was an old bar ying trick, with variations—it might be a watch, a ring, a bracelet, or a switchblade knife (apparently it had sentimental value, as she'd stabbed her ex-husband with it). Calvino leaned against the wall, thinking how he was going to deal with one woman in the kitchen and another in the bedroom. He walked back to the condo's entrance and held the door open. A security guard passed, flashing a broad grin. Calvino closed the door, resting his back against it.

"No," she said. "I must have lost it in the living room."

"Of course," he said, slapping his head. "Feel free to search the entire premises."

"Do you mind?"

Siriporn gave the impression of searching for the earring in the low light of the sitting room, working her way toward the kitchen. As the two women locked eyes, Calvino moved behind Tanny, who stood at the stove, stirring the pasta with a large wooden spoon. Siriporn offered a tentative wai, which Tanny didn't return. Maybe she still didn't know that in Thailand it was culturally more acceptable to pull a gun than not to return a wai.

"How's the pasta?" he asked.

Neither woman thought that this was a particularly helpful question.

"Siriporn this is Tanny Craig. Siriporn's my stockbroker," he said, almost convincing himself that it was normal for a stockbroker to show up at night searching the place for missing jewelry. The expensive bottle of wine wasn't lost on Siriporn. She had a stockbroker's nose for market value.

Siriporn switched into Thai, asking Tanny Craig where she was from, and was just getting into the question of her age—necessary to determine whether she had to call her *pee* or *nong*.

"I don't speak Thai," Tanny said, wishing she had the sentence on a tape recorder that she could replay every time the question was asked. "I'm a private investigator from New York,"

"Tanny's from New York," said Calvino.

"We're working on a case together," she said.

"Colleagues," said Calvino.

The out-of-town part and the American part and the colleagues bit provided enough comfort to satisfy Siriporn that Tanny wasn't a long-term threat. What came in and out of Thailand was rarely competition; it was only a temporary inconvenience. Siriporn's face softened, and she managed a smile. "Well, I can't find it. I guess it's lost," she said, exhaling as if she'd just experienced a near miss—like a snake falling out of a banana tree. It had been that kind of day. "I should go. It seems you two have business."

Tanny brushed catlike against Calvino's shoulder. It was a fine performance. Siriporn tried to mask her discomfort. The women locked eyes again for a long moment. Calvino turned down the flame on the gas burner. A couple of competitive women around knives and fire had started to worry him. He led Siriporn out of the kitchen and back to the door.

"Pleasure to meet you, Khun Tanny," said Siriporn.

"Have a nice day," said Tanny.

At the door, Siriporn's parting shot was aimed at Calvino, a Thai expression that translated to "A man with more than one woman has invested his fortune in grief." After she was out the door, Calvino walked back into the kitchen. Tanny had taken lettuce, tomatoes, and onions from the fridge and found a knife and cutting board. She glanced up from slicing a tomato.

"There's a Chinese saying that a banker who loses her earring in your bedroom will lose your investment in the street."

Calvino smiled. "I don't know that one."

"It's from Chinatown in New York." She grinned, putting the slices of tomato into a bowl.

Calvino checked the pasta, then a pesto sauce, and turned off the burner. "But you have a point," he said. "I've got a history of falling into uncovered manholes."

"You should look where you walk."

"That's what my mother always said."

He opened the wine and poured two glasses, handing one to Tanny.

"Here's to your mother," she said.

"Here's to Chinatown," said Calvino. "The smoldering hole in the financial center of the universe."

The rim of his glass touched hers, and they drank, drifting through a patch of silence as a new jazz piece came over the speaker system.

"I need to phone Marshall," Tanny said.

"It's eight in the morning in New York," said Calvino, glancing at his watch.

"In an hour, then," she said, sipping her wine, eyes half hooded.

"You impressed Achara with your speech about family," Tanny said, finishing with the salad. "Is that a sideline? Giving speeches about family values?"

He shrugged and removed the pasta. It was overcooked. He'd lost track of time once Siriporn had arrived. He thought about starting over but decided to go ahead, hoping the pesto sauce would mask the error. Tanny, though, wasn't letting go of the speech about family. As he topped up her wineglass, she pressed him for details.

"I'm curious about the speech you made. It must've had some impact."

He described Montri's mansion as making Achara's place look like a guesthouse for visiting Chinese cultural attachés, and the group of men in dinner jackets who'd attended a

133

private art exhibition's opening. When he'd been asked to speak, at first he was at a complete loss as to what to say. "If you think about it, the most important things about life and morality come down to family. It's what binds people in this part of the world. Ancestors are essential for them. Laws, rights, and justice get adjusted to fit the importance of family. It's the opposite of America."

"Meaning men run the show," said Tanny. The effects of the wine had opened the possibilities of all kinds of impressions escaping from her lips. She jabbed well, and as long as he kept weaving, Calvino thought he'd avoid most of the punches. It was difficult to believe that this was the same woman whom fear had stretched and pulled into a state of terror, unleashing a torrent of tears in the car.

"Respect and loyalty are the show runners. It's tribal. And the women let the men *think* they're running the show. Most people are happy with the illusion."

"I wouldn't be," she said.

"You're from here but not really from here. So why would you buy into how the place wires people? Family is part of their religion, their politics, and their legal structure. For the Thais, family is sacred. It's what they get taught in school. What's with the Sawyer family argument?"

"There's no argument. Just two different points of view of what's good business."

"Marshall doesn't want Achara's shares. You lied to him. My gut tells me that Marshall's got a plan to flip Brandon's shares in the Thai company because New York's bleeding money and he needs the cash. The problem is, Brandon doesn't want to sell. And Achara doesn't want to play along."

"Brandon told you what was in the envelope," she said.

Calvino nodded. "Achara doesn't want to sell his shares. Brandon isn't interested in selling. Digging up dirt on Achara isn't going to get Marshall what he wants."

"Marshall always gets what he wants."

"Yeah, then he's a lucky man. He'd be careful enough to arrange a Thai buyer for the company?" asked Calvino. "Because he'd need Thais to hold the majority interest. It's the law."

"Marshall has the best lawyers."

"And they help him do whatever it takes, even if it means fucking over his brother."

"And that was in your speech?" she asked as Calvino refilled her glass. The flush on her face from the wine gave her the radiance of a celebration in progress.

Calvino smiled, drank his wine. "Okay, you got me. I left that part out." He'd just begun to like her when she reverted to a New York hard-ass dead set on winning. For a moment he wondered if he'd pushed the wrong woman out the door.

Tanny followed him to a low table surrounded by rattan seat mats on the floor. Plates, cutlery, cloth napkins, water glasses, wineglasses—the table had been preset by a woman; another woman could tell in an instant. Tanny wondered if that woman might have lost an earring.

"And what do you say?"

It was the kind of open-ended question that a couple of glasses of wine could bring Tanny Craig to ask. They carried the food to the table.

"I have a few more questions," he said as he filled her plate with pasta.

"Such as?"

"Why you came from New York to close a share-sale deal? How did you know about the payment Achara made? What happens if Brandon and Achara won't play ball?" She toyed with her pasta. "Anything else?"

"Will you stay tonight?" He grinned, waiting for her reaction. It was a short wait.

"Isn't that crossing the yellow line around a blind corner?" she asked. "Not to mention the evidence of considerable traffic to your bed."

The Zen of Thai Traffic had the capacity for spilling off the road and into the bedroom, and he found himself nodding. "The banker?"

She nodded, too, squirming as if a scorpion had crawled inside her thong. "Broker. I thought she was your broker."

"We're talking fender bender," he said. "Minor damage. One lost earring."

"That's *your* way of looking at her damages. She might not agree."

Calvino didn't have an immediate answer, and Tanny liked that he stumbled to find one.

"Forget about your broker's damage, let's get back to your other questions. Brandon told Marshall about Achara's payment to the Thai official. He bragged about it to his big brother, as if Marshall were going to be impressed by corruption. Marshall's lawyers had reviewed the payment and said it raised flags. That's why he sent me all the way from New York. Marshall's a fair man. He wanted to give Achara a fair chance to clarify the payment. Whether he really paid the money. It's clear that he did. As for my own family in Thailand, that's not so easy. I was adopted as an infant. I was three months old when I left Thailand. My father found me in an orphanage run by missionaries. My mother had left me there. So you can forgive me if I have a slightly different view of Thai family values. If my father hadn't taken me from that place, what would have happened to me?"

There came a turning point when a woman's defenses thawed out and she opened to the possibility of something more. Sitting across from her at the table, Calvino saw up close the subtle change that had drifted over her. He warned himself about letting things get out of hand, getting personal with Tanny, issuing the regulation "Get in" message that led to the bedroom. He refilled his glass, facing resistance against strong natural impulses. It was like lighting matches to peer inside an open container of gasoline. The impulse won; he couldn't help himself from reaching across and touching her hand. She didn't take hers away. And from what he saw, it appeared to be a mutual feeling. He knew exactly what had gotten to him. It was like seeing a magician show how he does a trick, then still being fooled when the trick was done. Full-knowledge tricks did the most damage to a man's sense of free will. Tanny lived inside a Thai woman's body but never had a chance to learn what it meant to *be* Thai, to know what being Thai meant or how it felt, or to fully understand someone like Achara. She was a Thai without the brainwashing. Tanny was what you got when the official line had never been registered from the first day in school. Everyone in Bangkok looked like they might be relatives, but after three seconds it became clear to them and to her that something beyond genes and DNA had been responsible for her psychological wiring, the glide path of her destiny. She was a cultural freak. And there was some incredible appeal she had as a result. In time, he told himself, he'd figure it out.

Instead that night, he looked her in the eye, holding her hand, and said, "I might be able to find your mother."

It was as if she suffered a flashback of the green snake dropping from the tree. "I'm not sure. ..." Her voice trailed off and she reached for her wineglass.

"Not sure of what?"

"Whether I ever want to meet her."

"But she's your mother."

"I know. And all Thai daughters worship their mother. So why should I be any different. Isn't that what you're saying?"

"Why not let me check it out? It's not like I have a dozen clients knocking on my door. Finding people is something I'm reasonably good at."

"Finding *earrings* isn't something you're particularly good at," she said, smiling.

"I am if they're on the person I'm looking for."

"You want another client?"

He tilted his head to one side, pulled his hand away from hers, and leaned forward, elbows on the table. "You mentioned something about having a kid," he said, brushing off her question.

"A six-year-old boy. Jeffrey. Jeff's what everyone calls him."

"I remember. You talked about him with Ratana in the office. I was standing in the doorway listening."

In New York, Calvino had a daughter, Melody, who was no longer a kid but he remembered her at six, the age when every girl loved her father, looked up to him, held his hand, smiled when he read to her, and then one day something changed. "Growing up" was what they called it.

"You must be missing him," he said.

Her eyes glistened as she nodded. "I do."

"Maybe your mother feels the same way."

"Are we back to that?" she asked.

"I didn't think we'd left it."

Maybe he'd been pushing her a little too far; the shell now started to extend over her. He stopped short of telling her that her musical hero on the saxophone had thought it was the right thing to do, and instead he split the last of the wine between the two glasses. Tanny pulled a cell phone from her handbag. The spell was broken as she moved back into professional gear.

"I need to phone Marshall. Is there a place where I can have some privacy?"

"You can use the bathroom." He pointed over her right shoulder to a door opposite the illuminated globe. "You can turn on the shower if you want. No, it's not bugged."

Calvino sat on the sofa, telling himself it was just as well it had happened like this; it was a good way to end the evening. She'd finish her call, collect her files, and leave, and tomorrow she'd be back at the office. He'd have to look at her all day, trying to figure out how to deal with the fact that he'd held her hand, made a play for her. Time would stop. She'd immediately tell Ratana, who'd stick her head into his office and stare at him. He felt doomed; maybe that was how a state of emergency was supposed to make a man feel. It was how rejection by a woman made him feel.

FIFTEEN

TANNY WAS AWAY for no more than fifteen minutes. Enough time for Calvino to clean up the table, sit on the end of the sofa, and stare out at Lake Ratchada and the Queen Sirikit Center, the lights like night running lights on a car, creating shadows that fell away into an absorbing darkness. He thought about the state of emergency across town. It helped him put his own feelings in perspective. Would this be the night the police or the army waded in with batons and guns to clear the grounds of Government House? Or would they wait and wait—impose one of those medieval sieges that lasted years, until those inside succumbed from thirst, starvation, smallpox and cholera, leaving no survivors.

Then he heard something strange. It was the sound of the shower from behind the bathroom door. He smiled. Tanny had seemed so relaxed, her professional face back in place, but the reality was different; she was definitely being paranoid, running the shower to mask her phone call, he thought. He checked his watch.

Half an hour after Tanny had gone into the bathroom, she walked out wearing a fluffy blue towel knotted above her breasts. The light showed the outlines of her collarbone and shoulders—broad, strong shoulders that seemed to overshoot her armpits by a couple of centimeters from where they should have stopped. Using a builder's plane, a master carpenter would have trouble matching that perfect straight line. She smiled, seeing Calvino's jaw still hanging by a thread, as she switched off the bathroom light behind her and walked over to the window. She knew the impact that she had on men.

"I was going to ask how it went with Marshall Sawyer, but I'm not so sure I care," Calvino said.

She smiled and padded across the marble barefooted, held out her fist, and slowly opened it. A gold earring rested like a crown on her palm. "Is this what she was looking for?" She dropped it into his hand.

He closed his hand and slipped the earring into his pocket. For once he was speechless. The effect brought one of her rare smiles, like one of those flowers that bloom once every hundred years in the desert. Surprises came in many shapes and forms, but having her emerge from the bathroom wrapped in a towel registered at the outer limit of expectations. A state of emergency across town and a state of undress in his condo, with Calvino at a loss to know which presented the greater danger.

"You spoke with Marshall?" he asked, looking at her bare shoulders.

"He's disappointed but hopeful," she said. Outside, Asoke Road glistened with rain, cars taking the bridge over Rama IV plowing through a low spot and unleashing a spray as they briefly blurred inside a watery envelope before reappearing on the bridge.

"That could describe my life."

She walked back to the windows and looked out at the Bangkok skyline, rows of high-rises stretching from Sukhumvit to Sathorn Road in the darkness, thousands of tiny windows strung out like neoimpressionist dots painted by Georges Seurat.

"You got Marshall to understand that Achara's payment wasn't corruption? And that it was Achara's own money, right?

141

It had nothing to do with company money," said Calvino, edging close to her, his hand slipping around her waist.

She nodded, sitting on the sofa. "That doesn't matter. Marshall doesn't want to be involved in the company."

Calvino sat down beside her in time to see a dark shadow streak across her face and said, "Maybe Achara ought to sell his shares to his friend Zhang. That guy's rolling in money. They've been skiing in Canada together."

"Not a bad idea," she said. In the half darkness, she pulled him forward and kissed him on the lips. "I can think of something else that's not a bad idea."

She rolled onto her back, tilted her head to the side, looking out the window. She reached down with her hand, stroked his leg.

He gently squeezed her waist, leaning down to smell her freshly washed hair. It was the same scent as Siriporn's. They'd both showered using the same plastic bottle, he thought. It wasn't right. Women shouldn't smell exactly the same; it was confusing.

"Marshall's wife invited me to their apartment. She wanted me to buy jewelry for her in Bangkok. She'd heard about the high quality and low prices. You have any ideas about jewelry beyond lost earrings?"

"I guess I deserved that," he said.

"It could have been worse. It could have been *your* earring."

He lifted her in his arms and carried her across the loft, around a shoji screen, and into the master bedroom. The "Get in" sign flashed inside his head. "I didn't think you had a sense of humor."

"You can't do this job without one," she said.

He laid her down on the bed. "But we're not working now, right?"

Curtains drawn, the light from outside, dim and soft, was set ablaze by a jagged scar when lightning flared, then

142

thunder rumbled as if a camera flash had caused the skyline to growl like a lion in heat. The wall of light lasted a couple of seconds, long enough for Calvino to find her eyes, reflecting something between sadness and desire. Her hair was pushed over the sheets, and she lifted her hips as he slowly removed the bath towel and tossed it onto the floor. She sat up naked in bed, legs crossed. Nothing self-conscious as she reached out and pulled him forward until their noses touched. His hands ran up her stomach and sides, sliding over to cup her breasts. There'd been enough recoil in her passion to give a twelve-gauge pump-action shotgun a run for its money. As in everything else, Tanny was dedicated to getting the maximum from her effort.

Half an hour later, legs coiled together, they lay in bed, watching the rain outside.

"Those lions were weird," she said, turning her head and finding his eyes in the near darkness. "The state of emergency is weird. And so are most of the people. They think I'm faking it because I don't speak Thai. Why don't they believe me? It's stupid."

"It's called culture shock. All foreigners go through it. It's like boot camp, where a whole new way of thinking and doing things gets drilled into your head. It's difficult to adjust. Some people handle the stress; others crack up, go home. In your case you give the Thais culture shock. You're shocked, they're shocked. That generates an excess of electricity in the system, enough to run a citywide grid."

"If you've got plenty of money, it doesn't matter," she said. "You've got your own generator. Or a couple of them stashed away."

It was the earring left behind cropping up again. He ignored it.

"I didn't have much until a couple of years ago. Before that, I lived in a place that, depending on your point of view, was either run-down or a slum. Then I had some luck, things turned around, and everything changed. I no longer had to worry about paying the rent. I had a lot of memories in that place."

"Like what?"

"The people. Like this young American who lived in my old building. Jerry Hutton was his name. He came from Scranton, Pennsylvania. He was twenty-eight when the police fished his body out of Lumpini Park Lake with a necklace of wooden penises around his neck. I had to identify the body. He got mixed up with people way above his pay grade. We used to call guys like Jerry 'third-shifters.' The guys normal people never saw, people who worked the shitty jobs for shitty wages during the middle of the night while everyone else was fast asleep. I wasn't living much different from Jerry."

"But now you're set. You don't have to do anything. Just enjoy."

He thought about this in silence, running his hand over her body.

"Yeah, it does. Most of the time. Once you get used to the money, everyone ends up asking the same thing as a bar ying: 'Okay, got the cash, what's next?' "

"Maybe you'll never be content."

"Maybe." He stroked her hair. "Soon I'll be finished with my last case. Then I'll have no reason to roll out of bed. Kinda like how I feel now. We could hang here and let the world go by. Order in takeout, and with my money we can hole up for a hundred years. What do you think?"

"I think I'd end up finding a jewelry shop full of strange earrings."

Calvino laughed. "You're tough. But you make me laugh. That's a good thing."

"I told you that I have a six-year-old son waiting for me at home. I learned to be tough. And funny." A lonesome echo stayed in the room.

"Jeff, right? You make him laugh?"

"Yes, Jeff." She smiled, thinking he had remembered her son's name. "You bet I do."

Calvino thought how he'd been going on at Montri's exhibition about the meaning of family, and said much the same to Tanny, and now he's acting like her boy is an afterthought. She felt an immediate distance open up. From his face she saw that she'd driven a knife through his heart and twisted it. "Why don't you try to find my mother? I don't give you much of a chance. But you got lucky with your inheritance, you got lucky with me, maybe you're just a lucky guy."

He'd slammed face-first into a brick wall, and she'd picked him up and put his face back on, ignoring that for a minute it had been lost in the darkness. Tanny Craig had finally given a glimpse of a slipstream of Thai-ness flowing deep below her New York ground-level setting. He was inhaling the smell of sex as he traced figure eights on her hip, hoping that she'd forgive him, when the phone rang. Reaching up, he grabbed the receiver. Siriporn was on the other end, asking him if he'd eaten dinner. No matter that it was after ten at night. But a Thai often needed no better excuse for phoning.

He rose up on his elbow as Tanny rolled over and looked out of the rain-splattered balcony windows. "I found your earring," he said, clearing his throat.

Calvino slammed his forehead. "To tell the truth, I didn't find it. Tanny found it in the bathroom. Here, why don't you tell her where it was," handing Tanny the phone.

She brushed away the hair from her face. It went downhill from her first words. "After I finished my shower, I looked for a towel. You left it on the edge of the towel shelf."

Afterward the two women exchanged a couple of lines frosty enough to freeze a monkey's nuts against a coconut tree. Tanny handed the receiver back to Calvino. He turned, put the phone to his ear, but the line was dead. By the time he hung up, Tanny had bolted out of bed, wrapped the towel around her, and padded across the marble floor. A moment later Calvino heard her turn on the shower. She reappeared dressed, and he'd already dressed, too, and stood shaking a ring of car keys.

"It's late. I'll drive you to your hotel."

Her expression reverted to the one he remembered from Brandon and Achara's meetings; she returned to her default professional, doing-business face. It was like one of those before-and-after advertisements: The woman who wants to cook morphing into the woman who wants to kill. "I can take a taxi," she said.

"But you don't speak Thai. You'll end up in Cambodia."

Her eyes widened, as she'd obviously forgotten about that slight limitation. She raised one hand as if she were about to take some sort of oath. "Promise me that what happened tonight stays in this apartment."

"You think I kiss and tell?"

"It would be a mistake to complicate things beyond our control."

"I thought that's what women spent a lifetime doing."

"Bastard." She smiled.

He wasn't certain what he'd expected, but this wasn't it. Over his own lifetime, he had done a lot of less-than-noble things—hurt some people, killed more than a few—but he'd never been a snitch. That was where Italian and Jewish genes had reinforced themselves in his psyche. "I was hoping we might do this again," he said.

"We should get to know each other better," she said. Sex without intimacy for most women was like drinking wine without alcohol, but for most men sex without intimacy was straight bourbon that burnt all the way down.

He almost laughed. "I thought we already knew each other."

"Not really," she said. "I'd appreciate if you'd be discreet."

Raising his hand like swearing an oath in court, he looked her in the eye, lower lip quivering, doing his best. "It stays confidential." Then he hugged her, and, much to his surprise, she hugged him back.

Strange woman, he thought.

He took the long way to her hotel, turning left onto Soi 16. It was just after 11:00 P.M. Slowing the car down as hundreds of construction workers in yellow hard hats, long-sleeved blue shirts, and rubber boots, weary from backbreaking work, walked three, four deep, spilling from the pavement onto the street.

"Who are these people?" she asked. "Looks like a mob. Some kind of a demonstration."

Calvino registered a hint of panic in her voice. The headlights shone on the throng of roughly dressed people.

"They're construction workers," he said.

"It's late to be working construction."

Calvino watched them filing past on the shoulder of the road. "They've walked over a kilometer from the work site and still aren't home."

"Christ, that's terrible," she said as they passed a number of young women in the crowd.

The men and women, bone weary and gaunt, showed up in the headlights of cars coming from the opposite lane. Both sides of the road, gorged with the crowd, slowed the traffic to a crawl. "They've been working since seven in the morning."

He nodded at a couple holding hands the way lovers do on an evening stroll. "That's what passes for romance. Dead tired at the end of the day, walk to a shanty, holding hands on the road," said Calvino. "Anytime you start feeling sorry for what's gone wrong in your life, remember them."

She leaned over and kissed him. "I think you're an okay guy."

Some of the workers lined up for a motorcycle taxi, the first in the line climbing onto the back of a motorcycle, then another, and another. They'd had it; the kilometer walk was beyond the energy they had in reserve. "In a sixteen-hour day, they earn about eight dollars. You see the high-rise over there? The people inside spend five times that taking a friend to lunch at a fancy hotel."

"I don't understand. Shouldn't these be the people who are demonstrating? If it isn't these people, who are they?"

Calvino grinned, glanced at her, touching her chin. "Those are the people in the high-rises, who believe that people like these shouldn't vote."

"Where in the world don't the rich run the show?" she asked. "I'm starting to feel as if Thailand isn't that much different from Latin America."

Tanny had a point: Southeast Asia was the Latin America of Asia, Calvino admitted. Hot-blooded people, coups, street demonstrations, powerful military, arrogant elites, poverty, and corruption. But one point doesn't add up to the final score. "I'm showing you Zen Traffic Lesson number two: A luxury car has more right-of-way than a Honda City, a car has a bit more of the right-of-way than a motorcycle, a motorcycle trumps a bicycle and all pedestrians. Thailand isn't a place you want to find yourself as a construction worker or a walker."

SIXTEEN

CALVINO TURNED UP at the Lonesome Hawk around noon to find McPhail on his hands and knees on the table inside the booth underneath the stuffed water buffalo head—years ago a customer had shipped it to George from South Africa. George had been proud that water buffalo hadn't come from Isan. At the far end of the bar next to the kitchen, the cook, a couple of her teeth missing, grinned and called out, "I bring special for you, Khun Vinny," then disappeared like a spider into the kitchen.

Calvino ordered a drink and stood beside Bill, a sweet old man who'd cried at Old George's funeral. Bill's face looked like a badly bruised mango left out in the Bangkok noonday sun. Drink caused that kind of erosion, carving canyons and ravines in what had once been fine, smooth skin.

One of McPhail's knees bumped against a hammer and nails. A couple of nails fell off the table, bounced down onto the floor, making some of the drunks sitting at the bar jump. "Incoming!" shouted McPhail.

"It's crooked," said Bill, an eighty-year-old ex–army gunny, wearing his glasses on a chain like a half-blind librarian lost in the stacks. He rocked back and forth on his heels, his liver-spotted hand extended, lining up his thumb as a rough-and-ready measurement tool.

McPhail was hanging a framed picture on the ghost wall. In the photograph, Old George held up a bottle of Singha beer, his hair combed, a long strand woven by one of the yings into a micro-ponytail. He was smiling into the camera.

"What do you think?" asked McPhail. He spotted Calvino. "Hey, buddy, will you pass me those cigarettes?"

"If you ask me, it's still crooked," said Bill, hands resting on his huge stomach as if it were a prayer stool.

"Calvino, is it straight or crooked? You're the man with the art collection. You ought to know. Bill's got me moving this way, that way, and back again. It's like doing the tango with a drunk."

"I'm sober," protested Bill.

"We ain't getting anywhere," said McPhail, catching the pack Calvino tossed him. "Working with Bill is like trying to get change back from a whore."

"That's not true," said Bill. "I just think we owe it to George to get his photo hung straight. It's his bar. For at least one time in his life, he should be remembered as straight up. Not off kilter."

McPhail bounced a cigarette out of the pack and lit it. "You know, if Elvis had lived to eighty-four, he would have looked just like George. What if—"

"Shut the fuck up," said Bill, defending George's memory against McPhail's about-to-be-delivered conspiracy theory.

"Bill, I'm starting to think it's your thumb that's crooked. George's photograph was straight the first time. Jesus wept," said McPhail.

Bill had jammed his hand in the breech of an artillery piece and almost lost his thumb and forefinger, which had been stitched up in a field hospital. The doctors had done the best they could with what they had. But as a metric measuring device, Bill's thumb wasn't much use. It wasn't even—it was closer to the way the crooked bartender measured shots.

A couple of the other regulars, daytime drunks, came to stare at the photograph of Old George smiling like the fox that had raided the chicken coop. Bill tilted forward, glass in hand, squint-eyed, looked hard at the photograph. "Straight," he said.

McPhail said, "Fuck you, no wonder we lost the Vietnam War." He drained his gin and tonic and started on another one, and only then did the number of drunks expand, their eyes shifting from Old George to the half-remembered faces in the other photographs hanging on the knotty-pine-paneled wall. A former navy pilot, his eyes puffy, the fissures of broken blood vessels turning the whites of his eyes into an alien, lifeless moonscape, said a few words about how much everyone would miss Old George but that he would always be in everyone's heart.

McPhail rolled his eyes, holding the hammer and nails and standing next to Calvino. There was a moment of silence. One of the drunks farted. A belch escaped from the gaseous region, and slowly was released from a rum-and-Coke-bloated belly. All eyes focused on the smiling faces of a long line of dead men who had once sat at the bar, bullshitting about wars, sometimes proving that false memories outnumbered real ones, crying in their glasses about Thai girlfriends, weeping about some ache of the soul that they couldn't identify. Once Old George had died, in the ensuing couple of days, someone had the brainstorm, fired by Mekong whiskey, to regroup the photos and add one of Old George. Big Henry, whose highest accomplishment had been being chosen as the understudy for a village production of *Hamlet*, christened it the "Wall of Ghosts."

The Brits had a flair for language and soon everyone called it the Wall of Ghosts, or the Ghost Wall. Bill had paid to have the photo of Old George framed, and he claimed that his payment entitled him to the right to decide where on the wall to hang it. McPhail drove a nail into the wall next to a photo of the mustached Colonel Bob, an ex–CIA spook who had run the "secret war" in Laos. Then there was Gator, another mustached ex-warrior, teeth and fingers missing, hollow-eyed, holding up a beer; and Josh, one of two black faces on the Wall of Ghosts, another ex-Vietnam vet, who'd knocked around the Square as a cook, quiet unless the subject turned to baseball; and Joe, who said he'd been a prisoner of war in Vietnam, and who fell in love with every new waitress who came through the door, promising to marry her and support her family; and a ninety-year-old bald-headed man whose name no one remembered, his arms around two waitresses who were kissing the sallow craters where cheeks once rose. The only photo everyone immediately recognized was a grainy black-and-white of John Wayne in a cowboy hat and shirt, looking about thirty years old. A heroic cowboy was one of the honorary dead.

The dead men's club rattled the drunks, who were doing their best to ignore the work that McPhail and Bill were doing. They shuffled their feet, cracked their knuckles, and drank. No one said anything, but everyone wondered who'd be next to go up on the Ghost Wall, joining the club. The old Navy pilot had already reserved a place below John Wayne, the way people reserved cemetery plots in Louisiana: They paid the mamasan, who wrote down their names in a book that she kept under the cash box. Drunks had a knack for organizing a spontaneous memorial service. Given their lifestyle, they had a lot of practice saying good-bye to people who'd occupied the barstool next to them for years.

The cook came out of the kitchen and put a plate of tacos and fried beans on the table inside Calvino's usual booth. He winked at her, and she returned her toothless smile. Calvino slid into the booth, and a moment later McPhail joined him, putting the hammer and nails on the table. "If Bill had organized the crucifixion, they'd still be trying to get Jesus straight on the cross," said McPhail.

"I've got a new case," said Calvino, pouring hot sauce on the tacos.

McPhail let out a long sigh. "I thought you'd retired." McPhail was like a wife who remembered every word a man regretted and forgot everything of pride he wished she'd remember.

A taco came apart like a cheap tailored jacket in Calvino's hand, spilling lettuce, hamburger meat, onions, and sauce onto his plate. He reached for a paper napkin and wiped his fingers. "Retire? And then what? Sit around the Lonesome Hawk all day waiting for you to get my photo hung straight?" Calvino dabbed the grease from his knuckles and finished his whiskey, raising his empty glass until the bartender saw him and nodded.

"Okay, don't get a bug up your ass." McPhail lit another cigarette and blew smoke off to the side, which the fan immediately blew back over the shattered taco spill on Calvino's plate.

Calvino pushed the plate away. He was one taco from paying the bill and getting out the door.

"Hold on, buddy. You just got here. I thought you wanted to talk about something." McPhail flicked the ash from the end of his cigarette onto the floor.

Calvino slumped back against the booth. "You ever see a lion up close?"

McPhail's eyes widened as smoke curled out of his nose. "What are you drinking? I want a double shot."

"Yesterday I saw two lions. I was close to them—about the same distance as we are to Bill." Bill was ten feet away, balancing himself against the bar on his elbow, one ankle hooked over a barstool, mouth ajar like he was about to say something, only that was just the way he looked—nothing came out of his mouth. McPhail turned, looked over his shoulder at Bill, who purred as a waitress massaged his shoulders. When Bill turned maudlin his mood infected the other drunks, whose long faces and vacant stares registered new lows as if they had discovered that the cook secretly spit in their soup.

"Lions? You're sounding like Henry. Only he sees little forest fairies dancing around naked at four in the afternoon. So what's it got to do with your new case? One of the lions cheating on the other, and you've been brought in by Mr. Husband to investigate?"

Calvino took the fresh glass of whiskey from the waitress. "I could use your help in finding someone."

"Someone's cub has gone missing?"

"It's a missing-persons case."

"Yeah, who's missing?"

"The client isn't sure."

"You want me to find someone, but you don't know who? How does that work?"

"It's called private investigation. I have names, dates, and places. That should be enough to track the two Thais I'm looking for."

"Then you don't need me." McPhail blew smoke, his eyes glancing up at Old George's photograph. Bill hovered around, pacing back and forth, sucking his teeth and muttering.

"The problem is, the information is old."

"How old?"

"Thirty-two years old."

"And the trail's gone dead cold."

"You're right, McPhail. I doubt you'd ever be able to pick up a trail that old. Two hundred a day plus expenses is what I had in mind. Maybe I should ask someone else."

That set McPhail off. "Maybe you should do it yourself."

"I don't have much time. The client is in Thailand for less than a week."

"This isn't the same woman who kicked me out of your car at George's funeral?" A cloud passed across his face,

154

and his shoulders twitched as he picked up the hammer in a manner that suggested that suddenly the whole world looked like a nail.

Calvino nodded, thinking McPhail had a curious way of remembering what had happened in the car on the day of Old George's funeral. "She wants to find her mother. And father." The father was a whispered afterthought.

The smoke inhaled into McPhail's chest held tight like one of those storm fronts from Canada hovering above New York. "They abandon the family house without telling her? I couldn't blame them. She looked as tough as coffin nails." He picked up one of the nails, exhaling smoke.

"She was given away for adoption as an infant."

"I'd say the parents made the right choice. From what I saw, I doubt they could have sold her."

"Don't be an asshole, McPhail."

"Showing up at George's funeral. What the fuck was that? Strangers shouldn't hang around a stranger's funeral."

"She came because of me. We had an appointment."

"And you told her to meet you at a funeral?" He put the hammer down and launched into his drink with both hands, the wet paper napkin around the glass disintegrating in his hands.

"Are you in or not?"

"Two-fifty a day."

"There's a depression. You should be working for one and a half."

"You're loaded." McPhail stared at him through the cigarette smoke, waiting for an answer.

"And I got a world of people waiting to help me lighten the load."

McPhail picked the wet paper off his fingers, balling it up and throwing it at the back of one of the drunks slumped over the bar. "Look at Henry. It's not even one, and he's passed out. You remember that big lug of a guy named

Jailbird Hugh? He was from South Dakota and claimed he went to school with Tom Brokaw. He drank more than a bottle a day. He'd slump over the counter, slide off the stool, end up on the floor, snoring and shitting his pants. When that happened, people came to help him. Hugh's problem was, when he kneeled over with a heart attack at the bar, face on the counter, everyone in the bar thought he was sleeping. He must've been dead half the day before someone realized he wasn't sleeping."

The life of men with no purpose but drinking had the burn rate of a candle lit at both ends. The twin flame of boredom and regret ate up a wick faster than a bar ying downed a lady's drink.

Calvino lowered his head, looked McPhail in the eyes.

"Okay, I'm in, goddamn it."

SEVENTEEN

RATANA SAT INSIDE the day-care center, a book open on her lap, reading to children who formed a semicircle around her stool. Downstairs, Brandon had arrived outside Calvino's office to find it empty. Ratana hadn't been gone long. She'd temporarily relieved Meg, who had gone out to buy sliced pineapple from a street vendor. His pounding on the locked office door echoed up and down the soi. The rapid punch of fists indicated that their owner had no recent practice of the *dharma*. Only a farang would assault an office door; bar yings had been known to attack locked condo and hotel doors, but with less force than a frontal military attack. One of the yings who worked at One Hand Clapping massage parlor strolled by eating pineapple and complaining that a mean-looking farang had given her an ugly look as she passed him on the staircase.

By the time Ratana walked down one flight, Brandon, hands in his pockets, looked like a man in need of anxiety medication. He was in a sorry state, his hair wild, his eyes fired with the kind of booming anger that frightened most Thais. Ratana ignored his conduct the way she would a child's; she smiled, then waied Sawyer, who stepped to one side as she fit a key into the door.

"Where's Calvino? I've got an appointment. Why does he make an appointment, then leave a locked office? That's no way to run a business."

She held the door for him.

"Mr. Calvino will come soon," she said. "Can I get you coffee or water?"

"A whiskey. Make it a double. He keeps a bottle in his desk. But you know that."

He was a man with a long list of questions, an even longer list of demands, and questions and demands spelled trouble, and trouble led to dangerous possibilities. Brandon didn't care if others liked him; he ran no popularity contest and, like many rich people, went to pieces the moment anyone appeared to challenge his entitlements, which were multiple and, in his mind, inviolate.

Ratana felt she was in no position to argue with her boss's only client. Opening Calvino's bottom desk drawer, she pulled out a bottle of Johnnie Walker Black and poured until she had filled half a glass. It was more than enough to soften his rage. As her eyes followed the glass, she hoped that Brandon wasn't the kind of drunk who could drink a bottle and only get meaner before pitching forward and falling flat on his face, breaking his nose, and losing a few teeth. Calvino had had more than one such client in the past. Good payers, bad drunks. She handed Brandon the glass, and he took a slow sip, sighed, champed his lips like a horse too long in the stable, before gulping down the rest of it, shivering, holding out the glass. "One more," he said. Not asked but demanded. She unscrewed the cap on the bottle, and refilled the glass. She left the bottle on Calvino's desk.

By the time Calvino returned from lunch, Brandon was slouched in a chair, slurring his words and not making a lot of sense.

"You know how fucking long I've been waiting?" Then he burst out laughing.

Calvino crossed over to Ratana's side of the office. "He's drunk."

"He drank most of your whiskey," she said.

"She forced it on me," he said, smiling, looking at Ratana.

"Shape up, Brandon."

"Put the whiskey on my bill!" Sawyer yelled. "I'm good for it!"

Calvino sat behind his desk, pulled out his bottom drawer. "You've talked with Achara," he said, taking the bottle and putting it back into the drawer. It wasn't a question.

Brandon nodded.

"What about Marshall?"

His brother's name had the effect of attaching jumper cables to Brandon's genitals. He twitched, he squirmed, and he belched a gaseous cloud of Johnnie Walker Black. "My dear brother and I talked. Then he shouted. That was before he hung up."

"What is it with you and Marshall?"

"Ask our father."

"You told me he's dead."

"It was a figure of speech. You ever hear of a figure of speech?"

Calvino stared at his client, who was lost in the haze of a self-pitying drunk. He'd talked with Brandon the day before and briefed him on Tanny's meeting with Achara. But he'd edited out a few details—the snake, the lions, the lost earring, the way he had pulled the towel in the darkened room away from Tanny's body. Otherwise it had been, he was convinced, a full and complete report.

"What's Marshall's wife like?" Calvino asked.

"Don't even mention that bitch."

"Is their marriage, you know, okay?"

"I may be drunk, but you're fucking nuts. Why do you care?"

"I'm trying to build a profile. Understand the personality."

Brandon swatted the air with his hand as if to catch a fly. "Marshall's a controlling, selfish, arrogant, devious bastard. That's his profile. That's all you need to know. Marshall and Laura are perfect together. When they flush the toilet, they see the other one's image reflected as the water drains from the bowl."

Brandon had lapsed into drunk speak, a language that inevitably crawled out of the toilet bowl. Calvino pulled the whiskey bottle from the bottom drawer and refilled Brandon's glass. "It's about what's in that envelope Tanny gave you, isn't it? Are you going to tell me what Marshall wants?"

"The moon."

"He wants to sell your shares," said Calvino.

Brandon sprayed good whiskey over Calvino's desk. "He wants to interfere. He wants to destroy me. He wants to control the world. Only he doesn't have the balls. Marshall said, 'Let's give it a few more days, and then I can make a decision everybody can be happy with.' In other words, stay of execution for up to a week, then we sell the company. That's the way Marshall works. He can't look me in the eye and say, 'Brandon, I'm pulling us out of Thailand. We need the money; our credit line is canceled.' That would be simple, to the point, and no bullshit."

Calvino leaned back in his chair, wrapped his hands behind his head, watching the sweat beads form on Brandon's forehead. The combination of heat and whiskey cooked him slowly, like a pig rotating on a spit. "Brandon, there's nothing more that I can do. You sell or you don't sell. It's not my business. I don't see what else I can do for you."

"You want to abandon ship?" Brandon's jaw dropped, and Calvino wasn't certain if it was because he was drunk, or was having a seizure, or whether it was just a bad punch line from his days as a stand-up comedian.

"It's not a ship, Brandon. It's a business. Work it out with your brother. There's nothing I can do to help you on that score. I'm not going to be your buffer. And you've put yourself in this bind because of your mouth. You bragged to your brother about how Achara handed a suitcase of cash to the official who signed your permits. What did you expect him to do once you mouthed off? You handed him a bat to hit you with. Bragging on an open phone line about how your business partner in Thailand knows who to pay off. It's called corruption. He may have thought you were setting him up for some fall in the States, knowing that your ass would always be in the clear here. You fucked yourself."

Brandon clenched his jaw. "You sound just like Marshall. I can see now why you didn't mind his mole coming here and using your office. You've been working for Marshall. He turned you with more money. How much is he paying you?"

Calvino walked around his desk and hit Brandon in the stomach, hard, knocking the air out of him. His knees buckled, and he fell onto the floor, moaning as if a drawbridge had landed on his gut. Standing over him, fists clenched, Calvino said, "Drunk or not, no client walks into my office and accuses me of betraying him. I keep my agreements—all of them. Do me a favor and get the fuck out."

He helped Brandon to his feet.

"Can't we discuss this?" Brandon asked. The punch had sobered him up.

Calvino hooked an arm around Brandon's shoulders and walked him out of the office, to the entrance in front of Ratana's desk.

Calvino shook his head. Brandon shrugged his shoulders, sighed, turned, and murmured under his breath, "Fuck it.

161

I don't need you. I don't need anybody. Achara's my only true friend. He'll know what to do."

He was shaking a ham-hock-size fist at Calvino as Tanny appeared. She stopped on the stairs as Brandon staggered down, holding on to the rails with both hands. He locked eyes with Tanny. He looked unsteady, out of wind, the huge fist he'd shaken at Calvino clenched again into an ugly claw. Was he going to throw a punch at her? She stopped, waited for a punch that never came.

"My brother has made a big mistake," he said.

"Marshall doesn't think so." She stood her ground.

Brandon's eyes widened as if he'd had a moment of absolute clarity. "You should go into comedy. Marshall needs a straight man."

Shaky, his guts churning from the punch, his brain swimming in Johnnie Walker's pool, shoulders slumped, he looked defeated. She watched him fall down the stairs, thinking how he reminded her of Achara's lions, slipping and sliding in a tranquilizer haze, all roar and no bite.

"What was that about?" Tanny asked Calvino.

"I just fired my client."

She smiled. "What a good way to start the day."

Sometimes he wished that Tanny could be a little less New York.

EIGHTEEN

TWO DAYS AFTER Calvino punched Brandon Sawyer in the gut and threw him out of his office, he sat behind his desk memorizing the names of Roman emperors. It was something to do while Ratana was at the district office in Ayuthaya province, standing in a line waiting her turn to ask an official to assist her in finding the address of Tanny's parents; that meant access to the house registration files that contained their names and ID numbers. Ayuthaya was a good hour-long drive from the office on Sukhumvit Road. She had gone to the office twice before seeking information, but not much ever happened until Colonel Pratt placed a phone call, asking a friend to arrange for his friend Ratana to be given a glass of water on one of those tiny, shiny aluminum trays they use for VIPs. An hour later, an official slipped a copy of the mother's ID, including her picture, into Ratana's hand and refused any payment.

Ratana got back to the office and told Calvino about her success. She kept it simple. "Got it," she said.

He studied the photocopy but didn't see much resemblance between the mother in the picture and Tanny.

Ratana caught the perplexed expression on his face as he looked up from the photocopy. "Why don't you phone Tanny and give her the good news," she suggested. "The mother's registered at a house five kilometers northwest of the city."

"Good work," he said.

She paused. "I'll go upstairs in a few minutes and check on John-John."

"Did you talk with Tanny's mother?"

"She wasn't in."

She saw printouts of the Roman emperors laid out on his desk. "Those generals all look pretty much the same," she said.

"They look like Romans. Look at the nose. Look at my nose." He touched the end of his nose.

She smiled, thinking, same-same but different. But she didn't say that. Instead she said, "Phone Tanny. Give her the good news."

"I'll phone her."

Satisfied, Ratana returned to her desk. Calvino sat back at *his* desk and pulled out his cell phone. He glanced again at the photocopy of Tanny's mother. Ratana had gotten it right about how all the Roman emperors had a certain look. He wrinkled his nose at their stylized faces, hooded eyes, hooked noses, and solid chins. The generosity gene turned up less than one percent of the time. Ratana possessed that gene, and she used it to give others moral clarity when it came to treating people.

Calvino tried phoning Tanny at her hotel, but she wasn't in her room. He tried her cell phone, but it was turned off. He was like the man who craved a salami sandwich only to be told they'd run out of mustard and fresh rolls. He settled into his office, twisting his chair from side to side as if his mind were deep in concentration but his body had detached like a rotary blade with unused forward motion.

He looked down at a set of flash cards and repeated the names.

The five good emperors were Nerva, Trajan, Hadrian, Antoninus Pius, and Marcus Aurelius. Not one of them would have allowed Brandon to rifle his office bottle, get sloppy drunk, and then call him a traitor. Trajan would have exiled him. Hadrian would have sold him as a slave. Marcus Aurelius would have had him publicly executed. Calvino had a tradition to follow. But times had changed since the days of the Romans—Calvino accepted that a punch in Brandon's gut was sufficient retribution. He thought that Tanny would like to know she had something in common with the five emperors—like her, all five had been adopted.

Researching Roman emperors was a way of filling the time. And he had plenty of time. After an hour or so, he grew edgy, like a bear confined in a small cage at the Rangoon Zoo.

Calvino phoned McPhail and told him about his latest Google search of the five Roman emperors. An extended silence followed after Calvino finished, and McPhail finally said, "Do you want me to pretend to be interested? What's happening with Tanny's mother search?" McPhail didn't want to talk about Roman emperors; he wanted to talk about work. "The wheels are turning, but the car isn't moving," he said.

"Oh, yeah, that job. We found Tanny's mother."

"Man, you could have told me."

"I am telling you."

"Then why did you start off talking about fucking Roman emperors?"

Calvino didn't have an immediate answer. "Send me a bill."

"I will send you a bill." The connection went dead.

Calvino stared at the phone, McPhail's tinny voice fading as fast as distant footfalls from a cut-off, a retreating Roman legion. Calvino put down the phone, having decided McPhail was well through four vodka tonics and in no condition to discuss ancient Rome. There was always Colonel Pratt, who'd listen to his latest discovery into the politics of the Old World only to remind Calvino that he had enough to deal with in the politics of the current world. Shakespeare must've said something about Roman rulers. But Colonel Pratt's cell phone was switched off.

It was lonely in the office, and as silent as a meditation room after a bag of Prozac had been passed around.

Calvino stretched his arms and legs and kept walking around the room, the way a prisoner paces a solitary-confinement cell—happy to be able to move and at the same time sad for the restrictions on the space available. He started to miss Tanny and wished she were at the office. He had the radio tuned to Radio Thailand. An announcer spoke English in a strange accent that randomly switched back and forth between England, Australia, and America. The announcer read the latest report about the protest at Government House. The number of demonstrators occupying the grounds had stabilized at around three thousand. New recruits had been shuttled in like troop reinforcements from the rear to support the original protesters. The morning newspaper carried photos of a member of the self-appointed security detail pointing to the main grounds with a golf club.

Eventually Ratana returned from Ayuthaya, went upstairs and checked on John-John, then walked into the office. By way of greeting, she said, "Tanny must have been happy."

"I haven't told her."

Ratana tilted her head, lips firm. "Why not?"

"She's not in her room, and her phone is turned off."

"She's shopping. I forgot. She told me about going to buy some jewelry."

Calvino nodded. "Yeah, for her boss's wife."

"You talked about jewelry with Tanny?" Ratana looked amused as she sat down at her desk.

166

"She talked about lost earrings. But it's a long story. I want to know, what's her mother like?"

"Her mother wasn't home. A child answered the door. She said that Auntie had gone to Bangkok. Dressed in yellow and wearing a backpack."

"She's joined the demonstration?"

"That's what it looks like," said Ratana. Before the last coup, along with Colonel Pratt's wife, Ratana had been a fixture at the earlier round of demonstrations organized a couple of years earlier. But this time Ratana wasn't out on the street. Things had changed for her; she had followed the arguments, agreed with a lot of the frustration and anger people felt, but she worried about her place and that of her son in what the leaders of the protest promised was the "New Order."

Calvino slipped on his jacket. "I'll go to Government House and see if I can find her."

"Good luck."

She looked like she wanted to say something, but whatever it was, she kept it to herself. There was only so much a Thai could say to a farang who was about to walk into the middle of a major demonstration. On the way out of the office, he phoned McPhail and told him to meet him at the Phrom Phong BTS station.

NINETEEN

McPHAIL AND CALVINO hired motocyle taxis parked at the foot of the BTS station at Phaya Thai to take them to Government House. Both motorcycle drivers looked amused at the two farangs. One whispered to the other that the farangs were crazy.

McPhail overheard the remark. "Not crazy, brother. We're a couple of drunken tourists."

The drivers smiled as McPhail handed them cigarettes. They climbed onto the motorcycles, and the bikes gunned down the road as if avoiding incoming rounds.

Calvino's driver pulled ahead on the wide avenues. This part of the city had a different feel and terrain; old Bangkok with shophouses run as mom-and-pop operations selling paint, tires, and rice. No high-rises blocked out the sky. No tourists in shorts squinting at maps. No yings in high-heeled shoes and short skirts hooking their arms around a farang on their way to a shopping mall. On the government side of town, except for the presence of the traffic, the mature trees, the manicured bushes and lawns, the motorcycles might have shot through a portal to a time fifty years ago. This was how Bangkok looked before the Chinese-Thais and Indian-Thais discovered that stacking tons of concrete half a mile high on Sukhumvit Road resulted in mega profits. This area was the last refuge of the Thai-Thais.

The motorcycle-taxi drivers dropped them at the junction of Phitsanulok and Nakhon Pathom roads, parking their bikes outside the main entrance of Government House. Calvino stood in front of the open massive black gate. McPhail followed him, running his hand along a string that divided the pavement into two channels: Entry and exit. It was the first evidence of the demonstration leaders' planning and organizational skills. The second piece of evidence was the security guards, dressed in black T-shirts and jeans and easy smiles. McPhail raised his hands high, cigarette clenched between his teeth, like a suspect waiting for the police to pat him down and arrest him.

"You want to see my ID or something, buddy?" he asked.

Calvino walked past. "He wants to see the back of you," he said.

On the right, a wide road was lined with vendor stalls stretching half a mile. Vendors hawked plastic clappers with three molded clown hands, yellow T-shirts, wristbands, souvenirs, and trinkets—like any other open-air market. On the left, a security station had been cobbled together from dusty planks. The materials looked like they'd been lifted from a construction site—the floor was made by stacking wooden pallets on the ground. A handwritten sign in English advertised BODYGUARD SERVICE 24 HRS. On the bench, a man who was as huge and solid as a teak stump, slept with one hand over his eyes, his massive belly slowly rising and falling.

"You want a bodyguard?" McPhail asked Calvino. "There's your man."

In front of the guard post were several golf clubs tied to wooden slats, hanging like samurai swords. "Tiger Woods call home," said Calvino, looking at a seven-iron. "We've found your caddie." He was sleeping a chip shot away from the gate. But the man was a long-drive wood away from the green, where several bodyguards stood steely-eyed looking at McPhail and Calvino with the concentration of men aiming to sink a twenty-foot putt.

"Tiger is half Thai. Of course he keeps a caddie on the payroll in Thailand. He's got a caddie in every fucking country in the world where there's a golf course. I hadn't thought of that before. You are a genius"

"I wish Old George could've seen that bodyguard," said Calvino.

"It wouldn't have surprised him. Most of his staff are daytime sleepers. But so are a lot of his customers."

Calvino nodded, remembering the back booth where they sometimes curled up. "I guess Old George saw enough sleepers to last a lifetime."

He'd already lost McPhail, whose attention was now focused on a poster. McPhail drifted over to a bulletin board, lighting a fresh cigarette and blowing smoke out the corner of his mouth. Someone had stapled the photocopy of a Thai woman's ID card to the board. Calvino put a hand on McPhail's shoulder. "We've got work to do."

McPhail held firm, jabbing a finger at the poster. "That's Nueng," he said. "I'm telling you, that's her. What the fuck is her picture doing here?"

There had to be a hundred thousand women in Thailand named Nueng; it translated as "Number One."

"That's not who we're looking for," said Calvino, holding up the photocopy of Tanny's mother. There was no resemblance between the two women.

"Nueng, you know her. She works at One Hand Clapping. Don't you recognize her?"

The photocopy pinned to the board was a grainy blowup taken from her ID card; one side of the photo was one of those calibrated height charts, in this case showing that the woman looking into the camera was 159 centimeters tall. It wasn't a bad photo, thought Calvino. Not the usual scary official document photo. Nueng's hair, pulled back, revealed her heart-shaped face, the lips frozen in a sly smile. Calvino remembered her; he passed her on the stairs as she walked up to the floor above his office and went into the day-care center that had been Ratana's idea. Nueng's kid played alongside Ratana's John-John.

"Yeah, I remember her," said Calvino.

"So what the fuck is her picture doing here?" asked McPhail.

"Don't know."

There was a typed caption in Thai script, a paragraph below the photo. Calvino tore down the copy, folded it, and put it in his pocket.

A photojournalist named Somkit, a couple of digital cameras hanging around his neck, appeared out of nowhere. Calvino remembered seeing him around Bangkok. Somkit was a good crime-scene photographer for the *Bangkok Post*, and he'd come upon Calvino at more than one location where the police were kneeling over a dead body. He recognized Calvino and waved. He snapped several photos of a couple of demonstrators, a mother and daughter by the look of them, buying hand clappers.

"Vincent, you come to have a look at the protest?" asked Somkit, lowering his camera. His nose twitched as if Calvino smelled like burned flesh.

Calvino waied him. "Somkit, how you doing?"

"Good. Someone gets killed?"

"Not as far as I know," said Calvino. "But thanks for asking."

"It's just—" Somkit broke off.

"Soi 33," said Calvino. "I'd rather forget about it."

The last time he'd seen Somkit, the photographer was also working the street; in fact, he'd been shooting what remained of a couple of bodies on Soi 33 not far from Calvino's office. Two hit men, one riding pillion—who pulled a nine with a silencer—and his helmeted driver, had turned into the soi for a drive-by, but the motorcycle encountered a problem: Calvino had earned an assisted goal by redirecting a vendor's cart into its path. The motorcycle driver T-boned his bike at fifty kilometers an hour, smashing into another bike parked beside a banyan tree. The back of the stationary bike had been overloaded with gas cylinders. Somkit had been first on the scene to snap the charred remains of the two men. It wasn't in Calvino's vocabulary to call them victims. Instead he had said the only good thing coming out of the crash was that it had saved their relatives the cost of a cremation.

Now Calvino smoothed out the copy of Nueng's photo he'd taken from the bulletin board near the entry gate. "Khun Somkit, what's this say?"

The photojournalist slipped his reading glasses over the end of his nose, cleared his throat, nodded, and sighed before handing it back to Calvino. "Says that this woman is a prostitute and that she's been banned. Security found condoms in her handbag and a business card from a massage parlor. They said she was hustling for clients, giving the demonstrators a bad name. She wouldn't be the first to turn a trick on the grounds of Government House."

"You're a cynic," said Calvino. "But this is different. I know this woman. She wouldn't come here to hustle. That's crazy."

"It's crazy times," said Somkit, watching Calvino fold up the photocopy. "Everyone's on the hustle." He nodded at one of the vendors demonstrating a hand clapper for a potential customer.

"Commerce," said Calvino. "Everything has its price."

"You mean everyone."

"You've been on the job too long," said Calvino.

"Look who's talking. But at least you've got an out. You can go back to New York. What about the rest of us? We've got no place to go."

McPhail saw Somkit put the camera to his eye and snap a series of shots of a family, all dressed in yellow, walking hand in hand as if they were in a laundry-detergent commercial. "Hey, you've been walking around looking at people. Any chance you saw this woman?"

Somkit took a look at the photocopy of Tanny's mother. He studied it, touching his hand to his jaw, rubbing it for a moment, shaking his head. "No. Haven't seen her." He handed the photocopy back to McPhail, smiling. "She could be anywhere. But I'd start over there." He pointed at the far gate. "Go that way. It will lead you inside."

Somkit walked a few steps, took a few more shots, lowered the camera, and turned back around. He tilted his head to the side. "You don't have any more photos of women you want me to identify, do you?" He grinned, shading his eyes as the sun broke through the clouds.

"Lead us inside where?" asked Calvino.

"Where the prostitutes aren't allowed," said Somkit.

They watched Somkit stroll down the road, still smiling smugly.

McPhail said, "I thought we *were* inside."

They watched Somkit snapping pictures for a moment. "Let's try the next inside," Calvino said.

They walked ahead past a high black iron fence that until the occupation had symbolized power and authority. The sound of hundreds of clappers beating the air, filtered through the fence. And Calvino couldn't help but think about the massage parlor next to his office, One Hand Clapping—a good name for a massage parlor. The mamasan had been ahead of her time, and even though she didn't have a political bone in her body, she was the type to start scheming, huddled with her yings, inventing reasons to claim a royalty from the clapper sellers. Two baht each, one of the yings would say, another would say five baht, and before long the royalty on a clapper would equal the price of an ordinary hand job.

Opposite the iron fence, sprawling trees and lush lawns and winding roads covered the eleven acres of Government House. The main building was the size of a palace and topped with golden domes. It looked like a magical Disneyland fairy-tale castle. Hand clappers, but no amusement-park rides for the kids.

McPhail stood beside Calvino, shaking his head. "This doesn't look Thai. It looks like some crack headed European built the mansion in *Gone With The Wind*."

"The columns are from the Palazzo Ca'd'Oro in Venice. Fifteenth century."

McPhail rolled his eyes. "Man, you're not going to tell me your great-grandfather built this motherfucker? Or painted it?"

"Annibale Rigotti. That's the name of the 'crack headed European,' the architect. Does that sound like 'Calvino' to you?"

"It ends in a fucking vowel."

Calvino punched McPhail on the shoulder, hard enough for him to back off. He decided it was better not to mention that his great-grandfather's rival and enemy from Florence, Corrado Feroci, had decorated the building during World War II, when Thailand and Italy were Axis partners. "Fit for a doge or a Mussolini, but not a McPhail."

"I said it looked European. You're the one who started on about the Italians."

Calvino sighed, shaking his head, thinking that after enough time with anyone—man or woman—if you were working together, you ended up like an old couple, getting into stupid fights over who forgot to turn off the light in the kitchen. "Let's find Tanny's mother," said Calvino.

On the other side of the interior iron gate, the clappers' sound increased. It was like a swarm of locusts beating their wings as they settled on a wheat field. Calvino looked around and suddenly saw thousands of people shaking their

174

clappers, using them to applaud political speeches shouted from a stage. The stage had been erected about a hundred yards from the gate, and protesters sat in plastic chairs, row after row of plastic chairs, until those in the back watched the stage on TVs. The TV platforms had been strategically placed, like pillboxes along a coastline, ensuring that everyone could see. The sound system registered a white hiss of noise. A woman's voice cracked as she spoke into the microphone, the clappers welcoming her. She stood in front of a podium, a yellow headband holding her hair back from her face. Behind her a group of musicians erupted into a vocal version of "Happy Birthday." Their broken English filled the air as hundreds sang for the woman smiling at the podium. It might have been Woodstock, as the compound of Government House, in every direction, was filled with thousands of people, sitting on those plastic chairs perched on a sea of wooden pallets sinking in the mud.

"Find her where? Look at the size of that crowd." McPhail, hands on his hips, slowly turned 180 degrees; nothing but solid yellow.

It was easy to feel discouraged, overwhelmed by the size of the audience. If Calvino had a dozen men, divided the grounds into sectors, sent a man into each sector, then they might have a chance. But there were just the two of them. As he started to say something to McPhail, he turned and saw that McPhail was gone. Maybe he'd decided to split; looking at the size of the crowd, and the light rain that had started to fall, Calvino wouldn't have blamed him. Calvino worked his way through the crowd until he caught sight of McPhail standing near the end of a long line. Funny thing was, McPhail was the only farang in line, and the only person *not* wearing a yellow shirt, scarf, or headband. He stood out.

"McPhail, I thought I'd lost you," said Calvino. "Don't just take off. Check in first. We gotta make this a team effort or it's hopeless. Let's go."

"Free chocolate donuts," said McPhail.

"What's a donut got to do with anything?"

"I want one. That's why I'm standing in line."

"On line." Calvino thought about the recent lines he'd crossed, double-crossed, on the way to his bedroom. "Okay, get your donut. If that's what makes you happy."

McPhail pointed at a demonstrator who walked past carrying a large chocolate donut with a big bite taken out of it. He licked his lips and smiled at Calvino. "It's only one per person. So you gotta get in line if you want one."

"McPhail, the food's for protesters. We're here to find Tanny's mom."

"But she could be in line. Look at that donut lady ahead. I'll show her the picture. Maybe she saw her. Or maybe this guy." McPhail pulled out the photocopied ID card, the photo blown up to cover most of the page, and showed it to an old man in front of him. "You know her?" he asked, as if speaking broken English were somehow the equivalent of Thai. The old man smiled, sucked his lips, and shrugged his shoulders. Gaining strength, McPhail moved up the line, showing each person the photo, until he reached the table and put out his hand for a free donut. The woman, wearing an apron, sheltered from the rain under a wide blue canopy, saw McPhail's spattered face and put a donut in his hand. "Can I have another one for my friend?" He gestured at Calvino.

"Didn't find her. But I got you a free donut," said McPhail as he strolled past Calvino, gnawing on his donut.

The first order of business was to get out of the rain.

As rain dripped from a canvas awning, they stood next to each other, facing the stage, eating their donuts and looking like a couple of cops in Brooklyn. A chorus of clappers rose across the compound. A new speaker stood at the podium, waving a fist, getting the crowd to its feet with an attack on the government, demanding it dissolve parliament. Surveying the size of the crowd caused a bolt of hopelessness to travel through Calvino's gut and exit his brain, leaving him with a dull headache.

Finding Tanny's mother at Government House in normal times would have taken a shaman and a Brahman priest working together. But that would have been a cakewalk compared to finding one person in this large mob, all wearing basically the same thing. Calvino and McPhail hadn't raised suspicion among the rank and file or the guards who yawned as they passed; choosing two farangs who'd immediately helped themselves to the donuts would have been a sorry excuse for infiltration by the pro-government side. Since everyone else looked pretty much interchangeable, the two of them were a diversion, an amusement, a couple of farangs wandering among a sea of yellow-shirted people wearing matching yellow headbands and living like happy campers who'd found a good cult to join. Outdoor living had a way of erasing differences in size, age, and weight as everyone merged into a collective.

McPhail finished his donut, licking his fingers, which he followed with a loud belch that turned heads.

Calvino gave most of his donut to a dog, which slunk away with it, sat beside a banana tree, and wolfed it down in two gulps.

Finding Tanny's mother meant they had to divide up and split the crowd between the two of them—a lot of haystack for one needle.

"Impossible, buddy," said McPhail.

"If she's here, we'll find her," Calvino said, without much confidence. He wanted to find her for the strange woman who had come out of his bathroom wearing nothing but a towel, holding another woman's earring in the palm of her hand. She had given every indication, before that moment, that in her view Calvino couldn't find his hat if it were sitting on his head. He had started to doubt himself. Maybe Tanny's right, he thought.

TWENTY

THEY PLUNGED INTO the large mass of people, both Calvino and McPhail trying to keep dry by using photocopies of Tanny's mother's ID photo to cover their heads. They stopped people, showed them the photo, and asked if they'd seen this woman. None had. They walked on. Calvino stopped at a makeshift shelter made from scraps of wood, only to find the same response—a blank stare, an offer of food. He knelt down and talked to three women sitting crossed-legged inside a simple shelter built atop old tires, the gray canvas walls pulled up and fixed to the roof. A steady stream of rainwater ran off the canvas and into the ground. They peeled and chopped garlic and onions, taking them from a large bag; one of the women sharpened a long butcher's knife with the skill of the person assigned to maintain the readiness of the guillotine. It didn't look like the kind of knife designed to peel garlic with.

Two hours later McPhail, pale and sweating, sat on the edge of a pallet, resting his head on his knees, moaning.

"You okay?" asked Calvino.

"Man, I don't feel so good." He lit a cigarette, smoke coming out of his nose and mouth, and almost immediately flicked the freshly lit cigarette into the rain. He groaned, held his stomach, as if he were a hammer and nail away from having his photo added to the Ghost Wall. Behind

McPhail a bloated four-hundred-pound wrestler of a man slept soundly on a pallet, using his hands as a pillow. From a distance he looked like a gargoyle chipped off a Gothic rampart and abandoned by thieves. Beside him was a table bearing bottles of soda for sale. The sleeping vendor could have passed as the brother of the bodyguard with the seven-iron.

"Can you get me a vodka tonic? That cures just about everything," McPhail said, turning and addressing the sleeping giant. "Vodka tonic," McPhail repeated, but got no response.

"Guess not," said Calvino as the man rolled over to face away from McPhail.

All around them, from inside the shantytown of wooden shelters, the TVs were tuned to ASTV—the only channel they could receive—connecting all of them to the speakers and performers working on the main stage. McPhail covered his ears. The sound was too much—the TVs turned to top volume, the thousands of clappers, and the drumming of the rain.

"You look white as a ghost," said Calvino.

"Hey, buddy, I feel worse than shit."

"The donut?"

McPhail nodded, fumbling for another cigarette. "You think someone poisoned it?"

Calvino shook his head, happy that he'd thrown most of his donut to the dog. "I wouldn't take it personally."

"I don't know any other way to take it."

"Let's find—"

"A toilet," said McPhail. "I saw you gave your donut to a dog."

"You worried about the dog?"

McPhail groaned. "Fuck the dog. Man, I'm dying."

Calvino helped McPhail to his feet. Slowly they walked on a pathway between the temporary shelters, looking at the demonstrators huddled inside, squatting vacant-eyed in front of the TVs like children hooked on cartoons. Calvino had his arm around McPhail, who was near collapse. A man rode toward them on a tiny bicycle. Calvino moved McPhail off the path, watching the cyclist disappear behind a cannon on the lawn, an old cannon that shot iron balls in pirate movies, only this one had a green hedge shaped like a enormous green donut around it. McPhail contemplated the rain-soaked green donut and vomited. He retched again while he was on his hands and knees, Calvino holding an umbrella over him. A couple of minutes later, Calvino assisted McPhail, who stumbled over his feet, into one of the portable toilets and closed the door. Calvino stood outside and waited, listening to McPhail moan as if he'd been shot or stabbed. As he waited, Calvino showed the photocopy to everyone who passed; soon he started to feel like a tout showing a menu of tricks in Patpong. People looked at him, hearing McPhail in the toilet screaming that he wanted to die, and hurried along. Calvino finally gave up, seeing how the protesters were giving him a wide berth as if he were personally to blame for the bloodcurdling screams coming from the toilet.

"McPhail, are you okay?"

"I want to die."

"You don't look so good."

"My guts. The motherfuckers gave me a toxic donut. I hope the army comes and shoots them all."

"I wonder what happened to the dog," said Calvino.

"Oh, man, don't make me laugh."

Calvino waited a few more minutes until the portable toilet door swung open and McPhail staggered out, zipping up his jeans. He looked like a ghost.

"I am a little shaky. But I've decided not to die."

"Are you good for another hour? Then we'll call it a day," said Calvino.

"They've got poison donuts. I figure, yeah, they've got to have a drugstore."

A woman with a blue whistle around her neck, who'd looked quizzical when McPhail had earlier shown her the photocopy, pointed them in the direction of the first-aid station when they asked her for medical assistance. They walked back to the main Gothic building, like the castle in Frankenstein, with the torch-carrying villagers in occupation. People eating donuts looked away bored as they perched on the steps. McPhail retched again, balanced himself against one of the gilded columns. "I'm going to be fine," he said, wiping his mouth. A couple of minutes later, Calvino half dragged McPhail to the front of the first-aid station, where a yellow string was suspended between two plastic traffic cones anchored with tires. A Red Cross sign was draped over the side of a table loaded with pills, potions, ointments, and bandages. Behind the table a couple of nurses worked. A large fan rotated a few feet away. Calvino explained the problem while McPhail, doubled up with cramps, his knees rubbery, slowly dropped to the ground, knocking over one of the traffic cones. He hugged the tire like a scared child hugging a teddy bear.

"Stomachache," said Calvino.

"Tell her I've got the runs."

"He has the runs."

"And the sweats and I'm—" He vomited. No need to tell her.

The middle-aged nurse looked over the top of her glasses at McPhail, making a diagnosis and running her hand along bookshelf-like row of boxes. Calvino tried to smooth out one of the photocopies, the image damp and wrinkled. "I'm looking for this woman."

Calvino watched her study the photo. She nodded, half turned, and pointed. A few feet further back in the cobbled-together pharmacy, a row of cots had been set up.

On one of the cots a middle-aged woman, wrapped in a sheet, slept with her back to them. "That's Mem. But she's sleeping. Last night there was an attack by people from Isan. We had many casualties. We got almost no sleep. I hate these ignorant people. Why don't they stay home where they belong?" Her face twisted into a mask of rage. She clenched her fists. It hadn't taken much to work her up. But when people were dead tired, they were on edge, emotions raw like open sores. "Farang don't understand." She looked defiant in her conclusion, as if she were talking to someone beyond hope.

"I do my best," he said.

McPhail gobbled down a handful of pills that the nurse assured him would cure his stomach. Doubled up, he rolled onto one of the vacant cots, curled into the fetal position, and fell into a coma-like sleep. Calvino had his wallet out to pay for McPhail's medication.

"We don't take money for medicine. Or food."

"I'd like to talk to Mem."

The nurse frowned, like she'd already decided not to interrupt the woman's sleep.

"It's important. Her daughter has a problem." Those were the magic words in a culture where mothers were worshipped like goddesses and to have a child with a problem was an intolerable affront to their stature.

She gestured for Calvino to enter the inner sanctum. "Mem, wake up and talk to this farang about your daughter."

Mem shifted around on her cot, raised herself up, blinking the sleep from her eyes, and looked at Calvino, who sat on a low plastic stool no more than two feet away. Her startled expression changed to perplexed. "My daughter is dead," she said. The wrinkles around her eyes deepened, and her eyes themselves filled with tears.

Calvino shook his head. "She's very much alive. She's now a grown woman." He pulled from his jacket photocopies of Tanny's birth certificate and her passport and held them out.

She rummaged through her handbag for reading glasses. Once they were on, she flipped through the documents. She looked up as if she'd seen a ghost.

"Bum?" she whispered.

It was the first time Calvino had heard Tanny's Thai nickname. Of course, she would have had a Thai name on her birth certificate. He wondered if she knew that her daughter's name was Tanny Craig.

"Her new name is Tanny."

The foreign name confused her. "My daughter Jeab died five years ago," Mem said.

The nurse who'd been listening from behind the table chipped in, "Police kill her daughter. Police no good. Corrupt. Why you think we are here? We hate the police for what they do to us."

The list of hatreds added another category of people along with people from Isan.

"But you had another daughter," said Calvino.

Mem stared at him. "Bum?"

"She wants to meet you. Are you okay with that?" Calvino asked.

Mem nodded, shedding more tears. "Are you Bum's husband?"

Calvino smiled, shaking his head. "I'm a friend."

"I think I never see Bum again in this life. Maybe she hates me very much."

She was fishing for information. He couldn't blame her.

Calvino squeezed her hand. "Bum doesn't hate you."

"I think she does."

"Bum has a son. That makes you a grandmother."

The most serene smiled passed Mem's lips. Then she opened up with a barrage of questions. Calvino found himself answering questions that were not his to answer, the kinds of questions and answers she'd have to work through with her daughter. There would be hundreds more, and it would take many days of face time before the two women could come to terms with the past. The fact was, he'd found her, though McPhail would claim, with some justification, the full credit for finding Mem in the eleven acres packed with demonstrators; without the contaminated donut, she might have slept right through their attempt to locate her.

While he waited for the pills to work on McPhail's head, stomach, and bowels, Calvino listened to Mem, who told him the story of Tanny's adoption and what happened to her sister. The same story she'd repeat to Tanny, using basic English to convey a lifetime of regret and sorrow.

TWENTY-ONE

CALVINO AND TANNY entered the Government House compound at dusk. Passing the long queue, Calvino said, "Keep away from the donuts." Tanny wore a white blouse, dark slacks, and low-heeled shoes. With a yellow headband, she could have blended into the swarm as one more worker bee.

Calvino led her through the crowd, past pools of light from the individual campsites, until they finally arrived at the Red Cross station. Tanny's mother was wrapping a bandage around the leg of a boy of about ten or eleven. He'd been running in the dark, tripped over an electric wire, and cut his ankle as he fell onto a pallet. Mem wasn't dressed like a nurse; she wore jeans and a yellow shirt. A brown clip held her hair, streaked with gray, back. Her hands efficiently secured the bandage around his ankle.

"You be careful next time," she said.

The boy's mother and two other relatives looked on with worried expressions, while the kid continued to sniff back tears and snot, looking to them for sympathy.

Tanny was as anxious as a schoolgirl waiting to see the principal as they waited nearby, watching Mem finish up treating the boy; Mem patted him on the head and sent him and his family on their way. Watching her mother work as a nurse had oddly made Tanny nervous, as if she were next in line with an old, open wound that needed tending. She nearly stumbled over one of the traffic cones as she negotiated the cots lining the area beyond the station table. Except for an electric lamp beside Mem, the near darkness made it difficult to see the ground. But not so dark as to hide Tanny's tears, and thus the first thing Mem saw was her daughter wiping away tears. She'd looked up to see the grown woman—saw an old image of herself as if in a time-traveling mirror—and then Calvino, whom she remembered from earlier in the day.

Calvino nodded. "That's her," he said in Thai to Mem.

"Bum?" her mother asked, not quite believing her eyes.

Hearing aloud her Thai nickname had made Tanny laugh. "She named me Bum? Is that a joke? Because if it is, it's not funny." As in deadbeat, drunk in the gutter, a homeless person, and bag lady—a few of the associations that crossed her mind.

"It's not a joke. It means dimpled. Not dimple. Like pressing your finger into flesh, and you take it away. That's the Thai name for the little indent that is left. That's *bum*."

Calvino had asked Ratana to teach her how to deliver the "mother's wai" that all Thai women give to their mothers. Mem wrapped her arms around Tanny, hugging her daughter. Calvino understood how that same decisive and unflappable impulse to deal with a situation came to be inside Tanny. In the shadows of the great Italian-designed building, mother and daughter embraced for a long time, as if to squeeze time to a fresh starting point.

Tanny caught her breath, her hands still trembling, and said, "Thanks, Vinny. I didn't think you'd do it. But, you know, thanks."

"I'll leave you to catch up with your mother." He hadn't thought anything could have bored inside and rattled her to the core. Such a reaction wasn't expected from someone who reined in her emotions with such skill. Finding her mother had broken the shell, humanized her, and Calvino liked the new Tanny.

"Please, stay for a while," said Tanny. She reached out to him with a glimmer in her eye, the kind that makes a man sit, stay, and ultimately beg. He stepped forward and found a place to sit, a plastic chair at a small table in the back. Incandescent lights flickered across the way as other lights—candles, flashlights, and fluorescent tubes strung up in the canvas shelters—signaled nightfall. Darkness brought the possibility of police and military moving in to clear the demonstrators, or another attack launched by the pro-government demonstrators who were camped not far away. The relaxed atmosphere of the day had vanished with the setting sun, and now the security guards and bodyguards no longer slept on pallets next to their golf clubs. They were on patrol of the grounds. The night stretched endlessly ahead as the demonstrators watched the TV broadcast from the stage, waiting for a call to repel invaders. The drone of preacher like voices railing against evil and injustice and promising salvation. The TV voices buzzed across the night.

The two women sat on the edge of a cot. A couple of volunteers sat behind the table handing out tablets to demonstrators who looked more in need of vitamin injections. Calvino waited until Tanny asked what she'd told him would be her first question: "What happened to make you give me away?"

Mem shuddered at the words. "It wasn't like that."

"It's important that I know."

"You must hate me."

"Did you ever think about me? I mean afterward?"

"Every day. It was all a mistake. It wasn't my choice."

Tanny looked down, exhaled.

"Can I tell you how it happened?"

"I'd like that."

"My father was a senior government officer, conservative and strict. I have no doubt that he loved me as his daughter. But he was part of a government that we hated. I had just finished nursing school when Tee, my boyfriend, who was a young doctor, decided to fight in the jungle against the government. He asked me to go with him. My father refused permission for me to go. He said if I left without his permission, he would disown me. I left. The communists at that time occupied strongholds in many places in the south, north, and northeast. We took a bus to Chiang Rai province. I worked as a nurse and Tee worked as doctor. We worked side by side in a field hospital. Many times we operated by candlelight, listening to mortars rounds and M16s close by. Still, despite all the work and difficulty of living in the jungle, I got pregnant."

One of the women at the desk came back with a bottle of water for Mem. She filled three glasses and handed them out.

"Tee?"

"Yes. Your father was at first surprised."

"And then?"

"I guess he was happy. Proud. The way men are when they make a woman pregnant."

"But not proud enough to raise me."

"Bum, it wasn't his fault."

"It was your idea?"

"After you were born, we were constantly on the move. We couldn't live anywhere for more than a couple of days. The army was always close, tracking our movements, shelling us. One day a missionary came to our camp. He saw me nursing you. The fighting the day before had been particularly intense. Five of our comrades were killed on that day, when the missionary and a deputy *nai amphur*—he was a good man, someone who was, in his heart, on our side—slipped into our camp. He asked if I'd registered your

188

birth. Of course he knew that had been impossible. But he said that he'd take care of it."

Mem didn't know the English for nai amphur and turned to Calvino. "District officer."

"Thanit was his name, and he was a young graduate like us. Tee had known Thanit at university. It was funny seeing him in his uniform and us in dirty rags. How different our lives had turned out. Thanit had made some effort to find us. Looking back, I think he knew that we were about to be overrun and wanted to do something about the children. He'd been shocked to find us in our condition. There were other children, too. We decided to permit Thanit to evacuate the babies and children. That night they left the camp with you and the others. They thought we were sleeping. Thanit didn't want the mothers to see their children leaving. But I watched them walk away, the big missionary from America carrying you in his arms. It broke my heart. Three days later the army raided our camp, and I escaped with four others. Everyone else was killed. The government listed me as one of those missing and presumed dead. My parents were notified. They thought I was dead, too. When a mortar round made a direct hit, there wasn't much left to identify."

"Where was my father?"

"Tee had gone ten kilometers north toward the border. The men had been in a firefight and were almost overrun. A patrol followed a couple of our men straight to the field hospital. Tee was operating inside the tent when government forces captured him. When I heard what had happened, I went into hiding. It took me three months before I got a message to my parents. I told them that you had gone with an American missionary to somewhere safe. But by the time they'd received the message, it was too late—you'd been adopted, bundled off to America for a new life. Your father had been interrogated for days by the military; he barely survived the beatings and torture. They threw him into prison and it was two years later that he found out what had happened to you. And to me. They'd told him that we had both been killed in an air raid. It was to break his spirit. But Tee never broke. After the amnesty Tee came home, and we had another child, another daughter, we called her Jeab."

"I have a sister?" asked Tanny, eyes blazing, reaching out and touching her mother's face.

"You had." Mem's lower lip quivered; she tried to speak but couldn't. She raised her hand as if to stop Tanny from saying anything. "She was killed in 2003."

Tanny raised her hands to her face. "How did it happen?"

"It was called the war against drugs. The police killed many people in 2003."

"Was Jeab involved with drugs?"

"Never." It was a fierce, clench-jawed answer. "At night, after Jeab was murdered, I told myself it was a blessing that you had been adopted out of this land. We have too much blood and tears and corruption. So stupid and senseless."

Calvino wondered if others around her knew about her background with the communists. "You might have a problem if people here knew about your past," he said.

Mem shook her head, reached for a tissue from the small table next to her cot, and blew her nose. "It's okay. They know. It was a shock for some. One said I might be a spy. I said spies had better things to do than stitch up wounded demonstrators. Mostly my old comrades are on the other side. So they were right to be suspicious. But like in the jungle, practical things matter more than ideas. The leaders here have no experienced medical staff living inside the compound. And those staff who come during the day didn't have battlefield experience, so they took a risk on me. Things were much better after the night we suffered our first casualties. I'd seen lots of wounds. But these weren't combat wounds. What I saw was more like street fight damage—broken hands, noses, jaws. Nothing like what I had treated in the jungle."

Mem didn't have to say it, but she knew exactly what was required, and worked without complaint, without sleep. She had earned their respect.

"I don't understand," said Tanny. "It happened years ago. What can they do to help you?"

Mem broke into a smile. "Bring me justice by punishing the person who murdered Jeab. That's all I want."

"And they will do that?"

She looked her daughter over, touched her face with the back of her hand. "It is the only way left."

"Go to the police."

"It was the police who killed her."

Calvino had been quietly listening. "And you're sure that she was killed by the police?"

"I am a combat nurse with field-hospital experience. I know how to field-dress most kinds of wounds—knife, shrapnel, gunshot—and I can tell you how far apart the shooter was from the target. I can tell if the shooter was higher or lower than the victim. I saw Jeab's body after it was taken to the hospital. I personally examined her gunshot wounds. I'd seen it before—on the bodies of comrades executed on their knees. The bullets had been shot at an angle entering the skull from the top, and in my daughter's case two of the bullets had gone through her hands, which had been cupped over her head."

That had answered his question and a couple he hadn't asked. For Mem, joining the demonstration had a single purpose—bringing the killer of her daughter to justice. The daughter had died in a political pogrom. It seemed natural to Mem that the new group of politicians might move against the old regime that had sponsored the war on drugs, and there was no better way, in her mind, to discredit the old politicians than arresting and trying one of the killers who'd done their dirty work.

"And where is my father? Is he alive?"

"Tee?" Mem's smile faded into a bitter half grin. "After Jeab died, he left me for a younger woman. It's not a new story. I know. It seems to happen to others, and then one day it happens to you." It was a cliché, trite and empty as a wino's bottle until you came face-to-face with the wino or the abandoned wife and saw up close the accumulated loss in their eyes.

"Does he think people here can help you?"

"I haven't asked. We don't talk. He has a new wife."

Calvino stretched out, looking at the growing line of people waiting to see Mem.

"I've talked too much," she said, nodding at Calvino. "This farang will think that I don't love my country."

Calvino had long ago learned that no matter the personal horrors, indignities, or injustices, none of the suffering ever quite extinguished the Thais' love and loyalty to their country. "You don't need me hanging around," he said.

"Go on," said Tanny, "I'll be okay."

She'll be safe, thought Calvino. Her mother would be more comfortable telling the domestic secrets without a farang listening, judging, and reporting what was said.

Mem glanced up as a man crawled his way to the front of the line, holding up his wobbly wife, pale, eyes rolling, feeling nausea. Mem took one look at the woman, shining a flashlight into her eyes.

"You'd better go with him," she said, squeezing Tanny's hand. "I have to work."

Calvino waited for Tanny to decide whether to stay with her mother.

She squeezed her mother's hand in return, eyes pleading. "I can stay and help. Please."

Mem said, "Tomorrow we can talk again. One thing. Do you have a picture of your son?"

Mem's curiosity about her grandson had gotten the best of her. Tanny took out the picture of Jeff and showed her mother. Mem admired the little boy in a white shirt grinning behind a hint of Asian eyes and a farang nose. With his father inside a federal prison, his mother at an illegal occupation of Government House in Thailand, the kid looked innocent, like all children who had no idea of the circumstances of their parents.

Mem smiled, handing it back. "Keep it," said Tanny.

"What's his name?"

"Jeff."

Mem said the name slowly, looking at the picture. "He's very handsome."

Tanny thought about her son standing before his grandmother.

Her mother smiled and reached out her hand.

"I'll be back," said Tanny.

Her mother nodded, receiving her daughter's wai. Not even a rebel fighter would wish her daughter to abandon that gesture of respect, no matter that foreigners might label it as subjugation and an insult to the class struggle. Thai pragmatism never encountered an ideology that stripped it of the ancient gestures of respect giving. Finding her mother was the first piece of good luck that had come Tanny's way in many years.

TWENTY-TWO

THE LAWNS AND pavements inside Government House were wet and slick from the rain. Calvino thought about Thailand's vast library, shelf after shelf stacked with millions of hard-luck stories—not that the Thais had a monopoly on the genre. People played their best hand, knowing they'd drawn a couple of deuces, and it had taken long for the slowest of the green players to find out that they held a doomed hand. If Mem's father had had a famous family name, the cards would have dramatically improved. He'd have shuffled from the bottom of the deck to help his children, his relatives, his friends and neighbors. Some called the famous-name system karma—the good deeds from the last life earned a person birth into a privileged family—while others fled to fight in the jungles, figuring that karma was another delusion of the mighty worth fighting against.

Some lives had an abundance of luck, others a steep trail of tears and sorrow on a march that offered no good ending. Mem had been seeking justice for Jeab's death for years. As they walked out of Government House, Tanny said, "Will you help me find the man who killed my sister?"

"How do you know it was a man?"

"All the executioners are men. It's what men do best."

"I just found your mother." Mission creep was normal; this was mission gallop into the void. Calvino needed to decide whether looking for an upcountry cop who'd killed someone in the war against drugs was what he wanted chiseled on his tombstone. Helping to find Mem was one thing—he hadn't found her, Ratana had that honor, and besides, he told himself that he had retired from investigations—but looking into a five-year-old murder that happened as part of the war on drugs wasn't a different kettle of fish, it was an ocean patrolled by sharks.

"Will you?" She pressed against him.

Calvino's law: Once a man slept with a woman, he opened himself to the existential question of all relationships—Will you help me?

"I represent Brandon Sawyer. This could be a conflict of interest."

"You fired him. Remember, I was there when you threw him out of your office."

Of course she was right, he thought. That was the fallout from sleeping with an educated, smart woman. "But I've thrown him out before."

"That's sick."

Finding people who didn't want to be found, or who were lost, was much easier than being a referee between a couple of brothers who'd been trying to stab each other in the back since childhood because their mother hadn't given them enough time or love.

Calvino grinned. "That could be dangerous."

"If you're afraid, I'll find someone else."

"You've got to understand what you're asking for."

"I *know* what I'm asking for. A man."

She pulled her hand out of his, turned, walked across the street, and got on the back of a motorcycle taxi. He watched as she struggled to communicate her hotel address to the driver. And he wondered if she had any idea how far they were from the hotel, and how the ride on the back of a motorcycle that distance would have her head spinning for days. She didn't seem in any mood for his advice.

After a moment the motorcycle left with Tanny on the back. She didn't turn to look at him standing near the gate, hands in his pockets.

What she needed wasn't a private investigator—she needed a patron. A patron who came loaded with power and influence to shelter her as she sought information against people involved in the murder—and those people had their own network of patrons. It came down to whose patrons had more juice. Calvino might have been a lot of things, but he knew his limitations—he wasn't in a position to be anyone's patron. Digging into a murder carried out during the war on drugs could cause a problem for Pratt.

The following morning Calvino waited until Ratana walked downstairs from the day-care center. After she settled at her desk, he withdrew the copy of Nueng's photo and smoothed it out in front of her.

"I found this posted at Government House," he said.

Ratana's smile evaporated. She blinked back tears and turned away. She pulled out a handful of tissues, blew her nose, dabbed her eyes. Whatever had been written on the paper had been deeply troubling. "Do you know what this says? How could anyone do this?" Her voice broke. He almost never heard Ratana display anger.

Calvino had given considerable thought to whether to show Ratana the poster. But he had his reasons. It was possible the police could be coming around asking questions, and Ratana needed to be prepared. "I'm sorry," he said, as if the messenger were required to deliver an apology.

"How many posters did they put up?"

"I wasn't really looking for them."

"You should have looked and torn them all down."

"You want me to go back tomorrow and do that?"

She shook her head. "No. If you did that, something bad might happen."

She had a good point. A farang ripping down posters would likely bring to life the black-shirted security guards, golf clubs swinging as they chased him through the grounds. It wasn't an image he felt he wanted repeated outside his imagination.

"So she's banned from the grounds. What does she care? Yeah, she works at the massage parlor, but she's not a prostitute," Calvino said.

"It   says on the notice that they found condoms in her handbag and a business card from One Hand Clapping. But it's not fair. Nueng went to Government House to meet her older sister. The sister works as a secretary for the railway. She came to Bangkok to support the demonstration. She used her own money. Nueng was proud of her. They planned to have dinner, and her sister asked her to come to Government House to meet her friends."

"Some friends." He paused, sighing, shifting his feet. "It seems that Nueng didn't tell you about her little problem at Government House." The loss of face for her would have been so complete that no plastic surgeon would have been able to stitch it back onto her head.

"She never complains," said Ratana. "Nueng accepts too much."

Calvino thought about the sister walking into the grounds with posters of Nueng plastered everywhere, calling her baby sister a whore. Ratana ran out of the office and up the stairs, where she gathered Nueng's little boy and her son in her arms and wept.

The two sisters had planned on dinner. Nueng was a humble, friendly woman who had volunteered her time at the day-care even though it meant fewer customers at the massage parlor, and less money. If Nueng had any idea that Ratana knew about the poster, she would lose face. Once that happened, anything was possible from avoiding eye contact to replacing friendliness with a haunted, discouraged look—to something much worse.

"I am a bad person," she would say. "It's my work that is a sin. They look down on me. But they have a right to do so. I hope that I've not hurt my sister. I didn't mean to cause her a problem."

She might slit her wrists or take an overdose of sleeping pills. Or she might do nothing, because, like a slave who'd been trained to wear her chains without complaint, Nueng would have been taught to know her place and to stay away from decent people.

TWENTY-THREE

BRANDON SAWYER, ONCE he'd sobered up, bathed, and checked his e-mail, decided that he'd made a huge mistake. He phoned Calvino. His voice sounded mellow, contrite. "You've been drunk, Calvino. You know how things can get out of hand. Let's forget the other day."

Calvino's long sigh carried over the grid like a gust of mournful wind.

"Okay, I'll say it. I need your help, Vinny. I was an asshole. There. I said it. Now come out to my house and let's get drunk."

Calvino sat alone in the office. Ratana was working upstairs at the day-care nursery looking after her boy and a ragtag jumble of snot-nosed kids whose mothers worked at One Hand Clapping and other hole-in-the-wall operations in the sub-soi. Tanny had gone back on her own to Government House to be with her mother. In a way she had become detached from Marshall Sawyer's mission, and Calvino hadn't decided whether that was a good result. Sometimes clients gave up, shrugged off a loss, and moved on. Sometimes it also happened to private investigators.

At the other end of the phone, Brandon rattled ice cubes around the inside of his glass and barked for a maid to bring him a fresh drink. Calvino had nothing but Roman emperors on his desk; joining Brandon, kicking back, and forgetting about the rest of the day had a powerful attraction.

"Let's find a drink in town. On your tab."

"Thanks, Vinny. You won't regret it."

"Yes, I will. But that'll be tomorrow. And bring a replacement for my office bottle you drank dry."

"I only drank a quarter of it. Put four drinks on your next bill."

"Bring a bottle of Black or fuck you."

"Okay, okay. You got it, a bottle of Black. Anything else?" His voice, with an eager-to-please tone, remained unbroken by the demands.

Calvino said nothing for a few seconds.

"Well?" asked Brandon.

"I'm still thinking."

Brandon groaned, smacked his lips.

Calvino thought about asking him to make an appointment for another day. He was still sore at being accused of double-dealing. But it was an opportunity to find out what documents Tanny had handed over to Brandon. She'd been right about one thing: Brandon was the only person who would tell him what they were about. Also, this was Brandon's lucky day, and if he were truly lucky, he might find a way to get his brother off his back so that he could resume watching his pool yings giggling and splashing as they clung to rubber rafts at the shallow end. "Bring a couple of Havana cigars," said Calvino.

"Roger that."

It was two in the afternoon when Calvino arrived at Brandon's private club on the thirty-eighth floor of a domed steel-and-glass high-rise with sweeping views of the Chao Phraya from the bar, mid–Silom Road traffic moving like stoned ants escaping a hungry predator down below. Brandon had poached most of his pool yings from among the hostesses, who formed a long greeting line at the club's entrance. Other club members despised Brandon for harvesting the newest, most beautiful recruits, and there had been a half-hearted movement to cancel his membership.

"You should've come out to the house. All of them are going out on a *tamboon*." The entire staff—gardener, driver, maids, and pool yings—had piled into a rented van and driven two hours to a wat upcountry in order to make merit, and afterward line up to ask one of the famous monks to tell their fortune. "The usual superstitious tree-hugging bullshit," he said, finishing his drink.

Calvino had seen the ritual before. Women sitting in a circle around a monk, his eyes closed, a sign that he was performing his mind meld with rocks and trees and the world of spirits, transporting his consciousness to a niche in nirvana where the holy shouted at clouds and danced barefoot on tall elephant grass. And for an additional twenty baht, a guru would wave his hand and pluck winning lottery numbers out of the cool blue sky.

"It makes them happy," said Calvino. "Relaxes them."

"The sad thing is, it takes so little to make them happy but so goddamn much to keep them at that level. You ever notice how they're in a full-blown mania one minute, then you turn around to pour yourself a drink, and before you take a sip, they've flipped into a deep depression. That bored, glassy-eyed look—what's it called?"

"Catatonic," said Calvino.

"That's the word. But what the fuck do I care? There's always a chance that the new crop will be more stable." Brandon's eyes followed one of the new hostesses, who, having been briefed, steered clear of Brandon's table. Brandon chewed a piece of ice, swallowed the fragments as sharp as blades but didn't feel a thing.

The truth was slowly dribbling out as Brandon drank. He'd been as lonely and restless as Calvino had been. The house empty, he'd probably phoned the top half of his drinking-buddy list before he got down to Calvino's name. He reached into his bag and pulled out a one-liter bottle of Johnnie Walker Black and put it on the table in front of Calvino.

"Sex with a strange woman is still the best deal in town," Brandon said. "No history. A blank slate, and you can write whatever you want on it. She's all mystery. No baggage. But that only works for the first time. The second time, you know what you're getting. It's a steep falloff by the third time. By the fourth time, she's fucking you on her own script. Count on it."

Brandon was a little drunk, images and ideas bounced off the sides of his mind like mud bricks made with too much straw. Watching a barge on the river below, the new hostess hiding in the back, pretending to be invisible—Calvino understood the unwritten rule to never interrupt a drunk in the middle of a riff on the meaning of sex.

"What is it between Marshall and you? Did you beat him up when you were kids?" asked Calvino, turning the bottle over in his hand to find out in which duty-free shop Brandon had bought it in Singapore.

Brandon had now reached the cusp between drunk and too drunk to give him an honest answer. "He beat me up until I got bigger, and one day I kicked the shit out of him. You'd have thought it would have taught him a lesson. Changed the balance."

"But it didn't. And he's still doing it."

"Marshall has a Napoleon complex. He's five-nine, and that makes him a midget in New York. He should be living in Thailand, where his height would make him the star guard on the Thai Olympic basketball team."

Calvino held up his glass as a waitress filled it with one of Brandon's member bottles of single-malt whiskey.

Brandon raised his glass for a toast. "To Marshall, the family's little Napoleon, looking to take over Russia, China, and Thailand." He drank, rattled ice around in his glass, and said, "It's like he's lost his mind but still has all his teeth. Marshall likes eating. Thinking only makes him paranoid. He shouldn't attempt thinking."

"The state of emergency isn't helping." Calvino considered telling Brandon about going out to Government House, but it would only have fed his paranoia.

"Everything connected to Thailand worries him. I told Marshall to forget about the politics. Business is like an ugly woman with a good heart. You gotta shut your eyes and think of that pure heart beating inside."

"Marshall wants you to sell out. How are you going to change his mind?" asked Calvino.

"He hates controversy. He can't handle it. The thing with the journalist getting whacked…well, it fucked him up. If Achara did it, then he had an excuse to pull the plug on the deal. When he couldn't connect Achara to the murder, then he got the bright idea to jump on the corruption bandwagon. That's nothing but a smoke screen, though. You just figure out how to buy the bandwagon."

"Who's behind the screen?"

"Some people think that GM food causes infertility, turns babies into blind midgets, and curls their toes into claws. They're crazy. But it doesn't matter. For them there's a tumor incubating inside every cup of rice. They think our company is part of a conspiracy to destroy the health of the Third World by making them eat genetically modified rice. They've written letters, sent e-mails. The government. Congressmen. Governors. Mayors. Newspaper editors. Any gasbag with a web site. Who haven't they written? Fucking beats me."

A bottle of Scotch was opened, and Brandon mentioned that Marshall Sawyer had a larger problem. That caught Calvino's attention.

"Marshall's a cover-your-ass kind of brother. He learned it at home. My mother admires that. It reminds her of what a mistake her own life has been." He smiled, savoring the moment, his tongue darting into his glass. Then he smacked his lips and sighed. "Marshall's gone overboard." Brandon leaned across the table, his head only a couple of inches away from Calvino. He glanced around, as if anyone in the near-empty room were listening. "He's digging for any excuse to sell the company. Going from one thing to the next. And he knows I ain't gonna let him do it."

"Someone's got to blink first," said Calvino.

Brandon nodded gravely. He clenched his pinkish fist around his glass, turning his knuckles the whitish yellow of chicken gristle. "I'm not worried. I've got my brother by the balls. And he knows it."

"Then squeeze," said Calvino. "Or let go."

Brandon had given a revocable voting proxy of his shares in the company to his brother. With that proxy Marshall could pretty much control the company. What he said at board meetings wasn't just listened to, it was the law. "My brother needs my shares if he wants to keep playing the hotshot. I told him to go along with my GM deal with Achara or—"

"You'd revoke the proxy."

"You clever bastard. How did you ever guess that?"

"Whiskey and luck."

"He knows I won't sign the document his delivery girl delivered."

"Have you told him?"

Brandon's lip curled like a dog's that was about to bark. "I told him."

It had started to make sense. Brandon had made a threat, and his brother, playing for time, had dispatched Tanny Craig to dig up dirt on Achara. The best she could find was the money for the ancestral temple. Marshall must have known that Brandon wasn't going to back off just because his Chinese partner wanted to keep the souls of his dead ancestors from entering the bodies of his pet lions.

"I said, 'Marshall, maybe it's time for me to go back on the board. With all the bad financial shit, why don't I come home to New York and let's go through all the books and deals and decide what needs to be sold off.' "

"He didn't take it well," said Calvino.

"He fucking freaked out. It was like holding a cat over a swimming pool." His smile, menacing, had just enough of a whimsical element to throw his intentions into confusion. Brandon assumed that his brother was terrified that Brandon would tear up the proxy and return to New York. Calvino wondered if Brandon was overplaying his hand.

"How much time did he give you to come around?" asked Calvino.

Brandon reached across and slapped Calvino on the shoulder. "Wrong question, Calvino. It's how long am *I* giving *him*? He's got two more days." He pulled one of the paper napkins from the table and tore it in half, then tore it again, stuffed the pieces into his clenched fist, blew on his fist, pulled out a whole and undamaged napkin.

"Nice act, Brandon."

"Drunk or sober, there are certain things a man never forgets," he said, smoothing the napkin out on the table and grinning like a Cheshire cat.

"But I'm not the audience you need to work," said Calvino.

Brandon fingered the edges of the napkin. "You hit me pretty hard the other day."

"When I deliver a message I like to know it's been received."

Calvino didn't look away as Brandon stared at him. Violence, Calvino had learned, was never a matter of pride or swagger. A man carried the capacity of violence inside and released it only for a good reason—someone pushed you, you pushed back. It wasn't something that he thought about; it was pure instinct. Push. Shove. Leave out the period between the two. There was never time for a pause. The grammar of violence turned on a verb. And he used only enough to get the job done.

"Okay, I got the message," Brandon added. "Happy? Have another drink. I liked what you said the other day."

"What'd I say?"

"About keeping your agreements."

"A man's only as good as his word. I told Marshall I had agreement with Achara. I quoted you about keeping agreements."

"What'd he say?"

"He accused me of trying to get him sent to prison."

Calvino held out his glass as Brandon refilled it with the expensive Scotch, the color of ripe oak timber. He drank from the glass and set it down on the mysteriously reconstituted napkin. Brandon had reached out and grabbed a passing hostess and pulled her onto his lap. He pinched her cheek. She tried to maintain her dignity, balanced on Brandon's knee, as he wrapped his hands around her small waist. He bounced her on his knee, and she jerked up and down like she was riding a mechanical bull in a redneck bar.

"I feel the urge for a little rodeo time," Brandon said. "Some roping and bucking."

"There are two kind of cowboys," said Calvino. "One rides hard and chews up the trail behind him. The other just gets himself chewed up."

The glint in Brandon's eye made him look less like a cowboy than a circling shark. "I'm the kind of cowboy that will die with his boots standing straight up by the side of the bed."

Inside his jacket, Calvino's cell phone rang. He answered it as Brandon kissed and pretended to bite the hostess's neck.

"Where are you?" asked Colonel Pratt.

Calvino heard from Pratt's tone that this wasn't a call that had much to do with where he was. "What's happening?" He watched Brandon as he spoke on the phone.

"I'm at Khun Achara's house. You'd better come out to meet me."

"What's the problem?"

"Brandon's with you?"

"Yes."

"For how long?"

"Since two this afternoon."

"You've had a couple of drinks."

"That's what retirees do in the afternoon."

"Achara's dead. Don't say anything to Brandon. Not before I can talk to him."

Calvino clocked the time, feeling sober all of a sudden. "When did it happen?"

"We won't know until forensics does some tests on what's left."

"What's that mean?"

"See you in an hour." Colonel Pratt terminated the call.

TWENTY-FOUR

ACHARA'S ESTATE SWARMED with cops and emergency service people. Calvino locked his car. He continued along the driveway past four police cars. An ambulance slowly backed over the lawn, stopping around the corner from the gate and out of sight of the drive. The rear door of the ambulance was open. An attendant stood beside it, earphones in his ears, smoking a cigarette and keeping time to the music with his foot. No one was inside the ambulance. Two uniformed cops approached Calvino, smelled the whiskey on his breath, and ordered him back to his car. Colonel Pratt, dressed in his brown police uniform, walked along the path, telling the cops to let the farang come through. They exchanged a look with each other, then with Colonel Pratt, and the Thai cops reverted to their default setting in such circumstances—they pretended that Calvino no longer existed, as if he'd evaporated like a puddle on a hot April afternoon.

"What happened to Achara?" asked Calvino.

"We're still trying to work it out."

"You said he was dead."

Colonel Pratt started to say something, but words failed him. "Have a look."

The roar from one of the lions made the cops jumpy. One cop's hand automatically reached for his holstered handgun.

Neither Calvino nor Pratt said anything as the lion roared again. The colonel exchanged a hard look with one of the cops, telling him to get more plastic bags, the large black ones that gardeners used to bundle up grass cuttings and leaves.

They walked along the side of the mansion, keeping to the stone path that ran along the back, across the garden, through the ferns and the banana and coconut trees. They passed the tree where the green snake had almost fallen on Tanny. No snake eyes today, Calvino thought. Colonel Pratt entered first, through the two huge stone guardian lions, into the area behind the property where the lions were caged. Cops wearing surgical gloves combed the ground, putting bits of paper and scraps into large Ziploc bags. The ambulance attendants stood beside the cage. One leaned against a rake. The other hunched down next to the gurney, waiting.

A dozen cops loitered outside the lions' enclosure, covering their noses and mouths as they watched the lions and waited. A bellyful of death had made a couple of them sick. They vomited behind the banana trees. The sour stench from the retching and the stink of death thickened the air. Being good Buddhists, they had no desire to accumulate bad karma by shooting the lions. There was no good reason to do so. No ranking officer had given an order.

"We're waiting for the tranquilizer gun," said Colonel Pratt.

Calvino nodded. "When I was here a few days ago, Achara's vet had tranquilized them before treating them."

They looked at each other, silently calling forth the shared memory of another man who'd been killed by an animal. His name was Oxley. It wasn't a lion but a German shepherd named Joy that had ripped out Oxley's throat.

Something about the lions didn't look normal.

"What's wrong with them?" asked Calvino.

Achara's lions were sprawled with their paws stretched forward, claws extended on the concrete, parts of the remains a few feet away. They gave every indication that they'd eaten all they wanted. One yawned, shook its head, then lowered it, looking drowsy, bloated; the other raised its head skyward, tongue arching out of its open mouth, shaking its mane before settling in for a long post-banquet nap.

"They've overeaten."

Their bloated stomachs heaved under the dark, rainy sky—a couple of gluttons, their breathing slow and labored.

A cop came up and whispered in Colonel Pratt's ear. The colonel nodded and gestured to the squad with the tranquilizer gun to approach the cage. The other cops pressed in to watch as the gun was aimed and fired, then fired again. The lions flinched, convulsed; they let out nerve-jangling roars, licked the air, yawned, and after a couple of minutes slumped over, looking like rugs covering a hunting-lodge floor. The ambulance attendants, with some reluctance, escorted by several cops, entered the enclosure and recovered body parts. Bones and meat were loaded into black plastic bags. Neither Calvino nor Colonel Pratt said anything as the men collected Achara's remains. The lions had left a trail of gore splattered across the concrete floor of the enclosure. The attendants efficiently stepped over broken coils of greenish-brown intestines, severed limbs with shredded flesh attached, working as if they'd had experience in such cleanups. Flies, ants, and a United Nations' worth of tropical insects gorged on the remains.

Clinging to the body parts were bits of clothing. A shoe. More like a slipper than a shoe, the kind Chinese men wear in the house. Or used for tai chi. Mud was caked on the upturned sole. It was under the roof of the enclosure, which served to keep the rain off it. Calvino had seen bodies that had been shot, stabbed, run over, blown up, and drowned, but whatever had cut down those victims, in death they remained recognizably human in form. As in life, in death the image meant something; it carried a coded message of the transformation between the living person and the lifeless form that was no longer living. What remained in the enclosure looked more like tailings dropped on the floor as a butcher worked inside a slaughterhouse. The usual human structure was gone, making it difficult to identify as a human being.

"He was proud of his lions and gave them Chinese names," said Calvino. "He showed them to Tanny and me before our meeting."

"Bad meat, he told you?" asked Colonel Pratt, making a mental note. "You said they'd been sick."

"Looks like they recovered their appetites."

Calvino would have done anything to extinguish the smell from his nostrils and mouth. The bitter taste of his own rising bile mixed with the whiskey caused him to cough and spit in the dirt.

"We found this," said Colonel Pratt, handing Calvino a business card.

"Did you find any other business cards?"

Colonel Pratt shook his head, watching Calvino examine the card.

"Strange."

" 'This was strange chance,' " said Colonel Pratt, quoting *Cymbeline*.

Calvino turned it over in his hand; the middle of the card had been perforated. He guessed it was from a large tooth, leaving a hole underneath his name. It was his, all right. He'd exchanged business cards with Achara the night of the Chini exhibition. Pratt had been beside him as they'd studied the card for signs of rank and importance. Calvino had had new cards made. Only his name and phone number, in keeping with his retired status. The old cards said PRIVATE INVESTIGATIONS. Calvino's new card invited an investigation. Achara's card was gold-embossed and included his CEO title and the name of a listed company. When the stock exchange opened tomorrow, the shareholders could expect a bumpy ride once the news broke that the CEO had been collected into a series of black plastic bags.

Calvino handed the colonel the card, shaking his head.

"Any idea why, of all the people he knew, he'd have your card on him today? Did you have a meeting or an appointment with him?"

Calvino shook his head. "Nothing like that."

"His staff said he was in the garden for his daily tai chi."

Calvino figured Achara for someone disciplined enough to never miss his Chinese exercise. "Until he had a reason to go inside the lions' enclosure."

"Strange," said Colonel Pratt. " 'They that have the voice of lions and the act of hares, are they not monsters?' "

Calvino paced around the perimeter of the enclosure with Pratt's Shakespeare quotation ringing inside his head. He stopped to think about it, using a pen to nudge the large Yale lock. The same one he'd watched as Achara slipped his hand inside his shirt and fished out a chain that held a key he inserted into the lock, opening it. The chain and key had dangled around his neck. Funny thing about the lock—the key and chain had been left in it. Achara—or someone—had removed them from around Achara's neck. Calvino was careful not to touch the lock as Colonel Pratt stopped a couple of feet ahead and glanced back.

"You coming?" asked Pratt, waiting on the path.

"Achara's key is in the lock," said Calvino.

Colonel Pratt doubled back for a look. He pulled the key out of the lock.

"He unlocked it, left the key inside the lock to save time when he came out."

"He wore it on a chain around his neck. I saw him lean down and open the lock without taking off the chain."

"What are you saying, Vincent?"

"It's an observation. Maybe it means nothing. Maybe he pulled the chain off most of the time, but with me around he was worried I'd steal it, so he left it around his neck." Calvino told himself that many things in life happened without a reason; patterns didn't necessarily repeat themselves; evidence of intention was mostly blurred and inclusive.

"Was Achara having problems with Brandon Sawyer?"

"I know that conflict of business interests is a leading cause of death, but I just left Brandon telling me how important it was to keep his agreement with Achara. It doesn't make sense that he'd kill his partner."

"People kill each other over business issues."

"This isn't Brandon's style," said Calvino.

"I'd like your help, Vincent."

Two uniformed officers interrupted before Calvino could reply. He was glad for the chance to wander off and look around. He crouched under the awning, inspecting a sheltered spot on the gray concrete surface where the blood had pooled. The rain hadn't washed it away. A dozen feet from that spot, the lions' rib cages softly expanded as the drugs sent them racing inside their dreams across the Serengeti, chasing an antelope. The sharpshooter with the tranquilizer gun sat on a plastic stool, keeping the rifle pointed at the lions in case they might need a little booster shot. As he touched the concrete, Calvino had a feeling that Achara was the kind of guy who turned in for bed at night with the chain and key around his neck. With Achara's neck and head gone, it was impossible to determine if force had been used to remove the chain. Once Achara was inside the enclosure, the gate hadn't been locked. The day Calvino saw Achara in the enclosure, he saw a cautious, careful, and calm man, not guided by sentimentality. He had known the power of lions. Calvino tried to make sense of why Achara had removed the chain and left it in the lock. What did the key in the lock prove?

"Pratt, have you asked the staff if their boss ever took off the gold chain?"

Colonel Pratt turned away from the two officers and nodded that he'd include the question when it came time to interrogate Achara's household staff.

Calvino rose to his feet, stretched his arms, strolled past the police to the back of the enclosure, overlooking the canal. The water, the color of mud, ran swiftly in eddies and whirls, the current carrying leaves and branches. As he looked down at the canal, Calvino saw clothing, bloody and torn. Achara had been reported as going into the garden to do tai chi. The cloth might have been a tai chi outfit—black cotton—the rough remains a faint echo of baggy, loose-fitting Chinese pants with a cord tied and knotted at the waist; it had become a bloody lump, like a piece of cartilage chewed and spit out by one of the lions.

Why would Achara have been wearing a tai chi outfit and going into the enclosure? To perform a ritual to honor his ancestors? Was it an impulse to check on the condition of his lions? Achara was a man of honor and not a man of impulse, though, as far as Calvino knew, there was no dances-with-lions routine in tai chi.

Colonel Pratt found him studying the blood-soaked remains of the tai chi pants. "It might have been an accident," he said.

Calvino nodded, squinting at the pants. "Or it was made to look like one."

There were always other explanations, and Colonel Pratt understood that in policing it wasn't feasible to follow up every possibility, or the investigation would never end. But he also understood that keeping an open mind was no bad thing. "What have you got?"

"What's left of his workout pants."

Colonel Pratt squatted down and had a look, pulling his walkie-talkie out and ordering someone from forensics to bag the pant fragment. Calvino pointed at the length of pant leg. "Mud." He looked around the enclosure. "I don't see any mud. I'm not an expert on tai chi, but I don't think it's done in the mud."

Two lab men, hands covered with thin white gloves, arrived and took charge of the pants. Colonel Pratt watched them salute before they disappeared like ghosts. "It wouldn't hurt to look around," Colonel Pratt said.

"It wouldn't do any harm."

Enough cops had stomped on the grass to churn parts of the lawn into fresh mud. Given Achara's status, the brass had dispatched a full team. Those in the upper echelons had substantial experience in covering their asses. Whatever was left of the crime scene had turned into a crowd of staff, police, ambulance attendants—no body snatchers for the likes of Achara—and some people who'd walked in from the street to see what was going on, simply stepping over the yellow crime-scene tape. It wouldn't be long before the noodle and fruit vendors arrived and the lions woke up.

"The canal," said Calvino, extending his arm, "runs through his property."

A maid showed them where Achara performed his tai chi sessions.

He'd chosen a lovely, uncluttered spot no more than five meters away from the canal bank—his little piece of paradise near the water, his lions, the green gardens with manicured palms and banana trees. Colonel Pratt discovered evidence of a struggle ten meters from where Achara conducted his exercises. Several sets of footprints were pressed into the damp ground. Calvino slipped down to the canal bank, where he saw several half-washed-away footprints in the mud. "Looks like someone landed a boat over here," said Calvino.

Soon the rain would remove any sign of the footprints—there were several sets of prints left by running shoes. Colonel Pratt directed a man in his group to photograph the prints he'd found and the ones that Calvino had spotted on the canal bank. Calvino thought that it looked like Achara had been grabbed. They had docked their boat and rushed him while he was doing his exercises. One of Colonel Pratt's men found the spot where the boat had been docked. The bow had left an impression in the mud, half filled with brown canal water. The police snapped more photographs.

"Doesn't look like Achara had an accident," said Calvino.

"People are up and down this canal all day long. Prints on the bank could mean anything. Unless we find a witness who saw strangers with Achara, we've got nothing. These footprints aren't telling us anything except that some people walked on the bank. But we have no evidence of what they were doing on the canal or their reason for walking on the bank. It's like looking at a tarot card—you get different readings from different people."

By the time they'd walked back to the house, Achara's staff had been herded into a group alongside the enclosure. Colonel Pratt received the report from the officer who had led an interrogation team. Three members of staff—a woman and two men—had fled the compound. One member of the staff had a stunned, surprised expression like a man who'd shaved with a straight razor for the first time and survived. He was the one who had ratted them out—said they were illegal Burmese workers. The remaining staff huddled, terrified, drained of words. Only whimpering and wailing sounds came from their mouths, as if they were waiting to be taken out and shot or transported to a concentration camp in a jungle location. None of the staff had admitted to being near the enclosure. Or to having seen Achara go through his daily tai chi exercises. Nor could they explain why there would have been mud on one of Achara's slippers and on his pants.

No one in the group stepped forward when asked by Colonel Pratt if anyone had seen a boat dock and strangers enter the compound from the canal. They were too frightened to swallow their own spit, and in no condition to give information that would single them out from the others. They had no idea who had fed their master to the lions. Colonel Pratt threw up his hands and walked away. Calvino stayed back for a moment, looking at the gardener who had sung like a bird about the illegal Burmese; he had the kind of prison-trustee mentality, and Calvino made a note to himself that the gardener should be put on the short list for further questioning. If a man rats out those he works with, then betraying the boss is an easy hop, skip, and boat jump onto the bank away.

A uniformed cop came out of the house and walked straight over to Colonel Pratt. The cop, flashing the warm, sincere smile reserved for impressing senior officers, held in the palm of his hand an electronic bug. He'd found it crawling under the long teak table in the banquet room. They followed the officer into the room, and Colonel Pratt had the officer show precisely where he'd located it. The cop rested his hand on the table right in front of the chair that Tanny had sat in at their meeting. Achara had made a big deal about seating arrangements. Being a trusting soul, it wouldn't have occurred to him to sweep the room for electronic devices after the meeting.

"Any idea where this might have come from?" Colonel Pratt asked.

Calvino smiled, looking at the black listening device the size of a bullet. " 'It's like reading tarot cards, you get different readings from different people.' " He had a good hunch that Tanny had left it behind, but he had no proof. Achara would have used the room for any number of meetings, and any competitor wanting to get an edge could have placed it under the table. Anyone wanting him to divulge his true intentions would have an uncensored log to monitor. The same wheels turned inside Colonel Pratt's head as the black bug was bagged, labeled, and taken away.

Pratt checked the time. "You don't have to stick around," he said.

"What about dinner tonight? I miss Manee's cooking," Calvino said, knowing that Colonel Pratt's wife prepared a full Thai meal every evening.

Colonel Pratt cracked a smile. "I've stopped asking."

"Because I came into a little money?"

"I didn't say that. But it happened around that time."

"Walk me out, Pratt. I want to run something past you." Calvino looked around at all the cops in the area, making it clear he wanted a conversation without a group of ears tuned in for content.

As they walked to the front of the house, Calvino told Pratt about the death of Tanny's sister during the war on drugs. He explained how the mother had made a physical examination of the body. "Civilians don't know what they're looking at," said Colonel Pratt, his tone dismissive. Clearly he'd been disappointed, thinking that Calvino had some further insight about Achara's death. But he'd already moved on. Maybe he was moving just a little too fast, hitting the New York accelerator.

"I know that. But she's got a medical background."

"A doctor?" asked Colonel Pratt, eyes narrowed. Calvino was stepping onto his turf, and the colonel wasn't all that happy having Calvino's footprints where they shouldn't be.

"She's a nurse. And she's an expert on treating gunshot wounds."

Colonel Pratt stopped dead in his tracks and cocked his head. "A combat nurse? Was she in the army?"

"She worked in a medical unit."

"Vietnam," he said with some confidence.

"Northern Thailand. She was involved in the communist insurgency."

Colonel Pratt raised an eyebrow, slowly shook his head. It wasn't what he'd expected to hear; it wasn't what he wanted to hear. It gave him an unsettled feeling, considering that he had a good idea where Calvino was trying to lead him—down a trail from where people rarely returned. Tanny's mother hadn't been the only one to lose a daughter or son. Her daughter had been shot in the head twice. The chances were that shooter was likely either a cop or a local acting under the cops' authority and protection—subletting the hit to professional gunmen. She'd have been one more of those whose names had been crossed off the blacklist. There'd been an unofficial quota. Those who eliminated the most in their district stood to gain promotions and benefits. It had been a kind of competition to show efficiency and loyalty. The police wanted to forget about the war against drugs. There'd been no arrests. Not one. He glanced over Calvino. "She was a communist?"

"The murdered daughter?"

"No, the mother."

Calvino shrugged. "Don't know. Does it matter?"

"For some people."

"That's why I asked you. You're not 'some people.' You'd go strictly on the merits. Murder is the same thing. It doesn't matter about the mother's politics."

"It's not the mother's politics. Murder on the scale we're talking about *is* politics."

Starting an investigation meant no end of problems. It wasn't opening a murder case file and sending out investigators to find the daughter's killer; it was the possible opening of the floodgates holding back thousands of others who'd had relatives murdered during the war on drugs. "So

Tanny's mother should just forget about it. *Mai pen rai*," said Calvino.

"Let's assume her daughter was murdered. Do you think a colonel like me can start an investigation without asking for higher approval? Or go around my commander and start a private investigation without him finding out? Because if I did that, you can be sure something would happen to me, Manee, my children—not to mention you, Tanny, and her mother. Is that what you want?"

Calvino stared at his friend, trying to find the answers to his questions. It was that patron-client relationship he'd tried to explain to Tanny that night at Government House. He broke into a smile, accepting that Pratt had confirmed his own instinctive reaction. "You're right. Forget about it?" When it came down to it, inside Colonel Pratt's world, Tanny had approximately the same odds of finding justice as a sixteenth-century leper chasing a cure.

Colonel Pratt had come to understand what that smile meant. "Vincent, you've retired from private investigations. But say for some reason you're thinking of going back into business. This isn't the way to make a comeback."

"In circles," said Calvino. "Large, looping, endless circles."

Colonel Pratt nodded. Around the eyes, he looked sad, wounded, and discouraged.

"It doesn't matter, Pratt. I shouldn't have brought it up. My mistake." Calvino walked away as the rain started again.

"Vincent!" Colonel Pratt shouted after him.

Calvino turned around. "Yeah."

"Dinner's at seven-thirty."

Calvino smiled, flipped the colonel a salute before walking back through the parked cars. He took out his key, leaned over the hood, watching the cops in the rain. It had been ordinary cops who'd gone out on the hunt. Men just like these. Men who'd taken the oath to protect and uphold the law. But oaths, like old forgotten books, the pages devoured by mites, often turned to powdery dust, leaving only the cover showing over missing pages.

Once Calvino climbed behind the wheel of his car, he reached into the backseat and pulled out the new bottle of Johnnie Walker Black that Brandon had given him. Technically it was a replacement for the office bottle. Twisting the cap, he opened it, took a whiff. Touching the rim to his lips, he drank, then wiped his mouth with the back of his hand. Tanny had lost a sister in the war against drugs. He closed up the bottle and started the car engine. She hadn't been the only one who'd lost a family member to the wave of killings.

February 2004 had been a month of many killings. Faa (who shared the same fate as Jeab, Tanny's sister), a thirty-five-year-old mother, lived with her family in Phetchaburi. The police sent a notice saying her name had appeared on a blacklist for drugs and instructing her to report to the police to have her name removed from the list. Faa arrived at the police station thinking it would be a short meeting. Her name would be removed, and she could breathe easily. Once she was inside the police station, the police insisted she sign a document. But she was illiterate. When she asked the police what was in the document, they told her not to worry, that once she signed it, her name would be removed from the blacklist.

She signed the paper, touched the amulet that she wore around her neck—the one her mother had given her when she was fourteen years old. Less than a week later, several Thai males aged late twenties to early thirties, their hair cut military style, wearing wraparound sunglasses and black shirts and pants and polished boots, parked their pickup truck at the noodle vendor's stand next to Faa's house.

Two men from the pickup walked into the wood-frame house, the others taking up guard in front of it. One of the men pulled out a handgun and shot Faa at close range while her twelve-year-old daughter sat at the kitchen table. The girl also watched as the second man shot her mother four times in the upper back, hitting the lungs and heart. The house was twenty meters from a police call box on a main road, but when the family called, the police took two hours before they came to the house. The daughter was found crying, kneeling over her dead mother. There was blood splattered all over the kitchen, and it had stained the daughter's white school blouse. But the police, when they finally arrived, collected no evidence and asked no questions about the murder. The amulet was still around Faa's neck. The killers were never caught. Threats were made to keep the daughter quiet. Threats worked. Intimidation worked. Violence worked without fail. The message to the daughter and to the family was that they shouldn't cause a problem. They were told that Faa had signed a confession admitting to drug dealing. An illiterate woman, fingering an amulet for luck, had signed her death warrant with a smile.

The prime minister at the time said, "Because drug traders are ruthless to our children, so being ruthless back to them is not a big thing. It may be necessary to have casualties. If there are deaths among traitors, it's normal."

TWENTY-FIVE

RATANA USED A wet hand towel to clean John-John's face; he sat passively enough in a chair, happily dribbling a glass of coconut juice down both sides of his mouth and over his book, opened to a drawing of a dragon. Dinner at Colonel Pratt's house was a family affair that had become infrequent after the Chini collection was sold. The paintings were more than art; they had formed a history, a personal connection that deepened between all of them. Colonel Pratt had recovered the paintings on the night of the military coup, the same night Calvino shot the man who'd masterminded the hit on John-John's father—strong cables that bound them.

Calvino arrived carrying a huge wicker basket brimming with red and white roses, white orchids, pink carnations, sprigs of tiny white flowers, looking like a burst of stars against a night sky. Manee put the basket on the dinner table, but it was too big, and leaves and petals hung over the plates.

"Mother, how can we find our food?" said their eldest, Suchin, a boy in university.

The two of them moved the portable jungle scene into the sitting room.

Colonel Pratt came in late, slipping off his shoes at the entrance, wearing his policeman's uniform, then walked

223

over and sat in his favorite chair. He groaned as if the weight of the world had temporarily been lifted from his shoulders. "Sorry I'm late."

Manee managed a thin smile before disappearing into the kitchen and instructing the live-in maid to warm up dinner. Calvino brought along a bottle of Scotch, set it on the table alongside a bucket of ice and several glasses. He'd been the only one drinking, and once Colonel Pratt had settled into his overstuffed leather chair, Calvino poured him a Scotch and dumped in a handful of ice.

The colonel glanced over his shoulder to see if Manee was watching—she wasn't—then drained the glass.

"Hard day," said Calvino.

Every day is hard if you're a Thai cop, Colonel Pratt said to himself. But this day had transcended the normal definition of hardness, to the point where he wondered why he didn't retire.

"Did you touch the gate to the enclosure?"

Calvino shrugged, pulling a pen from his jacket. "I used this to lift the padlock on the gate."

Not that the yellow tape at the crime had stopped the curious neighbors, who'd climbed over it and into the crime scene to gawk at the lions in the enclosure, nudging one another, saying how clever and fierce the lions were. Eating a man gained their respect.

Working at the police lab with several technicians, Colonel Pratt had watched as the technicians ran tests on the scraps of clothing, the slipper, and the body parts. It would take days before the results of DNA samples came back. Meanwhile, one technician at the crime scene had found a fingerprint—one that hadn't belonged to Achara or anyone who worked at the house. The print had been left on the gate—a single thumbprint from a right hand. And the lab was running a check against a database of fingerprints, including those of criminals and ex-military recruits—a military lottery meant that most Thai males served in the army and were fingerprinted in the induction process. No positive match had turned up—so far. It was possible that the print belonged to a woman.

By the time everyone was seated at the table, Suchin, who was a second-year engineering student at Chulalongkorn University, asked, "Dad, is it true a lion ate a man?"

Colonel Pratt, eyes bloodshot, nodded. "Where did you hear that?"

"It was on the news," Suthorn said. As the daughter of the family, and a star on her university debating team, she came to life as the conversation at the table showed signs of turning into a lively debate.

"I heard it, too," said Manee. "As an excuse for being late to your own dinner party, it is a good one."

"Wasn't Khun Achara a guest at Montri's party?" asked Ratana. She had known the answer but raised the issue to change the subject of the matter of his death. "You gave me his business card, and I put his name in your client database."

"He wasn't a client," said Calvino. "Not directly. He was the business partner of a client."

"Brandon. Your only client," said Ratana. That fact vested Achara with a larger connection to Calvino's life, lending him special status.

Manee shivered, shook her head, and caught her husband's eye. "It must've been a terrible death." The more gruesome the murder, the more fascination she had with the details. And she wasn't alone at the table in her appetite for further information about the murder.

Suchin rolled his eyes. "What if it wasn't an accident? And someone threw him to the lions? That's a possibility."

Calvino thought Colonel Pratt's son had a tiny streak of rebellion, nothing anyone could easily point to, but enough of the challenge to authority and the party line that gave him hope for the new generation of Thais.

"Khun Achara owned the lions," said Colonel Pratt.

"And he let them roam around the garden?" Suthorn asked. "Like cats?"

She meant it as a joke, and the others at the table had a good laugh. Except for Colonel Pratt and Calvino, who'd seen what had been left of Achara after the lions got finished with him. There was nothing particularly amusing about the dismembered body inside the enclosure.

"The lions live in a large, enclosed, secure space on his premises. Khun Achara went inside the enclosure. The lions jumped him. So far that's all we know. How he got there, we're looking into it. I'd like to talk about something else." Colonel Pratt rubbed his tired eyes as if this would erase the memory of the day.

A silence fell over everyone at the table. John-John threw a dumpling that landed on Calvino's plate. "Two-point corner shot," said Calvino, sticking his fork into it and shoving the dumpling into his mouth as if such behavior were perfectly natural. The others kept their heads down, everyone chewing, lost in one collective thought: What does it feel like to be eaten by lions?

The colonel believed that this night would be his last before the carbon arc lamps had been switched on, throwing a spotlight on his investigation. Achara was a "somebody," a man who occupied a prominent position, owned a large house and grounds, had significant ties to the Chinese community, was a friend of the rich and powerful. The public was accustomed to such men dying in car crashes, or of heart attacks in the arms of their mistresses, or of some rare cancer, and occasionally by gunshot. But being chewed up and swallowed by lions, even by Thai standards for death, that was biblical, mythical, and, most important, newsworthy. A Thai devoured by lions was the kind of story with racetrack wheels good for the long journey to the front pages of the foreign press. It would be all over the Internet. Video clips on YouTube. There was no way to clean the stain left on the reputation from this far-flung unofficial public record that was both everywhere and nowhere at the same time.

And Achara's dramatic death couldn't have come at a worse moment for the police. Or the fragile government that sought to maintain the illusion of authority.

The top brass in the police department would turn up the temperature—that was what they did best—and the heat fell hard, burning some subordinates, threatening to fry others, as the lower ranks scrambled to commandeer resources away from the demonstrators and put them on the case. Colonel Pratt knew that the internal pressure had only started, and all he had was an unidentified thumbprint standing between a verdict of accidental death and one of murder. It did no good to point out that no investigation was being made into the death of a pro-government demonstrator the previous evening, or into the harm done to the forty people who'd been injured when the two sides clashed. Those were ordinary people. Those deaths, like the war-on-drug deaths, were political. Political deaths were the most difficult crimes to investigate. It was made worse by the atmosphere since the seizure of Government House and the declaration of a state of emergency. People halfway expected violence to erupt, and once it had, after surveying who'd been hurt and seeing no one important among the wounded or dead, everyone moved on. One Achara was worth hundreds of them.

Foreign governments from America, Canada, the UK, Japan, China, and Australia had been busy issuing advisories against unnecessary travel to Thailand. Stay away from demonstrations—the tone of the official warnings making Bangkok sound like a sister city to Gaza. People on the other side of the world would awake and, over coffee and toast, read about a man in Thailand eaten by lions as they'd slept. It was the kind of special feature news story that acted as a welcome diversion from politics. No government ever issued a travel warning about avoiding Thailand because of lions, elephants, snakes, and stingrays, though the chances of becoming a food treat or being shot by an off-duty upcountry cop who had too much whiskey and too little self-control were much higher than of getting caught up and killed in a political protest. People didn't need their government to warn them about the lions.

Colonel Pratt saw the faces around the table, and no one looked hungry, no one was joking or laughing. The children had lapsed into silence, and John-John ignored his food to play with a toy robot. Pratt and Manee had come to think of Ratana and Calvino as more of a couple than a boss and secretary, though neither one had said anything to encourage that idea. Wishful thinking was always a sufficient basis for a delusion. Manee had taken matters into her own hands by referring to Calvino as if he were the father of John-John, even though she knew perfectly well that John-John's father was a young American lawyer who'd been killed in Bangkok.

Pratt's children seemed largely disinterested in politics. The demonstrations could have been happening on the moon. It hadn't affected their lives or their studies. But lions, wild animals, fur around the mouth rimmed with coagulated human blood—that had drawn and held their attention. "I wish I'd had a video to put on YouTube," said Suchin. "You think anyone posted something?"

"Dad, did anyone take any video?" asked Suthorn, thinking her brother was quite brilliant to see the possibilities.

Colonel Pratt inhaled and exhaled like a horse that the jockey was trying to back into the racing trap. "That wouldn't be permitted."

Blocked for national security.

Suchin and Suthorn locked eyes, the way siblings signal to each other that a parent has just given them a brush-off. The children knew that no one needed permission to post a video on the Internet but, like good Thai children, would not contradict their father.

First Suchin disappeared from the table, and a couple of moments later his sister followed. Suthorn had her handbag and car keys and left the house without saying anything to her father or mother. Manee watched at the window as her daughter's car pulled out of the driveway. "The new generation," she said, turning away from the window. "Going out without a word. When they're little children, they are so happy to see you come home every day. When they grow up, you become invisible. They slip away without saying good-bye. It's what you and Vincent have to look forward to with John-John."

Manee and Ratana were at odds over the demonstration. They hadn't always disagreed. Before the coup they had attended demonstrations against the government together; they were like two sisters, committed, sure, and filled with the righteousness of their cause, and when the tanks came onto the streets of Bangkok, they believed they had won. But the coup hadn't delivered the victory everyone had hoped for—new elections—and suddenly there was a new round of demonstrations to overthrow the new government. "Liberal democracy isn't good for Thailand," said Manee. "We need to build up the people first so they cannot be fooled by corrupt politicians. Otherwise Thai people will lose who they are."

Their instinctive closeness had gone missing the day after Calvino had come back with the poster banning Nueng from the grounds of Government House. Nueng was a massage-parlor ying, a mother in her mid-twenties, who'd signed on at One Hand Clapping and had been on the job for less than a year. She had gone to Government House not to hustle a trick but to meet her sister, and had been summarily tried and sentenced to banishment by the black-shirted security guards.

None of the other yings at the massage parlor had followed the political events. It was too remote from their daily need to earn a living. So far, none of them were aware of what had happened to Nueng and why she had suddenly become quiet and withdrawn. Being labeled a prostitute in public was about the worst thing (other than being labeled a drug dealer) that could happen to any Thai woman. She was spending more and more of her time watching the children in the day-care center. Since she'd been expelled from Government House's grounds, she hadn't worked at the massage parlor at all. Ratana knew that soon Nueng would run out of money, and pride would stop her from asking for a loan.

Calvino had noticed something else that existed between the women, something that manifested itself in the cool, formal way they spoke to each other. There wasn't much he or Pratt could say or do. The thread of Thai politics was stitched from friendship obligations. People followed their friends. They didn't much care about the details of the debate. Whenever ideology raised its head, no one except for a few leaders stayed awake two minutes into such a discussion.

Once dinner was finished, Colonel Pratt and Calvino settled into the colonel's study. The colonel shut the door, pulled his saxophone from its leather case, tilted his head, and slipped the strap over his neck. His tongue touched the rubber mouthpiece, his fingers pressing against the keys. He played for five minutes, taking a Miles Davis riff to another level of despair. The selection of Miles Davis hadn't been random. Davis had been a heroin addict, and America's own war on drugs claimed Davis and Charlie Parker and a stadium full of other jazz players. They hadn't cleared the air about Calvino's involvement in the death of Tanny's sister and what it meant—everyone knew that Calvino was under his protection. Pratt found that his saxophone was the best way to put things right in the world, in a friendship, and in a heart filled with hurt.

"We asked them your question, Vincent," Colonel Pratt said, the saxophone resting on his lap.

Calvino scratched his head and wondered aloud, "I guess someone on the staff must have heard Achara scream. You get eaten by two lions, you're going to empty your lungs screaming in horror. A bloodcurdling scream like you hear in the movies. A bloodcurdling scream turns your guts with fear."

Calvino only needed a few words in Pratt's study: "Did anyone hear a scream?"

Colonel Pratt had carefully double-checked with the staff. "No one heard anything."

"There are two possibilities. Achara was either already dead or unconscious when he was dumped in with the lions," said Calvino.

The maid brought in a tray with two cups of black coffee. Only then did Colonel Pratt remove the strap from around his neck and tuck his saxophone back into the case. He sipped his coffee and waited until Calvino drank before picking up the conversation. "Maybe he had a heart attack," said Colonel Pratt.

"Do you believe that?"

"Or a stroke."

"Or he committed suicide," said Calvino, putting down the cup. "Fed himself to the lions."

"I'm trying to be open-minded, Vincent."

"Open-minded is good. But there's a limit. We've got to think about how a man is torn apart by a lion and no one hears a sound. Achara was in good health. He didn't seem depressed when I met him. And the way he was holding on to his business with Brandon Sawyer indicates he planned to be around in the future."

"We're working on all theories."

"I didn't like the look on the face of Achara's gardener." A rat-faced, grinning monkey looking for someone to turn his back before cleaning out his stash of bananas. "I got the feeling that he was holding back something."

"If people's looks were evidence, policing would be a far simpler matter. All the ones who look guilty, you lock up. All those who look innocent, you let them walk."

The colonel had, in a way, summed up the prevailing system: It functioned mostly on appearance.

Calvino checked his watch. "It's getting late. Ratana needs to put John-John to bed." He rose from his chair.

"About the sister of that Craig woman. Be careful, Vincent."

It was as close to a warning as Calvino could ever remember hearing from Pratt. He thought it would have been familiar to the woman, who'd watched two men walk into the kitchen and shoot her mother dead. The colonel saw that New York look of mild amusement cross Calvino's face, and he leaned forward, patting him on the shoulder. "You can go fast. Or slow. Ultimately you arrive, but one way takes a little longer. If that preserves harmony, we must take it, even though it may taste bitter in the back of the throat."

It wasn't clear whether Pratt was talking about Achara or Tanny's sister—he could have been talking about both of them. Calvino grinned. "Is your sax broken, or are you getting too old to play for more than five minutes?"

The words about preserving the harmony reminded him of how Chinese in attitude Pratt was—the sax, the Shakespeare quotes, the time abroad, shaping Pratt's way of understanding the world. How else could he understand it?

The half wail, half moan of Charlie Parker poured out of the sax as Calvino leaned back, thinking about harmony. Jazz had it. But it meant something else in Asia. In the nineteenth century, the British businessmen making money in the drug trade had a realization: What can we build to speed up the transportation of all this great opium? Someone must've looked over his pint glass and said, "Train." From that one word to a functioning railway, things moved incredibly fast. No one had bothered to ask the Chinese for permission to build a railway. The British had built a secret one. When the royal court found that a railroad had been covertly built, the Chinese bought the rail line from the British. The intention wasn't to run it as a railroad; they bought it so they could tear down and destroy every engine and track, reducing the lot to scrap. Nothing left was recognizable as a train system. Harmony had been restored.

That was Colonel Pratt's slow march forward, sheltering in the past, moving cautiously ahead, suspicious of outsiders with new ideas threatening structure of life that had always been. Pratt escaped through his music and reading. Most had no avenue of escape; they were caught on one side or the other, and harmony a distant dream.

The door to the study opened, and Manee peered in.

The evening had ended, and it was time for Calvino to leave. There hadn't been time to tell Pratt how Tanny's mother had gotten it into her head that Jeff, her grandson, was the reincarnation of her murdered daughter. That association had made it personal for Tanny. And as Calvino left the colonel's study, he found himself thinking of Tanny Craig and wishing she were waiting for him.

TWENTY-SIX

ON FEBRUARY 12, 2003, forty-five-year-old Surachai, his younger brother Komchai, their sixty-two-year-old cousin Paskorn, and fifty-nine-year-old Sahit, who was the village head, traveled by truck in Phetchabun province after having gone to talk with officials at the district office. Two of the men had received notices to report to the authorities the previous day. The district head said they'd been invited to clear the air. One of the men drove while another sat in the passenger seat and the two other men sat on the bed of the truck. Eighteen kilometers from the turnoff to their village, all four men were found dead. The doors of the truck had been left open. The invitation was on Surachai's body.

Like all of the other bodies, Surachai's had been dumped on the road. From the way the bodies had fallen, it looked as if they'd been lined up. One thing was for certain—the manner of their deaths. Each of the four had been shot, execution style, in the head. The guns had been close enough to their skin to leave powder burns. This happened on a public road during daylight hours. There had been witnesses who said they'd seen uniformed police kill the men. After a week, none of the witnesses could remember seeing anything. The family requested copies of the autopsy reports. They were informed the reports weren't available. Ten days later the crime evidence disappeared, including the police notice that Surachai had been sent. Komchai and Paskorn had similar letters. The police said they'd checked, but couldn't find who had issued the letters.

After the tally of people killed in the war on drugs was announced, the polls showed that the shoot-to-kill policy enjoyed a high level of public support. One university poll reported that 92 percent of respondents backed the government's approach.

The police had invited Brandon Sawyer to appear for an interview in connection with Achara's death. There were exactly two parts of this that Brandon didn't like. First, starting with the invite: You were invited to birthdays, weddings, bar mitzvahs, maybe, stretching it even to a policeman's ball, but he'd never heard of anyone getting invited to a Thai police station because someone in uniform thought you might be worth knowing. Instead they invited you if they had a hunch that you had something to do with the murder of a business partner. Second was the interview bit: You were interviewed for a job, for a bank loan, or, if you were a celebrity, by journalists and broadcasters, but cops interrogated people because they were looking for clues or, better yet, a confession. They had means of persuasion not open to a bank officer trying to collect on a bad loan.

"I'm topping up your retainer." That was the first thing Calvino heard when he picked up the phone. The next thing was the faint splashing of the yings in the pool in the background.

Calvino drew in a long breath. "What do you want?"

"Have you opened your new office bottle?"

Calvino had no intention of thanking him for the replacement bottle. "Why don't you get in the pool and swim twenty laps and call me back."

"Hold on. Don't hang up." A frantic strain colored his throaty voice. "Okay, I've got an invitation."

"Brandon, tell me what the fuck this is about."

"The cops. They've invited me for an interview."

"You applying for a job?"

"Vinny, I want you to go with me."

Calvino leaned back hard, his head banging against the headrest of his chair. He left his head there, rolling it from one side to the other, then leaned down and pulled out the office bottle and free-poured two fingers' worth of Black into a water glass. He blasted it, hiccupping like he'd swallowed a grenade. He smacked his lips and blew air into the receiver.

"They think I had something to do with Achara's death."

"Did you?"

"Are you fucking nuts?"

"That doesn't answer my question."

"I loved the guy. Why would I kill him?"

"When is the appointment?"

"Then you'll come with me?" asked Brandon. "It's tomorrow at ten."

"I'm going to regret this."

"No, it's an interview. I've been invited. What could go wrong?"

Calvino met Brandon at a coffee shop in a shopping mall near the police department. Brandon unscrewed the cap of his hip flask and topped up his coffee.

"You want a pull?" Brandon asked.

Calvino shook his head.

"You gotta be grateful living in a country where the politics gives you an ironclad reason to drink. By the way, you're invited to hear me speak tonight at the Foreign Correspondents' Club. I'm talking about our rice-growing project. Achara had planned to be on the panel. I'm a last-minute replacement. I've booked you a table. Bring a guest.

I'll need all the support I can get. That place is full of left-wingers who hate businessmen. What do you say?"

"You've got more than your share of invitations. My advice is to concentrate on the one from the cops."

"They're gonna waste my time, and for what?"

"They're going to ask you if you had any conflict with Achara."

"I loved him like a brother."

"Like Marshall loves *you*?"

Brandon frowned. "I take your point. Brotherly love isn't the way to go."

"When was the last time you saw Achara?"

Brandon pulled a diary from his briefcase and flipped through the pages. "One week ago." He looked up like a student who was expecting a gold star from the teacher.

"Where did you meet?"

"I went out to his place."

Calvino sighed. "You saw the lions?"

"I've seen them many times. He called them his babies. They were the biggest goddamned lions I'd ever seen." Brandon shivered, a gesture that reminded Calvino of Tanny's reaction to the green snake.

"What did you talk about?"

Brandon gestured using both hands. "We talked about hiring a couple of experts to manage our project. He had a doctor from China who was interested. We went over the budget, the résumés, and the timeline. We discussed Marshall, and I told him not to worry. Marshall wouldn't be a problem."

"Any arguments about hiring the guy? Or about Marshall?"

"None. That's why I liked doing business with him. No bullshit."

"Who do you think killed him?"

"Fucked if I know."

237

"You don't want to say that to the cops."

"What *should* I say?"

"You don't know enough about his other business or personal relations to give an opinion."

Brandon finished the coffee and poured another two shots into the empty cup. "His death was a tragic accident, Vinny." The way he delivered the verdict, Brandon almost sounded Thai.

"The police may have reasons to think otherwise."

"I was at my club with you, getting drunk when it happened."

That was Brandon's ace in the hole—during the time the lions had sent Achara to meet his ancient bloodline, Brandon had been in no shape to herd a couple of house cats to a litter box. In theory it was the game stopper, the point when the interrogation would end, but in Thailand every wealthy mastermind of a killing had an alibi, so it merely made the cops think there had been some good planning.

Calvino leaned forward and stopped Brandon from pouring another shot. "In Thailand you only have to re-enact the crime, not the alibi."

Three uniformed police officers were inside the interrogation room. The room was spartan—chipped paint, fluorescent lights, scuffed metal chairs, and a table with initials carved on the surface, plus a dragon and elephant. Maybe Brandon will carve a lion, thought Calvino. One of the uniforms, arms folded, stood beside the door, while another cop sat on the table, one foot planted on the floor, the other dangling as if ready to make a free kick. The third uniformed cop, who wore his sunglasses indoors—never a good sign—leaned against the wall smoking a cigarette, flicking the ash on the floor.

The cop moved off the table, walked around it, and took a chair.

"Sit down, Khun Brandon."

Still rattled, Brandon cleaned the ink from his finger pads as he lowered himself into the chair. It had been the only invitation he'd ever received where the host had fingerprinted and photographed him. Walking into the interrogation room, he winked at the translator, a young woman, who returned an icy stare, no hint of a smile. Hitting on a woman was an art—right place, right time. An interrogation room in the early afternoon violated both place and time.

"This is my lawyer, Vincent Calvino."

Calvino wasn't his lawyer, but let the phony introduction ride. He wasn't even Brandon's friend. Calvino had once been a lawyer. He had done a couple of criminal cases in New York. But that had been years ago. The interior of the room and the sight of the police had his heart galloping like a horse on steroids. Getting into a fight over his status in front of the cops would have caused complications. That didn't stop Calvino from kicking Brandon under the table.

"He can't be your lawyer," said the cop in Thai across the table. The translator explained to Brandon in English.

"Why?" He waited for the translator to finish.

The cop pointed at Calvino as if he were a heavily bruised mango in a wet market. "He's not Thai."

Brandon waied the translator, who lifted her eyes from her notepad, stared at him as if she were looking at a pedophile farang, and brushed a loose strand of hair out of her eyes.

He sheepishly grinned at her. "Tell him that Calvino's my alibi, then. Or does an alibi have to be Thai, too?"

The cop glared at him as the translator explained in Thai what Brandon had said. The failure of his irony had been obvious on the faces of the cops. That seemed to give the translator more satisfaction than it should have.

"You had an argument with Achara," the cop said in English.

"If every argument turned into a fistfight, there'd be hundreds of millions of fights every day, and if every fistfight turned into a homicide, you'd get a million murders a day. In the real business world, people mainly argue. It ends there."

Calvino slowly closed his eyes. Everything he'd told Brandon had gone out the window. He was sparring with the police. That was a battle no one outside the movies ever won. The rule was, never talk to the police. Except that rule was difficult to keep in Thailand, where the police used all means to make a suspect talk. The preliminary fingerprinting and photo session had wound up Brandon; that was a part of the deal—humiliate the person in small ways, haul him into a small room crowded with cops, and watch him fall apart. Cops weren't stupid. They knew how to break open someone like Brandon like a piñata and wait until all the secrets tumbled out.

"Is that how your argument with Achara ended?"

Brandon looked dazed. "I never said we had an argument."

"You said arguments turn into murder."

"I was making a joke."

"You think murder is a joke?" The cop had switched back into Thai. The technique of switching from Thai to English and back again sometimes worked to disorient the suspect. Brandon gestured for the translator to continue doing her job.

Luckily, he'd been drinking with Calvino, pulling yings onto his lap during the time the murder had happened, or they might have thought he had something to do with Achara's death. They were going through the motions because they had to, and nailing a farang for the murder would mean recognition, promotions, medals, and a sigh of relief that it hadn't been a Thai who'd killed Achara. The translator said, "You kill because it's funny?"

Calvino shook his head. If translation were an art, this translator was a graffiti artist. Calvino leaned over and whispered to Brandon what the cop had asked.

"I didn't say that," said Brandon. "Lions aren't a joke. I hate big animals. Besides, I'm American. We love guns. We invented them. We use guns to kill. Not fucking lions. That's just plain gross. I don't care who you are. Only savages kill people with lions. Or Romans. I'm going to have nightmares for the rest of my life. Achara was my friend. One of the few friends I could ever count on. We both collected Thai coins. I sold him coins, and he sold coins to me. He knew everything about the history of Thai coins."

"You killed him for his coin collection," said the cop.

"Was Achara's coin collection missing?" asked Calvino.

"You had a business conflict with Khun Achara," said the cop, taking another tack.

"They're fishing," Calvino whispered loud enough for the translator to hear.

The translator shot Calvino a hostile look, the kind that says, you'll pay a price. Calvino smiled and nodded.

Colonel Pratt had stayed away from the interrogation. He'd told Calvino he wouldn't attend. The Department of Special Investigations had been assigned to handle the case, and part of the reason Pratt thought this had happened was his friendship with Calvino. In normal circumstances the case would have gone to the Crime Suppression Department. And these cops turned up the heat, circling Brandon in the room, holstered guns brushing against his shoulder as they walked close to him.

Cops use intimidation because it works. It makes even the most smart-assed suspect sweat. And Brandon dabbed his forehead with a handkerchief, a large white billowy cotton rag that was soon drenched.

"You put him in the cage with the lions," said the cop as if it were a matter of fact.

"Not that, no. I would kill another human being, but I am fucking afraid of lions. And I was with Mr. Calvino. Why don't you ask him? He's sitting here. That would clear up everything. Wouldn't it?"

He sought reassurance from Calvino. "Can't you say something?"

But Calvino understood that holding back played to Brandon's ultimate interest: Walking out of the room and going home. Calvino shrugged. "The police will ask the questions they want. That's how it works." Then he repeated the same thing in Thai, not trusting the translator to butcher it into something like, "The police can do whatever they want with you. And there's nothing you can do."

It would have been true as statements go, but it wasn't what he wanted the police to believe had come out of his mouth. For the next half hour, the interrogator asked Brandon about how he'd spent the afternoon on the day Achara died. The time he'd left his house, the route his driver had taken, whether they'd stopped, if he'd made any phone calls, the time he signed into the club, what he'd ordered, where he'd sat, and what he'd talked about with Vincent Calvino.

"Your brother in America didn't like Khun Achara."

Brandon shrugged. "I don't like my brother."

"Blood is thicker than water."

"People always say that. But when you're thirsty, what do you drink? Water."

"Mr. Calvino, you've lived in Thailand a long time. You know that if you lie today, this will be a big problem. Not just for you, but for your friends."

He was threatening Colonel Pratt, dragging him into the equation.

"Check with the staff of Mr. Sawyer's club. I signed in, and so did Mr. Sawyer."

The cops huddled around the interrogator, a thick cloud of blue cigarette smoke hanging like a collective halo above their heads. "We will prepare something for Mr. Sawyer to sign."

After Brandon heard the translation, he said, "I ain't signing a fucking thing."

"Mr. Sawyer will be pleased to sign the document," said Calvino in Thai.

The translator shot him a dirty look. He flashed a winning smile. "I'd say that was a fair translation, wouldn't you?"

The cops and the translator left the room, closing the door on Sawyer and Calvino.

"What did you tell them?" asked Brandon.

"You'd sign the document."

"Shit, Calvino. In Thai?"

"They will do an English version. You sign that one."

"What if it's a confession to murder?"

"It won't be."

"How will I know?"

"Brandon, it's gonna be in English. You can read English, can't you?"

Brandon looked around the room. "You think it's bugged?"

"Does a lion like fresh meat?"

An hour later the cops and the translator returned carrying papers. They had hammered out a statement in English and passed it to Brandon. "Sign here," said the cop, handing him a pen.

"I want to read it," said Brandon.

The cop's face turned stormy, and he looked like he wanted to belt Brandon. "You think we make mistake?"

Calvino gestured before Brandon could reply. "Of course he doesn't think there's any mistake. He only wants to make certain nothing was left out."

"That's what I was going to say," said Brandon.

Together they read through the three pages of typescript. "Doesn't anyone edit this shit?" asked Brandon.

Calvino kicked him under the table. It didn't matter that every third word had a unique spelling and the grammar and syntax looked like they'd been boiled in a pressure cooker. Calvino asked the police for the Thai version. It was fished out of the file and slid over the top of the carved-up table. He would let Ratana and Colonel Pratt have a look later. "Can Mr. Sawyer keep a copy of the statement?"

"No problem," said the cop.

The English version had a slightly different take on what Brandon had said. "I scare of big lion. I no like. Big headache. I think I use gun much better. No bad ghost with gun. Murder like funny joke." The last words were the translator at her artful best; the English translation was passed to Brandon, who broke out laughing. The statement read like English subtitles flashed under a Thai movie.

"I used to be funny," he said. "But I was never that funny."

Not that no, he wouldn't kill another human being, but no, he was fucking afraid of lions. That was the statement in a nutshell, and Brandon Sawyer scribbled his signature at the bottom and slid it back across the table.

"Now sign the Thai version," said the cop.

Calvino shook his head. "He can't sign what he can't read. That's why he signed the English version. Unless you're unhappy with the translation?"

The cop pursed his lips, staring bullet holes into Calvino. "Don't leave Thailand," he said. "Either of you."

TWENTY-SEVEN

THERE HAD BEEN a long, noisy line at the buffet. Throngs of journalists, NGOs, embassy people, narrowly avoided colliding as they wove in and out, carrying plates loaded high with pasta, chicken, rice, vegetables, dumplings, pork balls, and *somtam*. Some of the meat had been harvested from no apparent known species. Someone in the line mumbled, "Genetically altered rabbit." Another replied, "Mutant cats." The line was divided between those who giggled and those who took the comments as sober cultural observations.

Calvino and Tanny found themselves at a white-cloth-covered table—a chrome stand held a piece of paper designating it as Number 9—within arm's reach of the upright piano. Calvino hovered for a moment, looking around the room. The table had been booked under Achara's name. His friends had failed to show up, and Calvino inherited the table. If it had been a nightclub, Calvino could have turned his chair and played some Ray Charles—if only he'd learned to play the piano. He put his plate on the table and sat down. Tanny sat on the opposite side, her back to the head table and the stage. It was as if she were happy to avoid eye contact with Brandon Sawyer.

The head table, positioned near the stage—behind which hung a large blue banner announcing THE FOREIGN

CORRESPONDENTS' CLUB OF THAILAND—was occupied by the panelists, club officials, and several journalists and VIPs.

Calvino's table, wedged like a bread stick between the head table and the piano, had a clear view of the stage. Brandon Sawyer sat a knife's throw away. He leaned back in his chair and nodded at Calvino, pointing at Tanny and shaking his head. He'd fully recovered from the sweat-drenched ghostly figure who had left the interrogation room shaken. From where Calvino sat, he had a view through half-open blinds out the window overlooking the balcony. Smokers, the bored, the conspiratorial, and the depressed congregated on the balcony, watching the rain streak through the canyon of high-rises on Ploenchit Road. Most of the tables at the club were filled. In the back were the bar and the pool table converted into a buffet table. Calvino recognized some of the faces among the crowd, and the odd tank commander assigned to protect Thai political operatives. The bar was randomly divided between the red-wine drinkers and the serious drunks.

Brandon, who occupied a place at the speakers' table, sat squeezed between the club vice president, a balding farang with a Lenin goatee, and a Thai newspaper journalist who never stopped smiling. Brandon worked his meaty fist around a whiskey glass and flexed his arm like the slide on a pump-action shotgun. The organizers had worked to isolate Brandon from the two other speakers, a member of the opposition and a green activist, both of whom avoided him. Every so often Brandon turned around in his seat, glanced across the room at Calvino, gestured at the other panelists, and rolled his eyes. Tanny caught his attention, and Brandon waved at her as if she were an old friend. She waved back before lowering her gaze and studying her plate. Maintaining contact with Brandon was tiring. He held up his glass like a quarterback making a Statue of Liberty fake, catching the attention of a waiter, which hadn't been difficult, as Brandon had repeated the action several times in less than half an hour.

On the elevated platform was a long table with name cards that identified each member of the panel. Brandon Sawyer was on the far right; Virote, the opposition member of Parliament, in the center; and on the left the green activist, Scott Baker, slightly built, red-haired, with a well-kept short beard, gold-rimmed glasses like an investment banker's, the classic eighteenth-century minor-royalty bone structure. Baker looked to be late thirties, early forties. A number of tables were filled with his friends and supporters.

"Brandon asked if you were going to take notes for his brother," said Calvino.

"He's a headcase," Tanny replied.

Calvino thought the Thai police had reached a similar conclusion before cutting him loose.

"He plans not to sell the company," said Calvino. "He told me that he has another Thai partner lined up. This one doesn't keep lions."

Tanny sighed, looking over the crowd. "To spite Marshall."

"What if he thinks it's a good opportunity?"

"Like a Somali pirate sizing up a passing freighter."

"That's capitalism."

"What does he know about genetically engineered rice?"

"We'll find out tonight."

"Brandon may expose the company to bad publicity by doing this. He should have asked Marshall first. This is a not a small thing, Vincent."

"We're all looking for something," said Calvino. "And when we find it, it's not really what we thought it was going to be."

Drawing no response, he ate in silence

Tanny picked at her food without much appetite; her attention had been drawn to the framed photographs on the opposite wall, an exhibition of war and natural disaster—a wrinkled old Vietnamese woman; bleached human bones in the dirt; three wailing women, white paper masks hanging around their throats; a family standing in front of rubble that had been their house; a Chinese tank flying a red flag. The one she couldn't take her eyes off showed a woman with red hair, mouth frozen in anguish, holding a framed photo of her smiling daughter—in front of a destroyed building. Calvino saw Tanny study the photo; lost in thought, her mind seem to float away. She was in the room but not in the room.

"You've been staring at that photograph. You must like it."

She looked away, searching Calvino's expression and trying to assess if he was being ironic. "Looking for one thing and finding another. Like when you were talking about finding my mother."

Calvino speared a carrot with his fork. He figured that the mother had known "how things went" as well as anyone who had taken up arms against the government, had fought in the jungles, only to return to society and find that her daughter had vanished and to have the second one killed in a police ambush years later. "I was thinking about what your mother's looking for at the demonstration."

"Nothing will stop her from finding the men who killed my sister."

"You inherited her fire. An emotion that can make you rich in one country can also get you killed in another."

"My mother isn't afraid of anyone."

"She's a brave woman."

Tanny had something else on her mind. "Ratana keeps saying how easy it was for her to trace my mother. Maybe she thinks I didn't try before. Which isn't true."

"She understands."

"You told her?"

Calvino nodded. "Yeah, I told her."

"I was going to, but …"

"You were afraid she wouldn't believe you."

"I never had any reason to question my parents," she said.

Tanny's adoptive parents had instilled in her their own version of how they came to adopt her, and it squared with what her real mother told her. The people she'd called Mom and Dad hadn't lied to her about the circumstances; it was just that they didn't have all the facts. Her American mother had said that Tanny's natural parents had been killed in a firefight in the north of Thailand. Her mother had been a nurse, her father a doctor. And both had been killed in action when the military overran their position. They had adopted Tanny believing that she was an orphan, to give her a fair chance in life. She hadn't searched for her Thai parents because it would have been pointless—she'd been told they were dead. Initially she thought that Calvino was wasting his time trying to track down two ghosts. But she let him try. She had nothing to lose—only a story to confirm.

"You're the first man who didn't ask me about my first name."

Calvino tilted his head, smiled. "What's with Tanny?"

"Tanny is my adopted mother's family name. Craig comes from my father's side. My mother said that made me special. If they'd adopted a boy, he'd have been Craig Tanny. Funny, isn't it? How my parents decided on my name."

"That's a new one. It makes you special," said Calvino.

Tanny Craig's ambiguity was complete. She'd lost her birth identity and had received, like a heart transplant, a new one cobbled together from two American families. Her story confirmed one of Calvino's laws: What may be a dinner-table anecdote for you can represent an entire life for someone else.

TWENTY-EIGHT

VIROTE, WHITE SHIRT and dark business suit, pushed back his reading glasses as he droned on about the importance of protecting people's health, and launched into the government's six-point program for national security. At just about point two into his lecture, even the wine drinkers at the bar switched to whiskey. Nothing he said had anything to do with the topic, but no one seemed to mind. The moderator pointed at his watch when Virote seemed stalled at point three and factions of drunks in the back openly threatened revolt. Virote wrapped up his little speech by saying he'd be happy to explain the remaining points during question time. The thought horrified the audience.

The next panelist, Thanom, whose catering experience at Government House, in a week, had qualified him as a food safety expert spoke next. He ended his speech by holding up and shaking a plastic hand clapper at the audience, and he appeared endlessly surprised when no one replied with a hand clapper.

By the time Scott Baker's turn came, the moderator said, "We're running late. Would you limit your remarks to ten minutes, Mr. Baker?"

Brandon Sawyer leaned forward, blew into the microphone. "He can use my time if he wants."

The audience laughed.

"Free," he whispered into the microphone, drawing more laughter.

Brandon's presence had drawn cold stares earlier in the evening. But his showmanship was gradually winning over the audience, and the more popular Brandon became, the more emotional it made Scott Baker. "You, sir, are a bioterrorist."

"I ate the same thing as you tonight. Am I in trouble?"

Again the drunks at the back of the bar laughed the hardest, supporting the man they clearly embraced as a fellow reprobate. Calvino leaned forward over the table. "Brandon's going to do stand-up. This should be interesting."

Tanny shook her head, whispering, "Is he drunk?"

"I don't have a baseline to answer that."

"Look at him. You begin to understand why Marshall wants to sell the company," she said.

The moderator raised his hand. "Scott, you've been involved as an activist against GMO for over ten years. Can you explain why the rice project planned by Mr. Sawyer's company should cause us concern?"

Scott cleared his throat, glanced at his watch. "I'll try," he said.

Brandon mouthed at the audience, "I'll try, if I can ever get this frog out of my throat—before I croak"

The bar had somehow organized into their laugh brigade. For people who lived exclusively on drink, they could be smug about food safety, thought it was a joke, seducing overworked sober people who were food-obsessed. These people didn't eat food. So long as the booze wasn't poisoned, they had no beef.

Baker waited for a break in the background chatter before leaping back in. "Excuse me. Consider this possibility: Someone injects a virus or an antibiotic-resistant gene into rice grown in Thailand? This becomes a public-health issue that we need to address. Is the political system strong enough against the large corporate giants who will exploit the relatively lax laws in Thailand?" He spoke like an Englishman who'd diverted his passion for sex and football into battling genetically engineered foods.

Like a cat tracking the movement of a bird, Scott pointed at Brandon as he continued his speech. "Your Defense Department is funding GM rice to make it a military-grade weapon system. Deliver infertility to a billion people. That's the evil you represent."

Brandon took a drink of water and grimaced. "Seems someone put water into my water glass. If I'm evil, does that mean I can't get a real drink?"

He had the entire back of the room hooting.

"And they're using clowns like you to front for them," Baker snapped. "You make everyone laugh so they don't take this discussion seriously."

"In the land of *sanuk,* 'serious' is a seriously bad word," said Brandon. "We don't want to create a new species of mutants, or superman soldiers, or make small children infertile. The farmers have better yields, pay less for fertilizer, use less oil, and the rice can be warehoused longer. Our technology adds vitamin A and iron and calcium. The Chinese showed that this was possible with 'golden rice,' which saves about a million kids' lives every year in the developing world. The health-cost savings alone to the Thai government is huge. The kids are better able to compete in sports and learn when in school. I don't know about you, but if that's evil, we should be fearful of good."

"You failed to mention the allergic reactions that children have had with the golden rice. No one knows how those changes work on human DNA. And we don't know what happens when your rice seeds find their way to other fields. You are enabling a mono-agricultural system that will destroy the Thai rice industry. The point is, you have no idea what dangers you are unleashing on the planet."

Brandon held up his hand and waved at the moderator. "Can I ask a question?"

The moderator nodded.

"Mr. Baker, what did you study at school?"

"I take that to mean university," said Scott, his English accent adding the tone of condescension. But he was up against a pro who was used to dealing with drunken hecklers in a New York nightclub.

"If you got that far."

"I read civil engineering. I've worked in Africa, Asia, and the Middle East as a water-systems specialist."

"What did that teach you about genetics, DNA, and biotechnology? Just because you know how to build a lighthouse, that doesn't mean you know anything about the shipping business." Brandon quietly unscrewed his flask and tipped the neck over the rim of his glass, screwed the cap back on, and took a long sip. More applause echoed from the bar.

"And what are *your* qualifications, other than money?"

"I have two degrees in biotechnology. A master's from Caltech and a Ph.D. from MIT. But I couldn't tell you how to build a lighthouse. An investor came to me because he knew my background. He asked me to help Thailand. I said I would."

"The point is, the evidence on GMO shows beyond a reasonable doubt that it is a ticking time bomb."

"No, but food prices skyrocketing *are* a ticking time bomb. We have a solution. You have fear. That's not a solution, that's burying your head in the sand and doing nothing."

"We can't risk allowing Frankenfood loose on the ecosystem."

"Did you have the buffet? I had the buffet. The rice we're planting won't be any riskier than those chicken legs. You have a higher risk of getting bird flu from the buffet than infertility from our rice."

"Accidents happen," said Scott.

Brandon flinched, going silent, his expression somber as he stared at his hands. Scott's reply had triggered the thought of Achara. "Accidents can be prevented," he finally said. "It takes time and money. Our company has invested both. We plan to avoid accidents."

Brandon, after the program ended, walked over to Calvino's table, giving him a pretend punch to the shoulder. "Let's get out of here and find a place where we can drink. Bring along Ms. Dick Tracy—she can talk into her shoe and report back to Marshall about the evening."

"He's taking me to see my mother and father," she said.

Calvino liked her style, and the line hit Brandon harder than the punch he'd stuck into Brandon's gut inside the office. "Yeah, Tanny's right. We're going to meet her parents."

Brandon winked, pulled Calvino a few feet away from Tanny, and whispered, "This is getting serious. Out of hand. What do you think?"

"It's not what *you* think," said Calvino.

"It's far more kinky." Brandon patted him on the back. "I never took you as a guy who'd fall for another sleuth. Go on, slug me again. This time I'll have witnesses to your brutality."

"Brandon, no question you can work an audience until you own them. Like tonight—I saw it. But when you go head-to-head, one-on-one, you stumble, shoot yourself in the foot."

"Let me give you some advice: Never get involved with a woman who wants to be best man at her own wedding," Brandon said, and turned away.

TWENTY-NINE

THE WIND, HEAVY with rain, caught Tanny's umbrella, turning it inside out as they reached the gate on Phitsanulok Road. Lights shone from the upstairs windows inside Government House. As they entered the compound, Calvino picked up on the different attitude of the demonstrators. After dark they were easily spooked, moving along the paths with an edgy suspicion of strangers, avoiding shadows, looking over their shoulders, giving anyone not dressed in yellow a long, hard stare. They walked past several security men armed with a variety of improvised weapons—butcher knives, cooking pots, golf clubs—with a preference for irons over woods. Calvino calculated they were about a five-iron chip shot from the pharmacy, and followed the pathway that ran along the front of Government House. The walls were plastered with anti-government posters and crude cartoons of the ousted prime minister with devil-like fangs and horns.

Twice security guards stopped them. They directed their questions to Tanny until it was clear that if they wanted to communicate, they had to speak Thai to the farang. They reacted with confusion and suspicion, their knuckles white as they clutched their weapons. But Calvino told them in Thai that Tanny was an American and had come to the compound to visit her mother. And the mother, Mem, was one of the heroes of the demonstration. He explained he'd come along as her translator. The security people finally let them go, but seemed unconvinced that they weren't spies.

An old woman appeared from the shadows and tied a yellow headband around Calvino's forehead. He leaned down and let her adjust it so that it didn't cover his eyes.

"How do I look?" he asked Tanny.

"Like the pirate in Peter Pan."

"Welcome to Never Never Land. Is that what I'm supposed to say to Wendy?"

"Keep the umbrella up. That's enough."

It was slow going in the rain and dark, avoiding puddles and being splashed by others who hurried as if chased by ghosts before disappearing into the night. More security staff stopped them, and again Calvino explained the purpose of their presence as Tanny shook her head and looked agitated. She had a New Yorker's lack of patience for bureaucratic roadblocks that slowed her down. Each time, Mem's name had proved to be the right passport. Everyone seemed to know who she was. And for Calvino, he was happy enough to be waved along without blocking a three-iron swung at his head. Patience was finishing the course without getting injured.

The ongoing state of emergency hadn't changed life inside the compound. Neither the senior officers in the police nor in the army had the stomach to use tear gas, let alone M16s against the grandmothers, office workers, students, housewives, and retirees camping at Government House. They had rightly figured that they'd be blamed for a bloodbath, and no officer wanted to load up an elephant train's worth of the bad karma that would result from shedding a fellow Thai's blood. Calvino studied the situation and shrugged; what spark would ignite the killing? No one ever knew in advance what caused the first man to aim his rifle and open fire. As they walked in the rain,

Calvino thought about Achara's lions. True violence meant lions tearing you apart. But here tonight, with everything soaked from the rain, with nothing looking flammable and no wild animals, Calvino thought the chances were they'd get in and out without incident.

Tanny squeezed his hand as the path darkened. "Are we lost?" she asked.

"Everything looks different in the dark. A couple of minutes and you'll see the Red Cross sign."

She nodded, pointing at a row of abandoned tents. "Maybe people are going home. Living rough like this in the rain is miserable. No one could blame them for leaving."

"Or they've gone to sit in front of the main stage to watch the band."

The sound of the guitars and drums rolled from the distant stage.

It was nearly midnight by the time they reached the pharmacy.

Music blared over loudspeakers, interrupted by an emotional speech by one of the leaders about corruption and betrayal. Midnight in the rain, but those onstage had kept the fire burning in the belly.

"The government's authority doesn't reach inside here," said Calvino.

"It's surreal," she said.

"It's Thai politics. Food, pop music, rants. Everyone feels at home. They call each other brother and sister, mother and father, grandfather and grandmother."

She shook her head.

"The government can't use Government House. So they're going to set up operation at the airport."

While there was technically a state of emergency, no one in the government, the police, or the military had taken any responsibility for said emergency, and once a certain delicate moment had passed, once the crowd settled in for the duration, it was like a boxing match with no one able to deliver the knockout blow.

"Why the airport? Are they planning to leave Thailand?"

Calvino laughed. "No, they are waiting for something to happen."

"Waiting for what?"

"A miracle."

The choice of the airport had been an inspired one; it fit the image projected: A government in transit, on its way to another destination. Thais predicted that the government would collapse or be removed. At least the government had one good plan—it was only a runway away from climbing aboard a Boeing 777 and flying off to England and setting up a government in exile.

Tanny's mood had relaxed by the time they reached the pharmacy. She freed her hand from Calvino's and waied the woman behind the counter.

"We're here," she said.

Calvino stopped cold.

"Something wrong?" Tanny asked.

He walked ahead, around the orange cones and the rope, to the back where the cots were folded out. Manee, Pratt's wife, sat on a plastic chair, a mug of tea balanced on her knee. Next to Manee was Ratana, who smiled, looking at the yellow band around his head, nodding as he walked up. Both women were dressed in yellow, each one sporting a yellow band. He pulled up two more chairs and sat in one.

Calvino faced Manee. He shook his head and grinned.

"Hello, Vincent," said Manee. "We've been expecting you."

"Maybe one of you can tell me what's going on. Does Pratt know you're here?" He could tell from her expression that Pratt probably didn't directly know. He might have picked up a possible clue, but that was work; he was at home, and he had absolutely no desire to resolve contradictions—such as she's in the house but she's not in the house.

Tanny waied her mother, then embraced her, sitting down beside her on the cot.

"This is my daughter, Bum," Mem told Manee, her face beaming with pride.

Ratana's umbrella was still dripping against a plastic chair. Calvino figured that they hadn't been waiting long enough for an umbrella to dry. But long enough for Mem to have covered Tanny's fate as an infant adopted by Americans and the second daughter murdered in the war against drugs.

Manee held out her hand, and Tanny was grateful for the gesture.

"And this is …"

Manee nodded at Calvino. "Yes, this is Vincent. "We're late. They're waiting in the meeting room," said Manee.

"Who are we meeting?" asked Calvino.

"General Suchart's wife, Khunying Tamarine. The meeting starts at three minutes after midnight," she said.

Calvino raised an eyebrow. "Sounds like Khun Tamarine's astrologer has been working the charts."

"I like midnight meetings. I like astrologers. I'll not cause you to lose to face."

The Thais loved meetings, couldn't get enough of them—talking, eating, joking—they were a kind of party that ended with a decision to hold another one. The possibility of losing face was about the worst thing for a Thai going to a meeting with an influential person. Meetings with the police, though, didn't always turn out for the best. It was a thought Calvino kept to himself. Ratana dropped back and walked beside him as he'd followed alone, guarding the women ahead of him. Their umbrellas touched as they walked with the easy rhythm of a couple, each accustomed to the other's walk.

"It wasn't easy for Manee to arrange the meeting. General Suchart. He has authority over the investigation of what happened."

They followed the path in front of Government House around to the back. The building looked medieval at night, haunted, light pooling in the shadows, rain falling, dripping from the eaves. Calvino walked alongside Ratana. "Manee did this for you, too," said Calvino. "It shows how much she values you as a friend."

Ratana shook her head. "No, she did it for you. You are her husband's friend. You asked him for something he couldn't give you. That is a bad thing for a Thai. Manee saw how her husband had suffered because he couldn't help his friend. And yes, maybe a little, she knew it would make me feel better after what happened to Nueng."

"I don't like it."

"The general's wife can help Mem."

It was that hope which was dangerous. Hope based on a connection through a friend. Ad hoc, uncertain, open-ended—lottery-ticket hope.

"What if it backfires? What happens to Manee and Pratt?" Calvino asked.

Ratana had been carrying a wicker basket in her free hand.

"Give the basket to the general's wife and follow that with a respectful wai. The one I taught you to give."

Ratana smiled and walked ahead, joining Manee.

At the back entrance, two security men blocked the path. Manee told them who she was and whom she was having a meeting with, and after one of the men confirmed permission with someone on his cell phone, the security detail let them pass into the main building. People talked in the corridors, ate and slept in the corridors. It looked like an emergency shelter zone after a cyclone had blown through, dragging along a two-mile trail of debris. People cocooned inside sheets and blankets. If the outside looked derelict, in here the evidence of bodies curled up, still and deep in sleep, littering the floors, made it look as if a massacre had just been carried out.

Calvino walked beside Tanny. "Do you know what to expect?" he asked her.

"My mother and I are meeting a woman who can help us find my sister's murderer," she said with the firmness of a guard shutting a prison cell's door.

He thought, Will this general's wife promise to find and catch Tanny's sister's killer? That kind of promise had more back doors than a Chinese gambling den. They proceeded like an overseas tour group through the foyer and climbed the stairs to the second floor. One of the security guys had taken point, walking with a firm, military clip—all that was missing was the little flag that guides wave overhead so their charges don't get lost—Manee marching behind, shaking her umbrella as she followed him like a raw recruit locking onto her platoon leader. They passed through the door of a conference room, where the general's wife and two other women sat at a table. Several candles were lit, decorating the battered conference table. The room looked like a good place to hold an inquisition. Security guards against two walls, looking like golf pros at a seedy Chonburi clubhouse. The judges seated at the table.

The woman in the middle, a small, thin woman of about fifty in a blouse and a yellow jacket, looking like the girl's racquetball team coach, spoke to the woman on her left before turning and speaking to the woman on her right. Then she went quiet, watching the stream of visitors, fighting back a yawn but failing as a crinkled web of lines scattered like buckshot around her eyes.

"That's Khunying Tamarine," Ratana said in a hushed tone. Her husband was rumored to having connections with one of the private militias financed by an upcountry powerbroker.

Tamarine looked exhausted, like a Marine who'd been on the front line a week too long. She nervously fingered a pen as they took their places by the table. The impact crater of age had buried most of Tamarine's girlish features—the pouting lips turned down like a sadly-made bed—that once resided on a face that still retained dignity as it dispensed with beauty. Unofficial meetings made for tension.

The first ten minutes were spent sorting out names and family connections to power and influence. After the rank was established it took only a couple of minutes to follow the power to the general's wife. "Is this the dead girl's sister?" she asked, looking at Tanny.

Manee corrected the error, nodding at Tanny. "This is her older sister. This is the mother." She looked at Mem. "She works at the nurses' station." She didn't bother with a list of distinguished connections because Mem's family had none.

"We've heard very good things about Mem. We are pleased with your valuable contribution to our cause. And if it weren't for that, I wouldn't be here tonight."

Mem smiled and waied the *khunying*. "It is my honor," she said. *Sakdina* rituals ran in the blood, humbling an ex-communist before a general's wife.

Tamarine's tired eyes shifted to Calvino. No man got to be a general without a wife talented in sweeping the terrain for traps; it became instinctive, something that could be done in her sleep—though from this woman's look, it didn't appear that the khunying was getting much bedtime.

She had to make a decision: Was this foreigner a possible hole that might swallow her and her husband in one belching gulp? She kept an eye on Calvino as if waiting for him to do or say something. Calvino stepped forward, keeping his head half bowed like a medieval courtier. He reached the table, using both hands to offer the basket filled with mangoes, bananas, kiwi fruit, and oranges. She nodded for him to set the basket on the table. Calvino positioned it on the table in front of the khunying so she could get a closer look. She moved one of the candles to the side of the basket and examined it. It was a dangerous game. If the demonstration succeeded in bringing down the government, the factions in the department who had supported the leaders would be rewarded; if it failed, then the police would need deniability. Wives were a perfect foil. No man was expected to control his wife, and her actions could be distanced from his in a way that every man understood. But they also knew how the game was played.

"He's our good friend. My husband has known him many years," said Manee. What she really meant in this roundabout way was clear: "I can vouch for Khun Vincent."

"And so can I," said Ratana.

Manee introduced Ratana as someone from a good family.

Looking around the room, he understood what was at stake. Manee and Ratana were offering themselves as guarantors; if something happened to cause damage because of Vincent Calvino, then they'd both be held accountable. And what was a guarantor other than a specialized type of hostage? On the scorecard of guilt, Manee and Ratana would have received a perfect score. In an odd way, it was almost reassuring to have a farang in the room to blame if whatever they planned fell apart, blew up, or faded away into nothingness.

Without asking him, two Thais had pledged their family as a guarantee for his good conduct. He felt imaginary handcuffs on his wrists, leg irons around his ankles, and a gag tight around his mouth. The general's wife smiled at Manee and Ratana. She motioned for everyone to sit at the table. At last Tamarine had been satisfied that Vincent Calvino understood the deal—and how things worked if the deal were broken.

"Do you have a Thai traffic lesson that explains what's happening?" Tanny asked in a whisper.

He smiled, his eyes hovering for a moment before they returned to Tamarine. "It's about the social status of someone passing on a blind turn. Rank determines who walks away, who gets left in the road."

Mem took the chair nearest to Tamarine and her two friends.

"Everyone is grateful for your work at the pharmacy," said Tamarine, repeating herself as though the purpose of the meeting had been to congratulate Mem. "If I can do anything to help, I can try."

Mem turned, nodded at Tanny. "This is my first daughter, from America. I've told her that you can find justice for my family."

Tamarine showed no emotion or acknowledgment, looking at Mem like a poker player glancing up from her cards. Manee had briefed Tamarine on the basic facts of the daughter's murder during the war on drugs. Tamarine's first comment was to pronounce a judgment about Tanny's appearance. "*Ouab un,*" Tamarine said. The others laughed. Mem explained to Tanny that the Thai saying referred to someone who'd grown up eating a lot of beef, milk, and eggs. The kind of diet that ensured a woman would develop a voluptuous body. Once the small talk was over, they reached the point where dealing with Tanny's dead sister could no longer be avoided.

All eyes in the room were on Tanny as she talked about how much her mother had suffered, and how she herself had gone through the evidence to see that clearly there had been a gross injustice. The general's wife never stopped smiling. How much of Tanny's fast, clipped English Tamarine understood wasn't clear, since by her expression she indicated that everything was understandable. And, in an odd way, it probably was. When Tanny finished, she sat back in her chair. A moment later the conversation switched back into Thai. Tanny discovered the hard way the importance of the language barrier—finding herself on the outside looking in, confused and frustrated, like a child shut out by the adults.

If Tanny had expected help, she would have been disappointed. She waited for her mother to lay out all the facts about her sister's death, not knowing that that wasn't the way things worked. It wasn't necessary. Tamarine had no reason to hold a meeting unless she'd been convinced that Mem's daughter had been a victim of an extrajudicial killing and that she might find a way to reward the mother who'd devoted her time to the cause with an inquiry. And there was another benefit—Manee would be in her debt, meaning that her husband, Colonel Pratt, would also owe the general a debt.

"Please, help my mother," said Tanny.

Tamarine smiled, and in English said, "I know how difficult it has been for your family. In Thailand we all love our family. And we feel hurt when something bad happens."

Real power and justice in a criminal matter weren't drawn from the conclusiveness of evidence gathered at the crime scene—the outcome was determined by the importance of the person who left the evidence, his connections and influence, which trumped eyewitness accounts. Calvino figured the chances were that Tamarine's husband might gain by going against the senior officer who had approved the murder. Whatever happened next, it would have little to do with how justice worked in other places.

Everyone had feet of clay, but on close inspection, some people were clay all the way up to the top of their heads. And it was this kind of people who were the first to be tipped over and hauled away, the ones swallowed up by a crack.

Nong, a thirty-two-year-old, had a lovely smile. Her friends complimented her on her clothes sense. She rose early in the morning and fed the monks who filed past her house. Nong had never missed a payment on her red Toyota, which she used to take her children to and from school. Her husband was named Gung. He worked for a local real-estate company. He was liked by his colleagues and had good relations with his neighbors. The police said Nong had been a major methamphetamine dealer.

Nong was shot in her dining room, in Korat, on February 11, 2003. She was eating lunch with two neighbors. They had been discussing a project to raise money to build a new sala in the grounds of the wat where the monks who came past their houses each morning lived.

The neighbors said that an "unidentified man" arrived in a pickup truck, walked inside the convenience store that was part of the house, and shot Nong five times. Police refused to pursue the case, saying they'd found court documents in Nong's house indicating that she had acted as a guarantor for more than two hundred drug suspects who had been released on bail. Her guarantee had been called in. There was no need to proceed further.

The ex-prime minister said that the first war on drugs had made the Thai public happy with his administration.

THIRTY

BRANDON DRANK WITH the recoil action of a double-barreled sixteen-gauge shotgun shoved into his mouth. Or so an American freelance travel writer reported. The reporter's name was Kincaid. After the crowd had thinned, leaving only a scattering of hardcore drinkers, Brandon heard his name being called. His fan club sat around a table, and they waved him over. Brandon crossed through a handful of stragglers. A woman asked him about a set of cancer-rate statistics she'd read in *The Guardian*.

"There's a link between increased cancer and genetically modified corn. It could be the same for rice. I'd like your opinion."

"Corn, rice, peaches, lobster—lady, you can find statistics that show anything will cause cancer," Brandon said as he brushed past. "Eyeliner, lipstick, bikini panties."

"I don't think that really answers—"

But he'd already sat down at the table, Kincaid slapping him on the back and introducing him to Harry, a wire-service hack from Berlin, and Ian, a TV cameraman from Denmark. Brandon liked the back of the club better than the front, with its TV cameras, platform, and guest table.

Kincaid bought Brandon a drink. When the whiskey arrived, Kincaid watched in awe as Brandon performed his seal-swallowing-a-whole-herring trick. Most of crowd had left the club. The hardcore drinkers had also dwindled, leaving only Brandon's fan club and a few other stragglers. The woman who worried about cancer walked up to the table.

"Can I get you a drink?" Brandon asked her.

"I don't drink," she said.

"I'm told that's good. Me, I eat genetically modified food and drink. I'll take my chances. Sure you won't have a drink?"

She had turned and walked away. Brandon shrugged and caught the eye of the skinny head barman, signaling another round.

"She's afraid of cancer," whispered Brandon.

"She doesn't trust the Chinese," said Ian, rubbing the side of his face as if it had gone numb.

"Blame the Chinese. Everyone does. But I think they're trying to improve their game," said Brandon. "The world's gotta eat." He paused, watching Gillian disappear out the door. "She has nice legs," said Brandon. "At least what I saw of them."

"You're not a problem drinker," said Harry. His Berlin accent made it sound like a stern cop's warning.

"I've got no major problems with drinking." He thought for a minute. "And no minor ones."

"You must be a single man," said Kincaid.

"Single-*malt* man," said Brandon.

After Brandon finished his drink—ahead of the others— he invited them to go drinking. "Two things that draw a big crowd: A dinosaur exhibit and naked women. If you could combine the two elements, the sky's the limit."

"You know a place like that?"

A radiant smile crossed Brandon Sawyer's face. Half an hour later, they cleared out of the club, leaving behind a half dozen others. Brandon phoned ahead, and his driver was waiting with the van outside the side entrance to the Maneeya Building. When he saw Brandon, he got out and slid open the door. Brandon was in the back, taking the top off an ice chest. He removed a bottle of white wine, opened it, and poured plastic glasses to the brim, handing them to his new friends.

By the time Brandon's van reached Sukhumvit Road, they'd polished off the bottle. Brandon climbed out of the van and led the way along a narrow neon-lit soi lined with bars and hole-in-the-wall massage parlors and restaurants. Near the far end of the soi, Brandon turned into a four-story shophouse where the neon sign out front flashed in red and green lettering—LOST HORIZON. Once inside the bar, Brandon nodded at a waitress and then a farang owner, then continued up three flights of stairs. At the top they entered a fake tropical jungle. A wet bar had been built in the middle of the jungle foliage.

"I don't see any dinosaurs," said Harry with childlike disappointment.

Brandon pushed back the plastic leaves on a fake tropical fern and pointed at a dinosaur about the size of a cocker spaniel. He pushed back a plastic green banana leaf to disclose another, slightly smaller stegosaurus skeleton that looked like the skeleton of a cat with tiny shark fins taped to the arched backbone.

"Aren't dinosaurs supposed to be bigger?" asked Ian.

They watched a waitress arrive to take their drink order; she wore an outfit that signaled she'd crossed the line between cheerleader and streetwalker. Kincaid stared after the waitress as she walked away and said, "I thought the second thing you told us about at the club was naked women. These all have clothes." Several yings began massaging Brandon's shoulders and back.

"Feels so good," Brandon said, his eyes half closed. "Stop complaining. 'The dinosaurs are too small, the women are wearing too many clothes.' You sound like a gay hairdresser screaming over a hair floating in his bowl of noodles."

His fan club had slowly begun to unravel. Brandon had managed to do what Brandon did best—break the audience's mood with a rapid-fire barrage of insults. Ian stared at his drink as if there were a dead mouse in the bottom, the German looked disappointed, and Kincaid ruffled his own hair in a gesture of tired frustration.

"Let me get this straight. You came for a good time?" asked Brandon.

The mood of the evening had been broken. Harry glanced at his watch. "Got to work tomorrow."

After Harry left, Brandon said, "The Germans give the work ethic a bad name."

Ian patted the head of the stegosaurus.

Brandon eyed him closely. "You're not leaving, too?"

"Got to," said Ian.

"I thought you guys were serious drinkers. But you're a bunch of pussies," said Brandon, pretending to be a little hurt. And that left Kincaid, who stood near the model of a sauropod, which had a neck and head shaped like a penis. The skeleton didn't look quite right but somehow it fit the atmosphere of the upstairs party room.

"Kincaid, it's only you and me, buddy. Fuck the Europeans. Us Americans gotta stick together. I have a story that will run with your byline in the *New York Times*."

"I'm a travel writer. I write features about full-moon parties. Vultures eating decomposing bodies left on a hill in Tibet. I can sneak in a story about lions eating people."

"Tabloid shockers," said Brandon. "That could work."

"Did I give you my card?"

"Three times so far. But I'm drunk. You can always give me another one." Brandon smiled and slapped Kincaid on the back, pulling him closer. "I'm talking about taking tabloid journalism to a lower level. And you seem the man with the talent to do that," he whispered in Kincaid's ear. "A story with all the elements people love—conspiracy, betrayal, lions, powerful forces, exotic locale, and controversial new technology."

Kincaid cocked his head as if engrossed in what Brandon had to say, listening to what appeared to be the set-up for an offer of some kind.

"Journalism that makes a reporter's reputation, Kincaid. You interested?" Brandon asked.

"I think I already have a reputation."

"Among the local boneheads. I'm offering a story that will make you an international reputation."

Kincaid rolled his eyes. "I'm unworthy."

"Yes, you are," said Brandon, ignoring Kincaid's smirk.

"Why me?"

Brandon sighed and removed his arm from around Kincaid's shoulder. "You're the only one left. That's why. See over there? That's the hall to the short-time rooms," said Brandon, gesturing with his hand. "See the tyrannosaurus rex skull next to the first door? Maybe something you can work into the story." From the number of teeth it was missing, the skull could have come from a hockey player or a betel-nut chewer.

"Exactly what's the story that's going to make me famous?"

"All in good time." Brandon grinned; he'd hooked his man, and now he just had to slowly reel him in.

Kincaid watched as Brandon lowered himself onto an overstuffed sofa and raised his feet, anchoring them on the sauropod's long neck. A couple of yings massaged his legs, and Brandon hadn't seemed to notice when Kincaid slipped down the stairs and into the night.

At 4:30 A.M. Calvino's phone rang. He fumbled in the dark to find it under the front page of the newspaper. When he finally answered it, Colonel Pratt asked him if he'd been sleeping.

Calvino said, "Kinda early, Pratt. You got insomnia?" He fought back a yawn, sending a shudder down his body. "Or have you got some other reason for being up at this ungodly hour?"

A long, aching silence filled the line. Calvino sat up, reached over, and switched on a reading light. On the mattress beside him, Tanny had rolled over, clutching the sheet close to her throat.

"It's Brandon," Colonel Pratt said at last. "Vincent, he's had a heart attack."

Calvino closed his eyes, rocked forward in bed, leaned over Tanny, pulled back the blinds, and stared out at the empty streets, slick with rain. "When?"

"A couple of hours ago."

She smoothed his hair, ran her fingers across his shoulders and back.

"His body's been delivered to the morgue," said Colonel Pratt. "I got a call a few minutes ago."

Pratt hadn't needed to say anything more. If there was any doubt that people far removed from him in the department were using his connection to Calvino, the phone call eliminated it. Being used was the other side of using. One hand washes the other, as Calvino's Uncle Mario said from his retirement home in Miami.

"You want me to identify the body?"

Tanny, foggy with sleep, slowly sat up, pulling up the sheet to cover her breasts. She searched for his eyes in the halo of light from the reading lamp. Calvino gently put his finger against her lips.

"You said something about a body?" she whispered anyway.

Calvino covered the phone with his hand. "Brandon's dead. Pratt needs me to identify the body."

"You're not the only person who can identify him."

Calvino shrugged and spoke into the phone. "Brandon's got a houseful of people who can identify him."

"It's short notice," said Pratt. "But the American Embassy prefers having an American body identified by an American." This appeared totally reasonable to Pratt. It never quite sank in that Americans came in all shapes and sizes and from all ethnic groups.

Calvino switched off the phone, his hand going slack as he sat on the edge of the bed. "I'm meeting Pratt at the Police Hospital to identify his body. You might want to phone Brandon's brother."

Her eyes were wide open. "What happened?"

"No details. Colonel Pratt said it was a heart attack."

"You want me to go with you?"

Calvino shook his head as he pulled on a short-sleeved shirt, smoothed his hair, and shook his head.

He leaned over the bed and kissed her. "Get some sleep."

"Go," she said.

He reached over and kissed her again. "I won't be long," he said.

"I'll wait."

On the drive to the Police Hospital, there was no traffic, the city emptied of people. It might have been another place—or the same place after a virus had wiped out the population. He thought about how Tanny had pushed him. It was a woman thing, and a woman trained in due diligence pushed better than most. A discussion about his relationship with Ratana was one he'd avoided even with Manee and Pratt. He told himself that there a kind of love that, once acknowledged, evaporated. Such a love flourished only in silence. Both of them understood that any attempt to address any feelings would have been as successful as tap-dancing on gravel.

THIRTY-ONE

THE INTERIOR OF the morgue had the chilled smell of death—chemicals that preserved bodies, doctors' washed hands, cleaning fluid used to scrub the doors and floors gathered like a force of nature, blending into an invisible cloud that stung the eyes and nose. It wasn't much different from any big-city morgue, except in the corner stood a platform with a Buddha statue, flowers, and incense sticks—the last of these functioning to appease the spirit of the place and fight a losing battle against the smell of death.

Colonel Pratt watched as an attendant opened the cold-storage locker door and pulled out the trolley on gunmetal-colored rails. Calvino stood at the foot of a body covered with a white sheet. Colonel Pratt nodded, and the attendant pulled back the sheet. Brandon's eyes were almost closed—tiny slits remained, exposing slivers of white. His head tilted to the left, and his hair was spiked like a punk's. Anyone who said the dead looked as if they were sleeping had not seen dead people in a morgue, thought Calvino. Brandon's lips were blue and swollen, black-rimmed. Four or five other uniformed police stood around waiting for Calvino to make the identification. None of them looked too happy at being called to the morgue at that time of morning.

Most of the time, merely looking at the body wouldn't reveal the cause of death. A bullet hole in the forehead or a knife sticking out of the back being the exceptions that proved the rule. Calvino quickly examined Brandon's body, looking for signs of bruises, scratches, or abrasions.

"Heart attack was the cause. But there's not been a full autopsy," he said.

"It's the preliminary cause of death."

Calvino pulled the sheet back to the waist. A whiff of whiskey came from the body. Brandon had already filled his tank drinking at the Foreign Correspondents' Club, and afterward he'd poured a great deal more down his throat. His blood-alcohol content had been way over the limit before he'd died. Calvino noticed on Brandon's chest two dark marks eight inches apart, one on each breast. Calvino leaned closer. They might have been love bites, but the indentations had slightly puckered ridges.

"What are these?" He wrinkled his nose. "Smells burned."

"Bite marks. Marks from kinky sex."

"If kinky sex caused a heart attack, Brandon would have been dead years ago." The marks didn't look as though teeth had caused them.

"A man's lifestyle catches up with him sooner or later. People age, Vincent. You can smell the liquor."

"Where they'd find him?"

"A bar on Sukhumvit called Lost Horizon. The owner called it in."

Calvino knew the bar owner, an American ex-cop from Ohio named Larry. He still had his old badge, which he flashed whenever the cops showed up at his bar looking for a white envelope. Not really a cop but a highway patrol officer, and to hear Larry's stories, the area he patrolled around Toledo was about as safe as the Mekong Delta in 1968—which happened to be the year Larry was born. The cops would smile, but the badge didn't give Larry any advantage. Calvino had gone to the bar a couple of times, once with Brandon. That's how he knew that Larry had taken a disability from the highway patrol after the doctors said he was bipolar. That was the right personality for someone renting a shophouse at the back of one of the odd-numbered sois on Sukhumvit Road, converting it into a bar. Kangaroo-shaped lights were strung across the soi—the lights flashed in a controlled sequence to give the illusion that the kangaroos were hopping. A few drinks were required until the 'roos morphed into muay Thai boxers performing their preliminary ritual before a bout.

"I have to formally ask, Vincent Calvino, can you identify the body?"

Calvino sucked in his breath, "Yes. His name is Brandon Sawyer. He's an American citizen." Facing Colonel Pratt, with his back to the other cops, Calvino raised his cell phone to chest level and snapped several photographs, aiming the lens at Brandon's chest, followed by a couple of full-body shots.

"What is your relationship to the deceased?"

"He was a client." Calvino slipped his cell phone into his pocket. Colonel Pratt said nothing.

The attendant, after Colonel Pratt gave him the nod, covered the body and pushed the drawer back into the cold-storage locker. They stepped into the corridor as the dawn broke outside. "It's stopped raining," said Pratt, glancing out the window. The others who'd been in the morgue had left for their offices or beds.

"I also asked Tanny to find out what the family wants done with the body."

"Practical," said Colonel Pratt. "Manee is always telling me how much she likes the way you get down to what needs to be done. Organize things. See things through."

Calvino tried to guess why Colonel Pratt was handing out compliments that time of the morning. And wondering if Pratt knew that his wife been at the meeting attended by a general's wife at Government House. It didn't seem the right time to bring up the subject. "I have two practical suggestions," said Calvino. "First, you ask the doctor who does the full autopsy about the marks on Brandon's chest. Was it some sex device or something else?"

"You said there were two practical things."

"What are you doing tonight?" asked Calvino.

Colonel Pratt looked away from the window and the street below. "I'm playing backup with a band on Soi 26."

"Tell you what. I'll come along and listen. Afterward we can go and have a talk with Larry, who runs Lost Horizon. I know the guy. Maybe he can tell you something useful."

Colonel Pratt pulled out a notebook and flipped through it, stopped and read a page, slowly turned through three more pages. "I talked with him already."

"Did he tell you Brandon was a regular customer?"

Pratt folded the notebook. "He left that out."

"Maybe he left some other things out."

"Thanks for coming down, Vincent." Pratt had a worried look.

"Something bothering you?"

"What are you going to do with the photographs?"

Calvino sniffed the air. It was stale and smelled faintly of cigarettes, but compared to the morgue it was the Swiss Alps. "Achara ends up in half a dozen body bags and inside the stomachs of two lions. Not two days later his partner ends up dead in a room surrounded by midget dinosaurs. Makes you wonder if there's some kind of connection or if it's just another week's worth of random casualties in the wild kingdom. They say a picture is worth a thousand words. I wanna see what words I can find to fit the pictures I took."

There were some words Calvino thought were appropriate to caption the picture of Khunying Tamarine on her perch at Government House. Words he'd like Colonel Pratt to review, just to check if he had seen the picture correctly. A crowded picture that included Manee and Ratana.

THIRTY-TWO

LOST HORIZON WAS at the end of a soi that looked like a blighted strip mall featuring a neon salesman's catalog's worth of bargain-basement lighting. In the dark spaces between the bars, vendors sold hot dogs on sticks, fried grasshoppers, scorpions, and ears of corn—a wide enough selection of creatures to satisfy about everyone's taste for Third World food. Mounted flat-screen TV sets blared with European football matches. As they walked down the soi, a hundred eyes from balconies, tables, and stools watched them—a farang and a Thai who looked like a *phoo yai,* someone who didn't belong on the soi. If not a cop, then someone close to officialdom. They passed the pizza place, restaurants, and just before the hotel an Arab in a long dark brown kaftan raced past them with one of those carved wooden frogs with a ridged-saw back of dull teeth, and he ran a small stick along its surface, unleashing the eerie sound of a frog in a nearby pond. He laughed hysterically. He ignored his large-framed wife, swathed from head to toe in several layers of black. She pushed a stroller, and inside it lay the offspring of this couple, wrapped like a mummy. The wife chased along, nearly striking Colonel Pratt with the stroller as she tried a sharp turn to keep up with her frog-noise-making, laughing-out-of-control husband.

"I always wondered who bought those wooden frogs," said Calvino.

The laughing Arab ran past again.

"If he's trying to lose his wife, he's not having much luck," said Colonel Pratt.

It was the kind of high-pitched laugh that shot out like tracer rounds, punching the night and causing those nearby to flinch.

The couple disappeared at the end of the soi, swallowed up in the crowd walking on Sukhumvit Road.

"I'd like to talk to Marshall if he comes to Bangkok," said Colonel Pratt.

Calvino nodded, feeling that Pratt had been saving up something. He'd been a little too quiet after they'd left Tokyo Joe's, where Pratt had played with the band for an hour.

"What'd you have in mind?"

Colonel Pratt stood to one side, allowing an elephant and mahout to lumber past.

"Marshall sends an investigator to Bangkok. She's been out to Khun Achara's compound and to Brandon's house. She keeps her boss informed. Marshall wants to sell the company. Achara wasn't selling. Neither was Brandon. That's what you told me."

"You think Tanny is involved in their deaths?"

Colonel Pratt walked a couple of steps before stopping in front of a noodle stand. "What do you think?"

"Not a chance," said Calvino.

"Is that a because-you're-involved-with-her 'not a chance' or a professional opinion?"

"Marshall's other companies are caught in a credit crunch. He needs cash. But who in America isn't in the same position? It's a stretch to stick a murder rap on someone who only wanted to sell the company."

"Murder is almost always a stretch. A person expands the range of possibilities. One option is to remove the obstacles. Murder does that in most cases."

When Colonel Pratt took this position, Calvino was never sure whether it was because he was a cop or because he was a Thai cop.

"Pratt, the Sawyers have business interests in seven countries. It was Brandon's choice to live in Thailand. If they had reason to kill every time they disagreed on a decision, one of them would have been dead before they hit their teens. Americans are combative."

"Combative people are more likely to murder someone. It's another reason we should investigate," said Colonel Pratt. That aggressive people committed aggressive acts was a police truism.

If Marshall could be connected to the death, the collateral benefit was substantial, because it would have let the Thais off the hook—farang killing farang, while bad, didn't reflect badly on the Thai cops or tarnish the image of the country. If anything, such a murder was a vindication, proving that other nationalities routinely shot, stabbed, drowned, axed, and suffocated each other on a regular basis and that it couldn't be helped if the bloodletting spilled onto Thai soil. A wrongful farang death attributed to the police during the state of emergency was the last thing anyone wanted. The higher-ups worried that the foreign news would feature the story and connect it to the political unrest. Brandon Sawyer wasn't some obscure backpacker, but from a prominent East Coast American family. Pratt felt the heat.

"Brothers murdering each other is something Shake-speare made a living writing about. Brandon and Marshall had differences. Who doesn't? American courts would be jammed with lawsuits if knocking off your brother was the usual way of settling a business dispute."

"I'd still like to talk to the brother," said Colonel Pratt, giving himself enough space to avoid getting into a pointless argument.

At the end of the narrow soi, Lost Horizon loomed on the right-hand side. The building was a frenzy of neon glitter—red dragons, jumping tigers, wheels of lights washing the wet street in gaudy shades of red, blue, and green. In the immediate area around the bar, there was less neon and fewer tourists. Calvino and Colonel Pratt walked behind a couple of foreigners. One unexpectedly turned around and asked Pratt if he knew which bar had the best girls. The question caught Pratt by surprise.

The colonel stared at the farang, wearing a baseball cap backward like a teenager. "The best girls aren't in the bars," he said.

The farang was about to complain when Calvino stepped in front. "You got a problem?" The farang took a swing at Calvino, who ducked and returned a punch hard enough to buckle the man's knees. Calvino watched him go down, gasping for breath. "Guess not anymore."

Colonel Pratt grabbed Calvino's arm. "Let's go, Vincent."

The man on the ground extended his arm to his friend, who pulled him up. He was unsteady on his feet and winded. He stared at Calvino, took a step forward, and the man stopped, brushing off his trousers. The party mood had evaporated as the two men turned around and shuffled past the yings calling out for 'handsome man' to come inside and have a drink. They ignored the yings as the injured one, walking slightly doubled over, brushed off the help of his friend. The one who'd taken the punch pulled his baseball cap back on his head, the distance he'd covered having given him courage enough to flip Calvino the finger and shout, his voice breaking with anger, "Fuck you!"

"He shouldn't be aiming so high," said Calvino.

Colonel Pratt walked the last few steps in silence. Calvino, two steps ahead, stood holding open the door to Lost Horizon. It was early, and a handful of customers, regular drinkers, the mainstay of bar revenue, bent over their drinks as if sooner or later the effects would allow them to invent a world much like this one only better, where they were featured as heroes. The ying behind the bar told Calvino that Larry was upstairs. The whole time she was looking Pratt over. Her boss had been expecting Calvino and a Thai police colonel. She thought Pratt didn't look like a colonel. They walked up the stairs.

Larry spent most of his time on the third floor in what he called the "VIP hospitality suite." The first time Calvino met him, Larry bragged that the suite contained everything, so a customer never needed to leave the floor. He even installed a karaoke nook with speakers hooked up inside two dinosaurs. When Calvino and Pratt entered the suite, it took a minute for their eyes to adjust to the dim light and the soft tone of jungle noises coming from a sound system in a ceiling draped with green vines. About a dozen yings wearing what Larry described as "jungle gear" crowded around them.

"We've come to talk with Larry," said Calvino.

"Boss over there," said one of the yings, tugging at her skirt. Larry never had an answer as to why he chose white tassels as a fringe around the miniskirts and zebra-striped bikini tops. It was his idea of caveman fashion.

They found Larry in the corner, half hidden by plastic-leaved plants. "Larry, how are you doing? This is Colonel Pratt."

Larry looked up from his plate, tilting his head as he tried to place Calvino.

"Hey, Vinny, glad to see someone isn't afraid of coming in for a drink. You won't believe the people coming in here asking about the dead farang. I've had an endless stream of gawkers, cops, and complete strangers wanting to know what happened. I'm telling you, it's been pain in the ass."

"Brandon would trade places with you," said Calvino.

"You're right. Things can always be worse. So what can I do for you?"

"I want to know what happened last night."

"Get in line," said Larry.

A private investigator was just one more person he added to the list of the overly curious. And now that same PI was in the VIP room with a cop in tow. Larry leaned over his food, chewing and shaking his head. This signaled that he'd entered a downer phase and was using food to fight off the depression. He'd gnawed a hole in a large taco. Licking off the melted cheese and tomato sauce, he stuffed the rest of it into his mouth. His fingertips glistened with grease. If food was a weapon, Larry had made a good choice for maximum destructive capability. He nodded, washed the food down with a long swig of beer straight from the bottle. Larry's caveman-like dining habits were a reflection of his jungle floor featuring stuffed-bear-sized dinosaurs, and yings whose hygiene was common in the early Ice Age.

"This is Colonel Pratt, Royal Thai Police Department," said Calvino.

"I've been up to my eyeballs with gators and cops, and I find that gators at least fight with a set of rules."

"Didn't know you had alligators in Ohio," said Calvino.

"Don't be so fast off the mark. Okay, a few baby gators got flushed down the toilets and lived in the sewers. That made us cosmopolitan."

"I'd like to ask you some questions about last night," said Colonel Pratt.

"I gave a statement about ten this morning. A guy in a uniform sits me down, and I don't get up for two and half hours. I figure he got hungry or he'd still be asking me something. I don't remember his name. Something like Somchai, Somkit, Som-enchanted-evening. But if you want to hear the whole story again, no problem. You are the boys."

"Pull up a chair. You, too, Colonel." He took another long hit from the beer bottle before setting it down. "Brandon dying here last night isn't good for business."

"You said the place was full of people coming in."

"And going back out after a look around. They didn't buy dick. What do you think that does for the morale of my girls? We want happy campers in our little piece of paradise. Look at them sulking. Not even the dinosaurs wanna be in the same room with them." He pointed at a fake hedgerow flanked by dinosaurs, and a dozen yings were bunched up in a ball in the corner. "Not to mention that they're scared shitless. They think Brandon's ghost is hiding somewhere in the jungle, ready to jump out and grab their ass. They loaded enough fruit on the spirit-house shelf to feed a village school. The stuff's been falling off the wall platform all day, decomposing on the floor, bugs and rats coming from every nest in Sukhumvit to eat the leftovers. Offerings. That's what they call it. It's like an Olympic relay. They take turns lighting candles and incense. Tiptoeing around the spirit house and stacking more fruit for the rats and bugs. It don't do any good talking to them. They just say, 'Farang not understand us.' "

"Can you show me the room where Mr. Sawyer was found?" asked Colonel Pratt.

Larry pulled a length of toilet paper from a plastic holder, wiped his hands and mouth, and rose from the table. "I'm familiar with law enforcement," he said. "I was on the highway patrol for almost eight years. I know something about murder. This guy died of a heart attack."

Larry's conclusion pleased Colonel Pratt. He nodded, even started to like Larry.

"You a doctor, too?" asked Calvino.

"You sound like a smart-ass lawyer. Always questioning, suspicious," said Larry, figuring Colonel Pratt might be worth having as an ally down the road.

"Did he have a girl with him when he died?" asked Colonel Pratt.

Larry nodded, snapped his fingers, and when that didn't work, he shouted out Nit's name. "Nit! Get your ass over here!"

After a long pause, one of the yings unknotted herself from her group. She yawned, uncoiled like a cat, extended her arms, cracked her knuckles one at a time, before getting up, walking over, and leaning against the staircase. She wore one of those "me Jane, you Tarzan," outfits, giving off a wild, untamed look. A look and an outfit that played better in one of the short-time rooms. "Nit, who did Khun Brandon bar-fine last night?"

Nit, who in normal times would have looked good sitting on a woolly-mammoth-skin rug inside any cave, now looked terrified. The blood had gone out of her hands, and they were ice cold as she touched Calvino's hand. "No, he's not a customer. At least not tonight, he's not," said Larry, winking at Colonel Pratt. "And this man is a policeman. He can talk to you in Thai."

"Were you with the farang when he died last night?" Colonel Pratt asked her in Thai.

The tune from the movie *Shaft* boomed from the jungle-themed floor. "Yes, I was with the farang. But not when he died. He asked me to go downstairs and bring back a bottle of whiskey. I go. I order the bottle. I talk with my friend, then a customer, and when I got back to the room, he was dead."

This matched what she had told the investigating officer, Major Somsak, a name that translated as "worthy of honor." No Thai expected a farang to remember Thai names and certainly had no expectation they had any idea of the names' meanings. When they reached the door to the short-time room, Larry took out a fistful of keys, selecting the one to fit the lock. He turned the key and opened the door. He leaned his head in and flicked on the light. The ceiling was webbed with vines and Christmas-tree lights—the tiny flickering bulbs floating over the bed in the shape of a heart. The decor was early Jurassic—plastic and canvas fabric appeared to have been used to make the dinosaurs and foliage. It looked like a firetrap, one short in the wiring away from an inferno. The kind of building violation for which an inspector would likely have given it a pass in return for a white envelope and a bottle of Black.

As they filed inside, Larry walked over to a table and picked up a remote control and flipped on CNN. "We've got cable," he said, pride filling his voice.

"No need ever to leave the cave, except for a pizza," said Calvino.

"Did he take another girl besides you to the room last night?" asked Colonel Pratt.

Nit shook her head, wrapping her arms around herself as they formed a circle around the bed. "When you came back, was the door open? Or was it closed?"

She squeezed her eyes shut, twitched her nose, as if thinking hard. "Closed," said Nit.

"Was there anyone else inside?" asked Colonel Pratt.

She shook her head once more.

"Did you see anyone leave the room?" the colonel asked.

She sighed, shaking her head yet again as if she'd lost her tongue.

"When you went inside, what happened next?"

Nit's face was passive, expressionless, like the doomed, like a peasant facing a firing squad. "I pour him a drink. I ask if he wants ice. He didn't say anything. I set the glass down.

287

Then I go over to the bed and slide down and massage his shoulder," she said.

"And then what happened?"

"He didn't move."

"What did you do?"

"I look at his face. I touch him, and he feels cold. I am scared something is wrong. I run downstairs and tell mamasan."

"Thank you, Khun Nit," said Colonel Pratt.

As far as he was concerned, the case was closed. Brandon Sawyer had died of a heart attack.

"When you came into the room, was anything different?" asked Calvino.

She shrugged, lips down turned as she stared at the pattern on the striped mattress. The pillow had also been removed. "Funny smell," she said.

"Why funny?"

"Smell like steak."

Larry had been quiet for about as long as was humanly possible for a man whose main job was talking to customers. "We don't serve steak," he said, an elbow resting on the head of a dwarf sauropod.

"Did Brandon bring any food into the room?"

Nit slumped down on the edge of the bed. "No, he only drink. Drink too much."

"When you came back, he was on the bed. Right? Was he undressed?"

She looked confused.

"What was he wearing when you came in?" asked Colonel Pratt in Thai.

"Shirt and pants. No socks or shoes."

No crime-scene tape had been used to seal off the room.

"Who else had access to the room before the police arrived?" asked Colonel Pratt. He was looking at Larry, waiting for a reply.

"I wasn't here when it happened," said Larry. "But I'd say it's safe to assume all the girls came in for a good gawk. You know what it's like. Thais love looking at dead bodies."

"*I* don't," said Colonel Pratt, waiting a beat before adding, "like looking at the dead."

"Okay, *some* Thais. Most Thais. The ones from up-country who can't speak English. A dead body turns them into natural spectators. Nit, you saw the body. What was the first thing you thought? I bet it was, 'My friends gotta see this. Dead farang. What's his birth date? Gotta buy a lotto ticket.' "

"How crowded was the bar last night?" asked Calvino, cutting off Larry's rant.

"It was fucking packed," said Larry. He saw the look of disbelief on Calvino's face. "I know, every bar owner says his place is loaded with customers. In my case it's true. But where else can you drink in a jungle surrounded by dinosaurs and lovely native girls?"

"Was it packed in the VIP area?"

Larry nodded. "Yeah, it was."

" 'Packed' meaning how many customers?" asked Colonel Pratt.

"I ran the tab this afternoon. We had a great night."

"How many customers do you estimate came to the bar last night?"

"Fifty, sixty. Maybe more. It's hard to keep track. They come in, have a look, go. A guy has one drink, doesn't see anything he likes, and takes off. Others stick around for the night and run up a tab. In and out all night long."

"Any of the customers stand out? Someone who looked like he didn't belong. Not one of the regulars, not a tourist, someone you wouldn't expect coming into the bar."

Larry thought about how extraordinary a man would have to be before he stood out in a crowd. "We get all types. Americans, Irish, Swedish, some Japanese, Koreans, and Chinese. Some Thais." The last category was said like an afterthought for the benefit of Colonel Pratt.

Calvino shrugged off the boast as unlikely; most nationalities remained tribal enough to frequent bars where their tribe represented the majority of patrons. Lost Horizon had the feel of an American-run place—a place run by an ex-highway patrol officer with a disability pension and a dream of being a big shot in the nightlife. When Calvino had been here before, the clientele had been mostly Americans.

"Any idea where the smell in the room come from?" asked Calvino.

Nit pointed at the empty bed. "His body. Smell bad."

Once they'd finished questioning Nit and Larry, they returned to the top of the soi, Calvino standing next to Colonel Pratt as the traffic passed along Sukhumvit Road.

"Heart attack," said Colonel Pratt. "Just like the autopsy report concluded, Vincent. I haven't heard or seen anything to challenge that result. When someone has a heart attack, they lose control of their bodily functions. That makes a foul smell."

"Even in Thailand, shit doesn't smell like burned steak," said Calvino. "Did the report say what food was in his stomach?"

"The Foreign Correspondents' Club buffet. We got the menu."

"That didn't kill him," said Calvino, grinning.

"Did he look ill last night at the club?"

Calvino tried to remember. He'd sat across from the guest-of-honor table and the podium. Brandon Sawyer hadn't looked a few hours away from suffering a fatal heart attack.

"He always looked the same," said Calvino. "Not quite ill, not quite healthy. He occupied the drunk zone, where being able to lift a glass was considered fit and ready for action. He bitched about a lot of things but never said anything about aches or pains."

A taxi stopped as Calvino waved it down. He opened the door and looked back at Colonel Pratt. "What did the pathologist say about those marks on Brandon's chest?"

"Inconclusive," said Colonel Pratt.

"At the morgue I thought I was looking at burn marks on his chest," said Calvino, climbing into the taxi. He waved off Pratt, leaving him to return to his car, parked around the corner. He hadn't wanted Pratt to drive him to the condo. Tanny would be waiting, and Pratt would do what he had to: Question her about Marshall Sawyer. Calvino wanted answers to the same questions, but he wanted to be the first to ask—and alone when he heard what she had to say.

The problem was that whatever had happened in the room had no witness. There were limitations in working any crime scene, and in one like the Lost Horizon's short-time room it was like trying to find an insurgent's fingerprints on a jungle trail during mating season. Larry had mentioned one of the problems—curious onlookers unable to resist touching everything in sight, sifting through pockets for valuables, helping themselves to loose change. The man was dead; what did he need money for? Once the crime scene had been tainted, no forensic staff could hope to find uncontaminated patterns that told the story of what had happened there. What it showed instead were layers of movement by the crowds, circling, picking up, touching, moving, and pushing back most objects in the room, leaving dozens of smudged fingerprints, strands of hair, DNA.

Colonel Pratt said what mattered was the available evidence, and that was that two men—Brandon and Achara, who had been business partners—had died within the same week. Two back-to-back bizarre deaths. Lions had eaten one; the other had had a heart attack—or, alternatively, had died by electrocution if Vincent Calvino had his way.

They both had tap-danced around that possibility, but it was apparent Calvino thought it worth exploring the electrocution angle. The method of death in both cases had made Pratt misty for the days when murders were solved by evidence of the entry and exit wounds, and from digging slugs out of the wall behind the victim. It was much simpler to unearth the weapon and, in most cases, trace the gun, hunt down the gunman, and convince him it made sense for him to confess to the crime and get a fifty-percent discount on his sentence. Electrocution could have been part of a sexual ritual. It needn't have been murder, Colonel Pratt thought.

If the two men *had* been murdered, someone had gone to a great deal of trouble to disguise the crimes so that the deaths looked like an accident in one case and natural causes in the other. The timing also troubled Colonel Pratt. Brandon wasn't whacked on the day his staff went on a temple outing to make merit for the head maid's birthday, where they got their fortunes told and ate endless bags of sugary *khanom,* custards, jellies, coconut rolls, dried bananas—and that was only the list of items consumed in the van. The thought of food made Colonel Pratt hungry, and he pointed at a plump, ripe mango, which the vendor skinned and sliced and slipped into a plastic bag.

Pratt popped one slice into his mouth as he walked to his car. This was the farang world, he thought. All around him were foreign faces of visitors who came from all over the world. People came to his country to have a good time. Some of them never made it back home alive. That's the way it was. It was their karma to die in Thailand. And if they died wrongfully, it was his karma to find their killer and bring that person to justice. Colonel Pratt slid another piece of mango into his mouth and chewed. One thing troubled him about Calvino's theory—it didn't fit the profile of a professional hit.

If *he* wanted to kill Brandon Sawyer, he would have had Brandon's house under surveillance from one of the shophouses located on the outside of the compound but with a view inside. He would have waited until everyone had left for the temple day trip. Then he would have gone inside and killed him. No witnesses. Brandon didn't die that day in his house. He died in a Sukhumvit Road theme bar, a bar filled with customers, dinosaurs, and bargirls.

THIRTY-THREE

A COUPLE DOZEN hungry, bored men sat at the bar of the Lonesome Hawk. The promise of free-food Saturday had drawn them. The word spread among a band of men who pretty much lived off free bar food. Their lives were less a moving feast than a journey from one soup kitchen to the next, living off the kindness of strangers. As for the hardcore regulars who gathered at the Lonesome Hawk, it appeared that drinking was their hobby, but mostly it had become a full-time vocation. Calvino had asked an ex-FBI agent named Mike Scully to meet him. He had a couple of good reasons for choosing Scully.

Scully had settled down in Thailand after thirty years at the Bureau under his belt. He had married a Thai whom he'd met at the Bureau. Anne—she'd adopted a farang name—had worked as the secretary to a deputy head, and that made getting Scully's papers through for retirement as easy as buying a lotto ticket. At first his wife had been happy about returning to Thailand, but not so happy once she'd talked to her girlfriends, who warned her about the dangers a wife faced from the local younger ying competition. Scully's pale blue eyes got him lots of attention. Thai yings were suckers for blue eyes, discounting age, money, and just about everything else for the chance to stare at them across a pillow. Anne wasn't stupid; Scully's eyes had done her in, and she rightly assumed that her Thai sisters would also find them irresistible.

Anne nagged Scully to wear his sunglasses each time he left the house. Even when he stayed home, she nagged him for details about whom he'd seen and where he'd gone since the last time he left the house alone. But lunchtime was usually a free pass. Calvino's call was one of the most important gifts one farang could give to another: A real cover story. Scully had been smiling ear to ear as he talked with Calvino on the phone, his wife listening to the conversation an elbow length way.

Mike was a detail man. Most retirees in Bangkok couldn't be bothered to remember faces, including the faces of the women they'd slept with. Others kept systematic accounts for each conquest—photograph, name, height, weight, place of birth, where they'd met, and what specific sexual activities they'd indulged in. Mike kept track, he was organized and still plugged into the law-enforcement grid, and that made him right for the assignment. McPhail couldn't remember whom he'd slept with the week before last, but he had other skills—like getting people to underestimate him and tell him things that they shouldn't because they thought he'd forget soon enough.

Calvino knew that as soon as Mike hung up the phone, he'd turn to his wife and say, "Got a private investigator who needs some expertise on a case. I think I may be able to help. But I might be a little late. Don't worry."

The odd thing about the truth was, it sometimes worked better than lies.

Sitting across from Calvino at the Lonesome Hawk, Scully couldn't help but feel grateful and wondered if there might be some way to spin out his usefulness.

Calvino told Scully about the wounds on Brandon's body. Then he showed him a blowup of the digital photos he'd taken at the police hospital. "The body has those two marks. Here"—Calvino pointed to the picture of Brandon's chest just above his heart—"and here"—he moved his hand to the right side of Brandon's chest. "Identical marks."

"What did the edges look like?" asked Scully, frowning as he adjusted his reading glasses. The resolution on the marks was less than Hallmark-greeting-card quality.

"Swollen like a bug bite." Calvino traced the outer edge of one of the marks on the picture.

"It's hard to judge the length."

Calvino said, "They were half an inch across."

"Anything else?"

"Look at the skin. It's torn. Like a fishhook had been yanked out."

"The wounds look puffy."

McPhail came to the table smoking a cigarette. Calvino slid over, and McPhail sat down across from Scully. "Thought you'd forgotten," Calvino said.

McPhail blew smoke. "Who me, forget?"

"Any smell?" Scully asked Calvino, ignoring McPhail.

Calvino removed an envelope from his jacket and, as if this were a perfectly normal gesture, stuck it into McPhail's shirt pocket. "That's another strange thing. His ying had gone downstairs for a bottle of whiskey, and when she returned, she said the body was clothed and lying on the bed. She said the air smelled as if someone had cooked a steak."

McPhail couldn't resist making a price comparison. "I wonder what she'd think this place smells like. Hamburger. Who can afford steak?"

"Brandon was rich," said Calvino. "But he wasn't cooking a steak inside the short-time room."

Scully rubbed his jaw; it was one of those habits he used to signal that he was thinking through a problem. "From what you've described, it might've been caused by a Taser."

"Tasers aren't lethal. That's the point of using one," said Calvino.

"Tasers can cause a heart attack," said McPhail. "There are stories all over the Net about people dying of heart attacks from being Tasered."

"Scully, you might be on to something," said Calvino.

McPhail touched the envelope, shoving it deeper into his shirt pocket, and raised his glass. He saluted Calvino. "Think I'll go over to Villa and buy some steaks for dinner tonight."

Calvino leaned forward, looking Scully in the eye. "Mike, what do you think? Do the marks look like something a Taser would make?"

He shrugged. "Can't be sure. But it's possible. Say the victim had a bad heart—a jolt from a Taser could kill him. You can't look just at the weapon; you gotta consider the medical history of the man who died. Maybe the sound of a car backfiring or maybe just watching a close baseball game would have caused the same result. No one uses a Taser to cause a heart attack. They're used to subdue someone who's aggressive. The idea isn't to kill the person."

Mike Scully was starting to sound like Colonel Pratt spelling out the official line. Law-enforcement personnel had a mentality that sought to explain a suspicious death as an accident, a freak of nature. It was human nature to look for an out to avoid a wrongful-death lawsuit.

"Is it possible that a man could be electrocuted by a Taser?"

"Where are you going with this?"

"I'm thinking out loud. If someone tinkered with a Taser and knew what they were doing, is it possible to juice up the voltage to a lethal dose?"

"What evidence do you have that he was electrocuted?"

"After the autopsy, I talked with the pathologist. He said he'd found tiny hemorrhages on the lungs and other internal organs. That's consistent with electrocution."

"And what do you do in the afternoons, Vinny? Sit around thinking how to turn a Taser into a lethal weapon?" asked McPhail.

Scully didn't blink an eye. "I've heard rumors about people who've fooled around modifying them. One guy came up with a battery that boosted the Taser to fifty thousand volts."

"That'd do the job," said Calvino, without confirming that that was the voltage number the assistant pathologist had used on the phone.

Scully nodded, drank his beer, and sighed. "It's better than a gun. No ballistics to worry about. There's no lab guy who can match a Taser wound to a specific weapon. There's no slug to identify and run through a database. The weapon would pretty much eliminate the usual blowback that comes from using a gun."

"Any idea how to find such a weapon in Thailand?"

Scully replied with a glassy-eyed stare, the one he used with Anne when she asked him where he'd been for three hours. "Thais like guns. But I'm told they think that Tasers are for pussies."

"How easy is it to bring one into Thailand?" asked Calvino.

"Everything can be bought in Thailand," said Scully. "If you have the money, you can find whatever you want. But like I said, a gun is much cheaper."

"Do you have any idea how many guns are floating around in Thailand?" asked McPhail.

"Enough to make America look like a country of pacifists," said Calvino.

"You got that right," said Mike Scully, flashing his blue eyes.

That sounded like an invitation. "I'm going to need some help here, Mike. If you've got the time, I'll make it worth your while to ask around and see if you can pick up any information about Tasers that have come into the country in the last little while. I'm just trying to find out if a friend of mine might have got himself on the wrong end of one. If you can't get out of the house, I'll understand."

The Lonesome Hawk regulars had pegged Mike Scully as someone whose wife kept him on a short leash.

Mike nodded. "I might have to do a little traveling. All of it in country, of course."

"I'll cover your expenses and throw in two hundred and fifty dollars a day," said Calvino. "And another twenty thousand baht for you if you come back with a lead to the importer."

Calvino could tell from Mike's eyes that he was interested. He was the kind of man who should never get into a serious game of poker—or try to lie to his wife about his interest in another woman.

"I'll see what I can do. Who can I say I'm working for? Vincent Calvino?" He waved the waitress over for another bottle of beer; the chits for the first couple had already been stuffed in Calvino's chit cup. Free food, free beer, and a job assignment; it really had been Scully's day.

He waited for Calvino to give an instruction.

"Tell anyone who asks that you're working for Jack Malone," said Calvino.

McPhail lit a cigarette and exhaled through both nostrils, a thick rope of gray smoke, violating the new non-smoking law on the basis that the Lonesome Hawk had diplomatic immunity, since Old George had landed in the second wave at Normandy. Jack had died in Hua Hin some years ago, a victim of mistaken identity. When Calvino or McPhail was asked for the name of a man who needed something special, they always used Jack's name.

"Jack Malone it is," said Scully.

"Be cool with that name," said McPhail. "Jack was one of the good guys."

As Calvino watched Mike get up from the booth and walk into the back to piss on ice, he was reminded of another Calvino's law: No man is ever as tough as he thinks, as truthful as he pretends, or as good in bed as he brags to himself.

"How do you know that Mike won't come back with some bullshit name that had nothing to do with Brandon's death?" asked McPhail.

"Scully understands we're moving around in a small world," said Calvino.

"They can feed Scully a line of bullshit, but does he know it? He gets his twenty grand either way. They might lead him to a dead end, and then you've got nothing for your dough."

"I wouldn't hire him if I thought he was stupid. He's ex-FBI, and he's heard enough bullshit to fertilize the rice crop in Thailand *and* China. Plus, he has an incentive to do the job. He's gotten himself into a hostage situation with his wife. If this case works out, he's in business, and if he's in business, he's got an excuse to get out of the house," said Calvino.

Scully returned, slipped into the booth, his hands clasped, still wet from the washbasin, dripping on the table, and drank his beer. "If this assignment pans out," said Calvino, "I have a nice little investigation business, and you can count on more work. With your background, you'd be a natural."

"What are you expecting in return?"

"Bring me one of the modified Tasers and the name of the man who's behind making and delivering them. And I'd like the information in a couple of days."

Scully rolled his eyes. "In a couple of days? And that's it?"

Calvino shook his head. "If you can get me the details on the guy who killed Brandon Sawyer, I'd say that'd be worth a hundred thousand baht. But I'm not expecting that information to fall into your lap."

"Have you at least got a lead?"

"I've got a couple of ideas."

"But you're not going to make my life easy and give them to me, right? It's like working for the Bureau again."

"What the pathologist told me was off the record," said Calvino. "It wasn't in the autopsy report. Because it had already been agreed that Brandon had died of a heart attack. Too much detail can get you into trouble. But you're an old pro, Scully. You know where to dig and how far to dig before the shovel hits a vein."

"Sometimes you strike gold, other times blood," Scully said.

McPhail held up the envelope, which had been glued shut and had Calvino's signature written across the seal.

"There's a thousand dollars cash inside," said Calvino.

McPhail stuffed the envelope back into his shirt pocket. "I'll keep it safe."

"No one gets paid until the work is done."

"The honor system," said McPhail. "That means *I* get the honor of holding the bills close to my heart."

Calvino stretched his arm over the table and snatched the envelope. He pressed it into Scully's hand. "Take the fucking money, Mike. I trust you. If Anne lets you out of the house long enough, I have a feeling you'll earn it. If not, then I'm out a grand, but the grand won't compensate you for the knowledge that you're just another farang husband hostage who'll never be rescued."

"You don't worry about me, Vinny. When I go to work, I'm my own man."

As Scully got up from the booth, stuffed the envelope in his pocket and headed to the door, McPhail sipped his vodka and tonic, sucking on a slice of lime. "Any man who's only his own man at work is fucked."

Before he'd left his office, Calvino had entered a number of names into a file marked "Possible Suspects": Marshall

Sawyer, Tanny Craig, Scott Baker, and Wei Zhang. Marshall had been in New York, and that should, in theory, eliminate him. Tanny had been with Calvino at the time of death, and that gave her cover as well. The Chinese businessman would have had his entourage around him. None of the people on the list would have done it themselves; they would have used a professional to do the job. Being on the scene at the time wasn't necessary. Most hits in Thailand were done when the mastermind was with a group of people a long way from the scene of the murder.

Calvino reviewed the possibilities. Scott Baker, who'd been humiliated by Brandon Sawyer at the Foreign Correspondents' Club in front of a large audience, was another possibility. Had Scott Baker taken his ideological commitment that one step too far, getting rid of Brandon Sawyer and also Achara because, in his view, the murders were necessary to achieve a larger good? Then there was Zhang, who Achara had said had been angling to worm his way in as a joint-venture partner. He had been disappointed when Brandon had been brought into the deal, excluding Zhang. Achara had never explained why someone with his roots in China, love for the culture, and admiration for the history, would have chosen Brandon over Zhang. But he obviously had his reasons. As he'd told Colonel Pratt when Marshall's name came up, Zhang was a businessman, and it was a rare deal that led a man to murder for business reasons. But it happened. Marshall, Tanny, and Scott would have appealed to the Thai police. Any one of them would have been slotted into the category of neutral to good news. No serious implications for the image of the department or of the country. Zhang, a Chinese national, would be another matter. The brass and the politicians went out of their way not to offend the Chinese. Accusing one of their nationals of murder guaranteed trouble from inside the government.

THIRTY-FOUR

ANYONE WHO CALLED Bangkok the Venice of the East must have been blind drunk when he visited Venice. A couple of generations ago, when there were hundreds of *klongs*, it was easier to pass off this counterfeit coin as legitimate. It was sometimes used as a marketing gimmick. Calvino understood that marketing and reality slept in different rooms and never bred anything other than mules.

He tracked down Scott Baker along the Saen Saeb Canal. Baker squatted on the Pratunam Pier, his outstretched hand touching the surface of the water—brown with the runoff from sewers, factories, and, farther out, chemicals used on large commercial farms.

"Hey, you found me," said Baker. "Foreigners can't get around because there aren't many signs in English."

Calvino squatted down beside the klong. "That smell doesn't bother you?"

"You get used to it," said Baker, wiping the sweat off his forehead with his sleeve.

"I want to ask you some questions about the other night at the Foreign Correspondents' Club."

"So you said on the phone. You were in the audience."

A ferry glided close, gently nudging, bumping, and finally coming to rest against a bank of old car tires that ran the length of the pier. Passengers who waited a few meters from where Calvino squatted had walked down from the garment district, Central World, or Pantip Plaza.

"Saen Saeb is one busy klong," said Calvino, watching the express boat's engines kick in and the propellers throw back waves, rolling out and splashing against the car tires and the pier.

"And one of the most polluted. That's why I'm taking samples. We're testing the water for lead and mercury content. If a kid eats fish from this klong, do you have any idea what that can do to his health?"

Calvino nodded. "Nothing he'd want on his résumé. The other night at the club, Brandon said some hurtful things. He picked on you. He poked fun at your arguments. Public humiliation can make a man do crazy things."

Scott Baker wrinkled his nose, making himself look like an elf with a short, reddish beard. "I promise not to sue him for libel," he said, flashing a smile. "Mr. Calvino, I went to boarding school. I understand bullies. The school I attended in England invented the term 'bully.' I learned to have a thick skin and never take their feeble attempts to humiliate me too seriously. That is one of the unfortunately few benefits of a public school education."

"Brandon Sawyer died later that night." Calvino watched him closely for a reaction. "You look surprised."

"I didn't know," he said, pulling in a vial on a piece of string, then capping the top and affixing a label. "He didn't look ill to me. But I'm not a doctor."

"You studied engineering at university. I bet you're pretty good with electrical things—fixing them, rewiring— someone who knows how to get the best out of an appliance. Juice it up."

"I can fix a toaster, if that's what you mean."

"Then you could modify a Taser if you wanted."

Baker carefully put the vial at the end of a row inside a

small padded metal case. "I've never tried. You have one that needs repairing?"

"After you left the club, where did you go?" asked Calvino.

"I hit a couple of bars in Nana Plaza."

"Never thought of Nana Plaza as a green meeting place. Circulating with all those large-carbon-footprint people ought to give you a guilty conscience," said Calvino. Lost Horizon was close by Nana Plaza. Fighting the pavement choked with vendors, hookers, johns, pickpockets, dwarfs, katoeys, and beggars, it still wouldn't take more than ten minutes to walk over to Lost Horizon, and about the same amount of time to get back. Thirty minutes to an hour hanging around the dinosaurs and fake tropical plants to catch Brandon alone. In theory the job could have been done in an hour. Scott Baker could have been in and out of a couple of stopovers and still had time to do the job.

"You came out here to call me a hypocrite?"

That hadn't been Calvino's intention. The stink of the klong, the motion of the pier bouncing up and down with each express boat, they'd distracted him. "Anyone at the bars who might remember you?"

"I don't really think that's any of your business."

"Brandon Sawyer's dead. He was my business."

Baker removed his glasses, wiped his arm against his face and put them back on. "I'm sorry he's dead. But what does it have to do with me?"

"The police say he had a heart attack. But I think someone made it look like one."

Baker stood up. "And what are you saying? I killed him because we got into it at the club?"

"Did you?"

"Are you barking mad?"

Scott Baker admitted that he'd bar-fined a regular squeeze, a ying who wore a plastic badge with the number 59 and not much else. That evening Calvino chased down Baker's lucky number. Her name was Taengmo, a pole dancer who worked at Lollipop, which meant she danced onstage hugging a chrome pole and making eyes with different customers. Number 59 was a pro at keeping them interested, like a juggler spinning plates on sticks. When her shift finished and the next shift shuffled onto the stage, Calvino tipped the mamasan and asked her to bring Taengmo over for a drink. She dragged her over to Calvino's table. Taengmo didn't seem all that happy that the choice of customer had been made for her by the mamasan. She'd had her eye on a farang who looked like he was in his early thirties, the basement of his brain flooded with testosterone. Taengmo saw the signs that he was going under and, like any predator, could spot an easy kill. But she did what the mamasan told her and joined Calvino. Half a smile was all she could manage.

"My name Taengmo. Buy me lady drink, okay?"

Calvino signaled the waitress and ordered the lady drink. "I know your name. I want to ask you a couple of questions."

"You pay me three thousand baht short time."

"How much did my friend Scott Baker pay you?"

The fire came into her eyes. "You know Scott?"

"He's my younger brother."

"You bullshit me."

"You're right. I am bullshitting you. Now I want some answers that aren't bullshit." He pulled a couple of thousand-baht notes from his wallet. "I don't expect you to give the non-bullshit answers for free. I'm paying for the truth. That may be a difficult concept, but do the best you can."

Her eyes grown large in the presence of the money, she took her lady drink from the waitress, sipped the cola, and counted the money again. "Okay, what you want to know?"

It turned out that Taengmo had been twenty-two years old when she'd left Surin province two years earlier. She danced dressed only in a permanent suntan and long eyelashes, and she had a waist the size of an hourglass with most of the sand above the fall line, and a client list and income that equaled a general's. 'Watermelon,' the English translation of her name, was no ordinary garden fruit. Calvino figured that she'd bought herself a truckload of face in her Surin village.

Calvino ordered her a second lady drink and she opened up, answering a few questions about Scott Baker. She admitted he'd bar-fined her three or four times (she couldn't remember the exact number but said the mamasan probably knew better than she did), and she thought Baker was a chump. He fell in the class of farangs that should have been required to apply for a pleasure permit before going out on the street. An official would first examine him, give him a test for his aptitude to find, experience, and appreciate pleasure, and if he passed, then he got a one-year permit. A pleasure permit was like a work permit, except for having fun. She said, "Scott not like fun. He thinks too much. He talk, talk. Make me have headache. Make me too bored."

Taengmo might not have been educated, but she was far from stupid. She knew the score.

She had gone with Baker back to his apartment on Soi 71 Sukhumvit, where he switched on a fan but not the air conditioner. He lived in a building where most of the occupants were bar yings. Taengmo felt immediately at home, and not a little disappointed. Farangs were supposed to live in expensive luxury units, not in a place where her fee equaled one month's rent. Rather than dragging her into his bedroom, he took her into his small living room and put on a DVD about a water recycling system that he'd help

307

build upcountry. She had fallen asleep ten minutes into the video, and he sat eating potato chips from a bag, watching the entire ninety minutes alone. The water plant had been built near her home village. The local officials had all bought new cars for their *mia nois* from funds earmarked for the project, so by the time the plant construction was finished, the concrete had started to crack and the machinery broke down. It had been abandoned four months after it had been opened.

As Calvino was going out the door, Taengmo said, "You think I am ugly?"

Calvino looked back, shaking his head. She looked small, young, no makeup, wearing shorts and a T-shirt, sitting on the sofa between her two friends with her legs crossed. "You're not ugly."

"I don't believe you. Scott, he not want to make love with me because I am ugly."

Calvino shook his head. "It's because he's in love with himself. And all he wanted from you was an audience to listen to his theories about water."

She knew that look on the face of a farang, the look that said the man had gotten what he wanted, he was done, and she was dismissed. "I dancing now," she said, finishing her drink, sliding off the seat, and disappearing around the back of the stage.

Getting information required a certain mind-set. The key was to cultivate indifference as a means to filter out the strangeness of the person or situation. He'd concentrated instead on what he had to do to get what he needed from Taengmo. Pay what was required. Anything else was a distraction. It wouldn't have mattered if Taengmo picked her nose with the end of her little finger, yawned and coughed up bad breath, had a bronze pin stapled to her lower lip, because all he wanted from her was a name, a time, a place. The rest of who she was hadn't mattered.

There was no need on either side to inject any emotion into the situation; emotions could backfire, and an investigator might lose what he'd come after in return for something he had no use for. Keep it cool, he'd told himself. Remember the reason you're talking to her. Get what you need and walk away. Forget the strangeness as if it never entered your mind. Deep down Calvino suspected that Tanny Craig had done the same thing to him.

Calvino had a certain hunger for the truth. Something real and genuine from the lips of Tanny Craig.

THIRTY-FIVE

FROM THE PHAYA Thai Skytrain Station, Calvino waved over a motorcycle-taxi driver who was parked under a pedestrian bridge with his seven-year-old boy seated on the bike, his face half covered in shadow, listening to his father tell him a story. It was a moment that every man wished he'd had with his dad. The driver lifted his son in his arms and slowly eased him over the front tank. Calvino climbed on the back, listening to the boy's father talking about planting rice upcountry and getting stung by a yellow jacket. Calvino told the driver to take him to Government House.

Once they reached the entrance, Calvino got off the bike and reached for his wallet. The fare was normally seventy baht. Calvino gave the driver two hundred and told him to use the tip to buy sweets and a book for his kid. The driver looked shocked, and so did the boy. As Calvino walked away, he thought that for one hundred thirty baht he'd given that kid a good impression of a foreigner, and this was a part of Bangkok that didn't have many farangs. It was one of those gestures aimed at the future. A man couldn't claim to have any sense of hope for the future unless he believed that such a gesture was an investment, one that created a lasting impression on the mind of a young boy. When, later in life, he came across the assholes, he could dismiss them as the exceptions to the rule.

As Calvino walked through the gate, two security men who wore ski masks with only their eyes showing frisked him in an unfriendly way, asking what he wanted at this time of night. Another couple of security guys wore bandannas wrapped around their faces. No one wanted to be recognized. Calvino figured these men, who had added sticks and slingshots to the golf clubs, had returned from the fighting that had started at six in the morning around Parliament and lasted through the day. The demonstrators had been bloodied and security increased. The smiles had vanished behind ski masks and bandannas, leaving in their place a trail of suspicious, hostile glares. Calvino saw the beginning of a standoff as a couple of the men started cursing farangs for writing and saying bad things about the demonstrators. The mood had changed. The time had come for Calvino to drop the general's wife's name. When he did, as in the Bible story of Moses parting the Red Sea, a gap opened and he was waved through.

Several demonstrators he passed on the pavement reeked of tear gas, and tears streamed down their cheeks. Most of the people had gone to hear speakers on the stage or back to their tents. Otherwise, the few who were out walking around avoided Calvino; one old man tilted his head to the side and spit. "The police, they tried to kill me," he stammered. "We were peaceful. We did nothing, but they want to kill us."

"You take care of yourself," said Calvino.

"They'll shoot a farang. Then the world will see the police for who they really are." He huffed, sucked his teeth, and walked off toward the platform in the distance. Calvino watched him leave, a frail, angry old man with a silver buzz cut. Someone's grandfather had joined pitched street battles. It took a great deal to push a man to such extremes when he could be home bouncing grandchildren on his knee. But there he'd been all worked up, railing and spitting and full of energy. Demonstrators had told him before that farang couldn't understand how they felt or thought, that you had to be Thai to understand. Calvino thought how, at the end of the day, all cults and true believers sounded pretty much alike.

The voices of the speakers on the stage echoed in the distance. The stage itself, cloaked in a hazy golden light, seemed to float in the night sky. A chorus of yellow hand clappers exploded through the crowds. The applause followed a point scored against the government, the police, the old prime minister, his family, and his cronies. It was unlikely the speakers were addressing the news reports about the three cops who'd been shot trying to break up the demonstration outside Parliament. No one wanted to talk about who had guns among the demonstrators or had used them against the police. There had been no point arguing in the dark with an old man about who was right or wrong, or who had guns, or who had the intention to kill. No one on either side would ever agree on what had really happened or who was responsible. The speakers onstage reinforced their own version of the facts. The words gave comfort to thousands. The crowd voted on the facts, and making it unanimous meant their facts must have been real.

Calvino understood the situation; for a foreigner there was no winning side—each group had its farang haters. Farangs had been billed as the evil demons. It might have been a professional wrestling match. The crowd knew whom to boo and whom to cheer. Like the old man who'd hobbled away said, "They'll shoot a farang." Calvino thought the old man was wrong, but looking at the distant stage, listening to the emotion of rage in full bloom, it wasn't hard to believe that the time had come when attention centered on the evilness of the outsider.

In most people's lives, there was a moment of realization that they had come to a fork in the road, a divide, and they had to make a choice. Tanny made her choice when she decided to spend the night on a cot near her mother on the grounds of Government House. Other people had made their own choice and fought the police. That fighting had left two people dead and four hundred injured. The ones who had lost a leg or an arm or a lot of blood were rushed to hospitals, but other wounded demonstrators limped or were carried back to Government House, where Tanny's mother worked through the night wrapping bandages, setting broken bones, stitching up wounds. Tanny pitched in, working alongside her mother.

Calvino found Tanny and her mother stretched out side by side on cots, sleeping. He pulled up a plastic stool next to Tanny and touched her shoulder. She sat bolt upright, her hands balled into fists. "Slow down," he said.

"You shouldn't be here."

"I thought you said that you'd wait."

She looked away. "My mother phoned."

"I wouldn't be here if you hadn't turned off your cell phone."

She looked for her handbag, reached over and opened it, taking out her phone. She turned it on and dumped it back in her bag, as if that solved the problem. She was becoming more Thai by the day. And night.

"I've been fielding calls for you nonstop."

"My mother couldn't cope with all the injured."

"Marshall phoned. Seems you are in popular demand."

She dropped her hands to her lap, her legs crossed as she sat on the edge of the cot. "It's been crazy here."

He pulled a fistful of phone messages from his jacket. "I took down these. You can go through them later. I told Marshall that you were busy at the embassy getting documents processed."

She reached up, wrapping her arms around his neck, pulling him closer. "Thanks, Vinny," she said, kissing him on the forehead.

"I've been working on Brandon's death. But I've hit a dead end. And figured you might be able to answer a couple of questions," he said.

Tanny's mother sat up on the cot, hooked her legs over the side, rubbing her eyes and yawning, her hair unruly, wild, spiked out from her head so she looked like a Zulu warrior after a fierce battle. "How did you get through security?" she asked.

He told her the story, whispering Tamarine's name, saying how he was her friend and a friend of her husband. The weight of his connection to it worked like magic on the guards. No one had the guts to test whether the farang was lying.

Mem said, "They're worried about undercover police coming to spy on us. That would be a big problem," she said.

"But I'm a foreigner," said Calvino. "No one's ever mistaken me for a Thai cop."

"People are tired. They're not thinking straight. I can hardly remember anything."

It turned out that Mem hadn't slept for more than two hours out of the last twenty-four. She was in better condition than most people would be after so little sleep. Her time with the communists in the jungles had prepared her to function without much rest.

"Let's take a walk," he said, standing up. He reached out for Tanny's hand.

She looked expectant, hopeful, waiting for her mother like a teenage daughter seeking approval. "Go ahead. I'm going back to sleep."

They walked around to the east side of Government House, stepping over puddles of rainwater and soggy signs that had slid down from the walls and collapsed into the mud. Tanny looked back at her mother, settling back on the cot. "You won't believe what she's been through."

"You admire her," said Calvino.

314

"A mother like this, who wouldn't? She's doing this work because she believes she can find justice for my sister. I've lived my life without ever facing the problems she's had to face daily."

"Justice," said Calvino, as if it were a foreign word.

She stopped on the pavement and let go of his hand. "Are you mocking her?"

"Never," said Calvino. "You ought to know justice is a personal thing."

"Isn't it everywhere?"

"You don't get it. Have they stopped teaching American kids that justice is universal? They don't throw you on some invisible social scale to see how much you weigh in the larger scheme of things."

"You're romanticizing America. You forget that you left a lifetime ago," she said.

"In some places you can't find justice with a flashlight. It's buried underground. And don't tell me that isn't true in America. Powerful people get their chops busted all the time and their asses hauled off to jail."

She'd never questioned the universality of justice. She'd never heard of anyone else questioning the idea either. "That's what you came out to tell me? To talk about the meaning of justice on the dark side of life?"

"I came to talk about us. Then decided that's another conversation. What I did come for has to do with Brandon Sawyer. It's business."

She looked confused. "Business."

"Business, justice, Brandon, your sister."

"What's Brandon got to do with justice for my sister?"

Tanny had folded all aspects of justice, as her mother had, into tracking down and punishing the gunman who'd killed Jeab. Her tone was consistent with letting the others find their own way, sort out their own problems, and make the compromises that required.

"What if I told you there's evidence Brandon was murdered? And it's being covered up. That's got something to do with justice."

"And you have evidence to show he was murdered?"

He withdrew the printouts of his digital photos, showing the two small wounds on Brandon's chest. He moved to a pool of light coming from a nearby tent. But it was still too dark for her to examine the marks. They walked far down until they came to a light shining from an open doorway, and stepped inside the door. Tanny looked up from the three printouts. "What caused them? And what do they have to do with his death? I thought it was a heart attack."

"That's the official version. I don't know. My theory is Brandon found himself on the wrong end of a Taser."

"And you've found such a weapon?"

"Not yet."

This was the same woman who had walked out of his bathroom with a towel wrapped around her. "The photos will help you remember how much you believe in justice. That's why you're here, right? And why your mother's here. Tamarine's husband promises to nail the hit man who killed your sister. Those are facts. Personally, I'd like to see Sawyer's killer found and put away. Murders of friends that go unanswered leave me with a bad feeling. What about you?"

"What do you want from me?" She tried to read his intention as they stood in the doorway, people walking past looking at the farang.

"Alice in Wonderland you're not. You still don't get it. The people who killed Sawyer and your sister aren't afraid. Ask your mother where that road leads."

She shoved the photos into Calvino's jacket pocket. "I don't need this. He was your client."

"A case can be made that you represent the family. It's your case. Not mine."

"I'm certain that Marshall—"

"Forget about Marshall. You can tell him I'm no longer in business. And what he does about Brandon is *his* business."

"You're finished?" she asked.

"I should ask if *we're* finished."

"Nothing personal is ever that simple."

"Justice is personal. You want it for your sister's death. Ask Marshall if the family wants justice for Brandon Sawyer's death. That'll give you the answer you ought to think over."

"I *will* think about it."

"You think like a farang."

"What's that supposed to mean?"

"In between my taking your calls, one of Tamarine's close friends—or at least he said he was a close friend—called. He said I was making trouble and I should lay off questioning Brandon's autopsy report."

"He threatened you?"

Calvino didn't reply at first, wondering if he ought to spell out the obvious: He could be written off as the unfortunate victim of an accident. But he decided to leave the nature of the threat vague, hanging in the air. Leave the words as markers to be sniffed around the edges. "It's all in the way you interpret it." The threatening phone call confirmed that his status was closer to that of a helium balloon drifting toward the sun.

Marshall had told Tanny to manage the details of the deal to sell shares in the joint-venture company to Wei Zhang. "When I said you were spending the day at the embassy getting the paperwork done for repatriation of Brandon's remains, you know what he said? 'Tell her Wei Zhang isn't happy. He wants to close the deal quickly. Tell her to get her butt over to his office.' I asked myself why you didn't tell me Brandon's shares were being sold before they cremated him. Even by New York standards, that's a rush job."

317

"I didn't think you'd understand," she said.

"I'm thinking you're right. There are a lot of things I don't understand. Such as getting me to tag along to the meeting with Tamarine. It was a good cover. Going to help with your sister's murder. I was the hero, right? Wrong. The plan was to compromise me. I have to admit, it was brilliant. I'm thinking, 'This woman knows nothing about Thailand or the culture. She's scared. Help her get through it.' Involve lifelong friends like Pratt and Manee, turn them into hostages of Marshall Sawyer's business deal. I join the ranks as another corruptionist working the system, keeping his head down, protecting himself and his friends."

"You seriously think I had something to do with Brandon's death?"

"I'm your alibi for that night."

"That doesn't answer my question. Do you think I could kill someone?"

He paused, trying long and hard to read her expression for a hint of an answer to her own question. "Why didn't you tell me about Wei Zhang?"

"I thought you wouldn't understand." She shook her head, removed Calvino's hand, and walked away. The heat, exhaustion, lack of sleep had broken her control, and she let slip an emotion that she had wanted to avoid. He stood on the pavement watching as Tanny's shadow was swallowed up in the night. He figured she would return to her mother, who would be working on a patient, believing that her work would gain her merit, and that merit would gain her the justice she wanted for her daughter. They'd become part of a cycle renewing itself day after day.

As he headed back to the main gate, a couple of security men walked just behind him. Close enough to let him know that they were there and were not going to lose him. He glanced over his shoulder and waved. One of the men

318

reminded Calvino of the men who hung around at the muay Thai center in Washington Square. Calvino smiled to himself. The two men trailed him. Patrolling the grounds was controlling the political space. The men behind him, like the ones wearing red on Sanam Luang, guarded their political space like a muay Thai fighter. Politics was the same—all elbows, knees, kicks and punches intended to knock an opponent down hard and keep him down. After the violence on the street near Parliament, the country had become a huge muay Thai match. People had been divided into two groups, and they circled each other, each waiting to land a winning blow.

"See you guys later," said Calvino, walking out to find the motorcycle driver.

Calvino sat alone in his office, opening a manila envelope. He found it with his name written on it at the bottom of the drawer next to his office bottle. When Calvino had taken out the bottle and poured himself a drink, he saw the envelope and opened it to find a copy of a sale-of-shares agreement. A gift left by Tanny. He sat back, sipped the Scotch, and read through the twenty-page document. Zhang had bought the shares of the Thai company, and the contract listed the names of the Thai nominee shareholders. Tanny Craig had signed under a power of attorney for the sellers: The Sawyer Corporation. He put down the agreement and poured another Scotch. He raised his glass to Brandon, then to Achara, and finally to Tanny.

He slowly typed out an e-mail. He attached his file with a dozen case histories documenting killings during the war on drugs. He wanted her to understand that Thais with no weight to throw around hadn't survived inside a system with a flaw in its design for rendering justice. He composed a short message: "Background information about the killings. Good luck. Vincent."

319

Then he remembered that there was a final traffic lesson she should know. He'd already sent the e-mail. It was the experience that normally happened after walking out of a room, remembering the one thing he'd wanted to say, but it was too late as he'd already left. He'd wanted to tell her about how the taxis sometimes stopped in the middle of the street, switched on their flashing taillights. How the car blocked the road, a back door opened, and a passenger untangled legs and arms like a slow-motion puppet dragon unfolding, as if time had stopped. The cars stacked behind the taxi don't honk; instead one of the other drivers automatically swung his vehicle into the oncoming traffic lane, without looking. Flashing headlights was a signal that the taxi driver had declared a personal state of emergency and had temporarily suspended the rules of the road. It happened every day throughout the city.

The oncoming driver had no choice but to stop or face a head-on collision. This wasn't limited to taxis. Delivery vans unloading bags of ice or rice for a restaurant, a BMW driver in blue silk and diamonds stopping to buy fruit, a van stopping while the driver phones to get directions. People stopped in the middle of the road. It never occurred to them that cars piled up behind them. That wasn't their concern. They never looked back; only what was ahead of them mattered, and how to stay ahead of those with large weight in a dangerous game of chicken. Rules had their price, too. Tanny had walked into his life as that oncoming driver. When she'd come out of his bathroom wearing only a towel, she'd flashed her lights. Only he hadn't bothered to see them. He thought it was an entirely different game that she wanted to play. But he knew enough about women: They liked to play by their rules. For once he was glad for his memory lapse. He would have been telling her about a rule she already knew.

THIRTY-SIX

CALVINO STOOD INSIDE the main lobby of Tanny Craig's hotel looking at his watch. He'd been pacing near the front door. He had wanted to surprise her with a gift to take back to New York—it was a Thai bullet coin, one that Brandon Sawyer had given to him. He'd polished it, studied it under a jeweler's loupe. The coin looked like a slug that had slammed through a body and smashed against a wall. Like people, Thai coins were valued according to their weight. For reasons he didn't fully understand, Calvino wanted her to remember Brandon, the night they'd gone to the Foreign Correspondents' Club and heard him speak, and the time they had spent together. But the surprise had been on Calvino; she hadn't been in her room, and the front desk said she hadn't been back that evening, nor had she checked out. That left Calvino floating near the door, deciding whether give her more time or forget the whole idea and go out for a drink.

It hadn't helped much—it made him edgy—that all the members of the security detail at the front door had taken their turns to give him a dirty look. They didn't like farangs who weren't guests hanging around the lobby. It smelled like trouble. The security personnel—four or five of them, in cheap suits, with earpieces and attitudes like the *luk nong* of an upcountry politician—did little to hide that they were clocking his movements. Besides the security were several bellboys dressed in wine-colored, Nehru-collared uniforms, who opened doors for people. Vans pulled up, people climbed out clutching cases, looking disoriented, walking through the open door into the cold air of the lobby. Calvino looked to see if Tanny Craig's was among the faces of those coming into the lobby. It wasn't. But the sudden chill of the air-conditioning revived the tourists as if they were wilted roses put in water. They cheered, smiled, and shed the burden of the thick night air, exhaling it from their lungs.

If the bellboys looked like a downscale boy band, the security detail, in their cheap black suits and shoes with plastic soles, hair cut short, were likely moonlighting cops, watching the people come and go. They watched as Calvino walked over and eased himself into a soft chair on an elevated area overlooking the front doors. Like a Roman emperor with a commanding view of the battlefield, he watched the men dressed like pallbearers at a gangster's funeral. They never smiled, never cracked a joke. Someone had switched off the feed to their sanuk valve, turning them into watchful, humorless machines, alert and suspicious.

A Japanese man with overly straight posture, combed-back white hair, and a dark suit stopped at the door and gave one of the security men a white envelope. The Japanese man bowed, the security guys, all four of them, bowed. Funny hotel, thought Calvino. It could be somewhere in Tokyo. A middle-aged clerk with reddish dyed hair who worked the transportation desk looked up and nodded to the man holding the envelope. Then he buried his head back in a large open ledger book, adjusting his glasses as he read. He glanced at Calvino, his thick, black, arched eyebrows like hairy banana spiders acting out a mating ritual on his forehead. He had a way of squinting and twitching his nose, making the spiders squirm. The clerk said something, a whisper out of earshot, to a member of the security staff. Then they huddled. A minute later a Thai woman with a tiny waist wrapped in a traditional silk dress and a ton of makeup came up to Calvino and asked him his room number. He told her that he was waiting for a friend. That was usually enough to satisfy hotel security. But it wasn't cutting much ice with the security of this hotel. Calvino felt as welcome in this fancy lobby as a uniformed Greyhound bus driver in a Las Vegas casino—assuming he didn't own the company. Then Tanny walked into the lobby. At first she didn't see him as he stood on the platform area to the side of the main door. Zhang followed a step behind her. He was dressed in a beige tailored suit with padded shoulders, and as he came inside, the security gave him the wais reserved for Buddha images. There wasn't a crease in the suit, not a drop of sweat on his brow, his hair perfectly combed. He carried a brown leather briefcase monogrammed with the Roman letter initials WZ. Tanny turned and faced Zhang, offering her hand, which he took, European style, and kissed.

It suited him perfectly well that she remained oblivious to his presence. But Zhang spotted Calvino on the platform, the newspaper now bunched up on his lap. "And that is our owner, Khun Wei," said the greeter who had been keeping an eye on Calvino.

A gradual smile crept over Zhang's face, causing Tanny to turn and look around. He walked over to Calvino. "Mr. Calvino, I am surprised to see you. I thought you'd be at Montri's with your grandfather's paintings."

"Great-grandfather."

"All grandfathers are great."

Tanny watched the two men talking, her face expressionless as she regarded Calvino. Then she looked away as if she'd just glanced at a stranger. "My security chief tells me you've been waiting for some time," Zhang said. "Patience is one of my favorite virtues. But, like any virtue, it can be misplaced, and when a virtue becomes lost, the universe is no longer in harmony."

"I once got the same fortune cookie. But I went ahead and ate it anyway."

"You are a brave and loyal man, Mr. Calvino. Your misfortune has been to serve men whose qualities do you dishonor."

"No need for the Flatiron Building when you have hotels like this as part of your personal empire," said Calvino, his eyes looking around the immense lobby, raising his hands in a sweeping gesture.

"If you will excuse me, I must go." Zhang turned away from Calvino, as if dismissing a servant. He said something to Tanny, and the security men and bellboys lined up, forming an honor guard as Zhang walked out and climbed into the back of a sleek black luxury van.

"He's taking me to the airport."

"Why do I have the feeling he's taken you to a few places in between?"

She slapped Calvino's face.

"Feel better?" he asked.

"Why did you come here?"

"I didn't know that Zhang owned the hotel. Google doesn't reveal every detail about a businessman. Only their major crimes and connections."

"What does it matter, Vinny?"

"I found the copy of the contract you left in the office. It took style to put it in the office whiskey-bottle drawer."

"Women have a habit of leaving things behind in your condo. I didn't have an earring to spare. I like you. I wanted you to know I'm not without sympathy. Brandon could have avoided the problem. Like Achara, he was stubborn."

"And Wei Zhang has a way of dealing with stubborn people."

"I didn't say that."

"You didn't have to. You've been working for Wei Zhang and Marshall Sawyer. It seems Marshall didn't waste any time after Brandon's death in getting a power of attorney authorizing you to sign over the company shares to Wei. I'd say you got bonus money from both ends. If you ever think about a second act, you ought to come and work in Thailand. You've got an interesting set of skills."

Tanny held out her hand. "Good-bye and good luck, Vinny. I mean that. Don't hate me." She searched his eyes, looking for something like understanding, if not forgiveness.

"You've picked up on what makes the Chinese tick. *Guanxi*. You go for the right connections to high places."

"You were my role model, Vinny."

He watched as her luggage came on a trolley and followed her out to Zhang's van. "I hope your mother finds the person who killed your sister."

Tanny stopped, slowly turned around. "She will. Wei has made certain of it. And thanks for your e-mail with the case histories. Illuminating."

Then she was gone. That had been the deal: She had turned to Zhang for a favor, and in return for his assistance she had delivered the shares. Achieving harmony sometimes meant special arrangements had to be made; Tanny Craig and Wei Zhang had come up with their own formula. He didn't hate Craig; he couldn't blame her for playing the card she knew would win the game. And maybe she was right—and he didn't want to face it—he had his own guanxi racket, and without Colonel Pratt he'd have his head underwater in some klong where a guy like Scott Baker was scooping out samples to check the pollution levels. Calvino told himself that no one working the streets had to bother testing the waters to find pollution, as it was mostly guanxi that contaminated the air, the water, and the land.

THIRTY-SEVEN

A HANDFUL OF young men—tall, slender and fit—wore black T-shirts and pants and stood in the shadows like a Special Forces team, disciplined and silent, assembled and waiting for the signal to carry out their mission. The men didn't look Thai. Too tall, too quiet, and too serious to pass as Thais. It didn't take an advanced university degree in personal security to tag them as Wei Zhang's private security detail, who'd been ordered to wait for Calvino in the hotel's underground parking garage. They stood about five meters from where Calvino had parked his Honda City. Men as combat fit as these didn't sign on to work as hotel security guards. The professional team loomed like an elephant's shadow on a mouse. Calvino prepared himself for getting jumped and stuck his right hand inside his jacket on his .38. He controlled his breath, counting his steps until he'd drop to one knee and assume the firing position, with the full recognition that a .38 would have little effect against the firepower he'd face from these men. Calvino smiled, thinking that this made about as much difference as fastening a seat belt while the plane spiraled toward the ground. His finger brushing against the worn leather shoulder harness, he kept on walking right past them. Nothing happened. None of them moved. Calvino stood beside his car and had to take his hand out of his jacket to get his keys. And he wondered if that had been the trap.

"Those Beijing Olympics were something," he said.

None of the men replied.

"You guys remind me of the Chinese basketball team. Except you're kinda quiet for basketball players. No ball. No hoop. Guess you're looking for a game, but the coach is keeping you back. That's a good call. Don't want to make a mess in the hotel parking garage."

They continued to stare at him, not revealing whether they'd understood a word he said or, if they had, giving no indication of what they'd do next.

Calvino took a deep breath and let another long minute pass before fishing his car keys out of his jacket. He got in the car, closed the door, and started the engine. The men stood passively, eyes on the car. He watched them in his rearview mirror until he turned a corner and they were gone. Then he waited a couple of minutes before driving down the ramp and handing the attendant his parking ticket. He checked his mirror again, but no one had tailed him, so he drove past the school on Soi 22 before turning right on Soi Sai Nam Thip 2 and followed the winding road that led back to his condo.

Calvino slowed as he started into the turn around the blind corner, hugging the gutter that snaked beside a sand-colored adobe condo wall as thick as a medieval fortress. A large black van with tinted windows and no lights veered into his lane, coming straight at him. Calvino pushed the accelerator to the floorboard and swung the steering wheel sharp to the right, clipping the front of the van. The van driver lost control and crashed into the condo wall. Calvino's Honda spun around and stopped along the edge of the road opposite the van. The driver's head, pierced with shards of glass, bloodied and raw, had gone through the windshield. Calvino got out of his car, pulled his .38, and ran across the street to open the door. He checked the driver, pushing him back from the steering wheel. He was dead. Two men in the rear hadn't been wearing seat belts, and their bodies were twisted at odd angles, both were alive but semi-conscious, groaning and moaning, leaking blood. One had a busted head. Calvino holstered his .38 and pulled out the man who'd been sitting directly behind the driver and sat him on the road.

Then he returned to the van and crawled inside. He saw boxes of fireworks—big Roman candles, rockets, and paper-wrapped crackers—scattered across the back of the van. The impact had thrown a bag against the window. Calvino saw a Taser exposed and grabbed the bag. The remaining man grimaced with pain; his shoulder was broken, and part of the bone had punctured the skin and the fabric of his black shirt. His thumb came down on a cigarette lighter. The flame moved toward one of the boxes. He smiled as he ignited a Roman candle. His eyes met Calvino for one long second. Calvino dived back to the front of the van and rolled out with the bag onto the street. The Roman candle showered the interior of the van with hot, white light. The van exploded into a huge fireworks display mostly contained inside it, with flares arcing out the open door and crashing against the side of the condo. Fire found the fuel line and erupted into an orange fireball that climbed up the fortress wall, illuminating the curve.

The neighborhood became awash in a fusion of red and green and yellow streaks of light as the larger pieces exploded, firing their load skyward through the broken windows, spinning wheels of color along the center of the curve and slamming against a retaining wall across the street. It was the kind of display reserved for major holidays. But there it was—no holiday, no parade. From the surrounding buildings, the cannon-like boom from the explosion and the spirals of light merged overhead.

Calvino stood the man he'd pulled from the van against the wall. He didn't look like a member of the team from the hotel; they'd looked professional—buzz haircuts, late twenties, muscled, and dressed in tight-fitting black T-shirts and training pants. He remembered the men from the underground parking lot.

"Who paid you to do this? Wei Zhang?"

The man glared at him like a wounded animal. "Go home, farang."

"Tell me, you asshole."

The man reached behind his back and pulled out a large knife, the blade catching the light from the flame. But his body hadn't fully recovered from the shock of the crash. He was unsteady on his feet, blinking away the blood that flowed from his scalp into his eyes.

"Wait for me in the parking lot. That's what you were told to do. Wei said make it look like an accident. He got his accident," said Calvino.

The man's injuries and the heat of the fire worked to give Calvino a chance to use one of the muay Thai moves he'd seen at the kick-boxing joint in Washington Square. Calvino swung the heel of his right foot, smashing it into the man's right knee, making him cry out as if he'd been shot, drop the knife, and collapse next to the wall. Another car came along the road, its lights shining on the burning van, the man still rocking back and forth against the wall of the condo and moaning. The car slowed, the driver rolled down his window. "You have accident? You need help?"

"Yes, and yes," said Calvino. He kicked the knife across the street, and continued, "Are you the one who killed Brandon?" The man spit blood, his eyes locked onto the ground. He slowly looked up, knowing that Calvino hadn't finished with him. "Or were you the one who got to have the fun with the yings? You even filled the short-time room with confetti." Calvino drove the toe of his shoe into the man's leg.

The man groaned in agony.

"I'll kick your ass over the Great Wall of China." Calvino nodded toward the retaining wall across the street.

"Go to hell," he said to Calvino.

"Your friend dies for Wei Zhang. Is that what you want?"

In the glow of the fireworks, the man's face was filled with hatred.

Calvino threw the bag with the Taser into the trunk of his car. The first police car, blue light on the roof flashing, stopped, blocking the road, and called in for backup. "Two guys in the van didn't make it," said Calvino.

"Make what?" asked the cop.

"The team. They got cut. They're dead. And this one, he got out just in time."

The cop began to write Calvino a ticket because his car was illegally parked in the wrong lane and, along with the van, was blocking traffic. He gave Calvino every chance to settle the ticket. But Calvino insisted that he preferred to pay it at the station. The cop frowned and shook his head, thinking the farang was stupid or crazy. As an ambulance came, along with a body snatcher's pickup to collect the dead, Calvino phoned Colonel Pratt and said he'd been in a little accident.

"The cop's deciding whether to throw me in jail or write me a ticket for blocking the road."

"Give him your phone."

Calvino held out his phone. "Someone other than your wife is about to change your day." The cop looked at the phone as if it were radioactive. "The colonel wants to talk to you."

The cop slowly put the phone to his ear, taking a long, hard look at Calvino.

The anger drained from his face after a couple of minutes. By the time the cop handed Calvino back his phone, he'd torn up the ticket and thrown the scraps into the flames. In the meantime the fire brigade arrived, and the firefighters were hooking up a hose as smoke curled from the wrecked van.

"Pratt, the van crossed the lane at the T-junction—that blind corner near my condo? The van shot into my lane, lights off. The three men inside were dressed for combat. It was a setup. The guy I pulled out of the van isn't talking about who sent them. Maybe you can get something out of him. Take him to a quiet place and ask him in that special way that makes not talking a bad option."

"Go home, Vincent. I'll handle it," said Colonel Pratt. It was a variation of what the survivor of the wreck had said.

A half dozen cops, their cars jamming the road, milled around the wreckage. As a fireworks show, the scene had become something of a letdown. The cops inhaled the smell of gunpowder, an ancient Chinese invention, which swept down the street.

None of the cops interfered with Calvino as he crossed the road to his car and drove the five hundred meters to his condo. Why hadn't one of them made an attempt to stop him? He'd just emerged from a major road accident, leaving behind two dead men in black tracksuits, another near-dead commando wannabe, and a black van that had lit up the sky. The problem was, no one could ever trust a cop, know who was a cop or who was an ex-cop working for a politician. Colonel Pratt understood that the line between criminal and humanitarian sometimes blurred. From the description of the scene from the cop at the scene, he'd made a field judgment that Calvino was on the wrong side of someone who had sent in his own private militia to eliminate the problem.

THIRTY-EIGHT

CALVINO PARKED ON the third floor of the condo-parking garage, sat forward, leaning over his steering wheel. He got out and opened the trunk, reached inside for the bag, and pulled out the Taser. He examined it, put it back, picked up the bag, and closed the trunk. He preferred his .38 police special. Zhang would know where he lived, thought Calvino. Had news gotten back to Zhang that his boys had caused some fireworks on Sukhumvit Road? Calvino thought how the cops had stood in several small groups across the street near the blind corner. They had no idea he'd taken the Taser from the van.

Closing the front door to his condo, Calvino flipped the dead bolt, switched on the lights, and examined the weapon in the front hall. A cartridge was loaded and ready to fire. He walked into the guest bedroom, switched on the light, looked around the room for a target. Fluffing a couple of pillows together, he set them on the bed like a headrest. He walked back a couple of feet, aimed, and fired. The probes slammed into the pillows, and dozens of tiny strips of confetti scattered across the room, floating like a mist, landing on the king-size bed, the parquet floor, dusting a couple of surreal paintings of twisted masklike faces, and leaving a residue on a chrome chair with a red cushion attached. Calvino rummaged in a drawer until he found a jeweler's loupe. He put a piece of the confetti under the loupe and wrote down what looked like a serial number. He phoned Mike Scully.

Scully picked up after the sixth ring. "Whoever the fuck you are, do you know what time it is?"

"It's Calvino. I've got a serial number I want you to check out with your FBI friends and see if it turns up in their database."

Scully backpedaled once he knew who was on the other end. Calvino could hear his wife complaining. But Scully ignored her as if he'd thrown a blanket over a caged parrot. "It's midday in Washington," said Calvino.

"I hear you," Scully said, his wife screaming in the background.

"Scully, it's a good time to make that call, and I'd like the information sooner rather than later. See you at the Lonesome Hawk for lunch tomorrow at noon."

Calvino hung up as Scully's wife ranted about "this little job is not little, only the money is little, and the risk," and listened to the peaceful silence of his bedroom. The fact was, Scully had contacts, but he'd qualified them as "not magical sorcerers who could conjure information from thin air," and Calvino had shrugged. Just get them off their asses to check the serial number and see if they can trace the origin of the knockoff Taser he'd taken from the van. Calvino had heard Scully's cover-your-ass excuses—in that department there was no separation from his personal and professional lives—which was why he'd given Scully one grand up front. Money stopped an excuse train from getting up a head of steam and pulling out of the station.

He put the Taser back into the bag and stored it on the upper shelf of a closet. When Colonel Pratt arrived half an hour later, Calvino was in the sitting room logged on to a Web site that sold Tasers. He was reading about the standard specifications when the colonel took a seat.

"It's taken care of," said Colonel Pratt.

Calvino nodded. "Pratt, it's like Whack-A-Mole. You knock off one and three more pop up."

"This time all three were taken out," said Colonel Pratt.

Before Calvino could answer, the doorbell rang. He looked at the colonel and shrugged. "I'll get it," said Calvino. He picked up his .38 from the bedroom, crossed back through the dining area, and squinted through the peephole. Siriporn stood outside, smiling and dressed like a movie star hitting the marks for her big scene.

He opened the door and pulled her inside, looked up and down the hall. "I tried to call you many times," she said. "Where have you been? And why are you holding a gun?"

"Shooting the breeze," he said. Behind her the elevator pinged, the pneumatic doors opened. Calvino closed the door, leaving only a crack so he could watch if there was someone following from the elevator. There was no one else. He holstered his .38. Siriporn stole a quick glance inside the hallway, checking to see if another woman might be behind him. She half expected to find "that Craig woman," as she called her. Instead she stood eye to eye with a Thai police colonel who had appeared behind Calvino. Siriporn smiled, looking half relieved.

"You make me nervous," she said, looking at the colonel. "Guns make me nervous."

"That's the main purpose of a gun." Calvino looked over his shoulder at Pratt.

"Colonel Prachai, this is Khun Siriporn."

She waied the colonel, glanced back at Calvino, and said, "You'll phone me tomorrow morning, there is a company I have been researching for you. I want to give you the information."

"I'll do that," said Calvino.

She left Colonel Pratt and Calvino standing in the doorway.

The entry hall smelled of Siriporn's perfume, sweet and soft like a spring day with the flowers in bloom. Except it was night and a couple of men had just been killed. Calvino and Pratt walked to the window overlooking the scene of the explosion. The fireworks had ended; the emergency vehicles and police cars had left. The street was again dark and wet in the rain. Calvino left Pratt brooding and staring into the darkness. He went into the kitchen and poured the colonel a glass of water and filled another glass with two fingers of single-malt. He returned with the two glasses, handing the water to Pratt.

"I can't decide if your timing is either very good or very bad," said Colonel Pratt.

"Tonight it's been both."

"Who's the woman? Was she in the car when all this happened?"

"She's my stockbroker. It's desperate times in the markets. Brokers are making late-night house calls."

"None of this is funny, Vincent. You left quite a mess tonight."

"You should be talking to the person who made the mess."

Colonel Pratt stared down at the street below before slowly removing documents from his briefcase. "There is a statement you need to sign." Pratt handed him a densely typed three-page statement written in Thai.

"What's it say?"

"That you witnessed an accident in which three men were killed."

"There's a slight problem. First, two men were killed," said Calvino. "And it wasn't an accident."

Colonel Pratt handed Calvino a pen. "Three men died," he said. "And it's best for all concerned, at this point, to keep what happened as an accident."

It didn't sound like Pratt.

"You've got orders from someone high up. Or you've forgotten what an accident looks like."

"You said on the phone that you'd been in an accident."

The colonel had a point. The crash had been set up to look like an accident. The plan had been for the van to crash into Calvino's Honda, for one of the men to jump out and zap Calvino with a lethal Taser blast, for the police to write it up as a fatal crash. It would have been no one's fault; he'd be written off as one more victim of Third World road design and feudally inspired driving practices. Only it hadn't turned out that way. To stay with the accident scenario required a little rewriting of the script. "They wanted it to look like an accident. But that doesn't mean it was one."

Appearance meant everything. If it looked like an accident, then that was the end of the matter.

Powerful people had the means to reward cooperation and punish disobedience. Mostly, Colonel Pratt found a middle way to keep his job, and cooperated only in those cases where he hadn't needed to wrinkle up his nose and turn away from a bad smell. The fragrance of this incident had entered his nose and lingered. Calvino had the choice to go along with the story or come up with a different version from that of everyone in authority who'd been on the scene. He looked up from the report Colonel Pratt had asked him to sign.

"One of the men in the van still had some fight in him when I left."

"Sign it, Vincent. Or not. But it's up to you. I can't make you."

"You've got someone pushing you hard, Pratt."

"Don't know about that. That curve is dangerous. You've said so yourself."

"Accident." Calvino nodded and leaned forward and signed the document; he understood that the man he'd pulled out of the van hadn't succumbed to the kick in the shin he'd administered. Someone had helped him into the next life.

Calvino handed Pratt the signed document. He thought about how someone had gone to the trouble of finishing off the sole survivor. And that was a succinct message intended for Colonel Pratt and for Calvino to think about. Someone had decided that it was better if no one from the van walked away from the scene of the accident. It was far safer in the long run to keep matters simple and neat. Things had gradually started to make sense to Calvino—why no one had questioned letting him leave the scene. Colonel Pratt was asking him to sign a document that he'd witnessed the accident involving three dead men and had tried to save them but failed. It also explained the absence of an English translation of the document.

"What happened to the Chinese guy I pulled out of the van?" asked Calvino, having a good idea of the answer. In the land of delusion and self-deception, the act of committing perjury had little meaning.

Colonel Pratt folded the document and put it in his briefcase. " 'Men were deceivers ever; one foot in sea, and one on shore, to one thing constant never.' "

"Since when did Shakespeare become a Thai cop's best friend?" asked Calvino.

"It's time you traveled outside the country," said Colonel Pratt. "Tonight luck was on your side. Next time you might not be so lucky."

"Google Wei Zhang and look for the article about him in Macao. There's a picture of him with a couple of Thai big shots sitting around a table. You might recognize the men. What kind of influence do you think Zhang has?" asked Calvino.

"Our world is suspended in the air, Vincent. Influence, power, arrangements that have stood the test of time are all being questioned," said Colonel Pratt.

"And friendship. Is that also up in the air?"

"I wouldn't be here if that were true. I'm speaking as your friend. Have I ever said to you, 'Leave. It's too dangerous. I can't control the situation. I can't protect you?' The answer is no. But there are limits to what I can do. You are looking to your world for answers. In that world, evidence and facts are used to solve problems in a different way. The world here has its own way, and you have to accept that. So yes, I am saying, for your own good, leave for a couple of months. The travel would do you good. Given a little time and things will have been resolved one way or the other. "

Colonel Pratt sipped his water, walked over to the window, and looked out at the city in the distance. The lights still burned in the string of high-rises circling Sukhumvit Road like a necklace of pointy teeth.

"Pratt, don't take this personally. But I'm planning to stay."

Pratt nodded. "You do what you wish, Vincent."

"Aren't Ratana and I invited to dinner this weekend? Or do you wanna cancel?"

The colonel smiled, put a hand on Calvino's shoulder. "Please come to dinner."

After Colonel Pratt left, Calvino called Siriporn and, with more velocity than a bull market, she walked into his bedroom. She removed her watch and her bracelet before slipping her dress over her head. Underneath, her naked body caught the lights from the street below. "I knew you'd call," she said with confidence.

She knelt forward on the bed and kissed him. He wondered if a curious tongue was a requirement for being a good broker. He hoped so, since she was also advising him on investing his money. Siriporn softly stroked a couple of blotchy bruises on his shoulder. "You're hurt," she said.

"You should've seen the other guy," he said.

"You were in a fight?"

"An accident."

"Serious?"

"It depends who you ask."

"I am asking you," she said.

He smiled. "It set off some fireworks."

And she smiled back at him as he leaned forward to kiss her on the forehead.

Later, as he lay in bed and looked out the window, with Siriporn curled up beside him holding a pillow against her stomach, he thought about Achara and Brandon and Zhang. Two of them were dead. And that included his last paying client, a farang who'd had the courage to keep going ahead after the death of his Thai business partner. Brandon had no longer looked happy; he must have had some suspicion that he wasn't safe. Someone had gone into that short-time room and shot him with the Taser, and in that instant everything would have become clear, the illusions and delusions exploded with the load of confetti from the Taser cartridge scattered across the bed and the floor.

He couldn't help but think of Tanny. The look of respect on her face as she'd glanced at Wei Zhang.

"You're thinking of her," said Siriporn.

Women seemed to know when a man was thinking about another woman. "I was thinking about the fireworks," he said.

She knew he was lying but said nothing, a little sigh escaping from her throat. "What kind of fireworks?"

"Roman candles and rockets."

The man he'd pulled from the van had been beyond a state of pain. He'd looked like a man who had been wrapped in barbed wire and rode an avalanche down the side of a mountain. His eyes had stared at Calvino like the eyes of a man who knew he was already dead. Calvino wished Tanny had seen those eyes.

THIRTY-NINE

SCULLY PASSED A row of whitewashed buildings, slabs of concrete with barred windows, shabby shophouses uniformly desolate, like a project or a prison. He wore blue jeans and a Boston Red Sox T-shirt, and a thin line of sweat covered his upper lip. Nothing about Scully said ex-FBI, and he was happy to pass as another late-middle-aged farang out in the boiling heat, his path flanked by massage parlors and bars. He used the back of his hand to wipe off the sweat, cupped the same hand over his eyes, scanning the lineup of parked cars. Halfway down, Scully spotted Calvino's white Honda with a bashed door and front fender. He continued walking, shaking his head as he assessed the damage the closer he got to the Honda. The daytime traffic in the Washington Square was light—a delivery van, a pickup unloading large bags of ice, another one unloading crates of soda, a taxi, motorcycles—and he grinned, catching the eye of a massage girl who sat with several others in the street near a vendor's cart. She looked up from her bowl of rice noodles and blew him a kiss. His smiled widened.

"Later," he said.

"I wait you," she said, giggling, covering her mouth with one hand.

Having exchanged lies with her, Scully continued walking until he stopped beside the Honda and rapped his knuckles on the window. Calvino opened the passenger door, and Scully walked around and climbed inside. The engine was on, keeping the air running. It was cool inside. Calvino was parked in front of the muay Thai school.

"Watch the guy in the red trunks," said Calvino, looking at a couple of men—one of them a foreigner—on the other side of the window, circling each other in the ring. The Thai boxer's right foot came off the mat, and he executed a perfect front knee kick. "That kick is called *kao drong*. And that one is *dtai kao*." The Thai boxer landed a kick to the side of the farang's left knee. It struck home, the pain registering on his face—just as the pain had registered on the face of the guy who, the night before, had pulled a knife on Calvino.

"You said you had something to show me," said Scully.

Calvino glanced at him, smiling. "Yeah, I've got something to show you."

Scully looked around, admiring the location that Calvino had chosen for the meeting. But it wasn't obvious what Calvino had in mind. "Kick-boxing moves?" asked Scully.

Calvino continued to watch the boxers. "To watch men in hand-to-hand combat is to learn something about how to stay alive."

"I've learned just about all I wanna know about my fellow man. In battle or peace, you never know who will stand his ground when you have the need."

"You know the Thai word *chok*?"

Scully shook his head.

"You should, as a married man. It means 'to fight.' I've got a fight I can't run away from. I could use a little help."

"I'm retired, Vinny. The fight's pretty much gone out of me." Scully paused, searching carefully for the right words. "But I'll do what I can. Though I can't see how, with the connections you have in the police department, I'd be of much help. You must be desperate."

It was a sobering moment when Calvino was forced to admit he was locked in a world of danger and had no choice but to reach out in order to limit the damage.

"Like a lot of people," he said.

"Yeah, I guess you're right."

Scully sat in the car watching the boxers throw punches, kicks, circle the ring, sweat dripping down their muscled bodies.

Calvino had parked in the open, in a public place. As long as they stayed inside the car, he thought the chances were good that no one was listening in. It was possible someone had a directional microphone rigged up from one of the buildings in the square. But it wasn't likely they'd have guessed that Calvino would park in front of the gym when his habit was always to park in front of the Lonesome Hawk. His parking was an advertisement for the staff hanging around the smokers' deck outside, who opened the door and leaned inside shouting an order to get Calvino's usual drink and lunchtime special.

"What have you got?"

"A possible murder weapon."

"Brandon."

"You remember the two marks on his chest. I may have recovered the weapon, or one just like it."

Mike Scully raised an eyebrow. "Shouldn't you hand it over to the police? You got your colonel friend. Give it to him. If you're in a jam, he's the man to get you a free pass out of the tiger's cage."

Lions' cage, thought Calvino. He thought about what had been left of Achara after the lions had finished. There was no time to explain that Colonel Pratt was locked inside the same cage. "Mike, if you don't have the time, that's okay."

Scully eye-rolled Calvino. "Whatcha got?"

"Open the bag in the back. You tell me what I've got," said Calvino, glancing over his shoulder.

Scully turned in his seat, reached over, zipped open the gym bag on the backseat. Calvino looked straight ahead, watching the two fighters. They wore red head protectors and plastic teeth guards, the combination distorting their features, turning them into alien-like creatures who danced barefoot around the ring, kicking and punching.

"I've never seen one like this," said Scully. He held the weapon low, resting against his lap.

"It's not one of yours?"

Scully shook head. "Not any weapon I remember ever seeing. Technology changes." He turned the weapon around, examining the grip. A raised lightning bolt was etched through a full moon on the side. He ran his fingers down the ribbed surface, slipped his finger against the trigger guard and eased the trigger back. Nothing. It was a dull, lifeless grayish blue, but a shade darker than a Taser. The barrel ended not with a hole for the bullet but with a stubby cube, blunt and ugly, the pug-nosed end that passed the current. "The heft is different. This weapon's got a Taser design, but it's something else. Some kind of knockoff is what it looks like to me. Where did you get it?"

"From a crashed van," said Calvino.

"Interesting weapon."

"If it's not a Taser, what is it?"

"I've got no idea. But it looks like it was professionally manufactured. I don't remember seeing anything like this. I'm going to have to report it." Scully had taken his sense of duty into retirement.

"You do that," said Calvino, reaching into the backseat for a plastic shopping bag. He opened it and showed Scully the contents. "A spent cartridge and a half dozen unused ones. "Take 'em."

Scully pulled out a cartridge. His eyes widened far enough to showcase the white all the way around the irises.

"The cartridges aren't regulation."

"Looks like the Taser's got some local competition," said Calvino.

Scully nodded. "You gonna tell me where you really got this stuff?"

"Mike, you're forgetting one thing."

Scully looked confused, racking his brain for what he'd forgotten.

Calvino reached over and squeezed his shoulder. "Mike, you work for me."

McPhail approached Calvino's car and slammed both hands on the rear window. Scully swung around with the electroshock weapon. Calvino had drawn his .38 from his shoulder holster. When they saw that it was McPhail, both men lowered their weapons. Calvino pushed the "down" button on his side window, and McPhail stuck his head in. "Baby Cook said she's put the special at your usual table and a double whiskey with ice. And she told me the soup is getting cold. The ice has already melted twice. And what do I get but two fucking guns pointed at me. Fuck you. Eat cold soup. Drink watered-down whiskey." McPhail weaved back and forth as if ducking punches from an invisible boxer.

"You don't look so good," said Calvino.

"I'm a little fucked up. Started drinking at ten. Hey, Mike, how you doing?"

Scully got out and shut the door. Calvino locked the car, and together they walked into the Lonesome Hawk and straight to Calvino's booth. McPhail crawled into the side facing the kitchen. Baby Cook came out with a bowl of soup for Calvino. She set it before him, looked him up and down. "Someone say they see you boxing. Muay Thai. That's why you late."

All eyes in Washington Square were public eyes, watching and reporting on who came and went; police CCTV cameras added another layer of watchfulness. No private eye could blend into the woodwork. The only way to work it was to become just another ordinary fixture nailed on the daily wall of life.

"I didn't start the rumor, don't look at me," said McPhail.

"Guilt by association," said Scully.

"You've got a good point. Exactly who are his associates?" said Calvino. He was thinking about Wei Zhang. Who *were* his associates? He thought of them as a weyr of fire-breathing dragons setting up their nests in Thailand. Not a pride, a swarm, or a flock, but a weyr. Dragons came in weyrs, even in Thailand. Calvino picked up his spoon and stared down at the soup. "Wei Zhang," he said, looking up as one of the waitresses circled to the booth behind McPhail.

"Whose associates we talkin' about?" asked McPhail. "Hey, honeybuns, scratch my back." He bobbed and squirmed under the pressure of Jum's fingernails running up and down his back. McPhail had forgotten his question.

"You see what's missing from the Ghost Wall?" he asked as he sent Jum off to get a lady drink.

Calvino, head bent forward as he ate his soup, looked up. "Old George's photo."

"What happened to it?" asked Scully, scratching his chin.

McPhail lit a cigarette as Jum came back with a shot glass filled with Mekong and a water glass filled with cola. She swallowed the Mekong, shuddered like she'd been harpooned, and washed away the blowback with the cola.

"Baby, massage my shoulders. Baby Cook said when she came in this morning, it had fallen down on the table over there. The frame and glass had shattered and were scattered on the floor. Freaked her out. She thinks it's Old George's ghost."

"What do you think?" asked Calvino.

"I told her it was Bill. He kept me moving the frame this way and that. It must have loosened the screw enough that the whole thing came down."

Calvino nodded, looking at the blank space where Old George's photo had hung on the Ghost Wall. "What did she say?"

"She said *I* had a loose screw." McPhail's eyes were half-lidded, as if he had gone into a transcendental state under Jum's experienced hands as she kneaded his shoulders like fresh dough. Soon he moaned with the kind of pleasure that only men of a certain age experience at the firm touch of a woman's hand unknotting old muscles. "You ever notice that no one ever sees a ghost during daylight hours? They only see ghosts at night. And why is it they only see one ghost? They never see a half dozen ghosts ring the bell at noon. I ask them these questions, and what do they say? 'Farang doesn't understand how Thai people think.' "

Scully smiled and looked away just as McPhail caught a flash of his grin.

"At least I'm not pussy-whipped," said McPhail.

Scully had heard this barb before. "If a man's gonna getting a whipping, he'd be wise to choose a pussy as the weapon to use. It doesn't leave any visible mark."

"Not like a fifty-thousand-volt jolt," said Calvino.

"That's the pussy I'm looking for," said McPhail.

Baby Cook arrived with the special—roast chicken, mashed potatoes and gravy, greens and stuffing—and scooped up Calvino's soup bowl to set down the hot plate of food in its place, executing the move in one graceful motion. Hands on her hips, her flabby upper arms covered in faded tattoos glistening with sweat, she flashed a crooked smile at Calvino. "I heat up twice already, Khun Winnee," she said. This was a woman who understood that some men were late for lunch, some men couldn't tie their own shoes, and some men plain and simple had a screw loose. Baby Cook had served them all and knew them for their true natures.

A German named Richter came into the bar dressed in a cheap Sunday-market pair of baggy shorts hung low on his waist with only his T-shirt covering the crack in his ass. He moved slowly from booth to booth, shaking each table. His clothes looked slept in for a couple of days. Round-faced, with green eyes, Richter had a bow-legged walk, feeble and bent over. He muttered to himself, sighing as he approached Calvino's table.

"What you do, Richter?" asked Baby Cook.

"Trying to find a table that doesn't wobble," he said.

"Go back to Germany," said McPhail. "The tables don't wobble in Munich."

Richter's eyes looked wild and slightly crazed. He had the look of someone the heat had tackled and knocked to the ground. A stream of sweat rolled off the end of his nose, leaving a trail on the tables and the floor.

"After a couple of drinks, they all wobble," said Richter. He stared at Calvino. "You need anything?"

Calvino shook his head. "I might have something for you. I'll give you a call."

Richter fished a cell phone out of his pocket. "You got my number?"

"Got it."

"Man, even your phone wobbles, Richter," said McPhail.

Richter shuffled off, testing tables.

The regulars at the Lonesome Hawk underestimated men like Richter. Calvino had taken some time to get to know that he was an electronics-surveillance expert. His crazy walk, sweaty clothes, and eccentric gestures led everyone to discount him as a crank—and that was his passport to hidden places.

McPhail had a point, thought Calvino. If you wanted to really understand a man, you had to go to where he came from, and the answer to who he was slowly emerged from his family, his neighbors, his school friends, his teachers, and his first love.

"You're suddenly quiet," said Scully.

Calvino sipped the Mekong and Coke. "I'm going to China."

"Take Richter with you," said McPhail. "Dump him over the side of Three Gorges Dam."

"Ah!" shouted Richter from the back, where he'd been listening to their conversation. "Chinese dam will wobble for sure."

McPhail somehow never got the emotional reaction from Richter he'd wanted. No outburst, no face red with anger. Like a lot of men who'd fallen, from time to time, into the gutter, Richter had managed to pick himself up and start again, happy-go-lucky. Falling into the gutter was one thing, falling into the abyss meant never hitting bottom, giving up any chance of starting over. Richter stared at Calvino for a minute or two, trying to figure out if his going to China was being dropped into the gutter or the abyss. It could go either way.

FORTY

TANNY CRAIG HAD been in New York a couple of weeks. Calvino had had no response to e-mails he'd sent her. His phone calls to her office went unreturned. He had thought about flying to New York and going to her office, sitting in the reception area, and waiting for her. But that wouldn't solve his main problem in Bangkok. Calvino turned his attention to Zhang's China connection. A Google search advanced his investigation to the edge of something promising about Zhang's business empire, but the searches always came up short. Gaps in the data and information meant that not even the Internet had made using shoe leather on the streets obsolete.

Colonel Pratt also had been skeptical about the ultimate usefulness of Internet research. The colonel was a traditionalist. The most useful information about a case was inside people's heads, not on a computer screen, and the challenge was getting inside those heads. "You scratch the scalp, but you never find the flea," he said.

"You've never heard of cyber warfare?" asked Calvino.

"I have other wars to worry me," he said.

Calvino understood that Colonel Pratt had taken considerable criticism over his protection. Though Pratt hadn't complained—he had said nothing—Ratana confirmed that the colonel had been given an order to put Calvino on a plane out of the country. If the Thai police decided to take a farang to the airport, it was highly likely no one would stop them from executing their plan. Calvino knew he had only a few days—enough time to fill in the blanks about Zhang's background and his burning interest in investing in Thailand—before he'd have to leave Thailand.

Twenty-four hours after Calvino had returned from China, he sat with a cup of freshly brewed coffee, the sound of Chinese still ringing in his ears, behind the desk in his office, hovering over his computer. He inserted his thumb drive and opened a file containing his field notes. For the first time in years, he was technically client-free. Meaning that only Brandon's ghost still visited him, asking for a drink from the bottle of Scotch in the desk drawer and needling him over why it had taken Calvino so long to connect the dots. He read through his notes, the dots beginning to connect themselves. He leaned back in his chair, hands stretched behind his head. The bone-tiredness of the journey had started to wear off. He looked out the window. It was too early for the yings at One Hand Clapping, and their plastic stools were stacked next to the building. If the rain didn't stop, they'd be forced indoors for the afternoon.

Calvino's presence in Bangkok hadn't made it easy for Pratt. Now that he was back, Calvino was aware that the problems would again emerge. He'd not phoned Colonel Pratt to let him know he'd returned. He found excuses to delay making the call. That the call would restart the chain of events troubled Calvino. Under the circumstances, he decided it was better to tell some lies, keep some secrets. Self-preservation was a general dumping ground to justify lying, but in some cases there was no other choice in order to stay clear of a bullet. Calvino causally mentioned over coffee with Ratana, that he'd planned to fly to New York and track down Tanny Craig and settle a little of his own unfinished business. He left the impression he was expressing his inner feelings—a man chases a woman for emotional resolution in order to find peace of mind. The very kind of self-searching that women liked to think men were as affected by as they were, unaware that men used the matter of the heart in a premeditated way as cover. Ratana would pass along the misinformation to Colonel Pratt. Instead he'd landed in Phnom Penh, where he'd applied for a Chinese tourist visa at the embassy, and caught a flight to Kunming.

His first order of business was to follow the money Achara had donated to the temple-building project. The temple turned out to be much larger and more elaborate than he'd expected. Polished porcelain surfaces, wind chimes and gongs, a pair of large stone lions, and hand-carved doors with red dragons and brass fittings. Calvino had recognized the mane, jawlines, and eyes on the Chinese guardian lions—it was like reading a man's signature you had seen before. Inside the temple an old monk showed him around, pointing out the photographs of clan members lining one wall. He had pointed at the faded photo of an old man with a goatee and rimless glasses and said that was Achara's grandfather. Another ghost wall, Calvino had thought. He turned to the old monk, and the question came to him: "Did a man named Wei Zhang have any relatives in the temple?"

The old monk, with gnarled hands and a serene smile, shifted his robes and told Calvino that Zhang had made the biggest donation to the temple, as indicated by a framed photo of an elderly Chinese man, his face wrinkled like a prune and sporting a braided pigtail flecked with gray. Although the other photos were covered with dust, this one was shiny and polished, and slightly larger than the others. It had been positioned on the wall facing the river below the temple compound. Wei Zhang's great-grandfather, firm jaw, piercing eyes, stared into the camera. He had a no-nonsense look that befitted a ship's captain, which is what the old monk told Calvino he'd been, one of the last of a generation who remembered British naval ships patrolling the river. Later this great-grandfather had kept horses and gotten into what proved to be a highly profitable business of supplying the army with horses.

The monk, with his black teeth and a face that looked like it had gone through several lifetimes, ignored the novices hurrying past without so much as a sideward glance. The abbot shouted after one or two of them to pick up a broom and sweep the courtyard. But the young boys in their novice robes ran away, knowing that the presence of a foreign visitor would offer a temporary safety net. With some gentle nudging by Calvino, along with a cash donation stuffed in the top of an offering box—a large wooden chest with gold lettering on the outside—the old monk spoke about Wei Zhang's great success. His empire proved how much good karma Zhang had accumulated from prior lives. It was also the result of his family lineage. No one would ever have thought that young Wei would grow up to have such large face, fortune, connections, and a footprint so long that it would stretch from China into Thailand. Like his great-grandfather, Zhang had parlayed connections inside the army—in Zhang's case the People's Liberation Army—to back him in business.

The abbot introduced Calvino to another man, a younger Chinese, in his fifties, who said Zhang had been a weapons specialist, and he explained how Zhang had used his Communist Party membership as a passport to advance along the road to becoming a big-shot businessman. The question in Calvino's mind was whether to trust this man who hadn't arrived at the temple by accident—someone had sent him. Was his role to keep an eye on Calvino and report back, or was he a new breed of freelancer who'd split a commission with the abbot?

Calvino looked him over. His haircut was a fresh military brush that gave him an official look. He wore a red polo shirt that tented over his ample stomach. He was from one of the ethnic minorities—half Tibetan and half Naxi. The kind of mix the Han Chinese viewed with suspicion. He went by his Tibetan name, Tagme. He was educated enough to know what "tag me" meant in English and told the joke on himself. Tagme agreed to act as Calvino's interpreter. He said, in a conspiratorial whisper, that many people in Zhang's village gossiped about in the number of Thai wives Zhang kept.

Calvino hired him for fifty dollars a day.

On day one, Tagme showed up wearing a green army cap, a yellow necktie, a purple shirt and black trousers. His face was puffy and round, with loose skin. The man looked totally different from the one Calvino had met at the temple. He sounded different, too.

Tagme was fond of homespun slogans that had a vaguely Mao-like cadence. "Take care of your body, Mr. Calvino. Because you will need to use it tomorrow." Or he would say, as he lifted his cap and scratched his balding head, "Keep your cap on and you'll always know where to find your head." Tagme smiled and clapped his hands together, applauding his own performance.

Calvino had a plausible cover story for his inquiry into Zhang's life. The price of the information inside China came at the cost of a small lie—he said that he was an American journalist doing a feature story for a financial newspaper about the rise of powerful business leaders from remote parts of China. He had taken Kincaid to lunch before leaving Thailand and arranged the cover should the Chinese ask. Kincaid received an official okay from an editor to use Calvino as a researcher on a Chinese business story. He also received a white envelope from Calvino. Yunnan province had filled the bill for the supposed story he had proposed: It was remote, and Zhang was a billionaire. Neither Calvino's interpreter nor the locals had come across a reporter asking about a famous native son. But no one was particularly surprised. Zhang was someone they thought everyone in the world had heard of, more famous than Warren Buffett.

Tagme introduced Calvino to an old woman, her back curved like a crossbow from a lifetime of carrying bamboo baskets filled with grass to feed livestock in the hills. Her rubbery face had gone slack, her neck sagging as she sat on the stoop in front of her simple wood-frame house. The woman had been a minor wife of Zhang's grandfather. She remembered Zhang as a boy. He had once blamed her son for stealing money left on the table by the father. In fact Zhang had taken the money. His father believed him rather than the boy whose mother was his minor wife. Near the end of the Cultural Revolution, a cadre had dragged her boy out of the house and beaten him. They'd sent him to a re-education camp and then to the army. If he'd been older, they might have killed him like they killed many others during that time. He loved his country so much. That's why he joined the army. She wailed how this was only one of many injustices she'd endured over her lifetime as a minor wife. She wiped tears from her old eyes as she said how the boy had been killed in a border war with Vietnam. The border was settled now, she said. Her boy had died for nothing. He had suffered, too. She unwound the scarf from her shoulders and patted her eyes, but the pouches under them continued to pool with tears.

Zhang had escaped from the sticks, the province where Mao's Long March had ended. His lineage included a great-grandfather who was a supplier of horses to the army. But it was his grandfather who had the wisdom to arm Mao's army. That wasn't just any family foot he'd planted in the door; Zhang's revolutionary foot could open a lucrative side door into the largest standing army in the world. All relationships that traced over a hundred years to the military would have meant nothing had his grandfather failed to see which way the wind was blowing and sold them weapons, then branched into electronics, mining, and shipping.

Several days later, they drove to a nearby village. Tagme pulled over to the side of the road, where the land sloped down into a valley. Rice paddies ran to the north in a uniform green blanket, with snowcapped mountains in the distance under a cobalt-blue sky. Tagme rolled down his window and spit. He pointed at the rice field. "A full belly never rests, because tomorrow an empty belly wants rice." He spit again, adjusted his hat, opened the door, and stepped out. He walked down the sloped embankment and stood on the edge of the field. "Wei Zhang's genius was to take ordinary rice and make it extraordinary. Stronger. No chemicals." Tagme sighed, coughed up a large glob of a thick tarry substance, which he shared with the crop.

"He had a problem with the government."

Tagme's mouth turned down in a frown. "So I hear."

Looking at the valley, Calvino could imagine the winds of gossip whipsawing from hamlet to hamlet. "What do people say?"

Zhang had engineered rice and had fields growing the crop throughout the province. Tagme filled in a gap in the picture. There'd been a rumor that someone in the People's Liberation Army or the Agricultural Ministry had raised doubts about the genetically altered rice. It was less a concern about the health of consumers or the environment than an attempt by Zhang's enemies to see him reined in, if not knocked down a couple of notches. There had been inquiry, investigations, and a hearing, all conducted in back rooms. Zhang came out bruised but had defeated the men who were behind the trouble. Yet it had cost him in a number of ways. Thailand was a card he'd played to stay in the game.

FORTY-ONE

THE INFORMATION CALVINO unearthed in Yunnan provided an early history of how Wei Zhang's power base had been nearly derailed. But the tracks had been laid on a solid basis from the time of his great-grandfather. Men like Zhang, like Mao, suffered setbacks, some small defeats, but after the smoke cleared, they remained standing while those who had fought to destroy them found themselves abandoned and exposed on the unprotected margins. Neither Tagme nor anyone else in the village could tell Calvino what part of Zhang's Thai ventures he had committed to deliver to the PLA.

Calvino had a theory. He saw Zhang looking out over a vast rice field and thinking of a way around the controversy the genetically altered rice had created. He shifted his attention to Thailand, another major rice-growing country, with a plan to redeem his vision of fast-growing rice crops. It remained a working theory, but one that was consistent with Brandon and Achara's experiment in Thailand's rice fields.

Acquiring another company was a time-honored shortcut in business. Their Thai company already had received all of the necessary government permits. But there was another piece of the puzzle with no obvious connection to the altered rice crop—Zhang's weapons-development program.

Was the rice-growing a cover for the weapons program? Or were they equal chips placed as business bets? Only one point was clear—Thailand was a good place to develop, test, and produce both exotic rice and exotic weapons.

Tagme shrugged off the notion that Zhang was an arms dealer. Calvino drew a picture of the Taser. Tagme patted his fat stomach, belched, and drank another beer, looking wall-eyed as he studied the drawing. He no longer bothered to dress up in his yellow necktie and purple shirt. Impressing the foreigner was no longer necessary. His eyes were unblinking as he studied the image of the weapon Calvino had sketched. Having a foreign financial journalist pump him about a weapons program was a surefire way to get Tagme a prison cell. He disappeared from sight for days. Calvino had looked everywhere for him. Then without any warning, Tagme showed up in his battered car, he had his dress clothes on and worked a toothpick on his upper molars.

"I have a new customer," he said.

"I want you to work for me," Calvino said.

"I work for you and maybe I get sent to prison. Tripping over your big boots to get money means you are working for the doctor and hospital."

"Double your fee and no more questions about weapons."

Tagme noisily twisted the toothpick, then spit. "Okay, two and a half times."

"Deal." And they shook hands.

"Should have asked for three times," said Tagme.

There was one condition: No more open talk about electroshock weapons manufactured to kill. That the new deal, and Calvino agreed to it. Tagme, whose inexhaustible knowledge about the history of Chinese rice, had no room for an interest in high-tech weapons. He replied with slogans each time Calvino tried to draw him out about Zhang's weapons development. It made sense in a weird way: Zhang's fortune was based largely on altering things—genetically altered rice and mechanically altered weapons. Zhang had followed in the footsteps of his ancestors in planning for the future and for their own place at the top of the pyramid.

Tagme wrote down the names and kinship relations of the people shown in the photos, which included Wei Zhang. Calvino asked Tagme to also write down the names of Zhang's school, his neighborhood, his childhood friends, his mother and father, aunts and uncles, classmates.

"Working for you reminds me of the Cultural Revolution," said Tagme.

"Keep writing," said Calvino.

Tagme looked up from the page, set down the pen, and lit a cigarette. "Then what?"

"We find the people."

Tagme guided Calvino through a game of house-to-house search. It took them a week to cover several villages, tracking down Zhang's family and friends, looking at old family photo albums—the ones that had been hidden during the purges of the 1970s. Zhang at eight years old, all teeth and snub nose, looking at the camera, was recognizable from the way he tilted his head to one side. Zhang at twelve, seventeen, and in his early twenties, filling out, more confident, hands on his hips, stared down the photographer. Every man had secrets. The more Calvino talked with people from Zhang's village, the more he felt they clammed up once he started to probe into Zhang's childhood. Then one morning an old woman he'd seen a couple of times before waved him over. She chewed a wad of tobacco and spit a foot ahead in the dirt.

"Find a Naxi called Tsier Qidgu and ask her. She knows a thing or two." Tagme had whispered that the old woman was half mad, and the other half wasn't all that sane. Something about the direct, focused look in her eyes, though, told Calvino that he should listen. "I want you to find this woman," he said to Tagme, who lifted his cap and scratched his head before carrying on a fifteen-minute conversation in Chinese about Tsier Qidgu. Afterward he slapped his thigh, sucked his teeth, and did about every gesture possible to relay his feeling that this was a wild-goose chase.

"Ask Tsier Qidgu about Chou." That was what the old woman had told Tagme. She'd laughed, shaken her head, and stuck another plug of tobacco between her teeth and cheek.

Doubt—and fear—registered in Tagme's eyes.

Truth, doubt, and anger showed in the eyes; there was no place for the eyes to hide those feelings.

In a chicken-scratching, flyblown Naxi village cupped like a fist inside Yulong, the name of the snowy mountains, located about thirty miles outside of Lijiang, Calvino found the house of the old woman named Tsier Qidgu. Her house was built from stone and soil; the courtyard was paved with cobblestones and blue and white tiles. She sat on a small bench, waiting for Calvino's arrival, as advance word had preceded him. For the occasion she'd dressed in a sleeveless black jacket over a blue blouse, a pleated skirt, and a black turban. She ate corn from a cob, looking up as Calvino entered the courtyard. Her weathered, lined face revealed a smile and the absence of several teeth, aging her another twenty years. She looked as old as the mountains framed behind her small compound. Tagme said the old woman lived in a good Naxi village. The bad villages were inhabited by evil men and were to be avoided even by other Naxis.

Tagme sucked his teeth and said that the Naxis could never keep a secret. And they believed in the old superstitions, and no one took them seriously in modern China. He admitted that the Naxi women were tall, strong as oxen, and good workers. But that was offset, in his mind, by the fact that they couldn't think straight or keep their thoughts straight, spending their lives supporting lazy men who lay around all day and played musical instruments and drank all night.

"Tell me about Chou," said Calvino through Tagme.

She fidgeted, tented her fingers, pouted, and slowly sighed.

"What's Chou's connection to Zhang?" Calvino nodded. He showed her three one-hundred-dollar bills and folded them into her hand, then balled her hand into a fist. She squeezed the notes even as Calvino removed his hand from hers.

"I can only report what I saw," she said. She swore that she'd never told another person for fear of the threat issued by Zhang's father that he would kill everyone in her village if she opened her mouth. The old man was long dead. The son was no longer in the region. No one cared much about such matters in modern times. She clutched the green notes in her hand as if they represented modern times.

She eyed Calvino, not saying anything. "Okay, we have tea first. Then we talk."

After small talk, Tsier Qidgu wiped her mouth and hands. Tagme translated.

Forty-five years ago, Tsier Qidgu had assisted the village midwife at Zhang's birth. She'd been young at the time. But she remembered the event clearly. Zhang hadn't been launched into the world alone. She smiled and fell silent. Calvino pressed Tagme to find out what the old woman meant. Zhang was the eldest son. But he was the eldest by default; his elder brother had been born dead. She had witnessed the face of his stillborn twin, eyes squeezed tight, a grim, sorrowful expression crossing the tiny lips, the fist a dull blue. The sexual organs had been only partially developed, but the child was recorded as a male. Zhang's twin came out first. The physical anomalies of the dead twin, and indeed the very existence of the dead baby, had been kept as a family secret. But in a village, secrets were difficult to keep. The midwife and her assistant, Tsier Qidgu, had witnessed the birth. Zhang's father paid both to seal their lips. The seal broke over time. Tsier Qidgu spoke to her sister about what had happened, making her swear never to repeat the story on pain of calling out the spirit of the dead twin. The chain didn't stop with the sister. Achara also had found out about Zhang's unusual birth. The midwife was his aunt. Tsier Qidgu said that the dead brother had haunted Zhang's life.

"I told you the Naxis were superstitious," said Tagme in English, shaking his head. He conveniently left out the superstition of the Tibetans and Han Chinese.

The old woman continued with her story. After Zhang's birth, his father organized a birthing ritual with some shamans, one of whom was Tsier's uncle, a man of great reputation for casting out devils, taming demons, and lifting curses. The dead baby was cremated and his ashes buried in a bronze urn. It was the location of the urn, the holding of the secret ceremony, along with her presence at the birth and ritual that she swore on pain of death never to reveal. It was said the spirit of the baby returned to haunt Zhang's family twice a year.

Calvino drove back with Tagme to his hotel in Lijiang. The ride had been mostly in silence. Tagme said he thought the old woman might be insane. Calvino shrugged, saying, "She looked sane."

"A Naxi trick played on foreigners."

Less than a week after meeting Tsier Qidgu, Calvino knew that the time to leave Yunnan had arrived when two uniformed police officers showed up unannounced. They approached him in the lobby of his hotel and asked for his papers. They looked over his passport, his visa, and the letter from the New York editor. They asked why he was so interested in Zhang's personal life if he were writing a business article? And specifically they asked Calvino why he'd been asking about exotic new weapons. And what was he doing talking to an old Naxi witch about superstitions? Someone with certain skills must have turned the toothpick on Tagme to get the background for those questions. Calvino wasn't allowed to leave his hotel until Kincaid's editor confirmed his assignment. Then he was told he had to leave the country. At the airport, he saw Tagme hanging around. He was wearing his hat, sucking his teeth, the toothpick firmly in the side of his mouth. His head remained on his shoulders.

FORTY-TWO

CALVINO HAD TYPED all the names and addresses of everyone he'd interviewed and put them into a database. The JPEG of Zhang in suit and tie was open on his computer screen. Calvino took a large red apple from the wicker basket that Colonel Pratt and Manee had sent to welcome him back from New York. He re-read Manee's handwritten note attached to the basket. He was glad to be home. He finished reading Manee's words again. He understood how McPhail had felt about avoiding seeing Old George at the hospital. It was easier to avoid others than to avoid living with yourself. It sounded like one of Tagme's slogans, he thought, looking for the whiskey bottle in the bottom drawer.

He hadn't been back in the office more than an hour before he told Ratana the truth. Then he phoned and told Pratt. "Glad that you're safe," said Colonel Pratt. Meaning he was happy that Calvino was still alive, and with the movement of events, no one talked about the van explosion or the three dead men or Wei Zhang. He didn't want to talk over the phone about what Calvino had found in Yunnan. He didn't say he was glad that Calvino was back.

Calvino picked up the phone to call Scully. He bit into the apple, cradling the phone in the crook of his neck, waiting for Scully to answer his cell. Calvino left a voice message saying he was back in town and suggesting lunch sometime during the week. He put down the phone and rummaged through the basket of cookies and fruit. Manee's note also said that she had made offerings at the wat for him, praying that his travels had fixed his broken heart. He thought about the people he'd met in Yunnan. They'd learned that despite suffering loss and pain, it did no one any good to whine to others. Everyone had a horror story to tell, every life had been shattered, glued back together, broken again.

Going through his e-mails, he found one from Tanny. It was a couple of weeks old. She had written, "I hope that you understand, I had to do what was necessary. Family is everything to a Thai person. But you already know that." She'd signed it "Love, Tanny." She included a photograph of her son, with a big grin, eyes squinting against the sun. Also a second photograph, taken in the compound of Government House with her mother, both women wearing yellow headbands, smiling, and each with her arm wrapped around the waist of the other. At the end of her e-mail was her Skype address. Calvino re-read the e-mail as if searching for a clue as to her intentions for writing. He'd seen enough of the boy's photo to understand what she had wanted and what he would have been unable to give to her.

Calvino showed Ratana the note and photos as he told her that he'd had no intention of going to New York. He'd expected a negative reaction from Ratana. But rather than showing hostility for being deceived, she looked positively elated.

"I thought you went to New York to be with Tanny. I assumed you would bring her back," Ratana said. Her sense of relief was overwhelming, and for moment it looked like she would hug him, but instead she rewarded him with a smile and then went back to her desk.

She looked up, still smiling. "I don't think you're over her."

Translation—shaving the truth was acceptable so long as potential rivals had not only gone from the front row of the picture but had been dumped from the frame. Calvino stood beside her desk, watching her type. His downcast expression was like that of a man who'd suffered a kind of honorable defeat.

"There was nothing to get over," he said. "*Phit faa phit tua.*" The lid doesn't fit the pot. It was an old phrase referring to a mismatched relationship. "I liked the lid, but the lid didn't like the pot."

Ratana smiled. She liked Calvino's way of falling back on a Thai phrase to explain a romantic misadventure even when it wasn't exactly the one she'd have used.

Relationships, like cooking utensils, were things close to the Thai heart—the breakdown in a relationship found its place inside the vocabulary used for stuff inside the kitchen. Ratana had seen a long line of his women flash like fireflies into his life before disappearing into the night; none of them were the right fit for her boss.

"Did you translate the Ministry of Commerce documents?"

"I e-mailed you the file," she said. "Kincaid phoned. His editor wants the story. He said you'd know what that meant."

That was the risk of a good cover story.

He returned to his desk, clicked back on his in-box. He scrolled down and found Ratana's. "Subject: shareholders and directors translated."

"What time is your meeting with Scott Baker?"

He glanced at his watch. "Three in the afternoon."

"Your getting involved in food safety is great," she said.

"If our food isn't safe, what is?" He thought about telling her he'd hired Scott Baker to go out to the two-thousand-

rai plot that Achara and Brandon had developed for the genetically engineered rice to perform tests on the soil and water.

"The food in China didn't make me sick," he said.

She smiled. "Of course not. That problem with milk and candy was stupid. Something the foreign media blew up to make China look bad."

"Because they don't like the Chinese competition," said Calvino in a flat voice.

"That's correct."

"And the Chinese like competition?"

Ratana sighed, her face clouded for a moment, and then she laughed.

"What's so funny?"

She looked over his shoulder, and Calvino turned in his chair, glancing out the window. A farang had tripped over a bicycle and fallen against three large trashcans, knocking them over, scattering the rubbish. He cursed and had trouble getting to his feet. The man was a morning drunk. Calvino pressed his hands against the window as he looked out and saw Bill from the Lonesome Hawk falling-down drunk in the rain. Seeing the state that Bill was in reminded Calvino that in Bangkok it was the wise man who never forgot the difference between falling into the gutter and a freefall into the abyss.

Bill had built a firewall out of booze, one that promised to protect him against life's despair and sorrows, but sometimes the wall collapsed and all that sorrow broke through like floodwaters threatening to drown him. No matter how much he drank, he couldn't stop the breach from catching him by surprise. He binge-drank when that happened. Ratana watched from the window above as Calvino helped Bill to his feet. The old man's eyes, hollow and red, were empty except for the void of sadness.

"Bill, where are you going?"

"McPhail blames me for George's photo falling off the wall."

"Don't let him get to you."

His old face tensed, his mouth narrowed as if he might howl. "I only wanted to help." Booze and self-pity filled Bill's shot glass in equal amounts.

Calvino guided Bill to the Honda and loaded him into the passenger side. He sat, arms folded like a scolded child, as they drove to Washington Square. When Calvino turned in to the parking space in front of the Lonesome Hawk, he opened his door. But Bill looked straight ahead. "Come inside, Bill."

"McPhail should know that I loved George," Bill blubbered, wiping away tears and snot with his hand. "I'm a vet. Just like George was."

Calvino patted him on the shoulder. "Let me buy you a coffee."

"Buy me a drink."

"You're already drunk."

"Not drunk enough."

Calvino understood what Bill meant. He'd heard it before. Drunks had no use for their sober self; better to bury it in liquor. Extinguish the memory of how it felt to be a sober man who'd reaped only failure. When Bill, like most drunks, said he wasn't drunk enough, what he really meant to say was that his drinking masked the pain that came from the realization that despite all his sober ambitions and belief in hard work, his life had amounted to an unbroken string of peacetime failures. It had been easier being shot at during the war, expecting to die. Being a drunk was much harder, but it had one redeeming benefit: No one expected much from a drunk.

After more encouragement that another drink was waiting for him inside the bar, Bill finally caved in and balanced himself on Calvino's arm, climbed out of the car, and staggered into the Lonesome Hawk, where he flopped into the first empty booth. McPhail was standing on top of the table next to the Ghost Wall with a hammer and nails. Old George's photo, in a new frame, leaned against the wall.

"Hey, buddy, I didn't expect to see you here," said McPhail.

Bill stared up at Old George's photo and blubbered.

"Bill, hand me a nail," McPhail said. "Stop crying and make yourself useful."

"Go easy, Ed," said Calvino. "Bill's got the strange idea you blame him for the accident with George's picture."

McPhail put down the hammer and climbed off the table. He hugged Bill and kissed his cheek. "You old fart. You're more sensitive than a woman going through the change of life," said McPhail.

"You said I screwed up. That it was my fault." The anguish of failure staring him in the face, Bill dropped his chin and shook his head. He drank long from his glass of gin and tonic.

"Okay, I admit it. But I got it wrong, you old goat. Baby Cook says the meat loaf special made the hungry ghost angry. I told her to take the meat loaf off the menu. Problem solved. What else do you want, you old bucket of spent ammo?"

"How about you buy me a drink." Bill's crooked grin reappeared, and he held up an empty glass the previous patron had left.

"You wanna drink on my tab, then you're gonna tell me how you and the other Rough Riders followed Teddy Roosevelt up San Juan Hill." McPhail snorted, lit a cigarette, and waited for Bill's drink to arrive.

"I'm old, but I ain't that old." Bill was coming around to the soldier self who clung on in the no-man's-land as his sober and drunken selves slugged it out. "But I admit I don't know too much."

McPhail exhaled from his cigarette. "So long as you remember your ATM card number, you don't have to know very much else to live happily surrounded by things and whores."

The firewall was being rebuilt, word-by-word, one glance, and one gesture at a time. Calvino slipped out of the Lonesome Hawk, leaving McPhail and Bill to hang the newly-framed photo of Old George. All it needed was more alcohol, and it would hold until the next suicide bomber of sorrow slammed into it.

FORTY-THREE

SCOTT BAKER'S WHITE lab coat made him look like a young professor or a doctor. He had in front of him a tray of beakers, slotted in rows of three. He'd been expecting Calvino since three in the afternoon. It was after four by the time Calvino had been cleared through three levels of security before being admitted inside the lab and office at Science Park. All the doors needed a personal ID card to open. Calvino walked down the corridor, past offices and labs on the cutting edge of the development of new technology— solar power, hydro engines, genetic research, and DNA and blood-analysis research. A security guard knocked on a nondescript frosted-glass door—WATER TREATMENT ANALYSIS SYSTEMS read a small sign in a metal holder, reinforcing the transitory, anonymous feel of the complex. They called it an incubator facility. The companies were like eggs; some would hatch, others would die inside the shell. Choosing doors that could have been copied from public toilets in New York reinforced the impression of Darwinian competition. Most of the experiments would never produce a commercial result.

Calvino liked the fact that there was no company name on the door. It fit his image of Scott Baker as a rebel, not so much without a cause but with no anchor, drifting in the commercial world to some distant shore that promised a better future. Like most idealists, Baker had a burning sense of mission. By middle age his mission would remain, but he'd likely be no closer to shore. He'd have the usual range of choices, disillusion, and drink or revenge and intrigue, or he could give up and sell out. As he approached the door, Calvino tried to guess what fate held in store for Baker.

A lab assistant opened the door. She smiled as Calvino handed her his name card. He saw Scott Baker, his back to the door, sitting on a high stool, working at a long bench.

"I have an appointment with Scott," Calvino said.

"Scott, Mr. Calvino's here!" she shouted across the room.

They were the only two people in the lab. "Would you like coffee?" she asked him.

Calvino smiled. "Black. No sugar."

Scott Baker climbed off his stool, his hand extended as he approached Calvino. "I thought you weren't coming," he said.

Calvino shrugged as if Baker hadn't been in Thailand long enough to know that one hour late was being on time. "You mentioned you had something for me. Something that was going to make me happy," he said. Anytime people told him they had something that was going to make him happy, it normally meant that it made *them* happy and he was expected to join in the celebration. It rarely worked out that way, except with a woman. He watched the lab assistant making him an instant coffee. She interrupted Baker to deliver the mug. Calvino took a sip and watched her settle into a chair behind a computer terminal. The sight of her made him happy.

"Getting what you asked for makes most people happy," said Baker.

"I'm happy enough," Calvino said. "And I rarely get what I ask for."

"I've got a report, and all the lab tests are attached," he said.

"Does this space belong to you?" asked Calvino.

Baker stroked his reddish beard. "Not mine personally. It belongs to Friends of Natural Food. They're based in Leicester. That's England. East Midlands."

"The lab is a long way from England."

"Food from Thailand, especially rice, is shipped to England. I can't think of a better place to have a lab."

Calvino, holding the coffee mug, followed Baker across the large, open space. Open but white. Everywhere. Scott lifted the tray of beakers and put them in a centrifuge, closed the door, and turned the machine on. Its low hum made the sound of a Tibetan mantra whispered in the wind. "You don't want to know what's in these," he said, glancing at Calvino.

"A whiskey mixer."

"It came from a klong. It's toxic."

"As you said, I don't want to know."

"But this water is from a test paddy. It is perfectly drinkable."

"The English drink anything."

Baker cracked an ironic smile. "I'm saying that the problem is basically solved." He pulled a file out of a filing cabinet and looked through it. "It's a contract with E-Dragon (Siam). They've agreed with each of our conditions. And best of all, they've agreed to limit the first generation testing to less than fifty rai." He handed the agreement to Calvino, who looked at the first page and then flipped to the last page. He wanted to know two pieces of information: The name of the two parties to the agreement and those who had signed on behalf of the companies listed on the first page. Wei Zhang's name was on the signature page; it was clear and elegant and somehow disconnected from the indecipherable man. Beneath the signature line, Zhang's name had been printed, eliminating any doubt he'd signed on the dotted line, and there was a signature by another company director—a Thai name that looked familiar.

Calvino stared at the second name and signature for a moment before he recognized the surname.

The director was a brother-in-law of General Suchart. Looking at the scribbled name, Calvino remembered the police general's wife, whose spidery web of power affiliations made her the big cheese at the Government House nighttime meeting, and the way the fear caused the Thais to bend over backward to pay her deference. He'd been one of them, handing her a basket of fruit. Ratana had supplied a map showing the relationship of family names of the new shareholders and directors after the shares were transferred following Brandon's death. The shareholders included nominees, four of which were other limited companies each holding ten shares, but the bulk of the shares were in the names of two individuals—Tamarine being one of them and her brother the other. They were both listed as members of the board of directors. It was public information—the one place to identify the masters of the universe, who inevitably were company directors. Ratana had spotted Tamarine and her brother's names immediately on new E-Dragon (Siam) directors' list.

Ratana had proudly printed out her research—while phoning a few friends and her mother—and put it on Calvino's desk. It wasn't that difficult. As in one large high school, everyone in Thailand seemed to know who had married into which family—at least any family with rank and privilege. Achara had said at a meeting that lineage, and ancestor worship, defined Asians. He'd been right: It sculpted Chinese identity, gave the living meaning, a sense of duty and obligation, and a composite, sober self they could live with. Lineage was their religion. Not to know the connection of people was to miss the transmission lines that carried the power from the generator into the field and beyond.

The company seal fixed to the signature page left a faded image of a dragon with bolts of lightning held in its talons.

As John-John's book had taught Calvino, dragons appeared in weyrs, and he'd stumbled into their nest.

"I told you that I had some good news for you. What if I told you that we'd won?" Baker asked.

"Depends on what you think you won."

"E-Dragon (Siam) agreed to scrap the rice project for the next eighteen months until more research can be conducted. The contract came in from England by FedEx yesterday. That's why I called and arranged the appointment. I thought you'd be over the moon," said Baker, his mustache and beard parting for a smile that emerged as a gaping hole in a thatch of red hair. "They've seen our position and gone out of the genetic-alteration business. That is a victory."

"Do I look like I want to take a victory lap?"

"I personally spoke with Wei Zhang, and if you don't mind my saying so, I think my arguments persuaded him," Baker said. "He was far more reasonable than Brandon Sawyer. Not that I wish to speak ill of the dead."

"I'm picking up a bad smell."

"It's the water from the beakers. Klong water. You get used to it after a while," said Baker.

Calvino shook his head. "There's something wrong. There must've been a problem using the land for growing rice."

"It tested as a perfectly good paddy."

Calvino had hired Baker to go upcountry and carry out environmental testing on the two thousand rai of paddy. Achara's connection had been instrumental in obtaining the licenses necessary to plant genetically altered rice. A test patch of rice had already been planted and harvested. It crossed Calvino's mind that Achara or Brandon had paid to get the results cleared. He counted on Scott Baker returning with contrary findings. Calvino expected a scary report documenting a case for massive contamination if the altered rice entered the food chain. What he was handed instead was a contract between Baker's NGO in England and the Thai company to voluntarily limit future planting.

"You checked the groundwater?"

Baker had started to put the contract back in the file.

"Make me a copy of the contract," said Calvino.

Baker hesitated. "It's confidential."

"Then you can refund the money I paid you."

Scott walked a couple of feet to the copy machine. He lifted the lid and slipped in the first page. "Let's say you genetically alter the rice so the paddy that has groundwater pollution leaching into the plant can be made to break down the chemicals and use them as a substitute for fertilizer. Good if it works."

"And if it doesn't?"

Baker stapled the copy and handed it to him. "You've got people eating nitrogen, mercury, zinc …" His voice trailed off as he watched Calvino study a clause in the contract.

"The stuff you can build cars out of," said Calvino, looking up from the paper.

"Yes, I guess you could say that. And that's what I expected to find. But the tests were negative. The groundwater is clean. Well, maybe not clean, but as close as you'll find in Thailand."

"You double-checked the results?"

"I triple-checked. Like you, I figured I might have overlooked something."

"When you talked with Wei Zhang, did he say what he was going to do with the land?"

"Funny you should mention that. He said they were putting in an industrial park—manufacturing, but clean and environmentally friendly. Nothing dirty like coal-burning plants. No activities that would harm—I mean, pollute or destroy—the soil or groundwater. It was more like research and development and testing of electronic systems."

"Electronic systems? A fridge is an electronic system."

"Fridges destroy the environment. You can be certain I checked there were no plans for fridge assembly."

"Any idea what *is* planned for the assembly line?"

"Electronic equipment."

"As in electroshock weapons?"

Baker's eyebrows did a red butterfly dance. His assistant, who sat across the room pretending to work, had been listening to their conversation. "He means like a Taser."

Calvino turned and saw her look up and focus on Baker, rolling her eyes. "And you are?"

"The brains in the lab."

"Don't go away. I may need to come back to you again."

"Zhang was quite open about manufacturing electronic crowd-control devices," said Baker. "Given what's been going on in the streets, God knows something to control crowds without injuring them would be an advancement."

The sad part was that Baker appeared to believe what he was saying, or he wanted to believe so hard that it amounted to the same thing.

Calvino turned back to the contract. "It says here that you will post on your Web site and send out a newsletter telling the world what a good corporate citizen E-Dragon (Siam) is and how they have contributed to your research into genetically altered rice." Calvino put the contract on the lab table. Zhang had successfully turned Scott Baker; he had successfully adapted the time-honored blueprint used by a pro who wanted to bar-fine a ying on her first day on the job, making her feel special, using soft, gentle words and throwing out big promises about tomorrow so she wouldn't feel like a whore once the money changed hands.

"That company is an example that will be used by a new generation of Chinese businessmen. It means that we've won," said Baker.

"That's the problem with intellectuals."

"What is?"

"You declare victory just as you're about to suffer a major defeat, one that you don't see coming. I should've seen what was going on."

"I told you what I found. Tell me what's wrong with my findings?"

Calvino pulled out his wallet and counted out the fee. He stacked and evened the edges of the notes, laid the stack on the table. "I pay you to answer *my* questions. It doesn't work the other way around."

On his way out, he stopped and gave his card to the assistant. "You ever get out to Sukhumvit Road, give me a call."

She took his card, while Baker, hands on his hips, the cash laid out on the table in front of him, waited. The money from Zhang had disabled his moral compass and his critical faculties. The funny thing about big money was its capacity to buy and use perfectly good minds. The magic was, it had bought Scott Baker without his even knowing he'd been bought. Zhang's money had also likely bought Tanny Craig.

Calvino walked out of the building, picked up his ID from the security desk, and crossed the parking lot to his car, thinking as he put up his umbrella how it had been that night at Government House. He'd seen a transformation in Tanny's mother—her body language, her eyes, even her posture changed. The regal, distinguished woman at the table had been like a god, a being who could part the sea of injustice that Mem had been drowning in most of her life, and let her walk through free, her head held high, the burden of her daughter's murder lifted. The fix had been in from the moment they'd walked through the door. Only none of the people except the general's wife understood the game and the hand that was in play. Calvino thought about phoning Tanny and asking her what her price had been. But he had a good idea of what she'd sold out for and wondered if she thought it had been worth it.

FORTY-FOUR

SOME WOMEN DEPART from a man's life within twenty-four hours after the first entanglement of limbs and mouths, exchanging bodily fluids like limpets; others lingered for days or weeks before falling to the wayside. Now and again there was a survivor who stumbled back from the front lines after years, knocking on the door and pleading to be let in. Siriporn, his broker, had all the earmarks of a survivor who was in for the long haul. The evening he opened the door, she stood smiling in a white spaghetti-strap dress, cleavage lifted from a push-up bra engineered like a suspension bridge. As an after-hours stockbroker, she knew how to influence a bull market. The plan had been to return to Calvino's condo and discuss information she'd collected and saved as an Excel file.

Calvino saw how much work she'd put into the job he'd assigned her. Siriporn had researched two-dozen listed Thai companies with earnings to justify the risk of a buy. She'd starred each strong buy recommendation and added columns spelling out book value, payout ratio, debt, P/E, and retained earnings. She'd also researched the three companies Calvino gave her; he didn't say they'd been listed on the shareholders' list of E-Dragon (Siam).

"There are three companies that aren't listed on the exchange. What did you find out about them?" Calvino asked her.

"Shareholders have big-shot names. And some Chinese names. Do you want to buy into a private company? That is quite risky," she said.

"You've got the names."

She nodded, turning on her iBook. "They're on my database."

He filled her wineglass and sat back on the sofa to watch as she opened the database and scrolled down an Excel file of names, ages, and addresses. She looked quite proud of herself as Calvino read down the list. She sipped wine and waited until he had finished. It was all there: The names of the people whom Zhang used to front for his companies.

"This isn't about investments, is it?" she said.

"Does it matter why I want the information?"

She brooded a little over his reply. "I have a sister who does weird things."

"Like what?"

"She finds private things about the people she needs to work with. She says it is profiling. Film says people leave evidence about their real intentions everywhere. If you look hard enough, you can follow their tracks and see what they really want. But she's looking at names of people she may decide to work with."

"Someone named Gaffer or Best Boy?" asked Calvino.

Siriporn pinched his hand. "You're making fun of my sister's nickname."

He read the information on the screen of her iBook again, absorbing the names.

"What was the nickname of that Craig woman's sister?"

Calvino looked up from the screen and found her smiling. "How do you know she had a sister?"

"You said that she had problem about a younger sister."

Women remembered everything. He had only a vague memory of a phone call with Siriporn and that he'd mentioned in passing he was helping Tanny with a family problem. It might have been a throwaway conversation for him, but Siriporn had stored it away for a rainy day. And it was raining outside now. It didn't end with the sister. Tanny's Thai name, the one on her birth certificate, appeared on the share registry of E-Dragon (Siam). Siriporn boldfaced the type just in case Calvino might miss it.

"You saw Tanny's name. But I'm certain she told you."

There was no point in arguing what he'd been told. Calvino shrugged it off. But Siriporn wasn't letting him off so easily. She enjoyed his discomfort in dealing with the help he'd extended to Tanny while all the time she'd been working to get the deal done with Zhang.

"She did tell you?" Siriporn pressed him.

"It didn't come up."

Siriporn smiled, savoring a small victory. "What kind of help did her sister need? Or maybe that didn't come up." Siriporn sat back, thinking he would let it drop. She assumed it was the usual family matter of hurt feelings and misunderstandings that occupied eighty percent of Thai domestic misery.

The price for associating with smart, educated women was that they saw through the evasions faster than a bat tracking a moth. "Her name was Jeab. She was shot. Tanny was after her killer."

"Oh."

The big "Oh" that registers just as you find you've stepped into something ugly and ruined a perfectly good pair of shoes.

Jeab was nearly twenty-three years old in February 2003 when she borrowed her friend's red Honda 150. She was running late for an appointment with a school inspector from Bangkok. The head teacher had assigned Jeab the duty of showing the inspector the premises and introducing her to the other teachers. The Honda belonged to Jeab's best friend from school, a woman named Moo, who had received a letter from the police station asking her to report. Moo had asked Jeab to go along, because a proper Thai woman would never go to a male-dominated place like a police station alone. It was only going to take a few minutes, Moo had promised. She asked the police why they thought she had anything to do with drugs. A neighbor had informed them that he'd seen Moo and her brother Dum deliver drugs.

The neighbor was a man named Vira, who had propositioned Moo and she'd refused to sleep with him. This happened as Vira's two friends looked on. She told the police that Vira lied and that he had tried to force sex on her. She had no friends at the police station. Vira did. Moo's interrogation took nearly two hours. They threatened to arrest her brother if she didn't sign the confession. They threatened to make trouble for her mother and father if she refused. They told her they could keep her in jail for as long as they wanted. So Moo signed. When she emerged afterward, Moo looked as pale as a TV soap ghost after signing a statement acknowledging that she was guilty of selling a small quantity of *yaa baa* and being told that by admitting her guilt, along with giving her promise never to sell drugs again, she was free to go.

Jeab waited patiently in front until Moo came out fighting back tears. Outside the police station, Moo said she was too upset to drive, that her head spun with black feelings, and she suggested going to the wat to make an offering. The spires inside the wat compound were visible from the police station. Jeab said she had a very important appointment to keep, telling Moo she should go to the wat on her own. Moo felt all the more dejected that her friend might be in trouble at school, so she insisted that Jeab take the red Honda. She was seven kilometers from the school. Too far to walk, and it was hot and sticky weather, threatening rain.

Two kilometers from the school, the road wound through open countryside. A pickup truck with two men in the back approached from behind. The driver rolled down the window and motioned for Jeab to pull over. He followed her until she had stopped then parked the pickup truck level with her motorcycle. One of the men in the back of pickup shot Jeab twice as she raised her hands. A witness working in a nearby field saw the pickup speed away and the red Honda motorcycle tipped over on the roadside. He ran across the field, his heart in his throat, and found Jeab dead beside the motorcycle. One of his relatives ran up a couple moments later and phoned the police to report the killing.

At the hospital the dead body was examined and the cause of death recorded. The results of an autopsy showed that two bullets had ripped through Jeab's brain. "Very professional," the doctor had written, as if to admire the marksmanship of the shooter. Jeab's clothes had been examined and recorded as personal effects. The following day, Jeab's mother was at the hospital, along with other relatives, looking at her dead daughter's body. Three police officers arrived and cleared the room. Fifteen minutes later they asked everyone to return, and displayed a small plastic pack of yaa baa pills and demanded to know why the attending doctor hadn't recorded this evidence when removing the clothing from the deceased. The doctor, nurse, and orderly all said the same thing: They hadn't seen the pills before. The police became irritated and asked if they might be covering up drug-dealing in the district. That shut everyone up. Except for Mem, Jeab's mother, who swore that day on her dead daughter's spirit to get justice.

The blue plastic packs were "found" by police officers on victims in every province in which people were killed during the period after January 28, 2003, when the prime minister signed what was called Order 29/2546. It morphed into a death warrant for suspected drug-dealers. The official name was firm but gentle: The "Concerted Effort of the Nation to Overcome Drugs." The reign of terror officially ended in April 2003, and a victory in the war against drugs was announced by the government and rewarded by the Americans.

In September 2004 the Bush administration removed Thailand from the list of major drug-transit or major drug-producing countries.

After Calvino had finished with the facts of the unsolved murder case, Siriporn said nothing for a couple of minutes.

"My father told me about the terrible things that happened then," she finally said, looking down at her wine.

Calvino refilled her wineglass to the brim, making her lean forward to sip the first inch; her throat felt constricted, and she looked up at him.

"I did what I could," he said. "It wasn't much. Tanny Craig did what she had to do, but it didn't work out the way she and her mother thought."

Siriporn didn't answer and turned back to her iBook. "Why didn't it work out with her?"

"I don't know. It just didn't."

"I should go," she said.

"You've done good," he said, leaning over her and kissing her on the forehead.

"Yes, better than you imagined. I know. But good for who?"

"I look for people. It's what private eyes do. Study patterns, because people can't help repeating themselves. They might try to disguise who they are, but sooner or later they stumble back into the old pattern and get entangled."

"You're right. Look, I want to show you something." She pointed at one of the Thai names on the screen. "Does it look at all familiar?"

Calvino studied the name. It meant nothing to him. "I don't recognize it. Should I?"

"She's a shareholder and director. Her family name is Craig."

He'd been prepared to accept that Tanny would move heaven and earth for her mother. But he asked himself if her side deal with Zhang came before or after the discovery of her mother and dead sister. She had needed a patron, and she knew that Calvino wasn't in a position to meet that need. Once that fact sank in, had she gone to see Zhang to shortcut an obstacle or two and in return gain the patron who could guarantee to catch her sister's killer? Calvino checked the date on the share-registry document; it was dated after the meeting with the general's wife at Government House. It could have been backdated. There was no way to know. He decided that whatever had happened along the way, Tanny had made a choice, and he'd like to think it hadn't included knowledge of what was planned for Achara and Brandon.

"It is easy to judge her, but what would I have done if it were my sister? What would you have done if it had been Film?" Calvino asked.

"Whatever I had to do," Siriporn said.

Calvino nodded, grinning. "I suspect that you would."

She rolled her eyes.

"This is very good work," he said, staring at her computer screen. His mind was already working out how to trace Tanny's Thai identity. How far back had this happened? What were the chances that she had set him up from the very beginning?

"You really liked her," she said.

"She was good, really good at what she did," he said. "Skillful."

"Was she better than me?"

He had invited the comparison. "Tanny Craig may have

turned out to be a better man than me."

Siriporn's frown easily slipped into a clownish pout. She brushed her hand against his cheek. She had won a clear victory and knew it. It showed in the way she held her wineglass, her firm confidence, and the glow of accomplishment in her eyes, like sunlight through a passing cloud.

"That means you won't be investing in these companies. Or am I wrong about that?" A warm smile opened as she took another drink from her glass, touching her tongue to the rim.

"I've been wrong about a couple of things. But that's all it takes to get blindsided."

Siriporn tapped her fingernails on the keyboard, shutting down the iBook. She had the cryptic look of a woman stranded in a no-man's-land between girlfriend and professional adviser. A look of sadness crept into her face, as if she realized there was nothing else she could do or say.

"I'll e-mail you the file tomorrow. Nice music," she said, listening to the music.

"Herbie Hancock."

"I like it," she said, closing the iBook. She finished her glass and started to stand up when Calvino pulled her down and kissed her.

"Why don't you stay?"

He felt sick deep in his soul, and somehow having her at his side would stop it from leaving his body and fleeing to another place. The place where Miles Davis went to compose music, thought Calvino.

"You still think about her?" she asked.

In the background Herbie Hancock's "Riot" drifted across the room; it filled the pause in conversation, kept her question unanswered. He looked over her shoulder at the rain falling.

"You're right, I'm being stupid. I need to go over some files. We can talk tomorrow," he said, kissing her on the forehead once more.

Pratt had always looked up to jazz greats like Herbie Hancock, John Coltrane, and Miles Davis, said these were men who took risks, never stayed in one place musically, men who were always experimenting, looking to break out of what everyone said was already a perfect, accomplished body of work. Mostly men who didn't live that long.

She stroked his cheek. "Are you okay?"

Calvino nodded.

"Bullshit," she said. "I want to stay. Are you blind?"

"Yeah." He raised an eyebrow. "As a bat." He listened to Herbie Hancock as the notes, bending and sharpening, blotted out the self-indulgence and foolishness he felt over Tanny. And in that moment he felt a pure moment of insight—he'd fallen into one of the oldest traps, and he could stay inside wallowing in self-pity or he could find a way out, turn things around before Zhang figured out that he had fitted the pieces of the puzzle together. That could wait until morning. Tonight he wanted to be with a woman who cared for him, had delivered him from that place no man wishes to find himself—in a state of confusion fueled by self-delusion. He liked to think that somewhere John Coltrane was smiling down on them.

Calvino waited to find the right words, but they weren't to be found, and he did the next-best thing—he said nothing as he took her hand and led her to the window. Outside, the rain was falling hard, runoff water swelling Asoke into an ankle-deep klong, traffic speeding up across the flyover, spraying a wall of water high in the air. Siriporn slipped an arm around his waist. The monsoon rains after dark had defeated their dining plan, or conspired with desire to the same end.

He put his arm around her, stroked her hair. She stared out at Bangkok, at the slanting rain washed in the golden glow of lights from the convention center across the road.

A driver lost control of his car and it spun out, snapping the front end of another passing on the left. The two cars collided.

"Accident," she sighed. "That's what I call bad luck."

"Before I left for China, I was in an accident in the same spot," said Calvino, watching steam come out of the engine of the damaged car below.

"Were you hurt?"

"No. I was lucky. As I said, it was almost a month ago. It's a dangerous corner. Sooner or later someone's gonna get hurt."

He told her about the damage to his Honda but glossed over what had happened to the men inside the van. There was no point in sharing the information. It was too remote from her life. She couldn't wrap her mind around the connection between private militias and what was uncoiling in Bangkok.

"It happened there?" She looked at the cars below. Her hands touched his face. They watched as the drivers climbed out of their cars to inspect the damage.

He pointed at the blind corner in the distance. "See that condo building at the fork in the road?" Raising her hand, he said, "Make your finger into a gun barrel. Point and fire. That's the blind spot."

"I had a dream a few nights ago that you were in a terrible crash. Ratana told me you'd been out of the country but that you were on your way back. She said your car was wrecked."

"I haven't driven it much since I got back. I'll get around to having the body work done."

She smiled, kissed his neck.

"Body work." He ran fingers along her neck.

"That feels good," she said.

"Glad to hear it."

"Wait, I have an idea. I know where to take your car,"

she said. "It's near where I work. They do a good job and not so expensive if they don't see your farang face."

They were halfway into the master bedroom, holding hands. He halted at the threshold. "Stop. Yellow line."

She looked down, frowning. "Where?"

"No yellow line and a green light."

Calvino slipped the spaghetti straps down over her shoulders, led her forward, and they fell into bed. He kissed her forehead. He worked his way slowly from the bridge of her nose to the side of her neck. What was it about a farang face that set off this tribal reaction? He was starting to trust her judgment. Not even Ratana had made the connection between Tanny and her Thai name on the record of Zhang's companies; and he'd also missed it. Overlooking something so basic troubled him. It made giving in to Siriporn easier than it otherwise would have been. Siriporn had her own agenda, but she'd earned a full tank of credibility. How was she going to use it? Getting his car repaired? That seemed simple and harmless enough, but there was a risk—she was using the little job as the next step on the road to a domestic, intimate relationship, doing stuff for each other the way couples did.

The fact was she was in his bedroom, asking to help him. What was he going to do as she took off her clothes? Say the banged-up car that needed repair was out of bounds? Looking at her body, he didn't much care at that moment if she kept the car. He agreed she could take the car in, and that made her happy. It was a little decision, a reversible one, he thought. He was happy to have her in bed; he thought of letting her help as a bonus payment. He was entitled to a celebration of life, for having returned from China or just for being alive. By all odds he should have been transported by the Chinese police to another place, the place of nightmares, the last frontier, where he'd find Achara and Brandon talking about the future and their plans.

A place of tracer rounds, a place where, in the shadows, Herbie Hancock and Miles Davis's music drifted from empty streets, a place filled with a rich tonality and emotion that delivered on the promise.

A strange noise entered his consciousness, and at first Calvino couldn't place the source. He opened his eyes and listened again. Someone was jamming his doorbell. He reached out for Siriporn and grabbed at an empty space. He sat up alone in bed, rubbing his eyes, feeling sore all over. Light leaked through small openings in the blinds. He reached for his watch on the headboard. The doorbell rang again, this time longer, more frantic. It was about seven in the morning. Calvino told himself that Siriporn had left something behind. An earring, a bracelet, a necklace, a piece of clothing, or maybe it was finally time to go through that Excel file, looking at listed companies who were looking for his money. He pulled on a T-shirt and a pair of tan trousers and walked barefoot to the door, thinking that he was going to find Siriporn standing on the other side, having locked herself out.

He opened the door, his arm coiled, ready to pull her close and kiss her. Instead he stared at a uniformed security guard, his face pale and drawn, eyes twitching as he shifted from one foot to the other. "You have a problem," said the guard through a bucktoothed smile that wasn't so much a smile as a smirk burned on a fright mask.

"What's the problem?"

"You come with me," said the guard.

"Where do you want me to go?"

"We go parking lot fifth floor."

"Is something wrong with my car?"

The guard nodded, his nervous grin twitching at the corners of his mouth like butterflies drinking nectar.

Calvino grabbed his keys and followed the guard to the

elevator. They stood in the corridor waiting for it to arrive. "Tell me what this is about."

The guard's head bobbed on his shoulders as if an invisible wire were pulling it. When he stopped shaking his head, he shuddered like a boy who'd tasted his first bad oyster. The elevator arrived, and the guard pushed the button for the fifth floor. When the doors opened, the guard bolted out, ran around a corner, and stood pointing at Calvino's car. The front left side of the Honda had taken a direct hit, as if a giant fist had smashed it. Calvino walked around the car, and on the right side seated up front, he saw a motionless body slumped forward, leaning against the wheel, the weight of the body against the steering column. The position of the body had drawn the guard's attention. When he saw that whoever it was wasn't sleeping, panic set in, and he'd raced upstairs to find the farang, the one who'd have to take responsibility.

Calvino opened the driver's door, knelt down, and slowly pushed her body to the side. Siriporn. Her eyes were no longer dreamy like the night before. Now, open and dull, they looked without seeing. He drew in a deep breath, reached out and pressed his finger against her neck, trying to find a pulse. He rested his ear against her chest and held his breath. He heard nothing but cold, stony silence. The smell of cooked meat in the confined space made him retch. The fingers on her left hand were black, swollen, the ring on her finger melted into the flesh. He looked back at the security guard, a young kid in a uniform two sizes too big. The current had gone straight from the ignition through her hand and into her body. Popping the latch, he climbed out of the car and was about to lift the hood when he thought better of it. What might be booby-trapped other than the ignition? He had no desire to find out. He walked around the car, rubbing his hands, the guard following his every move.

"She needs a doctor?" the guard asked, eyes wide, his hands shaking.

He was looking for reassurance that a doctor was the answer, but Calvino didn't give him any. He drew fresh air into his lungs. Then he leaned inside. The ying who'd found Brandon had reported a similar smell. He touched her wrist, and the skin felt clammy, cold. On the passenger's seat were her briefcase and handbag. And on the seat was her iBook. He grabbed the computer, glancing over his shoulder.

"Call an ambulance," he said to the guard.

Carefully he raised Siriporn's hand. The fingertips were burned, the plastic part of the car key dissolved and melted into her fingers. Calvino sat on the parking garage's cement floor, raised his knees, shook his head, looking at his car and then away. He should've sent her home last night, and now she'd be alive. At the same time, he knew that more likely than not, if she had gone home and he'd gone out to his car, *he'd* have been dead. Some dreams a man follows, and some nightmares follow a man, crawling out of his sleep and setting up a base camp to attack where he lived and worked. Tanny was back in New York. He decided it was a good time to call her and put a question to her: Was the pact she made with Zhang really about justice for Jeab? Whatever game she'd come to play was not much different from the one her sister had been caught up in. There was no time to call Tanny now or to weep for Siriporn. In a few minutes, others would notice and stop to gawk.

The security guard stood behind the car, waiting. He was no more than a kid in a billed cap trying to look as cop-like as possible. Only it wasn't working. He wasn't certain if he should stay by the car or do as the farang said.

"Go to the office and phone an ambulance. I'll wait for you."

The guard nodded, walked over to the elevator, and

punched the "down" button. He disappeared into the elevator, and the doors closed. Zhang's electroshock technology had shown no lack of creativity in its ability to mimic an accident. The man had resources, he had a firm commitment, and he had accumulated enough power to light up a city. When Calvino looked at the car, he understood the message Zhang had sent—he had no intention of backing off. The car had been parked, waiting for him to get in and turn on the ignition. The Chinese had patience. They could plan an ambush that would take days, weeks, or months to execute. It would be much easier to have Calvino killed with a bullet. Zhang, though, was going out of his way to finish him off in a fashion that not just eliminated the man but gave immense satisfaction in how it was done.

Calvino asked himself what he had to bring to the battlefield. Not much, he thought. The question was biblical—one asked by every David as he stared down and suddenly realized he was armed with only a wooden slingshot. But the answer was practical: Do whatever was necessary to surprise the opponent with overwhelming firepower. And remember that not all firepower came from the barrel of a gun.

Whatever the practical solution, Calvino knew he wouldn't be found in the parking garage sitting on the concrete waiting for the ambulance and the police. Colonel Pratt had been right. As every Thai understood, when faced with a greatly superior force, there was only one option— go underground, undercover, and under the protection of someone powerful. It was Calvino's car; the custom to flee the scene and think about what could be done in order to one-day rise to surface again and breathe air as a free man.

FORTY-FIVE

BEFORE THE POLICE arrived, Calvino slipped into the elevator, stepping off on his floor. He stashed Siriporn's iBook in a closet and laid a stack of *New Yorkers* on the top. He returned to the fifth-floor parking garage from the stairs, emerging from the elevator as the body-snatcher's pick-up, blue light flashing, angled to the back of his Honda. He walked over to the pickup and looked into the back. It was empty. The attendants waited, arms crossed, for the police. They didn't have to wait long. Two police cars, red lights flashing, powered up the ramp and screeched to a halt near his Honda. The officers piled out of both cars. He recognized two of them from the accident scene—they'd marveled as the black van delivered such an impressive, unscheduled fireworks display. One of the men getting out of the police cars was dressed in civilian clothes. He glanced at Calvino as he directed a uniformed cop to approach.

"Calvino," said the cop, his large hands hanging loose at his sides.

"I remember you, too." The line between being on the payroll of a militia and working on the force had blurred. Calvino couldn't be certain who was their boss.

They eyed Calvino suspiciously. Several more officers came over to him, as if to confirm that a miracle had occurred. Having satisfied themselves the farang was the same man they'd interrogated some time before, they set to work. They opened the car doors of his Honda. They checked the body for a pulse.

"She's dead," said Calvino.

The cop looked up. "You touched the body?"

"You find a dead body in your car, what would *you* do?"

Calvino reached inside the car, brushed his hand against Siriporn's cold cheek.

"Don't touch the body," said the cop.

"Don't touch the ignition," said Calvino.

He sighed, walked around to the other side of the car. All the time he kept his eye on the two police officers. There was something about their attitude that was disturbing. Neither cop seemed overly concerned about whether the car remained wired to deliver another fatal shock. One way to find out—he popped the hood latch. "Have a look inside."

One of the cops shone a flashlight on the engine housing. The key was in the ignition, and the back flasher lights blew red kisses on the concrete.

"We take your car to the station."

"You do that. Check the tires," said Calvino. "A tune-up would be good. Change the oil. Maybe get someone to wash it."

The cops were terribly interested in what Calvino had to say; one of them squeezed the keys in his palm. He was about to say something when the cop in civilian clothes put a hand on his shoulders. "We'll take your statement in a few minutes," he said in good English.

Nothing about them suggested they were in hot pursuit of the Four Noble Truths. Buddhism took the view that all things were, by their nature, impermanent, and these men stared at Calvino with a mixture of contempt and loathing, as if he'd escaped the inevitability of the rule. It also spoke volumes about the absolute certainty —if not arrogance—of those who'd organized and executed the mission, that they never needed to change personnel. It was called recycling failure. Or maybe it was more basic: Using a different set of men might have suggested they had something to worry about. What better way of delivering a message of confidence than sending the same officers to the crime scene? Vincent Calvino should have been on his way to the next life. "Mission accomplished" should have been forwarded to the right person. What should have been had an elusive history.

One of the officers focused a digital camera and snapped photographs—every angle of Siriporn, who remained slumped forward in the front. The ambulance guys stood in a corner waiting to be told when they could remove the body. Meanwhile two members of the forensics team dusted the exterior of car for prints. The senior cop who'd walked back to the silver-gray BMW police car, looked disappointed, as his men worked the crime scene.

To their credit, a fully prepared police response team had appeared in the parking lot in record time; they must have been nearby, expecting a call. Calvino figured they'd timed their arrival carefully, not showing up too quickly or too late. It was called the Goldilocks arrival schedule—a variation on the "meet and greet" system that welcomed new people to the neighborhood; only this wasn't a neighborhood anyone wanted to visit. It was a way of organizing police that had been perfected during the war on drugs. A dispatcher radioed in after she had talked with the condo security guard. The guard, who'd been upset on the phone, had neglected to give any details about the identity of the person found dead in a Honda City on the fifth floor of the parking garage of a condo located in Klong Toey district.

Two of the men shared a smoke, looked on with bored, listless expressions, hands on their hips, cigarettes in the sides of their mouths, smoke curling out of their noses. They'd assumed that this call would be to investigate the death of a farang and instead found a Thai woman dead in the car. They had nearly finished their report before the security guard had called in the job. Tearing up the paperwork and starting over again had put them in a bad mood. The two cops talked out of earshot, taking turns to gesture in Calvino's direction. They allowed themselves to show disappointment, masking a white-hot rage that lurked, boiling, occasionally breaking through the surface in their sideways glances, only to quickly recede, shoved back out of sight. The parking area around Calvino's Honda seethed with cops smoldering and uncertain of what to do next. There had been no Plan B.

Calvino had started his statement when Colonel Pratt arrived, coming up the elevator with the security guard who'd called in the incident. The interviewing cop closed his notebook, nodding for Colonel Pratt to follow him to the car. Calvino watched as Pratt and the cop had a discussion. The cop gestured with the notebook a couple of times, nodding at Calvino. They walked around the car. Colonel Pratt squatted down and looked inside. He knew Calvino's car well. It might not have been serviced regularly, but Pratt had never heard of a Honda, serviced or not, delivering an electrical current through the ignition system to kill the driver.

Colonel Pratt had a look inside at the body before walking to the front of the vehicle. "Maybe you should have stayed in China," he said.

"I was thinking the same thing about Wei Zhang," said Calvino.

"Are you okay?" asked Pratt.

Calvino shrugged and looked away, lips firmly compressed. She'd died in his place. How was he supposed to feel? Happy? Empty, sad, angry? He'd run through the emotions like doing scales on the piano. It was a warm-up for the program he had in mind. The other officers on the scene didn't seem happy with the way Pratt was handling the situation, but he outranked them. They said nothing as Colonel Pratt leaned over the engine and examined the wiring leading from a device the size of a landmine, menacing, homemade, covered in a green plastic casing, which had been expertly attached to the ignition wires. Someone had connected the device to the electrical system and made little effort to hide his work, a marker that the mechanic who'd rigged the device had expected a fluff team to arrive on the scene, remove it, clean up the system, and leave a mystery behind.

"It looks booby-trapped," said Calvino.

"The car, yes. The device, no." Colonel Pratt looked at his fellow officers. None of them disagreed with his opinion. The device had been planted in such a way as to allow for its easy removal. Pratt dropped the hood, and the sound echoed through the parking area. One of the ambulance guys, who'd been dozing on the side, jumped. Pratt walked over to Calvino as the police supervised a tow truck pulling into position.

"They're taking your car in for further inspection."

"You'll get someone to put a trace on that device?"

Colonel Pratt nodded.

"Good. Siriporn, Siriporn." Calvino shook his head, looking at her body. "Any chance the device will disappear between here and the station?"

They both knew the answer; the colonel had no need to confirm in the presence of the other officers that he had no control over the investigation once the car left the garage. "You're lucky. Those around you, not so lucky. Vincent, we need to discuss this in private."

Calvino locked eyes with the senior cop and his junior who stood beside the BMW. "Some of these guys look familiar. They showed up to investigate the van that night. We know how that turned out."

"Is there somewhere more private?" asked Colonel Pratt. "Not your condo. A place without windows."

He said "windows" as if it were part of an ancient riddle.

Calvino had started to feel the broad strokes of his life were starting to match the regulars at the Lonesome Hawk—men whose lives, like their stories, ended in skid marks and permanent scars.

Calvino walked in front, the colonel a step behind, on the stairs up to the pool and recreational floor. No one was around early in the morning. They silently passed the stone feature wall with its waterfall, pots full of large, leafy tropical plants, and goldfish swimming in a pond. They passed the kids' jungle gym, stopping in an open area near the pool. The gray clouds, knotted and frayed as a homeless man's blanket, rolled across the city, obscuring the high-rises along Sukhumvit Road, ghostly structures the color of old oyster shells.

"No windows up here," said Calvino, looking out at three tall condos under construction. The only building fully occupied in Bangkok was Government House, and that occupation was illegal.

The recreational area had a forlorn feeling, as if the inhabitants had abandoned the space in a hurry, leaving behind toys, plastic bottles, and a couple of shoes. The table and chairs sheltered under an awning were dry. They sat at opposite sides of the table.

Colonel Pratt had seen the way the police had stared at him, as if keeping Vincent Calvino alive had become his full-time responsibility. Fate interrupted the evil of men, thought Pratt, who no longer had any illusions about the forces confronting Calvino, their resources and intentions.

Sending him away hadn't worked. Having him stay away for months or years wouldn't work either. The colonel knew that he was going to have to deal with the situation the best way he could.

"One of those men was alive when I left him at the van," said Calvino, glancing at the smooth water of the swimming pool, clear and blue, an undisturbed volume. But when he looked away from it, he saw that Colonel Pratt was staring at the city below.

"Vincent, they aren't likely to give up. Double up their efforts, yes. A couple of the men in the garage aren't ex-cops. They're working elsewhere. You are aware of the situation."

"Militia. Only you've not been read into the program. They've left you standing on the outside looking in. Cops and mafia mixed together. See the way they closed ranks when you showed up? If there's something we can agree on, it's that I am aware of my situation—and yours."

The real cops had backed off as soon as Colonel Pratt had appeared. The same thing happened on the night the van crashed against the wall of a condo. But they weren't going to back off forever. Twice was about their limit. Colonel Pratt had talked with the plainclothes cop in the parking garage. That conversation lasted a couple of minutes. Long enough for Pratt to brief him on the choices open to Calvino. Pratt's problem was that the choices narrowed to one: Calvino had to leave the country and stay away. But Calvino had Bangkok in his blood; he would take his chances staying.

Colonel Pratt opened the conversation about the dead woman in Calvino's car. "I remember her. She came to your door. I was behind you. She saw me and left."

"She was my stockbroker."

Colonel Pratt raised an eyebrow, slowly shaking his head. "And nothing more?"

"Yeah, there was."

"A loss like this is personal."

"I'm not taking a pass on this one, if that's what you mean."

That was the problem, thought Colonel Pratt. He understood that stockbrokers don't normally take a client's damaged car into the shop for repair on the way to the office. The shock of her death hadn't settled at the scene. Sitting across from Pratt, Calvino felt the full weight of sadness roll over him. Pratt waited as Calvino seemed to withdraw into a mood of loneliness and hopelessness that robbed him of his voice and left him temporarily lost in his thoughts.

Pratt put a hand on his friend's shoulder. "You didn't know, Vincent. Couldn't have known."

"Pratt, I should have known. Seen it coming. They made it clear they were coming after me. The van was round one. Disappearing to China was no solution. Today was round two."

"They're preparing the final round."

Calvino's eyes hardened. "So am I." There was no bravado in his voice, only a sad firmness of intention.

"You're right, I've been walled off," said Colonel Pratt. "But I've narrowed down what happened to the fingerprint from Achara's lock. In a couple of days, I'll have a good idea who was behind it. You should have waited to come back. You've complicated my investigation. You poked a stick into someone's life, and that can be dangerous. Poke at a snake and it strikes."

The fragility of life, thought Calvino. Always just around the corner, an upside-down event came at you fast, too fast, and nothing could prevent the confrontation. In a moment it had been over for Siriporn. Whatever thought she'd had, the song winding through her mind, it had stopped.

"You're not going to take down Wei Zhang by yourself," said Calvino. "I can help with what I found in China."

"In *Julius Caesar*, Shakespeare wrote that 'the evil that men do lives after them,' and I used to believe that would keep evil in check. But it doesn't work that way. Maybe it never did. All that can be done is to separate yourself from that evil."

"You want me to turn and run?" asked Calvino.

Colonel Pratt shook his head. " 'Though the enemy be stronger in numbers, we may prevent him from fighting. Scheme so as to discover his plans and the likelihood of their success.' "

"Shakespeare?"

"Sun Tzu, *The Art of War*."

Calvino grinned. When Colonel Pratt shifted from quoting Shakespeare to Sun Tzu, the message was that a situation existed beyond what an Elizabethan playwright could be expected to imagine from Stratford-upon-Avon. Life was as fragile as glass in a landslide. Shakespeare was the glassblower. Sun Tzu put in the fine reinforcement wires to give it strength. In the end it came to a million pieces scattered down a nameless slope. Colonel Pratt worked on melting together the work of two great craftsmen, hoping to outrun what was about to come down on him.

"I would like to know what is making Wei Zhang so nervous. You didn't find this in China or you'd have told me." Pratt looked to Calvino for reassurance that he wasn't holding back information.

"How much time do I have?"

Colonel Pratt shrugged. "Stay in your condo. Don't go out. They'll be watching the building, tapping your phone, picking up your conversations from the vibrations of your windows."

"Zhang had Brandon and Achara murdered."

"You can't prove it."

"Lack of Evidence is a criminal's best friend."

This time Colonel Pratt said nothing to contradict him, adding only, "That's what people were saying during the war on drugs."

Calvino's face registered the defeat. "All the more reason to let me find the evidence."

Zhang had gathered his troops and put them in place, ready to strike. Calvino had a colonel who'd offered help but had no forces behind him. However, that wouldn't stop him from standing at Calvino's side. When you were surrounded, there was comfort in knowing that there was one person who would not break ranks.

"You seriously think you can force him to reveal himself?" asked Colonel Pratt.

"Can I get back to you on that?" Calvino asked, rising from the table.

His hand stuck in his trouser pocket, Calvino rattled a handful of loose change. There were only two reasons in Bangkok to do that—a makeshift mating call in a bar or a distress call when a man understood how much someone had wanted to kill him.

FORTY-SIX

CALVINO SAT ON the sofa where the night before Siriporn had been next to him, smiling, full of life, happy and hopeful. He'd taken her iBook from its hiding place and was scrolling through her files. He opened a personal folder. Reading through her diary, he found his name. She'd recorded her impression of Tanny Craig the night she'd returned for her earring. "She's using Vincent. Why are men so stupid? I saw contempt in her eyes. Hatred. This is a woman who is selfish, only cares about herself."

He reread the words; they made him shiver as if he were reading about some other fool who'd made the wrong decision regarding a woman. He made a mental note to delete a bunch of old personal files—"password-protected" suddenly meant nothing—from his office computer and his laptop. He scrolled through Siriporn's diary entries, her feelings about him, her sister, her parents, her friends and colleagues. When people wrote only for their own private reasons, it was unvarnished, raw, with none of the usual restraints, because no one else would ever see their impressions. The diary revealed the undisclosed face behind the one that Siriporn let the world see. He felt uncomfortable reading such raw, open sentiments. Thais were by nature indirect about their feelings. But, in private, Siriporn had written that she loved him and would wait for him, work for him, win him. In another folder were photos she'd taken with her cell phone. He studied his face. This was how she had seen him, looking into the camera smiling, giving the Winston Churchill victory sign. No cigar. What he saw was his own stupid, superficial smile, his tired, unhappy eyes staring into the camera as if seeing a demon on the other side. In the same file, she typed:

Four Rules for a permanent relationship with a woman:

Make her laugh daily,

Make passionate love weekly,

Give her security always,

Never make her lose face in public.

She had checked off each line with a "yes" and a happy face. He reread her rules, thinking that she had left out the final rule: Avoid getting involved with anyone, in Nelson Algren's words, whose troubles were greater than your own.

Calvino stretched back, exhaled long and hard, reflecting on how none of us ever imagined dying in the next ten minutes, dying before we had that last chance to cleanse away years of secrets and images that no other person should ever find. Who would be the first person to switch on *his* computer, comb through *his* old files, taking her time in the days following his own death, discovering inside each folder a different Vincent Calvino from the one she thought she knew? Or maybe she would pass on the job to Colonel Pratt. As he leaned back, arms folded, looking at the screen, looking at Siriporn's world, now dead, he thought about the world they'd briefly inhabited. There was never enough time to mourn. Old George, then Achara, then Brandon had passed through the gate. Colonel Pratt had all but said that Calvino had been handed a ticket for the same gate.

He told himself that Pratt had been right the first time and he was right this time, too—he should leave the country. It was a time-honored remedy that many accepted in similar circumstances, and they were the smart ones. The bullheaded ones, those who believed that friends or gods or spirits protected them, or who were deluded into a feeling of immortality, they stayed, and they most often disappeared, or their bodies were found in submerged containers, stuffed into barrels or buried in shallow graves. Calvino told himself he wasn't leaving and he wasn't going to let them punch his ticket to the next life. He leaned forward and typed in Wei Zhang's name for a search of the computer. A dozen folders came up. Gifts from a dead woman? he asked himself.

When Calvino tried to open the first folder, he got a prompt for a password. He typed in Siriporn's name, the name of her company, the condominium, his own name. If she had encrypted it, he figured no matter how many random attempts he made to guess it, he was doomed to fail. But private eyes knew a thing or two about human nature. Such as how most people stored their passwords. They created a file called "password." A simple search for a file using that word usually did the trick. No matter that the IT department sent around endless warnings about password security, people being people, they found it hard to resist the convenience. He found her password: "OneLoveSweet" was inside an unencrypted file labeled "password."

He read for several hours, taking notes as he scoured her memos, charts, graphs, reports, and Excel files. When Calvino turned around and looked out at the lake, it was late afternoon and the sun had broken through the clouds, gilding the gun-barrel color of the water with a skin of soft light skidding across the surface. In the kitchen he poured a shot of single-malt into a glass and walked over to the window, sipping the Scotch and watching the lake and the traffic below. Siriporn had assembled all the pieces. It wasn't clear whether she had fitted them into the pattern that Calvino saw as clearly as he saw the sun on the water. Zhang had established a network of officials, politicians, military and police brass. The builders of the black house—but not just construction workers, who would leave the premises, these people would also be co-inhabitants. As shareholders and directors, through a web of nominees—Siriporn had found and recorded the links—the companies would acquire licenses and permits for agriculture, weapons, mining, banking, airlines, casinos, land development. All the activity would occur offstage, inside the black house, a space with no windows, the doors locked, and Zhang held the master key. All he had to do was fund the election of his police general and his political party. The party promising democracy, a fresh start, and a break with the past—they had already worked out the talking points and the general's charismatic warrior image, the strong but fair man who would appeal to the upcountry voters who would sweep him to power. Calvino sat back, wondering whether Siriporn had seen Zhang's finished product from the blueprint she'd stitched together.

He checked the time. It was mid-morning in New York. Time to make that call he'd been putting off. He pulled up the menu for Siriporn's Skype account and typed in Tanny Craig's name. He dialed, and a moment later Tanny's face filled the computer screen.

"Using your girlfriend's computer," she said, smiling.

"She's dead."

That wiped the smile off the screen. Tanny's face contorted. "What do you mean, dead?"

"As in killed by Wei Zhang."

"Don't be ridiculous. He doesn't even know her."

Calvino hadn't intended to start the conversation with an argument about Zhang's prior knowledge of Siriporn. But sometimes there was no control over the direction of words uttered by people who had so much to say to one another and no clue about where to start. "I read your e-mail."

"I'm sorry we didn't have a chance to talk before I left."

407

He waited for a beat, studying her face on the screen. She had her hair tied back and sat in an office chair. There were books on a shelf behind her. A diploma framed on the wall. A framed photograph of her and her son was on her right. Jeff, that was her kid's name, thought Calvino. And a yellow hand clapper she'd taken back home from the demonstration. "The way that you left didn't leave much to talk about."

"You're not that different from Wei Zhang," she said. "Like Wei, you believe deeply that what you do is right. Most men don't. Doubt cuts them down."

"Seems that you got to know Zhang better than you did me."

"All men hide things from women."

She'd pried Calvino open like an oyster, one that felt the knife slide along the rim of the shell, cutting the muscles, but was powerless to pull away. "You could teach me a thing or two about sleight of hand."

When Siriporn had returned to search for her lost earring, Tanny had seen a crack in his world open. Siriporn's attempt to assert control over his space had him edgy. But maybe her return to his condo had nothing to do with control. It happened that people forgot things. They were easily distracted. In reality most people drifted through each day with only a sketchy plan, relying on half-baked reasons and assumptions, lurching from one lapse of memory or judgment to the next.

Tanny said, "You don't like it when a woman challenges your space. Arrives unannounced in your little kingdom. It's your secret fear. One that Siriporn didn't understand."

"What's *your* secret fear?"

"Being abandoned."

Two words bundled a lifetime of terror.

"How does that explain Zhang?"

"You were the one who said you couldn't help me. I needed a patron."

"You're saying I abandoned you?"

She shook her head. "I had no choice but to help my mother."

"Signing on as a shareholder and director of Thai companies was to help your mother?"

"It's public record. I knew you'd find out."

"But you didn't care."

"Vinny, there are levels of caring. Men don't understand. Caring isn't all one neat thing on one plateau. Choices are hard to make. But when it comes to helping her mother, every woman is clear about the choice."

"Even if it means betraying someone else who cares about you?"

She stared at the camera. "All you had to do was tell Brandon to sign the documents."

"He never would have signed. You knew that. So did Marshall."

"He was a hopeless drunk. But he listened to you."

In a lucid moment, Brandon had once said that it was easier to cure a man of his addiction to drugs and alcohol than to wean him off stereotypes. Brandon listened to no one.

"I need your help," he said.

The request made her blink, move closer to her desk, as if pressing her face closer to his. "What kind of help?"

"Does Zhang still go to Veera to have his fortune told?"

Tanny laughed, covered her mouth with both hands, and sat back in her seat. "Is that why you phoned?"

"I phoned because I can't seem to get you out of my thoughts. And I don't know why that is. I thought you might have an answer."

Her laughter stopped. All lives were scrap heaps composed of a paste-up job of messy details. Only a fool believed he could clean up the mess in his own life by finding the right broom. Only a saint would have enough faith to try to clean the debris of someone else's life with his bare hands. But before the screen went blank, she gave him a name, one that he'd heard before. "He's close to Ajarn Veera if that's what you are asking."

That was what he'd been asking and now he had his answer.

Around two in the morning, Ratana had gone downstairs to One Hand Clapping, woken up Nueng, and borrowed her ID card—no questions asked or answered. Nueng handed it over and went upstairs to look after the children. Ratana unlocked her silver BMW and backed out of the sub-soi onto Soi 33. The street was quiet. The usual service-car touts were absent from their squatting places near the mouth of the soi. She stopped at Villa, a twenty-four-hour expat supermarket, and bought groceries for Calvino. Then she drove a kilometer and a half to Calvino's building.

She pulled to a stop at the security gate and waited for a guard to approach as she rolled down the window. She flashed Nueng's ID card, saying she was booked to see a farang on the fourteenth floor. The guard looked at the BMW—the brand and model of the car broadcast that she had money. Women with money were always let inside the velvet rope wherever they went. Using the farang's name she intended to visit made it all the easier on the guard. She remembered the name Justin from the chattering heads in the front office who passed the time gossiping about the sex lives of foreigners living in the building. One lived on the fourteenth floor. She'd been in the office settling up Calvino's water bill. She paid it and listened to the stories about Mr. Justin. His name worked like a charm at three in the morning. Ratana assumed that someone was watching the building and had greased palms for any information about anyone who arrived asking for Calvino. They wouldn't have been looking for Justin.

Ratana slipped her car into Calvino's parking spot and sat behind the wheel, her heart pounding. She marveled at how much working for Calvino over the years had changed her—from a conservative middle-class Bangkok woman into one who borrowed a massage woman's ID card to pass herself off as a hooker to gain access. Working for Calvino had changed her in ways that made her understand the woman she'd become. She found her own way of handling a sudden snap of terror, by not giving into the impulse to panic. The way forward in an emergency situation was one step at a time, keeping the overriding fear in check, guarding against a reaction caused by surprise. From her years of working as Calvino's secretary, she'd learned certain skills from him, and they'd come in handy this evening.

She had just heard from Manee that Pratt had been shot. She'd cried, dried her eyes, only to start crying again. She told herself that controlling her emotions was important, because she didn't want Calvino to see her falling apart as she delivered the news about Pratt. Manee said it was bad but that Pratt probably would make it. Manee and the kids were at the hospital. Ratana thought of them standing around Pratt's bed, and she started to weep again. This was not good. She couldn't get out of the car looking like a nervous wreck. People remembered crying women. The image stuck in their minds even this early in the morning after they'd had too much to drink. In a few minutes she calmed down, composed herself as she freshened her makeup, then got out of the BMW to walk over and stand in front of the bank of elevators, waiting for one to stop. She told herself that she was nearly there, only a couple more minutes.

When the elevator arrived, Ratana found herself standing beside another woman, short and overweight, shaking water off her umbrella. The woman got in and pushed the button for floor eighteen. Ratana pressed the button for the fourteenth floor. The woman smiled, looked at Ratana as she sniffed the air and announced she was visiting her boyfriend who was very rich and generous. She commented on how foul the weather had been. Ratana nodded at her as she stepped out of the elevator at the fourteenth floor, waited until the doors closed, then used the stairs to walk down to the eleventh floor. She walked along the tiled hallway, windows overlooking slums on her right. Reaching Calvino's door, she glanced around, checking for any activity in the corridor—there was none. She set down the shopping bags from Villa and knocked on the door. Then she pressed the bell. When Calvino opened the door, she reached down and picked up the Villa bags and walked in. Calvino closed the door behind her. He hadn't been expecting her. She hadn't called. She wore her blue dress, the one she sometimes wore when they went to Pratt's house for dinner. Her hair piled into a bun, she might have passed for an average-looking Chinese-Thai housewife who'd just come in from shopping.

Single-malt whiskey, bread, cheese, olives, pickles, and yogurt spilled from the bags as she reached inside for file folders she'd removed from the office and hidden under the food. Calvino leaned down and picked out the whiskey bottle.

He stared at the contents of the shopping bags; it looked like a week's supply for a Mafia don who had gone into hiding. He glanced at her, marveling how efficient she was, how mindful and thorough.

It was then that she broke down.

A thick sob caught in her throat. "He's been shot."

"Who's been shot?"

"Pratt."

"When?"

"A few hours ago. He was outside a jazz club across town. He had sat in for a couple of sets."

"You talked with Manee?" he asked.

She nodded, sniffing. "Pee Manee said it had something to do with an internal investigation he was doing. Do you understand?"

"Yeah, he must've been close to a finding a missing fingerprint. How bad is he?"

"The doctors operated on him."

"Which hospital?"

"Khun Vinny, you can't go there. Impossible. He was shot because of you."

Calvino knew where they'd take a police colonel. "He's at the Police Hospital."

"Please, Khun Vinny. You will cause a bigger problem. Pee Manee said to tell you that she'll phone you when it's safe."

His mind raced as he downed two fingers of Scotch. "He was shot because of you," continued to career inside his head. Ratana was making a statement of fact; it wasn't an accusation. The truth of it rang like a medieval church bell, loud and clear, carrying across the commons, through the windows, and into the rooms for all to hear.

"Is he going to die?"

"Only Buddha can say."

"He's conscious?"

She nodded.

He went into the bedroom and found a box of Kleenex. He handed the box to Ratana, who'd followed him there; she took a tissue and blew her nose.

"I still can't believe it," she said.

The scent of Siriporn's perfume lingered in the bedroom, rising from the sheets and pillows like a morning mist. He turned Ratana around and walked her out of the room.

"I'll work it out. It will be all right," he said.

413

She stared down at the groceries on the floor, shaking her head. "It won't."

Calvino thought that if they had intended to kill Pratt, they could've done the job. But that would have caused them too much trouble. Questions would be raised, an investigation that might be difficult to control. Pratt was a colonel, after all, and killing police colonels was a serious business. Putting a couple of slugs into him would have been good enough for their purposes—it would take him out of circulation and send a clear message to his farang buddy Vincent Calvino that it was time to back off. Calvino's patron on the police force now had his own problems to deal with and was no longer in any position to offer the cloak of protection Calvino had become accustomed to sheltering under. Whatever move Calvino made, it would be on his own. And without Pratt to watch his back, he might find he had a bull's-eye painted on his forehead. That message was intended to keep him inside and out of the way.

He sat her down on the living-room sofa and brought her a glass of water. She unfolded a copy of the *Bangkok Post* on the table, then took the glass and drank. They talked about Pratt. It was decided that she'd go to the hospital and stay with Manee. Nueng promised to look after John-John, since it was too late for Ratana's mother to pick him up for the night. John-John would sleep with Nueng in a room above the massage parlor.

"I think of him," she said.

Calvino thought she was talking about Colonel Pratt.

"John," she said.

A few years before, Ratana's American boyfriend had been killed in Bangkok. Calvino had been having dinner the night John Lovell had been murdered. He had told Lovell to leave Bangkok, but Lovell didn't listen, and he didn't have anyone to cover his back. The pain of that loss hadn't ever gone away for Ratana; all it needed to fire up again was a reminder like Pratt's getting shot, and Ratana looked no different now from the way she had the day her boyfriend had been killed. The full load of that memory mingled with the knowledge that Colonel Pratt was in a serious condition. What bothered her at this moment was how she could go through each day so easily, mostly not thinking about what had happened to her life after the father of her boy had died.

Calvino offered her the guestroom. "It's late. You can leave in the morning."

"I've finished delivering my message," she said.

Calvino's eyebrows knitted.

"I told security I was going to Justin's unit. I'd been sent by an agency."

"Inventive."

"Careful. Please be careful."

"Get word to Pratt that I won't give up."

"Wait until he's out of the hospital before you do anything."

"That could be some time."

"It's better for him, better for you."

"Tell him."

"I'm not certain that's what he wants to hear." She took the keys to her BMW, her prized possession, and held them out to Calvino.

He looked at the keys. "What are you doing?"

"You will need a car." She dropped the keys on a table next to the door. "Be careful, Vinny."

"Yeah, I'll do that."

After she'd gone, Calvino opened the newspaper. Under a captioned photograph of General Suchart ran an article reporting a trial balloon from a well-placed source that the government should approach the Chinese government to borrow money to save the country as companies closed down and unemployment rose. The figure was a handsome

415

amount—ten billion dollars. What the article neglected to mention was that there were enough strings attached to put together a full orchestra of nothing but harps.

FORTY-SEVEN

MONTRI ADJUSTED HIS gold-rimmed glasses, as he stood tall and smiling at himself in the mirror. The glasses were imported and expensive, giving him a sense of mystery and authority. This evening he needed whatever edge he could muster. A current of cool air tousled his hair. The invitation he had sent to Zhang said that the ceremony started at precisely 8:23 P.M.—the time was auspicious, and the maw doo Ajarn Veera had insisted that Zhang bring something personal: Two dozen white orchids, and a photograph of his mother and father.

Several days after Colonel Pratt had been shot and refused to die, Montri had made the necessary arrangements. He whispered to Zhang what Calvino had told him: "Ajarn Veera was visited by a spirit calling himself Chou, who wishes to deliver a message. His spirit wanders. He's calling out for you." How else could Ajarn Veera know about Zhang's long-dead stillborn brother other than through a channel to the afterlife? Nothing would have kept Zhang from meeting Ajarn Veera after that message was delivered.

The ceremony would be held in the prayer room at Montri's mansion. Ajarn Veera was specific in his request for the appropriate place to perform the ritual.

Zhang was at first suspicious, obliquely asking what Montri might expect to gain from such a meeting—the idea of someone helping him without a hidden reason wouldn't have been believable. Montri replied that he had a business proposal he thought Zhang would be interested in. Zhang asked for details. Montri said the deal was a robot-manufacturing opportunity with a famous Japanese company, and he thought the investment might fit Zhang's portfolio. The Japanese company, though it had world-class technology, had been driven into distress by a couple of less-than-prudent financial investments. The chairman of the board would accept terms that were too good to pass up. Montri had the cash for the deal, but, like all good businessmen, like a bookie making big bets if he could lay off part of the risk, he'd have more resources for other deals. Montri used a shorthand that Zhang understood: The Japanese company was wounded, and Montri wanted someone else to help him make the kill. "We've always talked about doing business together, and now is our chance," said Montri. "After you and the *ajarn* finish, that is."

Calvino had to get Zhang into line, a huge challenge, and at the same time bring Montri in—that would cost something even larger. Without a convincing answer to the question of what was in it for Montri, his plan would fail. But there was something that Montri wanted badly enough to justify the risk of getting on Zhang's angry, vindictive side. The man, after all, had collected a ballroom of powerful Thai allies.

Calvino had told him that Zhang would owe Montri forever after the good ajarn performed an exorcism ritual. He'd give Montri whatever he wanted. That should have been sufficient, but it wasn't for Montri. He wanted something more. He couldn't help but negotiate the best deal he could. With a farang there was always the possibility of unpredictable emotions coloring the business, and that was fundamentally dangerous. It was a question of judgment. If the terms were sufficiently in his favor, even a deal with a farang might be worth the risk. Calvino had caught his attention by making him an offer that was difficult to refuse—the one Chini painting that Calvino had withheld. It was different from the others. The subject was a young nude woman turned away from the painter; her buttocks tight, firm, the curve of her spine in shadow, and her head turned to a profile, revealing a half smile, eyes flashing hot with passion.

He knew Montri's price, and Montri knew his.

Montri hovered for a while near a floral arrangement, filling his lungs with the scent of orchids and roses. When at last he moved across the room, he carried a glass of wine. Two maids trailed behind like pendants in the shadow of a holy man, a holy man with a tan, smiling face, a god incarnate who loved wine and women, dual forces driving the dogma of his personal religion. He was a cautious man, too. Standing on the wrong side of history's highway worried some men with large investments on that side; equally distressing was getting on the wrong side of those who engineered the lanes that history followed. Montri weighed the risks, deciding that the money involved would let him build his own highway.

Calvino sat at the table. Montri stopped behind him, placing both hands on his shoulders.

"Am I going to regret this favor?" Montri asked.

Calvino smiled, looking at him over his shoulder. "What do you have to worry about?"

"You might shoot Wei Zhang. But you won't?" He'd started as if making an order, but before he'd finished, it ended up as a question.

"That would be ungrateful of me," Calvino said. "Besides, I'm not armed."

"*He* might have a gun."

"If he shoots me, I'm certain you'll be able to handle the paperwork."

Montri laughed. "You, my friend, like to joke too much."

Calvino was conscious of Montri's dread, his position, the risk he was taking. Montri tapped him several times on the shoulder. Montri had converted the fist bump into the fist into the shoulder bump. The little taps felt like a man with lockjaw trying to gnaw off a piece of bread.

"Violence happens even when you don't expect it," said Montri. He'd told himself this same thing on the night of issuing the invitation, when he'd been crazy enough—unable to elbow away the pull of greed—to finally agree to go along with Calvino's request. Calvino had sweetened the bargain, making it irresistible to a businessman. Montri still owed Calvino twenty percent of the purchase price for the paintings. A deal made before the great financial crisis had collapsed the most secure of empires. Montri's own empire was leveraged like a pair of silicon breasts on a katoey, something he hoped to clear before there was a close examination. Meanwhile, the jaws of the credit crunch had clamped down like the business end of a garbage truck compacting trash. Forgetting the entire amount outstanding, though, wasn't enough. There was that one Chini painting that Calvino had kept back. Nothing had moved him to include the painting. Montri wanted that painting.

Calvino made it sweet by agreeing. Montri in turn agreed to invite Zhang to his mansion, escort him, alone, into the exhibition room where the Chini nudes hung from the walls. Calvino also asked Montri to leave them alone in the exhibition room, to lock the door, and not to let anyone in or out until an hour had passed.

"I never got a chance to say good-bye to my great-grandfather's work," Calvino had said.

"But I told you that you were welcome to visit anytime," Montri said.

The elastic in Montri's voice stretched under the weight of his polite lie. No one could be excused from believing that such an open-ended visitation right, as in a child-custody case, ever worked out in practice.

"Wei will understand why you invited me."

"These paintings explain everything." Montri grinned, sipping the wine and looking at the nudes.

"Your ass end of the elephant is fully covered."

"He asked about the other guests," said Montri, tapping Calvino's shoulder with another rapid series of light punches.

"You told him it was a small party."

Montri nodded. "And he asked if I'd invited any farang."

"And you said no."

"Technically you invited yourself," said Montri. "I didn't send you an invitation. You came out to see your great-grandfather's exhibition. What could I do? It was in our contract that you had access whenever you chose."

"You could be a lawyer," said Calvino.

"Not a lawyer." Montri pulled a sour face as a maid refilled his glass. "I feel more like one of the naked women your great-grandfather painted."

"And you're afraid of Zhang?"

"Why should I be afraid of him? Besides, it is, as you say, only a friendly talk. How can he complain?"

Had Achara asked himself the same question? Calvino wondered. This wasn't the time to raise questions about Achara or Brandon, the rice fields or the weapons-manufacturing operation. He suspected that Montri, with his sources, knew about Zhang's businesses in Thailand; he made it his business to know where the Chinese and others were investing.

Montri saw something in Calvino's eyes and grinned again. "You don't like him very much, do you?"

"Let's say we have a few issues."

"Okay, okay. It's a done deal. Just don't make him unhappy. At least wait until you're someplace else." Montri laughed, flashed a crooked smile, and punched Calvino's shoulder. "Can you do that?"

"I can," said Calvino. "Depending." He didn't finish the sentence.

Montri looked stricken. "Depending on what?"

"If he insults my host, I'd be forced to act out of honor. And the same in case he insults my great-grandfather's art."

"In that case, of course, you should kill him." Montri roared with laughter. He checked his watch, made a finger gun, which he aimed at Calvino's chest, then clicked his tongue before blowing on his finger and lowering his arm. "Ajarn Veera has set up everything. Our guest should be here any moment." And he left the room, having dispensed Thai-style justice between business associates.

The sun had set, and hundreds of kerosene lanterns were lit to mark the switchbacks as walkways twisted with the increased elevation. Far below, a river ran toward the horizon. Montri's vast estate created its own world, with jungles and rivers and lakes, forests and swamps. Calvino stood in near darkness. From the trees, cicadas sounded like a vast symphony with all musicians playing the same high-pitched stringed instrument. They consumed the silence, shredding the night with noise as sharp as a knife.

Calvino sheltered behind a large wooden boat with its several cabins gutted and turned into a guestroom suitable for a sultan and his harem. With one arm hooked over the bow, Calvino watched as Zhang emerged, illuminated in a pool of lantern light as he walked one step behind Montri.

Zhang had not disappointed, arriving a few minutes

before the auspicious time. The two men stood talking on a path leading to the sala, Montri gesturing, his hand sweeping along the horizon. Zhang nodded and walked the rest of the journey along the narrow walkway to the sala, a wooden pavilion with Khmer spires and a multi-tiered roofline rising like rows of pyramids. It was like a miniature Thai temple with the signature copper-colored wooden panels, gables and pillars, decorated with lacquer, gilt, gold leaf, mother-of-pearl. Large windows opened on all sides. The sala had a wraparound terrace from which orchids in pots hung over the lake. The door was open, and Ajarn Veera sat on a golden silk pillow in the lotus position. Frangipani graced a small teak ceremony table. Incense sticks burned. White lotus petals had been strewn along the floor leading from the doorway to the table. The voice of the maw doo rose above the roar of cicadas, his words forming into a singsong chant. Calvino could see the profile of Ajarn Veera, dressed in white, and kneeling at the table before him was Wei Zhang. The maw doo rocked back and forth as he burned pieces of colored votive paper, the ashes drifting out the window and across the lake.

Calvino hadn't hesitated to use the information about the unborn brother of Zhang as the bait to drag him to Montri's estate. There might have been a simpler, more humane way, but Calvino didn't have time to worry about such a moral dilemma. People used what they had available and made the best of it. Most of the time, the sharpest and most gruesome instrument was something personal, but not just any old personal thing—something black and deep and haunting that hammered in the background of waking moments and broke through the walls inside dreams. Tanny had lost a sister, Zhang a brother. Neither one had ever known the lost sibling. Maybe this had created some kind of bond that let them work as a makeshift team, put that hurt deep inside to some goal other than suffering. Something that had happened had made them see the other as if for the first time. Calvino had started to understand how little he'd known Tanny. Some say knowledge of that personal kind was better left unexplored.

After the chanting had stopped, the maw doo lit three candles, the light splashing across the lake as each candle was placed on an altar at the center point of the three windows. He burned more scraps of votive paper. Then the two men sat in the silence of people speaking their own privately coded language, one rich in the vocabulary of the night, and it filled the void. The deep bass from a gong broke the silence. The maw doo struck the paddle against the gong eight times. Each time, the sound cannoned off the surface of the lake like thunder, rolling through the forest before disappearing. Then Calvino saw Zhang's spiritual adviser stand, clap three times, wet his hands and rub them through Zhang's hair. Then he quickly moved to blow out each of the three candles before sitting back on his golden pillow.

Zhang opened a leather briefcase, working the brass latches with his thumbs, then reached in and took out two thick bundles of notes. He laid the money on the table and waied the maw doo. Their whispered conversation was masked by the sounds of the night, but that didn't much matter. When Zhang had pulled out the money, Calvino worked his way back to the Chini gallery. The lights illuminated the inside. The silence was total. Air-conditioning from the vents chilled the room. It wouldn't be long before Montri delivered Zhang to the gallery.

Zhang had brilliantly planned the company takeover, all the details—the contracts, the share transfers, everything done flawlessly. Tanny had made her contribution to the effort. It was clear they'd been using each other, but the more he thought about it, Calvino realized that they saw themselves in each other—damaged, used, haunted people who glimpsed their own reflection in the other. She had her own ghosts to bury. Calvino had been a good and proper shovel. Dumb as a dull blade when he should have seen the setup from the start. Coming out of his bathroom wearing a towel and holding Siriporn's lost earring. It had been too good to be true.

Both of them had had their lives bent in profound ways by the weight of personal tragedy; whether the loss warped them into greed and ambition and double-dealing or whether it was a smoke screen for how their minds worked, it all ended up the same. They looked for ways to offload their loss, and never quite succeeded in the task. What was it about tragedy that corrupted one person to the core but turned another into a saint? Standing before the gallery of naked women painted by his great-grandfather, Calvino asked himself where he stood in life, how much the accumulated losses in his own life had bent him. It wasn't the kind of question that invited messy, evasive answers; those were the kinds of answers politicians practiced in front of a mirror, because without practice the unease would be all too obvious.

FORTY-EIGHT

CALVINO WAITED IN Montri's gallery, half hidden behind a double helix fabricated from chrome, mirrors, and glass that spiraled from the floor to the ceiling. It looked like the space-age leg of a giant robot spider, a predator, hunting the women on the walls. The mirrors captured the nude images from the oil paintings and created a new expression, as they appeared to disappear into infinity, like reflections in a hall of mirrors. Calvino had stood in front of the sculpture the night Montri had opened the exhibition and turned to him, asking him to say a few words. Achara had been in the gallery, as had Brandon Sawyer and Colonel Pratt. Two of them dead, one of them shot. Zhang had also been in the audience, applauding with the others after Calvino talked. And Ajarn Veera, the maw doo, had been watching him with those small, unblinking eyes, alert and curious; calculating eyes, the eyes of a hooker assessing the benefits from a possible trick. His fame would only increase after holding an emergency session with Zhang. His bank account had been fattened. Just like a hooker, after all the ritual and ceremony, he got paid, too. Calvino had paid, and in ways that troubled him to think about. Taking down Zhang meant playing by the local rules. Feet, knees, elbows, fists—throw all of them, muay Thai, and aim for the throat. Calvino had found Zhang's weakness. And the main imperative was to convince Zhang that their meeting was accidental, a coincidence.

Calvino studied a public-gallery-size Chini painting of a woman, arms held out in supplication, legs together, with a timid smile. Her small breasts, slightly extended belly, curved hips suggested not just simple vulnerability but a more complex defenselessness, as if she'd been stripped and placed on display. Someone had told her not to move, and she'd complied except for the fingers on both hands—they curved so her fingernails brushed against the back of her hand. He examined her features and could find almost nothing in the face or body that existed in modern Thailand. But that had been the point; Montri was a traditionalist, a man who saw the beauty in the past, one that had gone extinct, but nevertheless its essence had been captured. And he owned that essence.

Montri and Zhang talked as they entered the room. Their conversation ended when Zhang saw Calvino. He suddenly looked like a submarine officer who had survived a depth-charge explosion, his combat-weary, agitated face housing two dull, dead eyes that looked at Calvino but somehow didn't see him. Zhang's mind remained inside the sala with the burning papers and the incense sticks, the bronze gong still echoing in his mind. Here was the same man who had been stalking in a hotel lobby when he was with Tanny. A man who was supposed to be dead; but wasn't.

"Vincent Calvino," said Montri. "When did you come in?" His timing was perfect, and he had mastered the shocked look of surprise from a thousand negotiation sessions and gambling tables, where such an expression could force the other side into a mistake.

"About half an hour ago. I'm missing a special painting. I wondered if you'd had time to hang it."

"Impossible to forget, isn't it?" said Montri.

Calvino smiled, glancing at Zhang and thinking that he seemed to be buying into the setup. But it was too soon to know for certain. "It looks good on that wall."

Zhang stared at his watch. "I will leave you to discuss paintings."

"Don't rush off. We need to talk," said Calvino.

"Good idea. I'll be back with a nice bottle of wine in half an hour." Montri waved and left them alone.

Calvino and Zhang faced each other, surrounded by paintings. It was one of those moments when silence became the loudest voice in the room.

Zhang walked ahead and stopped in front of a nude, a dancer, her belly round, her face clownish and sad. "Your grandfather made her ugly."

Calvino stepped back from the painting. "My great-grandfather found her beautiful."

Zhang showed no surprise. "I read where Galileo Chini once said, 'Siam is like a curse.' "

"Just think what he'd have said if he'd seen the van with the fireworks," said Calvino.

"This is a characteristic that runs in your family," said Zhang. He stared at the nude painting, for the moment ignoring what Calvino had said. "You knew I was coming here," he continued, a blade of steel flashed in his voice.

"Sometimes blind luck makes a man look a lot smarter than he really is."

"I remember asking Montri if he expected any farangs tonight, and he said there wouldn't be."

"I invited myself," said Calvino. "What does it matter? You heard him. I've got a right to be here. I should ask if *you* followed *me* here. I thought I'd lost your tail, but here you are. Proof of how one of us suffers from delusions."

"That seems to be a very bad habit you've formed, Mr. Calvino."

"What habit's that?"

"Playing the stupid farang doesn't fool anyone."

"Is there any other kind?"

"This false absence of ego makes you dangerous."

"Zhang, relax. This room contains my heritage. It's where I come to worship my ancestors," said Calvino. "You'll appreciate the importance of temples built for ancestor worship."

Calvino turned away, his back to the painting and focusing his attention on Zhang.

"What do you want?" asked Zhang.

"Money. And to have enough luck to live long enough to spend it," said Calvino.

Zhang smiled, slowly shaking his head. "You already have a great deal of money from the sale of these paintings." He gestured with his hand, pointing at the walls of Chini nudes. "And the length of a man's life depends on many things." Then he paused as if a thought had struck him. "And some men have more luck than others."

"Colonel Pratt had some luck. What do you think? Did the men who shot him intend to kill him? In which case he had some luck managing to survive. Or did they only intend to wound? In that case luck wouldn't have anything to do with his surviving."

"The destiny of some men is to bring bad luck to their friends." The purity and mystery of the sadoh kroh ceremony no longer pulled at him. Once again he was proud, imperial, in control.

"It could have saved a lot of time if you'd told me about your relationship with the general." Calvino decided that he didn't need to use the general's name.

Zhang produced a silver cigarette case, removed an unfiltered cigarette, and tapped it against the case before drawing it to his lips. He lit the cigarette, blowing smoke at the nude painting. A ring of smoke hit the woman's thigh.

He looked away in disgust. The reaction was intended to rattle Calvino, throw him off balance, force him into making a stupid mistake or move and fall flat on his face.

"I really don't know what you're talking about," said Zhang.

"You got yourself a good little racket. Packaged with a private militia and a general. But it's not that original. Your general models himself on another former Thai cop who parlayed some smart business moves into political power. The formula isn't that difficult—the right monopoly plus connections to men in uniform. You find a man with strong family ties to China. He agrees with your ideas about power. He clears the way for licenses, tax concessions, permits, and contracts. But I don't see you stopping at weapons. Not when there are so many other profitable businesses, from transportation to mining. One problem. The general can't get elected alone; he needs mountains of money, and that's where you come in. It's not exactly a trade secret that China has money. If you were to seriously invest in Thailand, owning the government is a good solution. Call it the Mongolia or Tibet model."

Zhang sucked on the cigarette, looking hard at Calvino, the way a Chinese judge looked at a political dissident. "China is the future. Everyone wants to do business with us. We don't need to own anybody," he said.

One factor that could be counted on to come into play was Chinese nationalism. "And the inside joke is that the future is in for a shock. In my old neighborhood in New York, no kid could've found China on a map. No one gave a shit about China. Overnight everyone cares about China's intentions. Whatever it is, it's way above my pay grade," said Calvino. "I'm more comfortable following bargirls to see if they're two timing their sugar daddy."

"Mr. Calvino, you have caused me a great deal of trouble. And this meeting tonight wasn't an accident."

"An accident? A van blindsides me on a hairpin turn near where I live. An accident? A close friend starts my car and is killed by an electrical shock. An accident?" Calvino was careful to maintain eye contact with Zhang, watching for a reaction. Specks of gold leaf from the ceremony had dusted his eyebrows and nose. He looked like a Hindu icon mask. The maw doo must have sprinkled him with the gold dust, confirming Zhang as the golden Yunnan boy, seeking the release of his long-dead brother's spirit.

"Even inside the trouble department, Mr. Calvino, you stand out from the faceless crowd. In Asia that is never a good thing. In the trouble department, you want to be small, hard to see, impossible to be heard."

"I want you to help me understand something," said Calvino. "Something I can't figure out. It's bothering me. Keeping me from sleeping."

Zhang glanced at his watch. He dropped his cigarette on the marble floor and crushed it under his shoe. "Understand what?"

"Why Achara didn't go along with it?" asked Calvino. "You had everything and everyone else lined up. The multi-million-dollar loan was in place, the paperwork signed to authorize payment of the funds to the general. My guess is Achara had some second thoughts. Maybe he thought what you had in mind was a raw deal for Thailand. He made a choice that wasn't Chinese enough. And Brandon refused to sign, because he wanted part of the money based on some crazy five-year earnings forecast. Brandon I can figure out. But Achara not going along with a Chinese deal, that I don't understand."

Zhang nodded, shrugging his shoulders, for a moment weighing Calvino's words, but his emotions and ego cut short the process. "Achara was more Thai than Chinese. He said the weapons violated Buddhist principles. He wanted nothing to do with financing any political candidate. He said, 'We've been down that road before. It didn't work out. You don't create another monster to get rid of the monster that haunts you.' If he were truly Chinese, he would have set aside his personal opinion. Instead he acted selfishly, thinking his private views were more important than the interest of China."

"And how much did Brandon want?" asked Calvino.

"He wanted a ten-million-dollar commission. Very Thai, don't you agree?" Zhang's lips spread into a smile of contempt. "He said China is rich. This was, as he called it, 'walking-around money.' "

"Brandon was an accounting detail you deleted from the balance sheet," said Calvino.

"He was greedy. Farangs lack patience. They want everything quickly. No trust. No harmony. That's my experience. Men who rush often fall down before they cross the finish line."

Brandon had said it was okay, though, because in Thailand it was a tradition for everyone to get a little cut from the gravy train.

What Brandon didn't know—or if he had, he'd done an incredible job of keeping it to himself—was that behind Zhang's rice screen, the Chinese had secured a technology base, one that would allow them to develop, manufacture, and finance an entirely new category of weapons. And the game-winning ticket: They would be the bankers of the new politics. It hadn't taken long before a handful of powerful people in China realized that if agriculture and guns were already in their shopping bag, what else from Thailand could they fit into the cart? Rumors had been around for some time that Zhang had a role in financing the general's political party in the next election.

"Brandon's demands were foolish. He would have been a never-ending source of demands in the future," said Zhang.

He was testing Calvino.

"He told me about a commission he was expecting from the financing, but he said he'd had some problems collecting it."

"Oh, that. Did he tell you that he threatened me?" said Zhang.

"He must've been drunk."

"He was sober."

"Brandon once was a comedian."

Zhang cared nothing about Brandon's background. All that had mattered was the present Brandon who threatened trouble. "Brandon told me that he had friends in the news business. And they might like a story about me."

"Basically that he'd expose the sham loan to the general unless you paid him."

"You said he was a comedian. But I don't find that very amusing."

"What Brandon would have found rolling-on-the-floor funny was giving a member of the general's family shares and a seat on the company board. But it gets better. You get a monopoly for your new generation of weapons and the exclusive right to export them. Next thing, Thailand's riding alongside Sweden and Israel in the weapons-selling business. Your general has enough money to buy an election. Your man becomes prime minister. And you own him. And there we are with history repeating itself, only this time China has found a way to offer a guiding hand to its little brother."

Calvino grinned, thinking what Zhang was trying to say in his fortune cookie way was that the colonel wasn't smart enough to be evil but intelligent enough to know he'd have a brilliant career as a tool of evil.

Zhang was reasonably sure that he hated the grin on Calvino's face, though he didn't dwell on the reason behind his hatred; he just struggled not to physically assault Calvino. He controlled himself, prided himself on remaining absolutely cool, his face a blank. It hadn't fooled Calvino. No question in Calvino's mind that Zhang would act on his hatred. He'd made a mental promise to himself, as if to say, I've pushed a pin through the eye of the Calvino voodoo doll.

"A hand provides stability. Something that Thailand needs," said Zhang.

"Stability is, if you look at the history, highly overrated by the Thais."

"I'd ask the real Thais if they agree with you."

"Achara seemed real enough to me. He lived in harmony and stability as far as I could tell. But the way he died was barbaric. Your ancient emperors buried ladies-in-waiting and court officials alive, but as far as I know, they never fed them to lions."

"That was an accident," said Wei Zhang.

"That word again, Zhang. Like Brandon had a heart attack. And I nearly missed having one myself. These weapons are tailor-made for guys like you. It's bad karma murdering people and then calling it an accident. People won't like you if you keep doing that."

Zhang raised his hands, palms out. "Now who's the comedian?"

"With the way your men have screwed up, who wouldn't be?"

"The Thai crew wasn't professional. What they did was frankly stupid." Then he stopped talking, dropping his hands to his sides, looking at the floor. "I was told that Khun Achara was unconscious when he was put in the cage."

"A guy docks his boat and then darts Achara. Ties up the boat, gets help to throw Achara to the lions."

"I loved him like a brother," said Zhang, as if Calvino had made him defensive.

"Like a dead brother."

Zhang averted his eyes. "We've talked enough. Return

434

the weapon you took from the van."

"And in exchange what do I get?"

"To realize your desire to live a long life."

Calvino smiled, nodded, hands in his pockets rattling loose change. "I'll see that it finds its way to you."

Zhang had been through an exhausting spiritual ceremony. The weight of the evening had worn him down. He stared at Calvino without returning his smile. "I'll send someone to your condo to pick it up tonight before you leave for the airport."

"The usual people you've been sending around to wish me good health?"

"You want money?"

Calvino didn't make an immediate response, leaving the offer in the air.

"How much?" asked Zhang. "Ten million, like your friend?"

Calvino shook his head, touching together his thumb and forefinger to form a zero. "That's what it all comes down to in the end. How much? General Suchart's already talking about how the government should borrow billions from the Chinese government. Good plan. You get him elected with seed money, and he kicks back, what? Twenty percent of the loan for research and development, along with the usual third-rate Chinese tanks and planes? But first you've got to finance him so he gets power."

"Watch the faces of any politicians and ask them about how they're going to raise money for the next election. You will see worry. Insecurity and fear."

"That means you've got General Suchart trembling in his jackboots?" asked Calvino. He scratched the side of his face, shaking his head as he stared at Zhang.

"The general understands our reality."

"If he doesn't get the picture, you'll fine-tune him until it's clear in his head."

Montri returned with a bottle of Château Latour 1966. He showed the bottle, waiting for a sign of appreciation. He looked disappointed at the lack of reaction; what did a farang private eye and a Chinese businessman know about fine wine?

"Let me show you my library," said Montri. "And we can drink this outstanding wine and toast Mongolia."

A flash of irritation crossed Zhang's face as he glanced at his watch. "I've got to go back," he said, waiing Montri, who, juggling the expensive bottle, made as elegant a return wai as possible.

"I'd like a few minutes for a last look at my great-grandfather's paintings," said Calvino.

Zhang walked a couple of steps, turned around, his hand touching the side of his cheek as if brushing away an insect. He stared at Calvino as he took away his hand. A smashed piece of white lotus petal touched with the flecks of gold leaf lay on his fingers.

"That's good luck," said Montri. "But it seems luck is on both sides. Vincent, I like your new BMW. It's nice what money can buy."

"I'd like a couple more minutes with Khun Vincent," Zhang said.

Montri sighed, glanced at the bottle, sucked his teeth, and strolled out of the gallery.

"Dismissing the host in his own house is an art," said Calvino after Montri closed the door. "The True Sons of The Soil is financed by Chinese money. I like the irony of that arrangement."

Zhang smiled, his attention moving from the petal to Calvino. "My associates will go to your condo. And one last thing: If you don't return the object we discussed, you will cause a big problem. I collected on my collateral. Colonel Pratt and his family might have less luck in the future."

"Something's been bothering me. Tanny told you about the meeting with the general's wife at Government House. You're the one who set it up, right?"

Zhang smiled. "You really thought it was Colonel Pratt's wife?"

"That's what I thought," said Calvino, exhaling.

"Tanny asked me for a favor. To help her mother."

"And in return you asked a favor of her," said Calvino.

"More than one." His face was smug, the glint from his eyes arrogant and hateful.

"You said, 'Why not take Calvino along to the meeting,'" said Calvino, flexing his jaw, thinking of the size of the wall that billions of dollars would build. High enough and long enough to rival the Great Wall of China, keeping out the barbarians and expanding the writ of the Chinese.

"And your secretary. To be strong, you need to turn men who are fearless into men who are afraid. And that has always been easy. Pinpoint the man's family and friends. It works like a charm, I think you stay in New York."

Calvino watched Zhang walk away, laughing as if he'd heard one of Brandon's jokes—not the one about the demand for money from a Chinese money launderer—but a punch line from some Chinese parable about how the stupid foreigner falls into the trap of being held hostage.

FORTY-NINE

CALVINO SWITCHED ON the reading lamp beside his computer screen and settled into the chair behind his desk. The only sound came from the low hum of the air-conditioner compressors on the balcony. The kind of white noise that wound through the consciousness an hour before the first patch of pink was smeared like cheap lipstick against an inky sky. At this hour the street was a dead zone, a space without people or cars. Bangkok was mostly still and quiet, asleep at four in the morning. The drunks, no longer able to bring their mouths to the rim of the glass, had rolled over for the night, and the hookers and their customers slept in the fitful way of strangers sharing a bed. Bars, restaurants, knock shops closed, offices, banks, massage parlors yet to open. It was the time when people talked to themselves because there was no one else to listen. It was the time when a man drank alone and thought about the past, about the people he'd loved, the people he'd killed. The full weight of those memories rode him hard. It was also the time when the full weight of loneliness that had no counterweight settled on him. Outside his window the neon sign for One Hand Clapping was dark and the soi as quiet as a cat stalking a house lizard.

A soft rain slanted against the window, blurring the streetlights mirrored on the wet pavement. He worked to edit himself out of the images. It was painstaking. He rubbed his eyes, sitting back and looking at the screen filled with Wei Zhang's face, his great-grandfather's nude painting a blur in the background. He'd given up his last Chini and started to wonder if it had been worth it.

He'd told Zhang that chasing down bar yings and deadbeats hadn't cut him out for unwinding complicated deals involving government officials, military officers, big-money types, regional gangsters, and powerful Bangkok families. He tried to list every category that Zhang had on his checklist. But the Chinese businessman failed to believe him. Blowing up the whole edifice, now, that was a possibility, and it focused Zhang's attention.

Calvino fought back a yawn, thinking how looking at someone on a computer screen was like looking at the TV. You never saw anyone you knew on the screen, just celebrities, politicians, models—that is, ignoring the thousands of faces of demonstrators or those in refugee camps. Wei Zhang's angular face, full lips, and high forehead might have belonged to a movie star. Zhang appeared to look at the camera as he talked. It was unnerving to see how perfectly the image had been captured.

Calvino slumped back, as if somebody had pushed him, as he regarded the image of Zhang, cigarette smoke frozen in the air. Calvino had positioned the camera on the double-helix sculpture. Behind Zhang was one of Galileo Chini's nudes hanging on the gallery wall, and the other paintings in Montri's collection surrounding it.

Looking at the image on the computer screen, Calvino thought that Zhang bore a slight resemblance to the man he'd shot in 2006. Or was it early-morning tiredness playing tricks on his mind? Look-alikes or not, they made Calvino wonder if his karma had gotten itself tied up in a bunch of Chinese knots that never seemed to voluntarily come undone. He stared at Zhang talking, unaware that he was being filmed. He was a natural: Self-confident, calm and

439

cool in the certainty that Calvino was just another Western fool who had no more of an idea of what was happening than a man trying to read time from a clock with only a minute hand.

Power of conviction lasted until the executioner raised his arms and the blade of the ax hovered a second before cleaving through the extended neck. After Calvino finished editing the video clip down to ten minutes' running time, he pulled a new office bottle from the bottom drawer of his desk and poured a double shot, splashed the whiskey around the inside the glass, took a deep breath, and emptied it in one swig. He poured a second round, checking the level in the bottle. He raised his glass, saluted Brandon's memory, thinking of him sitting on top of the ladder making people laugh.

Calvino used a proxy server to open YouTube on his Mozilla browser. He typed in the login information and waited a couple of beats. Clips of *The Daily Show*, Stephen Colbert, and David Letterman popped up on the screen. The funnymen had top billing. People needed a good laugh, to enjoy the folly of the human condition and to forget how serious and dangerous the world really was. Brandon had known better than most how humor worked as a temporary drug against sadness and despair.

Calvino had plugged the high-definition video camera directly into the USB port. All that was left was couple of keystrokes to upload it to YouTube. Next he opened the website Wiki Whistleblower in a separate screen and uploaded an eight-page report linking Zhang to General Suchart and listing the names of the shareholders as his close associates, documenting the history of Zhang's PLA connection, the electroshock-weapon manufacturing, and the transfer of three million dollars to E-Dragon (Siam). He headlined the article "Chinese Warren Buffett's Electrifying Journey On The Silk Road."

Calvino sipped the whiskey, felt the sting on his tongue, in the back of his throat as he set the glass down. He had no doubt what he needed to do. Zhang had, in a way, made the decision easy—daring him to build a window for anyone to peer into the black house where the Chinese mafia divided up the money.

Big decisions grew to massive proportions once a man understood the depth and breadth of the entanglements involved. Zhang's mission had been littered with casualties and fenced with lies and deceit, and in a world of funnymen the challenge for Calvino was untangling the relationships, reflecting on possible outcomes, and thinking about the consequences of exposing others at a time when emotions were raw and people were demonstrating in the streets. Zhang had no problem with letting Calvino walk out of Montri's mansion. Calvino had no choices left; every move he'd made had been checkmated, and now the game was over, and in Zhang's mind he had won. The ritual cleansing at Montri's mansion had given him confidence that his past was behind him. Zhang had stared at Calvino for the last time in the gallery, told himself that he was looking at a defeated man, a man who would submit to his will.

What he hadn't seen was Calvino's tiny video camera perched on the helix structure. It had been rolling from the moment Zhang came into the gallery.

The video was a couple of clicks away from an upload to YouTube. The Wiki page would be vetted and might take days before it was posted. But the YouTube video would appear immediately on the Net. He'd link the YouTube page to the Wiki article and hope for the best. But didn't everyone who uploaded a video? Calvino gazed at Jon Stewart's face on the YouTube clip. Eyebrows raised, a large ironic smile frozen in time as if he knew a secret millions of others wanted him to share. Would Zhang's confession be noticed in the vast digital sea of videos?

It was said that a butterfly flapping its wings in a Brazil rainforest might cause a hurricane along the Texas coast, or even more dramatically, change the orbit of the planet. Small events had potentially huge consequences, Calvino thought. A young woman in Isan was summarily executed in the war against drugs. Her death echoed through time, calling out to those left behind, including Tanny Craig. An unborn baby was incinerated in Yunnan province, but his spirit haunted his surviving brother. A political void had opened in Thailand, and money and lives and schemers tumbled in, head over heels—colonels, businessmen, players, dreamers, dealmakers, all entangled in ways no one fully understood. But like the butterfly, which required wings for flight, the Thai power brokers required influence to fly, one with another, flying in formation, and the misery of the world flowed from the realization of the near impossibility of changing the laws of motion. But it was worth a try, thought Calvino. He had no other plan in mind.

He smiled, watching the screen as the file loaded, sipping his whiskey. To start a media fire, he needed a reporter. A hack would do the trick, as most real reporters had long ago lost their jobs. Even the hacks he'd known from the old days were retired or dead or had packed up and gone back home to die. By the time the Europeans had set up enough committees to decide what to do with the story, Calvino told himself that he'd likely be dead. That left Kincaid, the American writer who'd hung out with Brandon the night of the Foreign Correspondents' Club panel discussion.

What writer wouldn't kill for an exclusive that had the potential to be picked up and broadcast around the world? Calvino figured Kincaid was his man. He'd spent a career getting freebie hotel rooms, buffets, and buckets of wine. He knew everyone in the press corps. And Kincaid would know where to feed the story—Reuters, DPA, CNN, BBC, and AP. He searched through his desk until he found

Kincaid's card, and, having forgotten the time, he punched in the number. When Kincaid answered on the fifth ring, he screamed into the phone, "You whore! I told you to stop calling me! It's the fucking middle of the night! And if you want money."

Calvino sensed that the "fuck-you moment," followed by the slamming down of the phone, had just about arrived, and interrupted, "This is Vincent Calvino. I met you at the Foreign Correspondents' Club the night Brandon Sawyer spoke."

"What the fuck do you want?"

"A political corruption story."

"Who cares?"

"Chinese funding General Suchart's political party. Government contracts. Kickbacks. Big money."

Silence. Kincaid's kick-ass anger dropped like an anchor. Calvino had hit the right sequence to speed-dial through to where Kincaid kept his ambition and greed under wraps. He described the video and what Zhang had said on tape, then e-mailed the YouTube link of the video to Kincaid, who watched it as Calvino heard him murmuring, "What is this?"

"A video confession from Wei Zhang, a key player."

Calvino opened his desk drawer, took out his passport and a wad of hundred-dollar bills. He stuck the passport in his inside jacket pocket and divided the cash, sticking it into various side pockets. Looping his arm into the leather shoulder holster, he secured it around his neck. It fit snug against the left side of his chest. He pulled out the .38 police special and checked the cylinder. Calvino always kept the .38 loaded—otherwise what was the point? Throwing it at someone wouldn't do much good.

Calvino had a good idea that Zhang was less interested in retrieving the prototype weapon than in finishing the business that had gone sideways twice, once in the botched job using a van and a second time when the device wired in his car had killed Siriporn. Zhang couldn't lose—either Calvino would run or he'd show up at his condominium for the appointment. And the Chinese believed that the third time was a charm.

But Calvino had a couple of ideas himself how to prepare for the next encounter. He'd given a security guard a thousand baht to borrow the CCTV tapes from the previous two nights prior to Siriporn's murder. He loaded the tapes onto his hard drive and studied each one—the faces of every delivery person, resident, friend, whore, gambler, and retiree who'd been buzzed into the lobby the night someone had wired Calvino's Honda.

One man stood out. His hair was closely cropped to a fine burr against the skull, and he had full lips right off a carved stone head from Angkor Wat. Calvino remembered this face, saw the man pull a nine-millimeter handgun out of a bulky red insulated carrier with a pizza logo and aim it at his head. In slow motion the gunman pulled the trigger. The sound of the round echoed in his ears. Calvino had awakened, sitting upright, covered in sweat. His gut told him that the Thai man in his mid-twenties who'd been captured on the CCTV tapes was more than the stuff of a nightmare. He thought the chances were good that he'd seen the face of Siriporn's killer on the tape. He asked himself what the odds were of meeting the man who had been in the tape; hit men in Thailand were as numerous as hookers, and just about as interchangeable.

As he sat in his office, getting ready to leave, he wondered if the face he remembered from the tapes was waiting for him at the condo. There was only one way to find out. He removed the compact video cam from the USB port and slipped it into his pocket. He checked the time. The fact that the police were no longer staking out his condo told him everything he needed to know. Zhang's general had a long reach. The fist had come out of the glove, and the knuckles had been brassed up, sent on a mission. Calvino switched off the light, locked his office, and walked down the stairs. He looked both ways as he reached the street level. The silent street yielded no one. A cat stretched, rubbed itself on the edge of the stair, and slipped away.

Calvino walked to Ratana's BMW, parked in front of the office; he had the keys in his hand. Zhang's security detail would have seen the car at Montri's. They'd be waiting for it at the condo. He pocketed the keys and walked up the soi, where he found a motorcycle-taxi driver who was both awake and sober early in the morning, and asked, as the young man pulled on his helmet, to stop within walking distance of the condominium. He paid the driver and cut through the back lane to the side of his building. A small walkway separated the building from a factory that manufactured stainless-steel industrial-size kitchen equipment—huge pots, sinks, worktables, and cupboards. He looked through a window, but the inside of the factory was dark and there was no movement. An outside light on the wall bounced off rows of steel sinks. A large rat ran over his shoe and disappeared under a stack of half-constructed basins piled high against the common wall. Halfway up the pile, a cat hunched down, eyes burning. Calvino climbed up, one kitchen fixture at a time—they made a natural ladder—until his hands touched the top of the wall.

Calvino pulled himself up, looking at the empty ramp leading to the first floor of the parking garage. After jumping down onto the ramp, he shook off the muscle burn in his shoulders and arms. He hurried up the ramp, pushed open the first-floor fire door, and walked up the stairs. By the time he reached the second floor, he no longer felt the cramp in his right shoulder, and had drawn his .38 from its holster. Leaning against the door as he reached the fifth-floor fire door, Calvino thought that this was how it was when there was no possibility of backup from Colonel Pratt. There was no question in his mind that Pratt would have wanted to be at his side. But the colonel was dreaming morphine dreams of sandy beaches and beautiful women—there was only one way the matter could be settled, and that was to run or settle it alone. He'd tell Pratt the full story later. Assuming he'd be around to tell it and Pratt to listen.

Calvino pressed his ear against the door. He picked up the low murmur of conversation from the other side. Two voices, two men talking about how the farang was late. He flattened his shoulder against the gray metal door. Through the small crack, he saw the two men. Both were young, slender, fit like men who worked out in the gym. One of them leaned against the back of a black Isuzu pickup, the kind with chrome mag wheels and a retractable roof that was cranked up, looming above the bed. He wore a black T-shirt tucked into his jeans, tattoos of a garuda and dragon chasing each other down his arm. He casually smoked a cigarette, flicking the ash with the nail on his little finger. He also had a gun holstered on his belt. The second man was positioned in front of the bank of elevators. His posture was picture perfect as he stood with his back turned to Calvino.

Slowly the man watching the elevators looked around at his friend beside the pickup. "Watch the ramp," he said, pointing at the ramp leading up to the fifth floor. Nothing was moving.

"He's not going to show. Come on, let's get out of here," said the man with the tattoos.

From the doorway Calvino made the sentry by the elevators as the same guy he'd watched on the CCTV tape walking in the lobby dressed as a pizza deliveryman. From the setup it looked like he was running the show, the point man delegated to make the decision on the ground—stay or pull up the tent and leave the area. "Give it a few more minutes," he said.

The man with the tattoos grumbled and flicked away his cigarette.

Calvino fixed the silencer on the barrel of the .38 and opened the door.

"Who you looking for?" he asked, standing in the doorway, training the gun on the man in front of the elevators.

"Zhang sent us. You got something for us." The guy didn't lie all that well. His eyes glanced at his partner.

The tattooed man standing beside the Isuzu saw the signal, and his expression changed as he slipped his hand down to reach for his sidearm. Calvino crouched in a firing position; he shot him twice in the chest. The man pitched forward and dropped chin first as if he were dead before he hit the ground. "You were here before," said Calvino to the survivor, who had raised his hands. "You fucked with my car." He stood in front of Ratana's BMW; the hood was open. "And you're trying the same thing again?" There was no mistake that Calvino projected what the Thais called *kliat khao kraduk dam*—hatred strong enough to go to the bone. "You shoot my friend, the police colonel? Well, did you, asshole?"

He was scared, and the predator's blood lust Calvino had seen in his eyes had been extinguished, replaced by not so much fear as desperation. Finally the man swallowed with difficulty, sighed like something jagged had gone down his throat, and he made the same futile reach his partner had, and Calvino shot him in the stomach. He let him fall to his knees. "Did you shoot the police colonel?"

The wounded man spit blood on Calvino's shoes.

"I take that as a yes."

"You have no friends," the man said.

"Maybe not."

447

Calvino shot him in the head. His body fell over.

Calvino holstered his .38 and pondered what to do about the two dead bodies. It was too early for heavy lifting. He dragged the first body from the area in front of the elevators and loaded it into the back of the pickup. He rested for a moment, pulling a cigarette out of the pack from the other dead body, found the lighter, lit the cigarette, took two hits, dropped it, and ground the long butt under his heel. He sized up the crime scene, thinking how the police would gather evidence and reconstruct what had happened to the two men. They'd look high and low until a bulb went on in someone's head that maybe the men had messed up their assignment. But that meant doing some rearrangement of both the bodies and the pickup in order to give himself some time.

Calvino flipped through their identification papers; both men carried old police IDs. They could have been real. Or not. They were a couple of years out of date. That pointed to ex-cops who hadn't kicked the habit of carrying their old IDs. He put their wallets back in the pockets where he'd found them. He fished the keys to the pickup from the front pocket of the tattooed man, and then he loaded the body into the back. He was sweating by the time he'd finished. He thought that since both men might be cops, things would turn ugly. In the back of the pickup, he found a black gym bag. Calvino unzipped it and looked inside. He pulled out a Ziploc tightly packed with white powder. There were half a dozen packages in the bag. That had been their play, he thought. The new war on drugs was taking a different direction: The cops decided that the person they hit needed to be a drug kingpin and required an investment of a couple of kilos of heroin. Like a Chinese loan, the white powder would find its way back to the source.

In the first war against drugs, the death squads had used a standard method to support the verdict of the dead person as a drug dealer—crude, but effective: Shoot the man or woman or child and plant drugs beside the body, in the pockets of the clothing, or inside a body cavity. Calvino threw the Ziploc packet into the bag and zipped it up. The cache of drugs gave him a moment of relief, until he remembered that rogue cops operated under the protection of influential crooked friends on the force. Two bodies with a duffel bag of drugs would normally make the news. Calvino figured that there was an even chance, using some creative forensics, that the two men would be reported as victims in the new war against drugs.

He closed the roof of the black Isuzu until it made a perfect cover on the bed like a lid on a pot. No one got shot in the chest without a rope of blood splattering the area. Shoot two men at close range and there's enough of that rope to hang a man. He pushed open the fire door, opened the doors to the utility closet in the hallway, and pulled out a bucket and mop. He worked against the coming dawn. It wasn't a professional job by any means, smearing blood around until it looked like something else had been spilled on the area. By the time he'd finished cleaning the floor and walls and put away the bucket and mop, he was running out of time.

He climbed into the pickup, inserted the key, and drove up to the sixth floor, all the way to the end. There were lots of empty parking places. It was far away from the elevators and people were too lazy to walk the distance. He parked the pickup, got out, locked the doors, and walked over to an SUV covered with a tarp.

The dust that coated it suggested that it hadn't been moved for a long time. Dragging the tarp to the pickup, he heard the muffled sound of a cell phone from the back of the pickup. He stopped, turned around, and thought for a moment. Better to leave it unanswered; whoever was calling was in for a disappointment. Someone would come

449

looking for them soon enough. He pulled the tarp over the pickup, knotting the tie holds in front and back. Moving the pickup to another floor and covering it with the tarp would only slow them down, but eventually they'd find it. The security guards would have a record of its coming in and not going out.

Calvino looked over the wall and saw a couple of workmen who had arrived for an early shift at the factory below. There was no going over the wall without being spotted. He couldn't go back to his unit. And he couldn't stay in the parking garage. He smiled as he pulled out his key chain and fanned through the keys like a card shark through a poker hand until he found the key to Siriporn's unit on the ninth floor. She'd left it on the kitchen counter with a note telling him not to be a stranger. That had happened not long after Tanny returned to New York. Siriporn said he could let himself in anytime. That time had arrived. He wondered if her relatives had changed the locks. One of them might even be inside.

He quietly opened the door, slipped inside, stood still, looked around, and listened. It seemed empty. He had the place to himself. By the time he had closed the door, the first rays of sun lit up the sky.

Calvino walked across the unit and into Siriporn's bedroom. He opened the closets and found her clothes still hanging inside. He sat on the edge of her bed. They'd always met at his unit. It seemed strange that the first time he'd sat on her bed, she was dead. Everything appeared to be untouched, left the way it had been on the last day of her life. He picked up her scent—a lavender and mint smell—a comb, a scarf, and a set of earrings. When he opened the dresser, he saw neatly folded panties and bras. On the floor of the closet, her polished shoes were lined up in neat rows. He leaned down and looked closer. One red shoe had a blemish, a scratch, a nick, making the shoe look like a neglected orphan. When he walked back to the bed, he found a file folder with his name lying on the nightstand. Inside were printouts of e-mails, Excel files, a matchbook from a restaurant where they'd eaten, and a couple of photographs printed on glossy paper.

Calvino thought about himself next to her on the wrong side of the yellow line, loving it, smiling—or he was smiling? And she was next to him laughing. It had been after Tanny had gone back to New York, and he'd told Siriporn a joke about how things had ended with her, using the Thai expression *kon maw mai than dam*. It struck Siriporn as funny, imagining Calvino as an old-fashioned rice pot whose bottom hadn't yet turned black from being held over the fire. That laughter captured in the photograph was the way he wanted to remember her. He lay back in her bed remembering how after they'd finished lunch at the Greyhound Restaurant, they'd run into one of Siriporn's colleagues, another broker, who had taken the photographs.

Being surrounded by her things, the full weight of her loss struck him.

People who cared enough to love you were not replaceable.

All he could do was stretch out on her bed and wait. He slipped into a deep sleep.

FIFTY

SIRIPORN'S SISTER, FILM, had arrived on a bus from upcountry. She had let herself into the condo at seven in the morning. She sensed immediately that someone else was inside and thought of turning around and going for help. Instead she pushed open the bedroom door and found Calvino sleeping in her sister's bed. She let out a scream, her hands automatically covering her mouth. She froze in the doorway, unable to turn and run, unable to rush forward to attack the man in bed before he attacked her. Before she could recover herself, Calvino had sat up, holding the .38 aimed at the source of the scream. Instantly he felt embarrassed, lowering the gun and sliding it into the holster as if it were a perfectly normal thing to do when someone came through the door. He tossed the holster on the pillow, smiling, holding up a forefinger as if to claim the right to speak.

Calvino recognized Siriporn in the woman's features: The high cheekbones, porcelain clear, smooth skin, and warm, full lips that took a hard edge when displaying anger.

"You're Film," he said. Siriporn had shown him family photographs. Thais always had photographs to show others.

"Why did you point a gun at me?" She spoke like someone out of breath.

"I wasn't expecting anyone."

"What are you doing in my sister's bedroom?" Her hands trembled.

"I was sleeping."

"I didn't see you at the wat. Not once did you come to pay respects. My mother and father asked about you. There was nothing I could say. Other than it had been your car that killed her. She died because of you." Her suspicion and dislike, if they'd been blades, would have sliced him into wafer-thin slabs. The flash of hatred twisted her mouth, and she ran forward, both fists clenched. *Kliat khao sai*, with hatred deeply lodged in her guts, would be an appropriate expression for Film's feeling for Calvino at the moment. He grabbed her arm and let her land a couple of punches with her free hand before pinning her down on the bed. Her hatred registered slightly below the hatred to the bone Calvino had felt as he shot the man in the parking garage.

"Someone tampered with the car."

"The police said it was an accident."

"It wasn't."

"Let go. You're hurting me." She struggled against his weight. He released her and she started to sob. "She didn't deserve to die. Why didn't you say good-bye to her? You should've been at the funeral."

Film worked in the movie business. Though from her performance in the condo, Calvino was convinced she wasn't acting. No one could have faked the kind of emotion that she'd uncoiled, rendering her helpless, defeated. "If you know who did this, why haven't you told the police?"

"The police are involved."

"*Farang baa*," she said, crazy foreigner.

He responded with a crooked smile. "You think it's crazy? I've got a friend who's a cop. He was shot investigating Siriporn's murder."

"Is this true?"

"Ask General Suchart's True Sons of The Soil Party," he said.

"My sister had nothing to do with politics. She wasn't political."

"You don't have to be political to get caught in the crossfire."

Film softened, puffing out her cheeks and slowly exhaling. Tears rimmed her eyes, and she looked away before wiping them with her hand. "My sister said that she loved you." She looked up, studying his face and trying to see what exactly her sister had found to love in this man. Nothing obvious came to her as an explanation. It was, like many things with Siriporn, a mystery, one that she had taken to her cremation.

Calvino let her words fall away. "I know," he said. "Can I tell you a secret?"

Film nodded.

"The men who did this are dead."

Calvino waited for a reaction. Her face clouded, thoughts rushing through her head. He watched her filtering through the options that suited the crazy-foreigner vision she possessed of him.

"How do you know?" She wasn't clear whether she wanted information about how he knew who her sister's murderers were or how he knew they were dead.

"Tomorrow morning there is going to be a news conference. Why don't you come along with me?"

"I want to know now. How do you know they're dead?"

Extending his right arm, Calvino pointed his forefinger, bent his thumb as the hammer, and pulled back his middle finger. She looked at his .38 in the holster and back at his finger gun. "I know."

She saw in his eyes that he had killed them. And as a teardrop escaped, she nodded. "Thank you."

Three days after Calvino walked out of Montri's gallery, a press conference was announced at the Foreign Correspondents' Club at 10:00 A.M. Three days was a biblical number, but in this case no one was resurrected from the dead. A news conference, though, was the next-best thing to happen for the living. Calvino and Film arrived late, edging into the back of a room packed with press, cameras, and lighting and sound equipment. At ten in the morning, a scrub of the correspondents still moved slowly, as if their blood wasn't yet fully circulating.

Kincaid sat alone at the table on the platform, hands folded, fresh haircut, the blue Foreign Correspondents' Club banner framing his solitary figure. He was hardly recognizable in a suit and tie, claiming journalistic privilege not to reveal his sources. Reporters jammed the room, lining up five deep behind two microphones. His statement was finished, and the club president opened questions from the floor. It was never too early for a journalist to belt back a drink, but this morning no one was drinking, and no one carried on the tradition of loud side-conversations that usually rumbled like an angry tide washing forward from the back of the room.

The correspondents understood that Kincaid had somehow managed to break one of those rare stories that a journalist worked a whole lifetime to find, the kind the major media players with large resources broke. The atmosphere at the club was like the one at the press conference when the footage of the Pol Pot interview had been released many years before. An American reporter then had hit the big time. Now it was Kincaid's turn at the brass ring. Kincaid, who blended into the room with dozens of other freelancers, had a Pol Pot–size exclusive. The others in the room envied him. China had blocked all YouTube videos, locked down its entire media, and ignored the overseas press, pretending that the video of

Zhang didn't exist. The Thais had blocked the video only on YouTube. But it was too little, too late—clips played on every major international channel.

"Do you have a book contract?" asked a reporter from one of the wire services.

"My agent has several publishers in New York bidding. But there's nothing firm. Not yet."

News reporting had moved online. Kincaid was living proof of a new era.

Kincaid grinned, looking like a fox with a mouthful of feathers. The BBC and CNN cameras rolled with close-ups of his moment in the limelight. He soon learned that the story wasn't about him. It was a big China story. The phrase Kincaid used circulated around the globe: "Disruptor Tycoon." Disruptor was the name of the weapon Zhang had planned to manufacture in Thailand. Other reporters labeled Zhang a "Chinese godfather."

Zhang had abruptly departed for Yunnan, flying direct to Kunming, looking forward to a homecoming—and before anyone could criticize the government for letting him escape, it was reported that he had been arrested and charged with misappropriation of state money. Chinese TV showed him being led away by uniformed police with their hard, blank faces as they escorted him from the airport. It had been a busy time for airport stories. The Thai government got a black eye when General Suchart and Tamarine slipped over the Cambodian border, then boarded a plane to Sweden. A spokesman for his political party said it was a fact-finding mission into bank-rescue plans. In Stockholm, General Suchart appeared before the cameras, grim-faced, exhausted from his overland escape and the jet lag from the flight, saying that he had been a victim of anti-democratic forces, that he didn't feel he could get justice in Thailand, and that his lawyers were drafting an application for political asylum.

Tamarine's astrologer told her over the phone as she paced in the first-class lounge at the airport in Phnom Penh that no one could have foreseen an asteroid coming out of nowhere to disturb the transiting of Venus as it passed through the Sextile Natal Sun. The general had been a victim of celestial mischief, knocking out the influences that had guaranteed his political and financial gain, and turning their happy travel for the year into a harrowing escape. He offered no refund on his fee. Tamarine phoned several friends in Bangkok complaining about the astrologer; the news of her disappointment rolled like thunder along the bamboo telegraph.

The general and his wife's escape to Sweden and Zhang's arrest in China had been linked, and the story played on BBC, which flickered on TV monitors around the room in the club. One of the correspondents asked Kincaid, "Any idea if someone tipped Zhang about the video?"

Kincaid said he didn't have that information. Meaning he didn't know how Zhang had managed the old Indian rope trick.

"Was it a political decision to let him leave?" another correspondent asked.

"You're asking the wrong person," said Kincaid.

"What do you think will happen to General Suchart's Party?" asked the same correspondent.

"My privileged sources say it's having a leadership crisis."

A polite way of saying that it was dead on the arrival of General Suchart's plane in Stockholm.

Calvino liked being called a privileged source as he sat at the bar in the back of the room. He had said nothing. It was Kincaid's show. A freelancer beside Calvino leaned over and whispered, "Kincaid must have had to blow a horse to get this story."

Calvino shrugged. "A whole stable of stallions."

"No one is so lucky in this life," said Film.

Calvino nodded. He knew she was talking about Siriporn. No amount of persuasion would convince Film that luck could account for Kincaid's break. The fact that anybody won recognition and fame was news; it was a miracle, and it was a promise of hope no matter how illusory. She accepted that Calvino had taken care of those responsible for her sister's death. He'd lifted the veil on that mystery, and regardless of the pain of the loss, she felt a sense of relief and closure as she stood next to Calvino and watched as Kincaid dug Zhang a fresh grave in China.

The blueprint for constructing a Thai black house had had two chief architects: Wei Zhang and General Suchart. But their plans never got off the drawing board; if they had succeeded, Colonel Pratt said it would have been only temporary before the house of cards collapsed. The government and the military had gone silent, like a cat fully alert, watching, waiting to see what rat would next run across the floor. They had no idea how to react, so they did what governments and the military do in such circumstances— nothing. First they needed time to regroup, find out who had been implicated, who could be protected, and how to tell the story without causing any more problems with the Chinese. The ministers and the police were eating enough aspirin to have the same economic impact as a small-scale infrastructure project. No one inside was talking to anyone on the outside. But they were all talking to their astrologers. Kincaid had said that ministers had been invited to the club to give a briefing; they'd all declined. The demonstrators were baying for blood, and the government, while still standing, had given the street leaders more rocks to throw at the wobbly black house even as its occupants tried to distance themselves from the scandal.

A government spokesman said the cabinet had agreed to set up a committee to investigate the licenses that E-

Dragon (Siam) had been granted and another committee to investigate the trail of money that Zhang had brought into the country. Investigation into the transfer of large sums from E-Dragon to General Suchart's party had been assigned to another committee. No one mentioned whether the Thai authorities would call the Chinese ambassador in for an explanation, as it had been agreed that both countries had been duped by rogue elements. The ten-billion-dollar loan from the Chinese had disappeared off the radar screen, vanished like Zhang into the twilight world, under the beds of Beijing politicos.

Ratana and Manee and John-John sat around the table after dinner. Manee had a coloring book filled with dragons, garudas, temples, and warriors, plus a box of crayons. John-John grabbed crayons with his fists.

"Color inside the lines," said Ratana.

John-John tried staying in the lines but soon gave up. She guided his hand and carefully positioned a gray crayon over the outline of an elephant. He sliced the crayon across the page. It didn't matter if he stayed within the lines, she told herself just as Manee said, "He's having fun." She was teaching a lesson to a future driver about life on Thai roads.

After a couple of minutes of drawing, the outline of the elephant disappeared in a maze of crisscrossed gray lines, pointless and sloppy. Let him be, she told herself.

Manee and Ratana, in effect, colored inside the lines as they talked about their mothers, their children, and an entertainer who was divorcing his wife. Nothing was said about politics. That was messy and all over the place. It didn't make for a pretty picture. But it was impossible to keep the outside world from invading the house. One of the kids had turned on the TV in the next room, and reports of demonstrators occupying the airport filtered through the house. The women pretended not to hear how the demonstrators had been bussed from Government House to Suvarnabhumi Airport, and all flights in and out of Thailand had been canceled. The demonstrators had agreed to allow foreigners to leave the airport, but none of the leaders had stepped forward to confirm their release. Politics was like love, in that it was possible to lose one's way, and also like love in that it sometimes led to obsessions, and the obsessed, by definition, never lost their way—they took down anyone who stood between them and the object of their desire.

Colonel Pratt, who'd lost five kilos, looked gaunt, like a man who'd survived a jungle ordeal. But his smile was still the same. He slowly moved toward his library, turned, and saw Calvino hanging behind. "We should have that talk," said Colonel Pratt.

Calvino followed Pratt inside, and they sat, poured each other drinks, and listened to Miles Davis in the background. "Zhang got out in time," said Calvino.

"Meaning he received a tip."

"Isn't that how it usually works?"

Colonel Pratt nodded, sipped his neat whiskey. "Listen to this riff."

Calvino listened, thinking that Miles Davis was mostly about the riff that opened time and space. It was hard to pick one riff from another unless you were a player like Pratt. But he listened anyway. He wanted to tell Pratt about the men in the parking garage and the fact that one of them had been the man who'd shot him. Pratt was back, but not all the way back; he'd taken a bullet in the shoulder and a second in the lower side of his body. Calvino also knew that the burden of such knowledge wouldn't help the healing process. He left it alone. When Pratt pulled out his saxophone, he moved a beat slower than before. Bullets did that kind of thing; they slowed even the fastest man down to a lower tempo.

"How are you feeling?" asked Calvino for the seventh time that night.

Colonel Pratt smiled. "Good. About the same as when you asked me twenty minutes ago."

"The arm's okay?" Calvino raised his right arm over his head.

The colonel lifted his arm level with his head. "I can lift it this far. But it will come back. Or so the doctors promise."

"Zhang's not doing so well in China."

Pratt lowered his saxophone, wiped his dry lips. "He got too greedy."

"If you were going to start a cult of the patriot, he was a perfect match for Suchart's ambitions."

Pratt nodded. "That was the problem."

"They nearly pulled it off. True Sons of The Soil were heading for a majority in the election."

"I doubt it," said Colonel Pratt. "Thais are smarter than you think."

"The weight of money makes smart people stupid."

Colonel Pratt sighed, opened the whiskey bottle, and poured two more glasses. He handed one to Calvino. They touched glasses and drank. "Have you heard anything from Tanny Craig?" asked Pratt.

"I talked to her briefly not long after I got back from China."

"You didn't mention it."

"There wasn't much to mention," said Calvino.

"It was an in-and-out job for her," said Pratt.

Calvino smiled, thinking that sometimes the colonel stumbled upon exactly the right expression that covered a whole range of activities. "There are a couple of ways to read her story. Either she had everything planned before she arrived and she used her mother as cover, or her world was turned upside down after she met her mother and found out that unless she helped the woman, no one would. She

461

wasn't going to let her sister's death mean nothing. It wasn't right, Pratt. Like you getting shot wasn't right."

"How do you read her?" asked Colonel Pratt.

"Like I read Latin. I'm half Italian. You'd think it would make sense. But I can't understand what I'm reading. And reading Latin's easier than reading a woman."

The two men fell silent, looking into their whiskey glasses as if seeking an omen.

"When something goes wrong in your heart, the pain doesn't go away until the wrong is fixed. The sadness of the world is that most wrong things can't be fixed. They stay broken. And you live with the mess, because you've got no choice."

"But the wrongs of traitorous men aren't just any wrongs," said Calvino, thinking he sounded like one of those Burmese generals who didn't watch television.

" 'Though with their high wrongs I am struck to the quick, yet, with my nobler reason 'gainst my fury do I take part: the rarer action is in virtue than in vengeance,' " said Colonel Pratt, quoting *The Tempest*.

"My father taught me that more crimes were done in the name of virtue than were done in the name of vengeance. But he wasn't a Shakespeare man."

"If we let go of virtue, where does that leave us, Vincent?"

Calvino refilled his glass, shaking his head in disappointment. He'd thought the colonel would be the first to want to put the likes of Zhang and Suchart against the wall. "You're going to let it go in the name of virtue?"

"There's nothing for me to let go of. It's finished. General Suchart's in exile. Zhang has fallen from grace and will never return. That's enough justice to satisfy me."

"You were shot because you found the fingerprint from Achara's padlock," said Calvino. "Are you going to tell me who it belonged to?"

"Zhang."

Calvino leaned back in his chair. "One fingerprint." It made awful sense. Achara's guard had been down that day as Zhang had come with the other men, the ones who would do the heavy lifting.

"*Nam phueng yod diew*," said Colonel Pratt. It was the old Thai expression that a small mishap could cause a large disaster.

"One drop of honey?" asked Calvino. "It was more like a bucket."

Calvino saw Pratt's eyes starting to narrow, nearly shut. He seemed at peace in his chair, the empty glass on the table in front of him. Calvino had expected bitterness. But the colonel had moved beyond bitterness, redemption, or forgiveness to a more detached understanding of the forces that had been at work, and things had not so much gotten out of hand as they became futile and meaningless. Men turned despite their best intentions into agents of harm; even though they loved their wives and children and country, they no longer were bound by the restraints that check violence. They wouldn't kill a fly for fear of committing a sin, but they would kill another to advance what they were told was the larger good. They didn't have to worry about coloring within the lines; the lines didn't apply to them.

"I think the Chinese will shoot Zhang. It's a good idea. It's a solution that the Chinese usually find works wonders. My worry is that he might have enough money to get out of the execution."

"I don't think the Chinese authorities care about the money."

"But he's got connections."

"Failure is an orphan. Its connections vanish," said Colonel Pratt.

"On principle he deserves a bullet."

Colonel Pratt nodded, smiling. "On principle I agree with you. The problem is that the principle is a difficult one to apply." The talk of Zhang's possible execution had breathed life back into the colonel.

"Your point?"

Colonel Pratt's eyes opened widely. "The problem is where to stop. There's an old Thai saying, *khah jet chua khot*. Kill not just the offender but kill seven generations of his line." Pratt sat up in his chair, reached out, and refilled the glasses with whiskey. He worried that he was picking up on Calvino's habit of reaching for a bottle. That was something wounded men did.

The colonel had it right, thought Calvino. "Tanny wanted justice for her sister," he said.

"I don't see that happening."

"But it has. The Department of Special Investigation has arrested three officers for her murder. A couple dozen other cases will follow," said Colonel Pratt. The department had gone into the cage and taken on the lions; the unresolved question was who would emerge from the flurry of teeth and claws and who would end up like Achara.

"General Suchart's *luk nong* must be feeling the heat," said Calvino. A number of junior officers were discovering out what happened to their career when a patron fled abroad. To be orphaned from the source of power was to be abandoned. "Someone in the department is trying to make up for what they did to you."

"There's a long list of people. I have no reason to think the arrest had anything to do with me getting shot."

They drank in silence.

"The cops will make bail," said Calvino, looking into his glass.

Colonel Pratt nodded. "That's how it works."

"The trial could take years."

"You're missing something, Vincent."

Calvino cocked his head. "Justice. That's what I'm missing."

"A colonel and two lieutenant colonels have been arrested. That may not amount to justice in your book, but it's a start down a road that's been blocked a long time."

Tanny's sister had caught a bullet, like thousands of others during the war on drugs. He wondered how she'd take the news about the investigation into the murders. Maybe she would think that she had delivered the justice her mother wished for; maybe she'd think about the large distance between the cup and lip. Calvino thought as he listened to the jazz and watched Pratt wiping down the saxophone. It had been called the war on drugs—that's what Tanny's mother had told her, and she believed her mother. But it wasn't a real war. In a true war, both sides sent trained soldiers into battle. In the war on drugs, only one side had the bullets and guns, and took to the field setting up ambushes. It had never been about drugs. It was all about power, relationships, and money arrangements—the brightly lit tail of the comet. He'd been convinced that the system would never try itself.

The black house had fallen on Zhang and General Suchart. Zhang's miscalculation was to believe that his patrons in the PLA would protect him. But he also had faith in Ajarn Veera's ceremony. There were too many possible loose ends that could, over time become embarrassing or dangerous, if Zhang were allowed to rattle around in Chinese prisons for decades. He was dispensable. Someone else down the road would try again. Perhaps he'd also fail, but sooner or later luck would be on the side of someone with the money, the right connections, and the determination never to give up.

Colonel Pratt adjusted the leather strap around his neck, resting the saxophone on his chest, his lips touching the mouthpiece. "Maybe you should phone Tanny and tell her about the investigation. Let her phone her mother with the news," said Colonel Pratt.

"I'll think about it," said Calvino.

Colonel Pratt smiled, nodded, and played a favorite Miles Davis riff. The melody filled the room. Calvino thought about pouring another whiskey but stopped himself. He had already drunk too much. He sat back, watching the colonel near the window, the curtain pulled open, the moon against the sky, playing as if the gods were listening and the walls and the ceilings, the whole universe listening to the sound of hope and anguish, pleasure and pain, love and hate. But all Colonel Pratt could be certain of was one thing: Calvino had heard him.

ACKNOWLEDGMENTS

There are a number of people who gave their time and counsel as I wrote The Corruptionist. Each one made a contribution that allowed me to write a much better book than otherwise would have been the case.

Les Rose, RCMP, film director, and screenwriter, pointed the flashlight along a couple of pathways I would otherwise have overlooked. He has a sense of narrative and story structure that only a few people are blessed with. And he used that talent to show me exactly where things could be improved.

Professor Charlie McHugh read and made detailed comments on a draft as he rode the train to and from work in Japan. His painstaking work helped me plug more than one hole in the road.

Richard Diran, painter, antique dealer, photographer and writer, devoted time to reading an early draft and providing his wise counsel and insight. Richard is an artist. And anytime you can nail an artist to the floor to read a book and give his opinion should be counted as a victory. In my case, the spoils of victory were Richard's opinions on what was working and what should be tossed down a very deep ravine and set afire.

Maureen Sugden arrived to do a professional job as copyeditor. She's one of the best in the business. I still have dreams of all the tracking lines on the manuscript; it looked like the sewer system blueprint for Bangkok. Richard Baker worked tirelessly as copyeditor, proofreader, and continuity master in the last stages of the book, at which point I thought (wrongly) that it was finished. To Richard's credit, the word 'finished' is only ever used once the book is frog marched to the printer.

Thanks to my agent Bridget Wagner at Rafe Sagalyn Literary Agency, for her support of the Calvino series. And thanks to my wife Busakorn Suriyasarn for her humor, and our many hours of discussions about Thai culture, language and history. I couldn't wish for a better guide along the rugged gullies and hills in the long march to understanding about Thailand.

What errors and holes that remain are despite the substantial efforts of those above merely illustrates that even with the best professional advice, an author still will be determined to commit mistakes that he alone must live with. Anyone who has ever written a novel understands the writer is not unlike a promising football player who has the benefit of the best coaches but still manages, on occasion, to kick the ball into his own net.

THE VINCENT CALVINO P.I. SERIES

Christopher G. Moore's Vincent Calvino P.I. series began with *Spirit House* in 1992. The latest, eleventh, in the series is *The Corruptionist* first released in Thailand in 2010.

Moore's protagonist, Vincent Calvino is an Italian-Jewish former lawyer from New York who left his practice to turn P.I. in Southeast Asia. Calvino's assignments take him inside the labyrinth of local politics, double-dealing and fleeting relationships. Unlike typical tough-guy sleuths, Calvino admits he would never survive without his guardian angel, his Shakespeare-quoting and saxophone-playing buddy, Colonel Pratt, an honest and well-connected Thai cop who helps him find hidden forces, secret traps and ways to keep him alive in a foreign land.

The eleven novels in the Vincent Calvino P.I. series are: *Spirit House, Asia Hand, Zero Hour in Phnom Penh, Comfort Zone, The Big Weird, Cold Hit, Minor Wife, Pattaya 24/7, The Risk of Infidelity Index, Paying Back Jack*, and *The Corruptionist*. The novels are published in Thailand by Heaven Lake Press (www.heavenlakepress.com), in the United States by Grove/Atlantic (www.groveatlantic.com) and in Great Britain by Atlantic Books (www.atlantic-books.co.uk).

The third installment in the series *Zero Hour in Phnom Penh* won the German Critics Award for Crime Fiction (Deutscher Krimi Preis) for best international crime fiction in 2004 and the Premier Special Director's Award Semana Negra (Spain) in 2007 or the author's website: www.cgmoore.com.

SPIRIT HOUSE
First in the series
Heaven Lake Press (2004) ISBN 974-92389-3-1

The Bangkok police already have a confession by a nineteen-year-old drug addict who has admitted to the murder of a British computer wizard, Ben Hoadly. From the bruises on his face shown at the press conference, it is clear that the young suspect had some help from the police in the making of his confession. The case is wrapped up. Only there are some loose ends that the police and just about everyone else are happy to overlook.

The search for the killer of Ben Hoadley plunges Calvino into the dark side of Bangkok, where professional hit men have orders to stop him. From the world of thinner addicts, dope dealers, fortunetellers, and high-class call girls, Calvino peels away the mystery surrounding the death of the English ex-public schoolboy who had a lot of dubious friends.

"Well-written, tough and bloody."
—Bernard Knight, *Tangled Web* (UK)

"A worthy example of a serial character, Vincent Calvino is human and convincing. [He] is an incarnate of the composite of the many expatriate characters who have burned the bridge to their pasts."
—*Thriller Magazine* (Italy)

"A thinking man's Philip Marlowe, Calvino is a cynic on the surface but a romantic at heart. Calvino ... found himself in Bangkok—the end of the world for a whole host of bizarre foreigners unwilling, unable, or uninterested in going home."
—*The Daily Yomiuri*

ASIA HAND
Second in the series
Heaven Lake Press (2000) ISBN 974-87171-2-7

Bangkok—the Year of the Monkey. Calvino's Chinese New Year celebration is interrupted by a call to Lumpini Park Lake, where Thai cops have just fished the body of a farang cameraman. CNN is running dramatic footage of several Burmese soldiers on the Thai border executing students.

Calvino follows the trail of the dead man to a feature film crew where he hits the wall of silence. On the other side of that wall, Calvino and Colonel Pratt discover and elite film unit of old Asia hands with connections to influential people in Southeast Asia. They find themselves matched against a set of farangs conditioned for urban survival and willing to go for a knock-out punch.

"Moore's Vinny Calvino is a worthy successor to Raymond Chandler's Philip Marlowe and Mickey Spillane's Mike Hammer."
—*The Nation*

"The top foreign author focusing on the Land of Smiles, Canadian Christopher G. Moore clearly has a first-hand understanding of the expat milieu ... Moore is perspicacious."
—*Bangkok Post*

ZERO HOUR IN PHNOM PENH
Third in the series

Heaven Lake Press (2005) ISBN 974-93035-9-8

Winner of 2004 German Critics Award for Crime Fiction (Deutscher Krimi Preis) for best international crime fiction and 2007 Premier Special Director's Award Semana Negra (Spain)

In the early 1990s, at the end of Cambodia's devastating civil war, UN peacekeeping forces try to keep the lid on the violence. Gunfire can still be heard nightly in Phnom Penh, where Vietnamese prostitutes try to hook UN peacekeepers from the balcony of the Lido Bar.

Calvino traces leads on a missing farang from Bangkok to war-torn Cambodia, through the Russian market, hospitals, nightclubs, news briefings, and UNTAC headquarters. Calvino's buddy, Colonel Pratt, knows something that Calvino does not: The missing man is connected with the jewels stolen from the Saudi royal family. Calvino quickly finds out that he is not the only one looking for the missing farang.

"Political, courageous and perhaps Moore's most important work." —*CrimiCouch.de*

"Fast-paced and entertaining. Even outside of his Bangkok comfort zone, Moore shows he is one of the best chroniclers of the expat diaspora." —*The Daily Yomiuri*

"A brilliant detective story that portrays—with no illusion—Cambodia's adventurous transition from genocide and civil war to a free-market economy and democratic normality. A rare stroke of luck and a work of art."
—*Deutsche Well Buchtipp*, Bonn

COMFORT ZONE
Fourth in the series
Heaven Lake Press (2001) ISBN 974-87754-9-6

Twenty years after the end of the Vietnam War, Vietnam is opening to the outside world. There is a smell of fast money in the air and poverty in the streets. Business is booming and in austere Ho Chi Minh City a new generation of foreigners have arrived to make money and not war. Against the backdrop of Vietnam's economic miracle, *Comfort Zone* reveals a divided people still not reconciled with their past and unsure of their future.

Calvino is hired by an ex-special forces vet, whose younger brother uncovers corruption and fraud in the emerging business world in which his clients are dealing. But before Calvino even leaves Bangkok, there have already been two murders, one in Saigon and one in Bangkok.

"Moore hits home with more of everything in *Comfort Zone*. There is a balanced mix of story-line, narrative, wisdom, knowledge as well as love, sex, and murder."
—*Thailand Times*

"Like a Japanese gardener who captures the land and the sky and recreates it in the backyard, Moore's genius is in portraying the Southeast Asian heartscape behind the tourist industry hotel gloss.
—*The Daily Yomiuri*

"In *Comfort Zone*, our Bangkok-based P.I. digs, discovering layers of intrigue. He's stalked by hired killers and falls in love with a Hanoi girl. Can he trust her? The reader is hooked."
—*NTUC Lifestyle* (Singapore)

THE BIG WEIRD
Fifth in the series

Heaven Lake Press (2008) ISBN 978-974-8418-42-1

A beautiful American blond is found dead with a large bullet hole in her head in the house of her ex-boyfriend. A famous Hollywood screenwriter hires Calvino to investigate her death. Everyone except Calvino's client believes Samantha McNeal has committed suicide.

In the early days of the Internet, Sam ran with a young and wild expat crowd in Bangkok. As Calvino slides into a world where people are dead serious about sex, money and fame, he unearths a hedonistic community where the ritual of death is the ultimate high.

"An excellent read, charming, amusing, insightful, complex, localised yet startlingly universal in its themes."
—*Guide of Bangkok*

"Highly entertaining."
—*Bangkok Post*

"Like a noisy, late-night Thai restaurant, Moore serves up tongue-burning spices that swallow up the literature of Generation X and Cyberspace as if they were merely sticky rice."
—*The Daily Yomiuri*

"A good read, fast-paced and laced with so many of the locales so familiar to the expat denizens of Bangkok."
—*Art of Living* (Thailand)

COLD HIT
Sixth in the series
Heaven Lake Press (2004) ISBN 974-920104-1-7

Five foreigners have died in Bangkok. Were they drug overdose victims or victims of a serial killer? Calvino believes the evidence points to a serial killer who stalks tourists in Bangkok. The Thai police, including Colonel Pratt, don't buy his theory.

Calvino teams up with an LAPD officer on a bodyguard assignment. Hidden forces pull them through swank shopping malls, run-down hotels, the Klong Toey slum, and bars in the red light district as they try to keep their man and themselves alive. As Calvino learns more about the bodies being shipped back to America, the secret of the serial killer is revealed.

"The story is plausible and riveting to the end."
—*The Japan Times*

"Tight, intricate plotting, wickedly astute ... *Cold Hit* will have you variously gasping, chuckling, nodding, tut-tutting, oh-yesing, and grinding your teeth throughout its 330 pages."
—*Guide of Bangkok*

"City jungle, sex, drugs, power, but also good-hearted people: a complete crime."
—*Zwanzig Minuten Zürich*

"Calvino is a wonderful private detective figure! Consistent action, masterful language ... and Anglo-Saxon humour at its best."
—Lutz Bunk, *DeutschlandRadio*, Berlin

MINOR WIFE
Seventh in the series
Heaven Lake Press (2004) ISBN 974-92126-5-7

A contemporary murder set in Bangkok—a neighbor and friend, a young ex-hooker turned artist, is found dead by an American millionaire's minor wife. Her rich expat husband hires Calvino to investigate.

While searching for the killer in exclusive clubs and not-so-exclusive bars of Bangkok, Calvino discovers that a minor wife—*mia noi*—has everything to do with a woman's status. From illegal cock fighting matches to elite Bangkok golf clubs, Calvino finds himself caught in the crossfire as he closes in on the murderer.

"What distinguishes Christopher G. Moore from other foreign authors setting their stories in the Land of Smiles is how much more he understands its mystique, the psyche of its populace and the futility of its round residents trying to fit into its square holes."
—*Bangkok Post*

"Moore pursues in even greater detail in *Minor Wife* the changing social roles of Thai women (changing, but not always quickly or for the better) and their relations among themselves and across class lines and other barriers."
—*Vancouver Sun*

"The thriller moves in those convoluted circles within which Thai life and society takes place. Moore's knowledge of these gives insights into many aspects of the cultural mores. Many of these are unknown to the expat population. ... Great writing, great story and a great read."
—*Pattaya Mail*

PATTAYA 24/7
Eighth in the series
Heaven Lake Press (2008) ISBN 978-974-8418-41-4

Inside a secluded, lush estate located on the edge of Pattaya, an eccentric Englishman's gardener is found hanged. Calvino has been hired to investigate. He finds himself pulled deep into the shadows of the war against drugs, into the empire of a local warlord with the trail leading to a terrorist who has caused Code Orange alerts to flash across the screen of American intelligence.

In a story packed with twists and turns, Calvino traces the links from the gardener's past to the doors of men with power and influence who have everything to lose if the mystery of the gardener's death is solved.

"Calvino does it again ... well-developed characters, and the pace keeps you reading well after you should have turned out the light."
—*Farang Magazine* (Thailand)

"A compelling, atmospheric and multi-layered murder investigation set in modern-day Thailand. The detective, Calvino, is a complex and engaging hero."
—Garry Disher, award-winning author of *The Wyatt Novels*

"We enjoy the spicy taste of hard-boiled fiction reinvented in an exotic but realistic place—in fact, not realistic, but real!"
—*Thriller Magazine* (Italy)

"A cast of memorably eccentric figures in an exotic Southeast Asian backdrop"
—*The Japan Times*

THE RISK OF INFIDELITY INDEX
Ninth in the series
Heaven Lake Press (2007) ISBN 974-88168-7-6

Major political demonstrations are rocking Bangkok. Chaos and fear sweep through the Thai and expatriate communities. Calvino steps into the political firestorm as he investigates a drug piracy operation. The piracy is traced to a powerful business interest protected by important political connections. A nineteen-year-old Thai woman and a middle-aged lawyer end up dead on the same evening. Both are connected to Calvino's investigation.

The dead lawyer's law firm denies any knowledge of the case. Calvino is left in the cold. Approached by a group of expat housewives—rattled by the "Risk of Infidelity Index" that ranks Bangkok number one for available sexual temptations—to investigate their husbands, Calvino discovers the alliance of forces blocking his effort to disclose the secret pirate drug investigation.

"Moore's flashy style successfully captures the dizzying contradictions in [Bangkok's] vertiginous landscape."
—Marilyn Stasio, *The New York Times Book Review*

"A hard-boiled, street-smart, often hilarious pursuit of a double murderer."
—*San Francisco Chronicle*

"Humorous and intelligent ... a great introduction to the seamy side of Bangkok."
—Carla Mckay, *The Daily Mail*

"Taut, spooky, intelligent, and beautifully written."
—T. Jefferson Parker, author of *L.A. Outlaws*

PAYING BACK JACK
Tenth in the series
Heaven Lake Press (2009) ISBN 978-974-312-920-9

In *Paying Back Jack*, Calvino agrees to follow the 'minor wife' of a Thai politician and report on her movements. His client is Rick Casey, a shady American whose life has been darkened by the unsolved murder of his idealistic son. It seems to be a simple surveillance job, but soon Calvino is entangled in a dangerous web of political allegiance and a reckless quest for revenge.

And, unknown to our man in Bangkok, in an anonymous tower in the center of the city, a two-man sniper team awaits its shot, a shot that will change everything. Paying Back Jack is classic Christopher G. Moore: densely-woven, eye-opening, and riveting.

"[*Paying Back Jack*] might be Moore's finest novel yet."
—Barry Eisler, author of *Fault Line*

"*Paying Back Jack* is so tightly woven and entertaining it is hopeless to try to put it down. Not only was it new and fresh, but I feel like I have taken a trip to the underbelly of Thailand. It is impossible not to love this book."
—Carolyn Lanier, *I Love a Mystery*

"A vivid sense of place ... the city of Bangkok, with its chaos and mystery, is almost another character. Recommended."
—*Library Journal*

"Moore clearly has no fear that his gloriously corrupt Bangkok will ever run dry."
—*Kirkus Review*

Mick Elmore © 2009

Canadian Christopher G. Moore is the creator of the award winning Vincent Calvino crime fiction series and the author of the Land of Smiles Trilogy.

In his former life, he studied at Oxford University and taught law at the University of British Columbia. He wrote radio plays for the CBC and NHK before his first novel was published in New York in 1985, when he promptly left his tenured academic job for an uncertain writing career, leaving his colleagues thinking he was not quite right in the head.

His journey from Canada to Thailand, his adopted home, included some time in Japan in the early 1980s and four years in New York in the late 1980s.

In 1988, he came to Thailand to harvest materials to write a book. The visit was meant to be temporary. More than twenty years on and 22 novels later, he is still in Bangkok and far from having exhausted the rich Southeast Asian literary materials.

His novels have so far appeared in a dozen languages.

For more information about the author and his books, visit his website: www.cgmoore.com. He also blogs at International Crime Authors: Reality Check: www.internationalcrimeauthors.com.

CPSIA information can be obtained at www.ICGtesting.com
Printed in the USA
BVOW011139010512

289132BV00005B/17/P